Starting Out

Starting Out

The Essential Guide to Cooking on Your Own

Julie Van Rosendaal

whitecap

For Aaron, who will have to feed himself very soon.

Many thanks to Mike, Mom & Dad, Sue, Rachel & Scott, Reith & Eddie,
and AnnMarie MacKinnon, Ben D'Andrea, Diane Yee, Kate Zimmerman & Joan Tetrault at Whitecap Books.

Copyright © 2006 by Julie Van Rosendaal
Fourth printing, 2007
Whitecap Books

06 07 09 10   05 04 03

All rights reserved. No part of this publication may be
reproduced, stored in a retrieval system, or transmitted in any
form or by any means, electronic, mechanical, photocopying,
recording or otherwise, without the prior written permission
of the publisher.

The information in this book is true and complete to the best
of our knowledge. All recommendations are made without
guarantee on the part of the author or Whitecap Books Ltd.
The author and publisher disclaim any liability in connection
with the use of this information. For additional information,
please contact Whitecap Books Ltd., 351 Lynn Avenue,
North Vancouver, BC V7J 2C4.

Visit our website at www.whitecap.ca.

Edited by Kate Zimmerman & Lesley Cameron
Proofread by Joan Tetrault
Cover and Interior Design by Diane Yee
Illustrations by Tom Bagley

Library and Archives Canada Cataloguing in Publication

Van Rosendaal, Julie, 1970–
    Starting out : the essential guide to cooking on your own /
Julie Van Rosendaal.

Includes index.
ISBN 1-55285-706-9
ISBN 978-1-55285-706-9

    1. Cookery. 2. Quick and easy cookery. I. Title.
TX833.5.V364 2006   641.5'12   C2005-906770-5

The publisher acknowledges the support of the Canada
Council for the Arts and the Cultural Services Branch of the
Government of British Columbia for our publishing program.
We acknowledge the financial support of the Government of
Canada through the Book Publishing Industry Development
Program for our publishing activities.

Printed in Canada

Contents

Introduction

No one is born with the ability to cook. Unless you had a parent or grandparent or good friend who taught you how (squeezing cookie dough out of a tube doesn't count), or took an interest in it yourself, you likely have become skilled at opening packages and reheating things in the microwave. Or perhaps most of your meals are prepared by the good folks at McDonald's. If this sounds familiar, sooner or later you should probably learn how to cook. Let's face it, you have to eat. Learning a few cooking skills will make life easier. It will also save you money, benefit your health, and come in handy if you're ever asked to bring something to a party. You may even become responsible for feeding someone else properly. Besides, man cannot live on toast and cereal alone, although many have made a valiant effort.

It took me a while to understand the saying "you are what you eat"—it applies not solely in terms of health, as in if you eat junk you'll feel like junk—but culturally, emotionally, and socially. We eat for so many reasons other than to satisfy ourselves nutritionally—food is a source of great comfort, to ourselves and each other, and is an inextricable element of any celebration or social event, whether it be a special gathering of friends or just your family (or even yourself) at the dinner table on a regular night. Few and far between are those who solely eat to live.

You don't have to *be* a cook to be *able* to cook. Most people who are convinced of their ineptitude in the kitchen are held back largely by intimidation. The best way to get past this is by doing it—fixing yourself something to eat on a regular basis is really the only way to become comfortable in the kitchen. Try something new, trust your instincts, even if you think you don't have any—and don't be afraid to experiment. Competence leads to confidence, and vice versa. And remember, even the best chefs have kitchen disasters.

The recipes that follow are meant to act more as guides, to encourage culinary independence rather than instruct how to follow a recipe. Start with the best ingredients you can find or afford, and you're halfway there. If you're not sure of something, look it up, call someone who knows, or taste your way through it. Food is one of life's greatest pleasures—cooking it can be, too. Just Do It.

Buying tools, gadgets, and appliances for your kitchen

When pondering what you're going to need in your own kitchen, consider how much space you have (particularly storage space), how often you cook, and what you like to cook most. There are some things you just can't live without, some you can probably get by without, some that will make your life easier, and some that are just fun to have. You be the judge.

Bits and pieces

Essential

Box grater: They aren't expensive, and they'll last forever. Buy one with four sides that has different textures on each side.

Colander: Unless you have a large sieve you'll need one to drain pasta properly.

Corkscrew or bottle opener: Makes it easier to access wine.

Measuring cups and spoons: They are cheap and will last you forever, so there's no reason not to own some. It's important to note the difference between dry and liquid measures— dry measuring cups come in a set of individual cups that you can level off; liquid measuring cups are glass or plastic and have the measurements printed on the side. A Pyrex measuring cup is great to have—you can measure ingredients and mix them right in the cup, and it's microwave safe. A set of measuring spoons is important too, particularly if you plan to do any baking. Slim spoons will slide more easily into spice jars and other small containers.

Oven mitts: They can range from really cheap to really expensive. Buy some nice heavy ones, the longer the better to avoid burns on your arms from the oven door. The new silicone ones are nice, but traditional fabric ones work equally well.

Spatula: A spatula is the best tool for stirring almost any combination of ingredients, especially when you're baking—you can scrape the sides and bottom of the bowl as you stir. Spatulas are also perfect tools for folding ingredients together. Heatproof spatulas are more expensive, but are great when you need to use them on the stovetop.

Tongs: They cost only a few dollars and are perfect for flipping things, transferring hot ingredients, and tossing salads. Stainless steel tongs are the best.

Vegetable peeler: Only essential if you're going to eat vegetables.

Whisk: Great for blending liquid ingredients, whisking eggs, mixing pancake batter, and making salad dressings.

Will make life easier

Garlic press: Makes the job much easier when you need to crush or purée a clove of garlic. You don't even need to peel the papery skin off first.

Kitchen scissors: Great for opening packages and cutting all sorts of ingredients.

Ladle: Very useful when you want to serve soup or stew, and can also be used to pour pancake or waffle batter onto the griddle.

Potato masher: Inexpensive, and the easiest way to produce mashed potatoes. If you want to invest in a potato ricer, which looks sort of like a giant garlic press, it's worth the cost if perfectly smooth mashed potatoes are important to you.

Salad spinner: Really nice to have if you have room for one. It's the best way to wash and dry salad greens quickly without damaging them.

Slotted spoon: Comes in handy when removing food from water or other liquid.

Pots and pans

You'll need pots and pans. You don't need to buy every size and shape available, but you'll need the basics—a medium-sized (about 2 L) pot, a small pot, and a large (7–8 L) stock pot (also called a Dutch oven) for cooking pasta, soups, and stews. You'll also need at least one skillet (also known as a frying pan) —preferably non-stick. An 8-inch or 9-inch (20–30 cm) skillet is ideal. A roasting pan and a double boiler (just an insert that fits into your medium pot) are pieces you don't need right away but should consider buying.

Most good pots and pans are fairly expensive, but think of them as an investment.

You'll use them every day, and if you buy cheap pots you'll only end up buying more a year or two down the road. When shopping, look for pots and pans made of stainless steel with nonoxidizing surfaces. They should be heavy, with thick, flat bases and handles that are riveted to the pan and ovenproof (not plastic) with tight-fitting lids. There are a lot of nice ones out there—buy what you like and what feels good in your hand.

Cutting board

You'll need a cutting board. Again, these range from a few dollars up to hundreds for nice wooden chopping blocks. If you want a cutting board you can put away between uses so it won't take up valuable counter space, buy a small one that's easy to move around and slide into a cupboard. Larger cutting boards generally stay out on your countertop, and traditional wooden ones look nice.

But which to buy, wood or plastic? It has long been believed that wooden boards are so porous that harmful organisms such as salmonella, E. coli, and listeria soak in and are difficult to remove. There's a general belief that plastic, because it's not porous, can be more easily and safely cleaned, but that's not actually true. Food scientists have published many studies that show wooden cutting boards are as safe as plastic ones—some say even safer—and better for your knives as well. Whichever you buy, just make sure you keep it clean. Wash it with hot soapy water and rinse it well. Non-porous acrylic, plastic, glass, and solid wooden boards can be washed in an automatic dishwasher. Sanitize both wooden and plastic cutting boards regularly with a diluted bleach or vinegar solution consisting of one teaspoon (5 mL) of bleach to 4 cups (1 L) of water, or a one-to-five dilution of vinegar. Flood the surface with the sanitizing solution and allow it to stand for several minutes, then rinse and air-dry or pat dry. If you use your cutting board to cut raw meat, make sure you clean it well before using it with other foods.

Knives

It's difficult to cook without a knife. There are many different kinds, but all you really need is a good basic chef's knife, a small paring knife, and perhaps a long serrated knife for cutting bread. You can build on your collection from there. Small paring knives cost only a few dollars; larger chef's knives are more expensive (they can range from tens to hundreds of dollars), but a good quality knife will last you a lifetime. Choose a knife that you like and feels great in your hand.

Sooner or later, your knife is going to need sharpening. You can buy inexpensive knife stones, or a tool called a "steel" that looks like a long, round sword with a handle, and is used to keep your knife sharp between uses and maintain its original condition. You could spend more and buy a knife sharpener, but they aren't necessary unless you're fanatical about keeping your knives razor-sharp.

Bakeware

You'll need a baking (or cookie) sheet not only for baking cookies but for baking biscuits and loaves, roasting vegetables, broiling fish or chicken, and a ton of other things. Buy a heavy baking sheet that is light in color (darker colors absorb heat better and tend to burn the bottoms of your cookies), with a rimmed edge. Buy two if you can afford it.

If you like to bake, you'll need to buy more baking pans. I'd start with an 8- × 8-inch square pan, a set of two 9-inch round baking pans, a rectangular 9- × 13-inch baking pan, a 4- × 8-inch or 9- × 5-inch loaf pan (or both), a 12-cup muffin tin, a glass pie plate, and one or two baking racks for cooling your baked goods when they come out of the oven. I like to have a 9-inch springform pan too, which you'll need for cheesecakes and some other types of cakes. Non-stick pans are nice, but not essential; just make sure they aren't too dark in color.

You'll also need a casserole dish of some description, or preferably a few, to accommodate a variety of recipes and quantities. Casseroles that come with lids are your best option, even though you won't always use the lids.

Small appliances

Appliances are fun to have and sometimes make life easier, but aren't essential to your success in the kitchen. Which appliances you buy will depend largely on finances and what you like to cook most. Most kitchens aren't without a toaster and microwave; food processors are very useful for a wide variety of recipes, and you'll need an electric mixer if you like to bake. Hand mixers can be very inexpensive, or you could spend more on a stand mixer if you do a lot of baking and will make use of the whisk, paddle, and dough hook attachments. A blender can come in handy too, especially if you like to make smoothies.

Appliances such as waffle irons and slow cookers are worth the cost if you have extra storage space—you may not use them all the time, but you'll enjoy them when you do. A hand blender (also called an immersion blender) is a great tool to have to blend, emulsify, or purée soups, sauces, and salad dressings. (The best part is you can plunge the blender right into your pot of soup to purée it without having to transfer hot soup to your food processor or blender.) A coffee mill may come as an attachment to your food processor, or you can buy it separately to grind your coffee, whole spices, or flax seed.

Stocking
your pantry

Starting out with an empty kitchen and having to do your first big grocery shop can be daunting. There are a lot of things that have always just been in the pantry, that you may never have had to go out and buy. Here is a list of basic ingredients that are good to keep on hand. Adjust the list, of course, to suit your taste and needs.

There are a lot of ingredients you'll probably only need to buy once or twice a year. It's important to remember that some products with long shelf lives, such as spices, can lose their flavor or become inactive over time. Leavenings such as baking powder and baking soda can also lose their effectiveness (see page 235). If possible, purchase small amounts of these ingredients from bulk bins and store them in small plastic containers or jars—not only is it cheaper, it ensures your stash is always fresh. If you have a deep pantry, it's a good idea to dig around once in awhile to see what's there and what should be tossed.

For your pantry

Baking

Baking chocolate: unsweetened and semi-sweet

Baking powder

Baking soda

Chocolate chips: semi-sweet and any other kinds you like to bake with

Cocoa powder

Corn syrup

Cornmeal: yellow or white

Cornstarch

Flour: all-purpose white (bleached or unbleached) and whole wheat

Honey

Molasses

Oatmeal: quick-cooking or old-fashioned (also called large flake)

Raisins and other dried fruit, such as apricots and cranberries

Salt: non-iodized sea salt or kosher salt is best (fine salt for baking, coarser for cooking with)

Sugar: white, golden brown or dark brown, and/or muscovado (the only difference is the amount of molasses each contains; the darker the sugar, the more molasses), and icing sugar (also known as powdered or confectioners' sugar)

Vanilla extract: imitation vanilla is much less expensive and fine for baking with; pure vanilla is better for desserts in which the flavor is dominant

Walnuts or pecans, chopped or in halves (Because nuts contain oil they can become rancid; store them in the freezer if you don't plan to use them soon.)

Oils and condiments

Canola oil: a great neutral oil for cooking and baking with, also very low in saturated fat

Olive oil: great for cooking and for salad dressings (see page 85 for more information on how to choose olive oil)

Ketchup

Maple syrup

Mustard: Dijon and yellow

Soy sauce

Tabasco sauce

Vinegars: white, red wine, balsamic, and any others you think sound good

Worcestershire sauce

Dried herbs and spices

Basil

Bay leaves

Black pepper

Chili powder

Cinnamon

Cumin

Curry powder

Dried red pepper flakes

Nutmeg

Oregano

Paprika

Rosemary

Sage

Thyme

Dry goods

Couscous

Dried beans (legumes)

Dry pasta and noodles in a variety of shapes and sizes

Grains such as quinoa or bulgur

Rice: long-grain white, brown, Arborio and/or wild rice

Canned and jarred goods

Beans (legumes), such as kidney, white beans, black beans, and chickpeas (garbanzo beans)

Beef broth

Canned tomatoes: diced, stewed, and crushed

Chicken, beef, and/or vegetable broth

Evaporated milk

Jam and preserves

Peanut butter

Salmon

Salsa

Spaghetti sauce

Tuna

Miscellaneous

Coffee: buy whole beans if you have your own grinder, or buy freshly ground and store it in the fridge

Crackers

Non-stick spray

Popcorn

Tea

For the fridge

Butter: salted is most commonly served and used in recipes

Cheeses: cheddar, feta, cream cheese, and/or other cheeses of your choice

Eggs: most recipes are based on large-sized eggs. There's no difference between brown and white, but free-range or organic eggs are usually much more flavorful. Omega-3 eggs come from chickens that have been fed a special diet containing flax.

Grated Parmesan

Margarine: non-hydrogenated tub margarine for spreading and/or stick margarine for baking

Mayonnaise: reduced-fat is best

Milk

Salad dressings: if you don't want to make them yourself

Reading
labels

These days we're finally seeing more useful nutritional information on packaged foods. Unfortunately, the labels aren't always easy to understand. Here's a guide to help you decipher food labels and understand what they mean.

Nutritional facts

The "nutritional facts" part of the label breaks down the calories, fat content (usually including some sort of distinction between saturated fat, polyunsaturated fat, monounsaturated fat, and sometimes trans fat), cholesterol, sodium, carbohydrate, fiber, sugars, protein, calcium, iron, vitamin A, and vitamin C per serving. These are nutrients that consumers, health professionals, and scientists consider important to your health. You'll find a breakdown per serving, and what percentage of the daily value each nutrient represents in the context of the total amount recommended in a balanced 2000 calorie diet, based on Canada's Food Guide.

Try to choose products with more fiber, vitamins, calcium, and iron, and less saturated fat, cholesterol, and sodium. Too much saturated and trans fats can increase your risk of heart disease.

Serving size

Pay attention to the serving size, which is usually given in grams (you'll have to look at how big the package is and do the math), but sometimes given in quantity, such as 2 cookies or 10 crackers. A package that appears to be a single serving often actually contains more than one serving. Keep in mind that the nutritional facts correspond to the serving size, so if you eat more than the recommended serving size you're also eating more calories, fat, etc. You may have to adjust the numbers accordingly.

Ingredients

Ingredients are listed in order of the quantity contained in the product. If sugar is the first ingredient on the list, then the product has more sugar in it than any other ingredient. Remember that sugar can appear in several different ways, such as molasses, honey, syrup, corn syrup, fructose, glucose, sucrose, and fruit juice concentrate. Fat can also be listed in different ways—hydrogenated and partially hydrogenated oils, palm oil, canola oil, margarine, butter, shortening, and lard are all types of fat. Avoid any products containing tropical oils such as palm or coconut oil, or hydrogenated fats, which contain trans fat. Fat has more calories than any other component, and limiting saturated and trans fats is especially important. When shopping for bread, remember that "wheat flour" actually refers to white flour—"whole wheat flour" contains the entire grain. Very often, breads labeled "whole wheat" or "multigrain" have white "wheat flour" listed as the first ingredient, rather than whole wheat flour.

Food additives

The ingredient list will also tell you what food additives and preservatives the product contains. Food additives are natural and synthetic chemicals that help preserve and flavor food, and add color. Some additives prevent spoilage, and others are enrichments that increase the nutrient value of a food. Additives often make it possible for foods grown in one part of the world to be shipped to consumers on the other side of the globe, and eaten weeks or months after being packaged. In Canada, all additives are subjected to laboratory screening by Health Canada before they're approved for consumption.

Best before date

Always check for a "sell by" or "best before" date, which indicates the latest date food can be safely consumed. If a product is past its expiry date, it may have lost some of its nutritive and esthetic value, may taste stale, or may even be spoiled. Although there's often some leeway, it's particularly important to pay attention to the dates on dairy products, mayonnaise, and meat.

Nutritional claims

There are two types of nutritional claims: nutrient content claims and health claims. Nutrient content claims describe one ingredient, such as fat, sodium, or sugar. Health claims tell you how your diet can affect your health. Nutritional claims can be deceiving—it's best to make your own assessment by reading the nutrition facts and the ingredient list. For example, "light" may refer to color or flavor, and not necessarily calorie content. If "light" or "lite" refers to the color or flavor of the food, the label must make that clear.

A "fat-free" product may still be high in calories and even higher in sugar, making it inappropriate if you are watching your weight. Often products with less fat than their regular counterparts still contain the same amount of calories from other ingredients they've added to make up for the loss of fat. "Low fat" means 3 grams of fat or less per serving size listed on the label. For a product to claim it's a "source of" something, it must contain an amount designated as significant. For example, a product labeled "source of fiber" must contain 4 grams or more per serving. For a product to be labeled "free" of something, such as cholesterol or sodium, it must contain no more than a trace amount.

In Canada, manufacturers are only allowed to make diet-related health claims about the following diet/health relationships:

- A diet low in saturated and trans fat reduces the risk of heart disease.

- A diet containing adequate calcium and vitamin D combined with regular physical activity reduces the risk of osteoporosis.

- A diet rich in vegetables and fruit reduces the risk of some types of cancer.

- A diet low in sodium and high in potassium reduces the risk of high blood pressure.

Produce
101

When it's in **season**,
how to **shop** for it,
how to **prepare** it,
and what to do with it
once you **get it home**.

When shopping for produce there are a few factors to consider, the most important being quality and price. When fruit and vegetables are in season they're generally at their prime, and because they're plentiful, you can usually get a good deal. Some vegetables, potatoes and onions, for example, are available year-round. Others, such as berries, can be bought frozen when they aren't available fresh. Frozen fruits and vegetables are just as nutritious as their fresh counterparts, but remember that once delicate produce is frozen and thawed, it loses much of its texture. Dried and canned fruits and vegetables are also available year-round, and are a perfectly acceptable alternative to fresh. The downside is that canned fruit usually has sugar added (in the form of syrup), and canned vegetables often have both added sodium and a mushier texture than their fresh counterparts. Legumes are also available dried, in which case they're cheap and have a virtually indefinite shelf life, but they require soaking and cooking before use, unlike the canned varieties.

Vegetables

Artichokes

Artichokes are in season year-round but fresh ones are most plentiful in the spring. Artichoke hearts are always available canned. When shopping for fresh artichokes, make sure they're heavy for their size, and keep in mind that larger ones are sometimes woody. Good artichokes should be plump and squeak when you squeeze the leaves together, and the outer leaves should snap off. They can be stored in a plastic bag in the refrigerator for up to 3 days, but are best the day you buy them.

Best cooking methods: Fresh artichokes are generally steamed, sautéed, or braised. Canned artichoke hearts are usually used in recipes: they don't require cooking and are good in dips and salads. If you're wondering how to eat a whole cooked artichoke, break the leaves off, dip them in melted butter, vinaigrette, or hollandaise sauce, and draw the soft meaty portion between your teeth to remove the flesh. Throw out the rest of the leaf. After the leaves have been eaten, the prickly "choke" is cut away and discarded, and you can eat the tender artichoke heart.

Asparagus

Asparagus comes in shades of green, white, and purple; all are delicious. Some people prefer very thin asparagus, but bigger stalks are just as good. Just remember that thinner stalks will cook more quickly than thicker ones. When shopping for asparagus, don't buy wrinkled, shriveled, or damaged spears. Store them loosely wrapped in plastic in the fridge and use them as soon as possible. Before preparing them you'll need to snap off the tough ends—break each one individually by hand so you can feel the point at which the end naturally breaks off the rest of the spear.

Best cooking methods: Asparagus is best steamed, braised, roasted, blanched, or grilled.

Avocados

An avocado is actually a fruit, but we treat it as a vegetable so I'm classifying it as such. When shopping for avocados, avoid ones that are blemished or have mushy spots. Avocados will ripen on the countertop at room temperature, so feel free to buy them even if they're rock hard. Generally, the darker its skin, the riper it's getting; you can tell an avocado is ripe when it yields to gentle pressure. If you want to slow the ripening process, keep avocados in the fridge. Otherwise, store them at room temperature.

Best cooking methods: Avocados are generally eaten raw. They're great in salads, sandwiches, and mashed to make dips.

Beets

Beets grow from spring until fall but are usually available year-round. Size doesn't matter, but avoid blemishes and mushy spots. Sometimes the greens on top are an indication of freshness; you can trim these and cook them as you would cook chard (see page 25).

To store, trim the greens to about 1 inch (2.5 cm) of the top of each beet. Store them with your potatoes and onions in a cool, dry place, or in a plastic bag in the fridge for weeks.

Best cooking methods: Beets are best roasted, steamed, pickled, or sautéed. They're rarely eaten raw.

Broccoli

Like other members of the cabbage and cauliflower family, broccoli is generally available year-round, but is at its peak between October and April. It's also available frozen, but fresh is far superior. Buy broccoli with a tight head, a deep color, tightly closed buds, and no yellow areas. Refrigerate it unwashed, in an airtight bag, for up to 4 days.

Best cooking methods: Broccoli can be steamed, simmered, stir-fried, blanched, microwaved, or eaten raw.

Brussels Sprouts

Brussels sprouts are a member of the cabbage family, and they resemble teeny cabbages. They're a winter vegetable but are available year-round. Look for small, bright green sprouts with compact heads, and avoid buying any that have blemishes or yellow leaves. Keep in mind that smaller ones are more tender. Any loose outer leaves can be trimmed off. Store unwashed Brussels sprouts in an airtight plastic bag in the refrigerator for up to 3 days; after that they will develop a strong flavor.

Best cooking methods: Brussels sprouts are best braised, steamed, pan-fried, or baked.

Cabbage

Cabbage comes in many forms, ranging in color from white to green to red, some varieties with compact heads and some with looser leaves. Most cabbage is available year-round; look for tightly packed heads with no yellow or loose leaves. The head should be heavy for its size with fresh, crisp leaves and no soft areas. Bags of precut coleslaw are great for all kinds of recipes, and save you a lot of chopping. Cabbage should be refrigerated, tightly wrapped, for up to a week.

Best cooking methods: Cabbage is usually eaten raw, steamed, braised, stir-fried, or stewed.

Carrots

Carrots are available year-round with their tops, without their tops, and pre-peeled in bags. One isn't necessarily better than the other, but thinner carrots tend to be sweeter and less woody. Don't buy them if they're flabby. Store carrots unpeeled in a plastic bag in the fridge, or peel them, cut them into sticks, and store them submerged in a jug of water in the fridge.

Best cooking methods: Carrots are best steamed, braised, roasted, stir-fried, or eaten raw.

Cauliflower

When shopping for cauliflower, choose firm heads with compact florets. Don't buy any that have brown spots or yellow areas. You could cut those spots off, but they're usually an indication that the flavor is already lost.

Cauliflower should be creamy white and firm, with its leaves tightly wrapped around it. Store it tightly wrapped in plastic in the fridge for up to 5 days.

Best cooking methods: Cauliflower is best eaten raw, steamed, baked, or sautéed.

Celeriac

Celeriac, or celery root, is a brown, knobby vegetable that tastes like a cross between celery and parsley. It's in season from September to May. Choose a small, firm celeriac with no soft spots. Store in a plastic bag in the fridge for up to 10 days.

Best cooking methods: Celeriac is best eaten raw, braised, sautéed, or baked.

Celery

Buy celery with the leaves on if you can; it should be bright pale green and crisp. If you like, wash and trim your celery and store it in a container of water in the fridge. Otherwise, leave it whole, wrapped in plastic, in the fridge, for up to a couple of weeks. If it starts to get flabby, it's sometimes revivable if you trim off the end and put it in water for a few hours.

Best cooking methods: Celery is usually eaten raw on its own, sautéed with other vegetables, or simmered or braised in soups and stews.

Chard

Chard, or Swiss chard, is related to the beet—in fact, it's like a beet grown for its leaves rather than its root. Chard is available year-round but is best during the summer. The kind of chard with dark green leaves and red stalks has a stronger flavor than that with lighter stalks and leaves. Look for crisp, deep green leaves and stems that have no bruises. Buy thick-stalked chard if you like the stalks (you can always trim them off), or thin-stemmed chard if you're after the leaves. Store either loosely wrapped in plastic in the fridge for up to 3 days.

Best cooking methods: Chard is typically steamed, sautéed, or wilted and added to recipes. The greens can be prepared like spinach, the stalks like asparagus.

Corn

Corn is available canned and frozen year-round, and is typically available on the cob during the summer months. When buying fresh corn, people are divided between what color and shape indicate a sweet and flavorful kernel—small, pale kernels or large, deep yellow ones. Either way, make sure they're firm; pull back the husks to make sure there are no shriveled kernels or moldy patches. Store corn on the cob in the fridge for several days; it won't go bad, but will lose its sweetness with time. To remove the kernels from the cob, scrape them off with a sharp knife. If you have a tube pan, hold the cob upright in the hole in the middle and scrape the kernels off into the surrounding pan. Corn kernels can be frozen in freezer bags (remove as much air as possible) for up to 4 months.

Best cooking methods: Corn on the cob is best steamed, microwaved, or grilled; off the cob

it can be steamed, sautéed, roasted, or stirred into soups.

Cucumber

Cucumbers come in many varieties, the most common being regular "garden" cucumbers, which are shorter and stouter with larger seeds and thicker skins, and English cucumbers, which are long and thin with small seeds and thin skins. English cucumbers are usually wrapped in plastic and are more expensive. Small "pickling" cucumbers are, as the name suggests, generally used to make pickles. Buy cucumbers with smooth skins and no blemishes or soft spots. Store whole, unwashed cucumbers in the fridge for up to 10 days; cut cucumbers can be wrapped in plastic and refrigerated for up to 5 days.

Best cooking methods: Cucumbers are usually eaten raw but are often pickled and sometimes sautéed.

Eggplant

The eggplant is related to the tomato and potato, and is actually a type of berry. It comes in many shapes and varieties, but is most commonly large and pear-shaped, with glossy dark purple skin. Choose a firm, smooth-skinned eggplant that is heavy for its size; avoid those with soft or brown spots. Eggplants should be stored in a cool, dry place and used within a day or two, but will keep in the fridge for a few days longer. The skin of a young eggplant is usually tender and edible; older eggplants should be peeled. Eggplants become bitter with age and so some recipes require you to slice the eggplant and salt it heavily and then rinse it; a process that draws out some of the bitterness.

Best cooking methods: Eggplant can be fried, baked, roasted, sautéed, or broiled.

Endive and Escarole

Endive is very closely related to chicory, and is often confused with it. There are three types of endive: Belgian (small, cigar-shaped with white leaves), curly (loose heads of curly, lacy leaves), and escarole (broad, pale green leaves). Belgian endive is available from September to May, and at its peak from November to April. Curly endive and escarole are available year-round, but are at their best from June to October. Endive should be fresh and crisp, with no blemishes. Avoid any that are limp or wilted. Store wrapped in plastic in the fridge for up to 3 days.

Best cooking methods: Endive and escarole are typically eaten raw, but can also be braised, sautéed, or grilled.

Fennel

Fennel is similar to celery, with a mild licorice flavor. It's available from the fall through to the spring and is bought for its bulb rather than its stalks. It should be tight and crisp, with no discoloration. Store it loosely wrapped in plastic in the refrigerator for up to a week.

Best cooking methods: Fennel can be eaten raw, braised, roasted, sautéed, or grilled.

Garlic

Garlic is available year-round fresh, minced or puréed in jars, and dehydrated in flakes, granules, and powder form. When shopping for fresh garlic, look for firm heads that haven't begun to sprout and have no soft spots or blemishes. Size doesn't matter, nor does color—the papery skin generally ranges from white to light purple. Store garlic as you would potatoes and onions—in a cool, dark, dry place. Whole heads will keep for up to 6 weeks, but may begin to sprout. You can still use it at that point, but the flavor may not be as intense.

Best cooking methods: Garlic is generally used in other dishes raw, roasted, or sautéed. To roast a head of garlic, wrap a whole head in foil (if you want, you can cut a thin slice off the top and drizzle the exposed cloves with a little olive or vegetable oil) and pop it in the oven for an hour, or until it's soft. This can be done while you roast chicken, meat, potatoes—anything that won't be ruined by a garlic odor. Roasted garlic can be kept in its foil in the fridge for a week.

Green and Yellow Beans

Fresh beans such as green beans (as opposed to legumes like kidney beans) are sold fresh in their pods. Wax beans are available fresh year-round, but are at their peak during the summer. They're also available frozen and canned. Shop for beans that are crisp (they should snap, not fold, if you bend them in half) with no dark spots. Store loosely wrapped in plastic in the refrigerator for up to 5 days. Their flavor starts to diminish right away, so use them as soon as possible.

Best cooking methods: Beans are eaten raw, steamed, braised, stir-fried, sautéed, grilled, roasted, and microwaved.

Kale

Look for dark green kale with firm, unblemished, and unwilted leaves. Small leaves with thin stems are more tender than the bigger leaves. You may want to remove larger stems. Kale and collard greens are sturdy and keep better than other greens. Keep them loosely wrapped in plastic in the fridge; they may start to yellow after a few days but will still be okay to use.

Best cooking methods: Kale is typically eaten steamed, stir-fried, sautéed, or added to soups and stews.

Leeks

Leeks are related to onions, but have a much milder, more subtle flavor. They're available year-round, but are most plentiful from late summer to late fall. Choose crisp, plump leeks that have plenty of white, since you are going to cut off and throw away most of the green part. Make sure there are no wilted or yellow leaves. Loosely wrapped in plastic, they can be stored in the fridge for weeks, although they're best used within a week. Make sure they're trimmed and cut lengthwise down the stalk before you wash them thoroughly—lots of dirt and grit tends to work its way between the layers.

Best cooking methods: Leeks are usually sautéed, braised, roasted, or grilled, and are often sautéed along with, or instead of, onions in soups and sauces.

Lettuce

Different varieties of lettuce are in season at different times of the year. The most common year-round types are iceberg, romaine, butter, and leaf lettuce (which comes in shades of green and purple), all of which have many varieties. When shopping for lettuce, choose heads that are heavy for their size with crisp, blemish-free leaves. If you're paying by the head instead of by the pound, tightly packed heads are a better deal. Lettuce can be stored washed and dried, or unwashed in a plastic bag in the fridge for up to 5 days. As with all greens, lettuce must be gently dried after washing—salad spinners are great tools for drying greens without damaging them.

Mushrooms

Mushrooms come in many varieties, the most common being the button mushroom, sold fresh year-round and in cans. Portobello, cremini, shiitake, oyster, chanterelle, enoki, porcini, and morel mushrooms are also available fresh and dried year-round, and have unique, more intense flavors.

Look for mushrooms that are firm and evenly colored with tightly closed caps. Avoid those that are broken, damaged, or have soft spots or a dark-tinged surface. Fresh mushrooms should be stored in a breathable paper bag, unwashed, in the fridge for up to 3 days. Mushrooms stored in plastic tend to go slimy. Because they're like sponges and absorb any liquid they come in contact with, it's best to wipe them with a damp paper towel to clean them. If you wash them in water, do it right before you use them or dry them well afterward. Trim the stem ends if necessary. Dried mushrooms can be stored in a cool, dry place for up to 6 months.

Best cooking methods: Mushrooms can be eaten raw, sautéed, grilled, and added to soups and stews.

Okra

Okra is an unusual vegetable, typically available from May through October and usually available frozen and canned. When buying fresh okra, look for firm, brightly colored pods; the smaller the better. Avoid any that are limp or blemished. Refrigerate in a plastic bag for up to 3 days.

Best cooking methods: Okra is typically braised, baked, fried or added to soups and stews, where it acts as a thickening agent.

Onions

Onions also come in many shapes, colors and varieties. Green onions (also called scallions) are long, thin, and green, with a small white bulb. They're available year-round but are at their peak during the spring and summer. Choose crisp green onions and store them loosely wrapped in a plastic bag in the fridge for up to a week.

Common yellow or white cooking onions and purple onions are available year-round. Size doesn't matter, but it's nice to have smaller ones if you're usually only cooking for one or two. Purple onions are usually larger and have a much milder flavor than cooking onions, which makes them the best choice for salads. Sweet Vidalia and Walla Walla onions are typically larger but otherwise look the same as yellow or white onions, and are much sweeter. Pearl onions are tiny, sometimes as small as a marble. Buy onions that are heavy for their size, with no soft spots or moldy areas. Store them in a cool, dry place for up to 2 months. Cut onions can be kept tightly wrapped in plastic in the fridge for a few days.

Best cooking methods: Green onions are best eaten raw or sautéed in cooked dishes. Cooking onions (yellow, white, purple, and sweet onions) are also eaten raw, or sautéed, roasted, grilled, caramelized, or battered and deep-fried. Pearl onions are usually blanched to remove their skins, then roasted with or without other ingredients, and are often used in soups and stews.

Parsnips

Parsnips are a root vegetable, available year-round but at their peak during the fall and winter. Like carrots, smaller parsnips tend to be more tender; the larger ones can be woody. Avoid any that are limp and flabby or have blemished areas. Refrigerate them, loosely wrapped in a plastic bag, for up to 3 weeks.

Best cooking methods: Parsnips can be baked, roasted, sautéed, steamed, or boiled and then mashed like potatoes.

Peas

Peas are available fresh in their pods, frozen, and canned. Snow peas and sugar snap peas have sweet edible pods and tiny peas inside; you have to shell the ones with bigger peas inside before you eat them. When shopping for any kind of fresh peas, make sure they're bright green and crisp with no visible damage. Don't buy any that are rubbery. Store them, loosely wrapped in a plastic bag, for up to a week, but keep in mind that they lose their sweetness over time.

Best cooking methods: Peas are typically eaten raw, steamed, sautéed, and stir-fried or added to soups, casseroles, and stews.

Peppers

There are essentially two kinds of peppers: sweet and hot. To roast peppers, leave them whole or cut them in half lengthwise and remove the ribs and seeds. Place them cut side down (or whole) on a foil-lined baking sheet and roast them at 475°F, flipping them if they're whole, until they're black and blistered all over. (It doesn't matter if there are still a few red areas.) Remove them from the oven and put them in a bowl; cover them with the foil from the baking sheet, a plate, pot lid, or tea towel and set aside to cool. When they're cool enough to handle, peel the skins off the peppers and remove the seeds, if there are any. Roasted peppers can be frozen in zip-lock bags or kept in the fridge, covered with a drizzle of olive oil, for about a week.

Hot peppers are often called chilies; they're much smaller and usually have a longer shape than sweet bell peppers. Bell peppers come in shades of green, yellow, orange, and red; the yellow, orange and red varieties are mellower in flavor than green peppers, and are usually much more expensive. Hot peppers have a wider variety of shapes, sizes, and colors, and range from mildly to dangerously hot. The most common hot peppers are jalapeño, poblano, Anaheim, banana, serrano, Thai, ancho, cayenne, and the hottest of them all—habanero and Scotch bonnet. Some are more widely available fresh than others, and most are available dried, powdered, or canned in small tins. Most peppers are available year-round but they're at their peak during the summer months. Choose peppers that are brightly colored, firm, and heavy for their size with no soft spots, bruises, or wrinkled areas.

Best cooking methods: Peppers are usually eaten raw, roasted, sautéed, grilled, or stir-fried. Hot peppers are often added to cooked dishes as a seasoning. Remember when preparing hot peppers to wear rubber gloves and to remove the seeds if you don't want your dish to be too hot.

Potatoes

Potatoes, probably the most popular of all vegetables, come in many varieties. Most common is the russet or baking potato, which has rough, dark brown skin and is mealy and starchy, making it ideal for baking, mashing, or turning into french fries. Yukon Golds are smaller, rounder, and have thin, yellowish skin. They're waxier and have more moisture than russets, with a buttery flesh that makes them perfect for mashing as well as roasting or making potato salad. Long or round white potatoes are similar to Yukon Gold, with thin white skins. Red potatoes are round and waxy, with thin red skins; they tend to produce gummy mashed potatoes but are well-suited to boiling, roasting, and making potato salads. Baby long white potatoes are referred to as fingerling potatoes, and new potatoes are simply any variety of young potato that still has a waxy texture and thin, underdeveloped skin. They're perfect for boiling, steaming, or roasting.

Potatoes are available year-round; new and fingerling potatoes are usually more plentiful during the summer months. Look for firm potatoes without any soft spots or mold, and make sure their eyes aren't sprouting. Some potatoes develop a green tinge as a result of prolonged exposure to light. This part is bitter and can be scraped off before using. Store potatoes in a cool, dark, dry place for up to a month, but do not refrigerate them. New potatoes should be used within a few days.

Best cooking methods: Potatoes are typically baked, roasted, deep-fried, boiled, steamed, or mashed.

Pumpkin

Fresh pumpkins are generally available during the fall, when it's pumpkin carving season. When it comes to baking, canned pumpkin purée is the preferred choice. Not only do you save yourself the mess of cleaning out seeds and goo, canned pumpkin has 20 times the beta carotene of fresh. If you're cooking fresh pumpkin, smaller ones are more tender and succulent than larger ones. Choose those that are free of blemishes and are heavy for their size. Store at room temperature for up to a month or refrigerate (if you have room for it) for up to 2 months.

Best cooking methods: Puréed pumpkin is most often used in baked goods; fresh is typically baked, microwaved, braised, or prepared any way that you'd prepare squash. The seeds can be used raw in baking, or oiled, salted, and roasted.

Radishes

Radishes are available year-round, both trimmed in bags and loose in bunches with their greens and roots attached. Choose firm radishes with crisp green leaves—those that yield to gentle pressure are probably woody inside. Store in a plastic bag in the fridge for up to a week. To crisp them up, trim the tops and ends off and soak the radishes in ice water in the fridge for an hour or two.

Best cooking methods: Radishes are usually eaten raw, but are also sometimes braised in butter.

Rutabagas

Rutabagas are similar to turnips, with pale yellow skin and flesh (turnips are purple-tinged) and a coarser texture. They're available year-round but are most plentiful from July to April. They should be smooth, firm, and heavy for their size. Store in a plastic bag in the fridge for up to 2 weeks.

Best cooking methods: Rutabagas are usually simmered, roasted, or cooked in any way that you might prepare a turnip.

Spinach

Spinach is available fresh year-round, but is at its peak in the spring. It can also be purchased in frozen blocks. Choose leaves that are dark green and crisp and avoid those that are limp, damaged, or have yellow spots. Bags of washed spinach are more expensive but are worth the price—because they're prewashed, you don't have to worry about getting all the grit off yourself; usually you have to be pretty thorough when washing spinach. When buying bagged spinach, you usually have the option of baby spinach leaves, which are smaller and more tender. Keep spinach in a plastic bag in the fridge for up to 3 days. If your bagged spinach is starting to go limp, pop the whole thing in the freezer and use it in recipes that call for frozen spinach. If the leaves must be chopped, crunch them up in the bag with your hands—the frozen leaves will shatter easily.

Best cooking methods: Spinach is usually eaten raw, sautéed, or wilted and added to soups, sauces, and dips.

Squash

Squash varies widely in size, shape, and color. They're generally divided into two categories—summer squash and winter squash. Summer squash have thin, edible skins and soft seeds. The most widely available varieties are zucchini, crookneck, and pattypan. Summer squash is best from early through late summer, although some varieties are available year-round. Choose smaller specimens with bright-colored, blemish-free skin.

Summer squash is more perishable than winter squash and should be stored in a plastic bag in the fridge for up to 5 days.

Although winter squash are more plentiful in the fall and winter, they're generally available year-round. Winter squash have hard, thick skins and require longer cooking than summer squash. The most common varieties are butternut, acorn, and spaghetti squash, which was named for its stringy, spaghetti-like interior. Select firm winter squash with no soft spots. Store in a cool, dry, dark place, as you would store potatoes, for about a month.

Best cooking methods: Squash is best baked, steamed, roasted, braised, or microwaved. It's also often used in soups and stews.

Sweet Potatoes

Also known as yams, sweet potatoes resemble large potatoes with tapered ends and light tan to bright orange flesh. They're available year-round but are at their peak during the fall and winter. Select them as you would potatoes; choose firm ones, without any soft spots. Store in a cool, dark place for a few weeks. They don't last quite as long as regular potatoes do.

Best cooking methods: You can cook sweet potatoes any way you can cook a potato. They're best baked or made into oven fries.

Tomatoes

One of the most popular vegetables, the tomato is actually a fruit. Tomatoes are available year-round, but are at their peak during the summer months. They're also available canned and sun-dried. Beefsteak tomatoes are larger, plum tomatoes are smaller and egg-shaped, and both are available in yellow or red. You can also buy cherry or grape tomatoes in pint-sized containers. Sometimes you can find heirloom tomatoes, which are pricey but worth it; they come in varieties ranging from pink and purple to green and yellow, sometimes with striped skin. When buying tomatoes, "vine-ripened" are usually more flavorful than hot house tomatoes. Choose firm, deep red tomatoes that are fragrant and are free of blemishes and soft spots. Tomatoes should be kept at room temperature and never refrigerated—the cold temperature ruins their flavor and makes them pulpy. Left on the counter-top at room temperature, green tomatoes will ripen and turn red.

Canned tomatoes are available whole, crushed, diced, stewed, and seasoned. Tomato paste is a thick, intensely flavored tomato concentrate available in small cans and tubes.

Best cooking methods: Tomatoes are typically eaten raw, stewed, sautéed, broiled, or roasted. They're often used in soups, sauces, and stews.

Turnips

Turnips are available year-round, but are at their best during the winter. Choose turnips that are firm and heavy for their size, with no soft spots. Small, young ones are sweeter and more tender—the larger turnips tend to be pulpy. If the greens are still attached, they should be fresh-looking. Store them in a cool, dry place as you would potatoes and onions, for up to 3 weeks.

Best cooking methods: Turnips are best boiled, braised, sautéed, steamed, or roasted. They're often cooked and then mashed or puréed.

Zucchini

Zucchini is a type of summer squash. Although it's available year-round, it's most abundant during the summer months. Zucchini can be yellow or green and its skin is very fragile, which makes it difficult to find one without any blemishes. Choose small, firm zucchini with as few dents and blemishes as possible. Store them in a plastic bag in the fridge for up to a week.

Best cooking methods: Zucchini can be eaten raw, steamed, grilled, roasted, sautéed, deep-fried, or stir-fried, and is often grated raw into cake or muffin batter.

Most fruits continue to ripen once they've been picked, if you store them at room temperature. Refrigeration slows the ripening process. To speed ripening, place the fruit in a paper bag to trap the naturally occurring ethylene it gives off without suffocating it. To speed it up even more, add a banana, which gives off more ethylene than most fruits, to the bag.

Fruit

Apples

Apples are undoubtedly the most common fruit, for eating as well as for cooking. The countless varieties available will vary according to where you live and the orchards in your area. The most common varieties are Red and Golden Delicious, McIntosh, Granny Smith, Gala, Fuji, and Spartan. McIntosh and Granny Smith are best for baking because of their tartness and their ability to hold their shape when cooked. Although they're available year-round, apples are at their most flavorful and plentiful in the fall. When choosing apples, make sure they're firm and heavy for their size with no bruises, and wash them well before eating or cooking with them. Store them at room temperature, in the fridge, or in a cool, dry place for weeks.

Best cooking methods: Apples can be baked, sautéed, cooked into applesauce, or baked into pies, cakes, muffins, and desserts such as apple crisp.

Apricots

Apricots are most commonly purchased dried, but fresh apricots are delicious. Unfortunately, they're generally only available for a short time during the summer. Fresh apricots should be deep orange and faintly fuzzy, fragrant and firm, without bruises. It's difficult to tell if an apricot is going to be juicy or pulpy, so sometimes it's just the luck of the draw. Store them at room temperature or in the fridge for up to a week. Dried apricots keep in a well-sealed container for a year or more.

Best cooking methods: Apricots can be stewed, roasted, simmered into sauces or preserves, or baked into pies and fruit crisps.

Bananas

Although there are over 400 varieties of bananas, only one is commonly found in grocery stores in North America. Buy them slightly green; bananas sweeten as they ripen at room temperature. The more black spots (also called "sugar spots") a banana has, the riper and sweeter it will be. If they get too overripe and you aren't in the mood to bake, throw whole bananas in the freezer to use later in smoothies, banana bread, muffins, and cakes.

Best cooking methods: Bananas are usually eaten raw, but can be sautéed, broiled, or mashed and stirred into cakes, breads, and other baked goods.

Berries

All types of berries are fragile and should be handled gently and eaten quickly because they're so perishable. (Cranberries are the exception.) Blueberries, raspberries, and strawberries are in season during the summer, beginning at the end of May. Blackberries reach their peak at the end of the summer. Berries are also available frozen, both dry and in syrup. When shopping for fresh berries, be on the lookout for mushy and moldy ones. Store them in the fridge. If you are going to wash them, do it carefully, just before eating. Fresh berries can be frozen on a baking sheet as is and then transferred to a freezer bag to store for months.

Best cooking methods: Berries can be stewed, simmered into sauces and preserves, turned into ice cream or sorbet, stirred into bread and muffin batter, or baked into pies, fruit cobblers, and crisps.

Cherries

Fresh cherries are usually only available during the summer months, and are available canned in syrup year-round. Look for cherries that are firm and dark, and store them in a plastic bag in the fridge for a few days.

Best cooking methods: Cherries can be stewed, simmered into sauces and preserves, or baked into pies, cobblers, and crisps.

Cranberries

Cranberries are most commonly found fresh during the Thanksgiving/Christmas season, but are available frozen and dried year-round. They differ from other berries in that because they're so tart they're generally not eaten out of hand, and because they're firmer and not as juicy, they keep very well. Their texture and tartness make them ideal for use in sweetened baked dishes and sauces. Buy firm, whole berries and keep them in the fridge for weeks or throw the whole bag in the freezer for months.

Best cooking methods: Cranberries can be stewed, simmered into sauces, or stirred into breads, muffins, cakes, pies, and fruit crisps.

Dried fruit

There are more varieties of dried fruit on the market every day. Raisins, dates, prunes (actually dried plums) and apricots used to be the most common; now dried cranberries, cherries, blueberries, mango, apples, and pears are all commonly available. Dried fruit keeps very well, but make sure it's plump when you add it to recipes—dried-out fruit will suck the moisture from your batter. Plump it up by covering it with hot water or other liquid for at least 10 minutes, and drain it well before using.

Best cooking methods: Dried fruit can be eaten as is, stewed, or stirred into baked goods or oatmeal.

Figs

Fresh figs are becoming easier to find, usually between June and October. They're also available dried year-round. They range in color from dark purple to pale green, and the most common varieties are Calimyrna and Black Mission. Shop for figs that are soft (a sign of ripeness) and unblemished. Figs won't ripen after they're picked, and if they aren't ripe, they won't be sweet. They're very perishable so it's best to use them right away; if you don't, store them in the fridge for up to 3 days. Dried figs should be plump and soft and can be stored well wrapped at room temperature for months.

Best cooking methods: Figs can be stewed, poached, roasted, baked, or stirred into baked goods.

Grapes

Grapes are available year-round. They range in shade from green to purple to almost black. When shopping for them, make sure they're labeled "seedless" unless you don't mind seeds. Buy grapes that are plump and firmly attached to their stems with no sign of mold. Store them unwashed in the fridge for up to a week, but make sure you wash them well before eating—most grapes have been sprayed with insecticides.

Best cooking methods: Although they're usually eaten out of hand, grapes can be baked into pies or onto focaccia, or turned into preserves.

Grapefruit

Grapefruit comes in shades of pink and white; pink is generally sweeter. Buy fruit that is heavy for its size and store it in the fridge for up to 2 weeks.

Best cooking methods: Grapefruit is usually eaten raw, but can be stewed or cut in half, sprinkled with sugar, and broiled.

Kiwis

Kiwis are usually available year-round. Buy kiwi fruit that are firm or tender without being mushy; you can ripen them at home at room temperature.

Best cooking methods: Kiwis are generally eaten raw, but can be turned into compotes or preserves.

Lemons and limes

When buying lemons and limes, look for firm, thin-skinned varieties, which will have more fruit and juice inside. They should be heavy for their size. Named for the Florida Keys, Key limes don't resemble the green Persian limes we're used to seeing in the supermarket; they're small, round, usually pale greenish-yellow in color, and have a distinctive flavor. Store all lemons and limes in the fridge or at room temperature and make sure you wash them if you plan to grate their zest.

Best cooking methods: Lemons and limes are almost unlimited in their versatility: they aren't typically eaten on their own but can be used to flavor countless dishes from sweet to savory. They also make great pies, lemon meringue and Key lime being the most common.

Mandarin oranges, tangerines, and clementines

Tangerines and clementines are two of the more popular members of the Mandarin orange family. All Mandarin oranges are loose-skinned and easy to peel. Clementines are the smallest variety, with tangy red-orange flesh that's usually seedless. Tangerines have thicker skins and sweet flesh. Mandarins are also known as Christmas oranges because they're available during the winter months. Select Mandarin oranges that are heavy for their size, have loose skin, and no soft spots. Store them at room temperature for a few days, or in the fridge for up to a week.

Best cooking methods: Mandarin oranges are usually eaten raw, and their zest can be used to flavor recipes. They can also be used to make juice or preserves.

Mangoes

Mangoes are best fresh, but are also available canned, frozen, and dried. When shopping for mangoes, color isn't an indication of ripeness—they can be shades of green, yellow, red, and/or orange. When a mango is sweet, it will be fragrant and yield to gentle pressure; hard mangoes will ripen at room temperature. To get at the flesh of a mango, cut it in half with a large knife, and in doing so run the blade along the flat side of the pit, which is large and roughly the same shape as the mango. Do the same thing on the other side—you should end up with two "cheeks." Score the flesh of the mango, making sure you don't cut through the skin, and turn each mango half inside out to easily release the cubes of flesh. It's easier than it sounds!

Best cooking methods: Mangoes can be roasted, poached, stewed, sautéed, or turned into preserves, chutneys, ice cream, or sorbet.

Melons

Melons come in myriad varieties, the most common being watermelon, cantaloupe, and honeydew. It's difficult to determine whether or not a melon is sweet and ripe, and unfortunately they don't ripen very well once they've been picked off their vines. The best way to check for ripeness is to smell the fruit—a sweet odor is a good sign. You can shake it, too; loose seeds are also an indication of ripeness. Some melons will yield to gentle pressure when squeezed, but you don't want them to be mushy or have soft spots. Although they don't ripen as well as other fruits, store an unripe melon at room temperature until it seems ripe; store a ripe or cut melon in the refrigerator to slow the ripening process.

Best cooking methods: Melons are usually eaten raw.

Oranges

Oranges come in thin-skinned and thick-skinned varieties, and both are available year-round. Oranges don't actually have to be orange to be good; their skins vary in color from yellowish-orange to greenish-orange to purplish-orange. Be sure they're free of blemishes, and remember that an orange that is heavy for its size is probably nice and juicy. Oranges keep very well in the fridge or at room temperature and need not be washed unless you plan on grating the zest.

Best cooking methods: Oranges are typically eaten raw and their zest is used to flavor recipes. They can also be used to make juice, or preserves such as marmalade.

Papayas

Papayas will ripen at room temperature, so you can buy them firm and eat them when they soften. Buy papayas that are richly colored and yield to gentle pressure when squeezed. If the papaya is already ripe, refrigerate it until you're ready for it.

Best cooking methods: Papayas are usually eaten raw.

Peaches and Nectarines

Peaches and nectarines are in season between May and October, and are always available canned and frozen. The difference between peaches and nectarines is their skin; peaches are fuzzy and nectarines are smooth. Both are typically yellow, blushed with varying shades of pink or red, but their color is not an indication of sweetness or ripeness. All are either freestone or clingstone, named for whether or not the flesh clings to the pit. Peaches ripen very well at room temperature, so they don't need to be perfectly ripe when you buy them. Make sure they're firm and heavy for their size; that means they're probably juicy rather than pulpy. Store them at room temperature until they're ripe, or refrigerate those you want to ripen more slowly.

Best cooking methods: Peaches and nectarines can be broiled, roasted, grilled, poached, stewed, made into preserves or chutneys, or baked into pies, cobblers, crisps, cakes, and muffins. To easily peel a peach or nectarine, first blanch it by dropping it into a pot of boiling water for about 30 seconds, then plunging it into cold water to stop the cooking. The skins should slip right off.

Pears

Pears are unique in that their flavor and texture actually improve after they've been picked. They're available year-round, but are at their peak from late July until early spring, and they're also available canned. The most common varieties of pear are Bartlett, Bosc, Anjou, and Comice, which range in color from green to red, and like apples, the different varieties have subtle differences in flavor. Ripe pears will be fragrant and yield to gentle pressure when squeezed; green pears tend to turn yellow as they ripen. Keep pears at room temperature until ripe, or store them in the fridge to slow the ripening process.

Best cooking methods: Pears can be poached, sautéed, simmered into sauce, or baked into pies, cakes, muffins, and fruit crisp.

Pineapples

Pineapples are available fresh and canned year-round, and are at their peak from March to July. Sweet, ripe pineapples are sometimes difficult to choose. Because the starch in a pineapple will not convert to sugar once it's picked, it won't ripen on your countertop. Buy pineapples without any green areas or soft spots, that are fragrant and yield to gentle pressure when you squeeze them. Try tugging gently on a small inner leaf—if the leaf pulls out easily, it's an indication of ripeness. Once the pineapple has been cut, refrigerate it, wrapped in plastic, for up to 3 days.

Best cooking methods: Pineapple can be eaten raw, broiled, grilled, roasted, sautéed, or baked into an upside-down cake.

Plums

Plums are available from May through October and are also available canned, although the canned variety doesn't compare to fresh plums. They're also available dried, in which case they're called prunes. Fresh plums can range in shape from round to oval and can be yellow, green, red, purple, blue, and shades in between. Choose plums that are plump and firm but not hard, with no soft spots or blemishes. The silvery film you see on some plums is natural and not a sign of spoilage. Harder plums will soften at room temperature. Keep them at room temperature until they ripen, or store loosely wrapped in a plastic bag in the fridge for up to a week.

Best cooking methods: Plums can be broiled, grilled, roasted, stewed, sautéed, turned into preserves, or baked into pies, cakes, fruit crisps, and even muffins.

Rhubarb

Rhubarb is actually a vegetable, but because it's tart and must be sweetened, we usually treat it as a fruit. Rhubarb shows up in gardens from April to June. The stems are the only edible part; the leaves can actually be toxic. Choose rhubarb with stalks that are crisp and not flabby. Store it loosely wrapped in a plastic bag in the fridge and use it within a few days. Before cooking rhubarb, pull out the celery-like strings that run lengthwise down each stalk.

Best cooking methods: Rhubarb is very tart, so it's best stewed, made into preserves, or baked into muffins, pies, cobblers, and crisps.

Strawberries

Strawberries are in season from April to June, but are often found fresh year round. They're always available frozen, dry or in light syrup. A good grocery store strawberry is sometimes difficult to find; for the most flavorful berries, go to a farmer's market or a U-pick farm and pick them yourself. It's difficult to tell if a strawberry will taste good without actually tasting it. Small ones tend to be sweeter, and larger ones are usually watery without as much flavor. Choose brightly colored berries with crisp green leaves, and always be on the lookout for moldy berries, which quickly infect all others around them. Store them in the fridge, preferably on a layer of paper towel to absorb excess moisture, for up to 3 days. Don't wash strawberries until you're ready to eat them.

Best cooking methods: Strawberries can be stewed or simmered into sauces, made into preserves or ice cream, or baked into pies, muffins, cobblers, and crisps.

Applying heat 101

You can apply heat to food in two ways: dry or with liquid. Methods of cooking with dry heat include baking, roasting, grilling, and sautéing. Boiling, braising, poaching, steaming, and frying use liquid, such as water, broth, or oil, as a heat conduit.

Dry heat

Applying heat

Baking and roasting

Baking and roasting are essentially the same thing: both are done in the oven (a closed environment) using dry heat that is applied from all directions. Baking is a term usually applied to breads, muffins, cakes, and pastries, and we tend to use roasting when describing meat and vegetables. You can roast all types of poultry, tender cuts of meat, fish, most vegetables, potatoes, and fruits. (Ham appears to be the exception—it's usually described as "baked" ham, yet we "roast" chicken and beef. What gives?)

Grilling and broiling

Grilling is most likely the oldest cooking method, and uses direct heat from a gas or electric grill or an open flame. Ideally, whatever you choose to grill should be an inch (2.5 cm) thick or less; because it's cooked over high heat, a thick cut will burn on the outside before fully cooking through on the inside. You can usually lower the heat somewhat, however, by moving food further away from the flame or to the cool side of your grill. Grilling is ideal for all kinds of meat, poultry, fish, vegetables, fruit, and anything that benefits from a charred surface and slightly smoky flavor.

The only difference between grilling and broiling is that when you broil, the heat source is above the food rather than underneath it. Broiling is generally done in the oven under high heat. Meat, vegetables, and fruit are often broiled, as are dishes that require a final browning on top.

Sautéing

Sautéing refers to a method of cooking food quickly in a hot, shallow pan set over direct heat with a minimum amount of fat. Add your oil or a combination of butter and oil (the milk solids in butter make it burn too easily to use alone) to the pan once it's hot, then add the food you want to sauté and move it around in the pan as it cooks.

If your goal is to have flavorful browned bits on the bottom of the pan, which are ideal for deglazing (see page 116) to make a sauce or gravy afterward, don't use a non-stick sauté pan. I love using non-stick pans—you can get away with using far less fat to cook with—but they don't produce as many of the yummy browned bits that come from food sticking to the pan.

Stir-frying

Stir-frying is very similar to sautéing in that food is cooked quickly over high heat in very little oil, but generally stir-fried foods are chopped into small pieces so that they cook even more quickly. Ideally, the food you stir-fry should be chopped into fairly uniform sizes so that the pieces cook evenly.

Wet heat

Blanching

Blanching is the process by which foods (usually fruit and green vegetables) are submerged in boiling water for a few seconds and then quickly plunged into cold water to stop the cooking process. It's a technique often used to keep veggies brightly colored while partially tenderizing them, or to make them easier to peel. Fruits such as peaches and tomatoes are easily peeled after blanching—it causes the outer layer of skin to break down, making it easier to slip off.

Boiling

Water acts as a heat conduit when you cook with it, and provides a constant and even temperature to foods as they boil. A "full rolling boil" is one that cannot be dissipated by stirring. This is important when cooking pasta; the constant motion and pressure washes away excess starches. Pasta, eggs, and vegetables are often boiled.

Braising

Braising is a cooking method by which meat or vegetables are browned in fat, then tightly covered and simmered in a small amount of liquid over low heat for a long time. Browning the food first caramelizes it, creating a flavorful crust and browned bits on the bottom of the pan that will add even more flavor to the finished dish. The slow cooking in liquid over a low temperature tenderizes tough cuts of meat by gently breaking down their fibers and connective tissues, and develops their flavors. Generally the liquid should come about halfway up the meat or vegetables. Braising can be done in the oven or on the stovetop—either way, make sure the pot or pan has a tight-fitting lid so the liquid doesn't evaporate.

Best cuts for braising:
Beef: Chuck, bottom round, rump roast, round steak, eye of round
Pork: Boston butt, picnic shoulder, blade end, ham hocks, pork leg, shank
Lamb: Shanks, shoulder, neck, leg, sirloin

Frying

The only difference between sautéing, pan-frying, and deep-frying is the amount of fat you use. Sautéing uses the least amount of fat—just enough to lubricate the pan. Pan-frying is done with enough oil to come about a third of the way up the side of the pan, and the food isn't moved around as it's cooked, which would be dangerous with hot oil. Deep-frying is the process by which food is submerged in hot fat in order to cook it.

Parboiling

Parboiling is similar to blanching in that you only partially cook food by boiling it briefly in water. Vegetables that take longer to cook (such as carrots) are often parboiled so that they can be added at the last minute to ingredients that require less cooking time.

Poaching

Poaching is a cooking method where food is gently cooked in liquid that has been heated just until the surface begins to quiver—not at a simmer or a full boil. It can be done in water or in any liquid that has been heated to just below the simmering point. Eggs, fish, chicken, and fruit are common candidates for poaching.

Simmering

To simmer is to cook foods in water heated to the point at which tiny bubbles break the surface. Although there isn't much difference in temperature, a simmer is not as turbulent as a full rolling boil, so foods cook more gently. Simmering can be done on the stovetop or in the oven. Rice, grains, and dry beans all benefit from simmering.

Steaming

When food is steamed it's set above, not in, boiling or simmering water, using a rack or steaming basket in a covered pan. Steaming is a gentle cooking method and it retains the flavor and shape of foods, and many of the vitamins that are often lost when vegetables are boiled. Vegetables and delicate foods such as dumplings benefit from steaming.

Stewing

Stewing differs from braising in its ratio of meat to liquid. In a stew, the meat is typically cut into pieces and submerged in liquid, but the long, slow simmering aspect is the same.

Tips
from Mom

Ingredients

To determine whether or not your eggs are fresh, immerse them in a pan of cool water. If an egg sinks, it's fresh; if it rises to the surface, toss it!

To soften hardened brown sugar quickly, put a small amount in a dish with a slice of apple or bread, cover, and microwave for about 30 seconds. To keep brown sugar soft, keep a slice of fresh bread in the bag or canister.

If you don't like grating small amounts of ginger for a recipe, buy several knobs, peel them, and grate them or purée them in the food processor. Transfer the grated or puréed ginger to a zip-lock bag, push all the air out, and flatten it as thin as you can. Pop the bag in the freezer for up to 6 months, and snap off a piece whenever you need it.

Honey that has hardened or crystallized can be softened in the microwave. Remove the cap and nuke it for about 30 seconds to liquefy it. When measuring honey (or corn syrup or molasses), spray the inside of your measuring cup with non-stick spray to help it slide out more easily. Honey stored in a cool place will last for 2 years or more.

To stabilize whipped cream, add 2 Tbsp (30 mL) of dried milk powder to every cup (250 mL) of whipping cream before you whip it.

To prolong the freezer life of fish fillets, pull them out of the freezer within a day or two of freezing them solid. Dip them in cold water, wrap them well, and return them to the freezer. This process is called glazing, and it should double their freezer life.

Slice bagels before you freeze them—it's very difficult to slice a frozen bagel, and microwaving tends to dry out the middle. Frozen bagel halves can be toasted from frozen—there is no need to thaw them first.

Bread goes stale faster when stored in the fridge. Store bread well wrapped in a plastic bag at room temperature for up to 3 days, or slice it and freeze. For breads that contain perishable ingredients such as meats or cheese, freeze what you don't eat the first day.

Use stale bread to make stuffing, or cut it into cubes, toss with oil and garlic powder and toast on a cookie sheet to make croutons, or grind in a food processor to make bread-crumbs. Store in a plastic bag in the freezer.

Leftover cookies can be crumbled or ground in the food processor and added to fruit crumble toppings or used to make crumb pie crusts.

Leftover pancake or waffle batter can be frozen in an empty milk container. It's easy to thaw the batter, then pour it out directly onto the griddle or waffle iron and toss the container when you're done.

After you cook potatoes, save the water (it will keep in the fridge for a few days) and use it in soups, breads, or anything that calls for extra liquid. The potato starch adds body and nutritional benefits.

Salvage hardened raisins or other dried fruit by covering them with hot water or other liquid; let stand for 10 minutes and drain well before using.

To sour milk, add 1 Tbsp (15 mL) white vinegar or lemon juice to every cup (250 mL) milk, and let it stand for about 10 minutes.

Place dollops of leftover whipped cream on a sheet lined with wax paper in the freezer. Once frozen, transfer to plastic bags to store them. When you want a dollop of whipped cream on a dessert or in a hot drink, pull one out and plop it on top.

Keep the rind of flavorful hard cheeses to simmer in soups and stews. Toss the rind out before serving.

Make sweet or savory butters by adding flavorful ingredients such as crushed garlic, finely chopped shallots or jalapeños, fresh herbs, horseradish, cinnamon, chili powder, grated citrus zest, curry paste, finely ground toasted nuts, or honey to softened butter. Refrigerate until firm, then roll into a long, thin log, wrap in plastic, and freeze. Cut off slices as needed.

Techniques

Use a meat baster to squeeze pancake batter onto your griddle.

Use an egg slicer to cut mushrooms easily and evenly.

To dry fresh herbs, keep the leaves on the stems and lay them in a single layer on a baking sheet, or tie small bunches and hang them upside down, out of the sun, until they are completely dry. Rub the dried herbs between your fingers to release the leaves onto a sheet of paper, and funnel the paper into a small airtight container. Dried herbs are more potent than fresh, so 1 tsp (5 mL) dried herbs can be substituted for 1 Tbsp (15 mL) fresh.

If you're having a hard time skimming the fat from your sauce or soup with a spoon, try folding a paper towel and dragging it across the surface to absorb excess fat. If you have time to refrigerate your soup or sauce, the fat will rise and solidify so that you can lift it off the surface.

To season a cast iron pan, wipe it clean and rub well with a light, flavorless vegetable oil. Canola oil works well. Put it in a 250°F (120°C) oven for 2 hours, and let it cool completely before using. To maintain your cast iron skillet, clean it while it's still warm by rinsing with hot water and scraping as necessary. Avoid using scouring pads or soap, which will break down the pan's seasoning. Dry the pan well and store with the lid off. Should rust appear, the pan should be scoured and re-seasoned.

To prevent cream from curdling when you add it to a hot sauce, remove about ½ cup (125 mL) of the hot sauce from the pot and whisk the cream into it; remove the pot from the heat and stir the cream mixture back into the sauce.

To scale a fish, first run it under cold running water or rub it with white vinegar. Scrape off the scales with the edge of a spoon, working from the tail toward the head.

Cleaning

To wash your blender, fill it halfway with warm, soapy water and pulse to thoroughly clean hard-to-reach spots. Always wash the blender right after you use it if possible— dried-on food is difficult to clean from around the blade area.

To clean mineral deposits from your coffee maker, fill it with water and 2 Tbsp (30 mL) of white vinegar. Brew it as you would a pot of coffee, running the solution through twice. Rinse the coffee maker by running plain water through it twice.

To clean the inside of your microwave, place a bowl of hot water (add a slice or two of lemon if you have one) inside and microwave it on high for 30 seconds. Let the bowl sit for 10 minutes to steam and soften any dried-on food, then wipe the inside of the microwave clean.

To get all the citrus zest off your grater, brush it with a pastry brush.

Keep an old toothbrush by the kitchen sink for cleaning beaters, graters, peelers, and other kitchen utensils with nooks and crannies. It's also useful for cleaning around the sink faucets.

To disinfect slimy, smelly sponges or dish-cloths, soak them overnight in a mild bleach solution or a mixture of half vinegar and half water. Run them through the dishwasher, or soak them and nuke in the microwave for a minute. Careful—let them cool before you pick them up!

To eliminate odors from your cutting board, sprinkle it with fresh lemon juice or cut a lemon in half and rub the cut side over the surface.

To remove garlic odor from your hands, rub your fingers with the bowl of a stainless steel spoon while holding them under warm running water.

Sprinkle kitty litter in the bottom of your garbage pail to absorb odors and any liquid that might leak out of the bottom of the bag.

Aluminum foil is great for lining your roasting pans to avoid a burnt-on mess to clean afterward, or for sealing pots and baking dishes that don't have lids. If you're worried about food sticking, spray the foil with non-stick spray first.

To remove burnt-on food from pans or casserole dishes, fill them with water and let them soak for at least 15 minutes; scrape off what you can and repeat as necessary. For food that just won't come off, add warm soapy water and cook it on the stove for about 10 minutes, then let it sit until it cools down enough for you to handle again. You could also try generously coating the surface with baking soda, then combining ¾ cup (180 mL) hot water

and ¼ cup (60 mL) white vinegar, and pouring it onto the soda. Let the mixture sit until it loosens any burnt-on bits. (Next time, line your roasting pan with aluminum foil!)

If something you're baking has overflowed in the oven, sprinkle the spill with salt as soon as possible. Wipe it all away once the oven has cooled.

Miscellaneous

To prevent sticky jar lids, dip a paper towel into vegetable oil and wipe the threads of the jar or bottle before replacing the lid, or cover the top of the jar with a square of plastic wrap before screwing on the top.

You can sterilize jars for jams and other preserves in the oven instead of looking for a giant pot to boil them in. Wash and rinse the jars well, place in a shallow roasting pan or on a rimmed baking sheet, and put them in a 250°F (120°C) oven for about 20 minutes.

If you stack your glasses and two get stuck together, fill the top one with cold water and set the bottom one in hot water. They should come apart easily.

When you're baking, keep a plastic bag by the telephone to slip your hand into so you can answer the phone without having to wash your hands first.

To make your house smell wonderful, sprinkle cinnamon on a square of aluminum foil and place it in a hot oven; turn off the heat and open the door slightly. It's better than potpourri!

Clean out a dish detergent or other squeeze bottle really well and use it to store cooking oil by your stove. It's easy to squirt some into the pan whenever you need it.

If your cookbook won't lie flat, lay a glass baking dish over it—you can read through the glass.

If you're having a hard time opening a jar, slip on your rubber gloves or wrap an elastic band around the lid to get a better grip. It also helps to tap the edge of the lid against the corner of the countertop or run it under hot water.

When sharpening knives on a stone, lubricate the stone with liquid dishwashing soap instead of machine oil, which is toxic.

Make your own icing decorating bags by rolling a piece of wax paper or parchment into a cone shape, taping the edge, and snipping off the tip. Slide in a decorating tip or leave it as is and fill the cone with frosting; twist the end closed before you begin to decorate.

To melt chocolate for drizzling, place chopped chocolate or chocolate chips in a plastic zip-lock bag, seal, and place in a bowl of warm water until the chocolate has melted. Snip off a tiny corner of the bag and squeeze out the melted chocolate.

Make a giant cookie by pressing cookie dough into a round cake pan and baking until golden. Once the cookie has cooled, decorate it with icing to make a cookie card. Cut into wedges to serve.

To keep a cutting board from slipping as you chop or a bowl from sliding as you mix, dampen a tea towel and lay it under the board or twist it under the bowl. When you're done, use the towel to clean the counter.

Crush crackers or nuts by putting them in a zip-lock bag and rolling with a rolling pin or bashing with a mallet or bottom of a can.

To prevent yogurt from separating under heat, stir a little cornstarch into the yogurt first and add it to a recipe at the last minute. Never let the yogurt boil.

Break an egg into a funnel to separate the white from the yolk.

When a recipe calls for only egg whites or yolks, store the egg whites or yolks you don't use in the freezer for up to 3 months. For faster thawing and easier measuring, freeze each white or yolk in an ice cube tray and then transfer to a freezer bag. When freezing egg yolks, add a pinch of salt or 1 ½ tsp (7 mL) sugar for every 4 yolks to prevent them from becoming gelatinous.

If you need to scald milk, rinse your pan first with cold water to make cleaning it easier afterward. This also works well when making scrambled eggs.

Peel garlic by placing the flat edge of a knife blade over a clove set on the countertop and whacking it with your hand. It will slightly crush the garlic, making the papery skin easy to peel off.

To remove olive pits, whack whole olives with the flat side of a chef's knife on the countertop, using the palm of your hand. This will split them open so you can easily remove the pits.

To chop onions without crying, place a lighted candle nearby. The flames burn the sulfuric fumes that cause tears.

When juicing lemons or limes, mirowave them for about 20 seconds or roll them on the countertop, pressing with your palm to yield more juice, then squeeze the juice through your fingers to catch the pits.

Washed-out vitamin jars and film canisters are great for storing spices. Remember to label them so that you remember what's inside.

When making one-pot dishes such as soups and casseroles, it's just as easy to make a big batch as it is to make a small one. Freeze it in individual containers or double the recipe and freeze the second batch so you always have a quick dinner or lunch to bring wherever you need to go.

Breakfast

When it comes to the most important meal of the day
we are all for the most part creatures of habit—most of us don't
like to stray from our favorite brands of cereal
or usual tea and toast. Not many people have the gumption
to cook that early in the morning, and we're usually
pretty short on time. But ask 10 people what their favorite
meal of the day is, and 8 will reply "breakfast."

It seems to me all foods are segregated into two categories: those that are acceptable for breakfast consumption and those that are not. Such strict parameters aren't imposed on lunch and dinner, so why are roast chicken and salads discriminated against in the morning? What's wrong with a stack of pancakes for supper? If breakfast is the most important meal of the day our parameters should relax a little, but then again in the wee hours, precious minutes are best spent sleeping so it's usually a rushed affair. On the weekends, the rules change. One of the best ways to celebrate a morning when you don't have to wake up to the alarm is by lingering over waffles or eggs. Just remember: whether you're scarfing something down on the way to wherever you need to be, or observing the ritual of Sunday breakfast, it's still the most important meal of the day. And admit it—no matter how sleepy you are, it's just as easy to eat something that doesn't come out of a package.

How to boil an egg

Yes, this is a recipe for a boiled egg. Eggs can be boiled to any degree of doneness you like if you time them just right. When cooking large eggs, 4 minutes will give you a soft-boiled egg: the white is set and the yolk runny; 5–6 minutes will give you a medium-boiled egg: the white is set and the yolk cooked but still soft; and 10–15 minutes will give you a hard-boiled egg: both the white and yolk are firm. (Note that the shorter time for a hard-boiled egg leaves some of the yolk slightly underdone.)

To boil eggs, submerge them in enough gently boiling water to cover them without crowding. If you are boiling several at a time, make sure they're lying in a single layer in the pot. You can use a pin or needle to gently poke a hole in the broad end of each egg before you put them in the pot to alleviate the pressure created by the swelling egg white and eliminate cracked shells. Start the timer as soon as you lower the eggs into the water. When they're done, plunge them into cold water to stop them from cooking. Leave them in a bowl of cold water if you want to cool them completely.

How to poach an egg

To poach one or more eggs, bring about an inch of water to a boil in a skillet big enough to accommodate the number of eggs you want to cook. (It's best to do no more than 3 at a time.) Add a good sprinkling of salt and, if you like, a teaspoon (5 mL) of vinegar, which isn't at all necessary but it's what restaurants do to lower the pH of the water and prevent the whites from becoming ragged. Reduce the heat to a simmer—the point at which the water softly bubbles. Gently break the eggs into the water and, as they start to set, spoon the water over the tops of the eggs to help them cook. If they stick to the bottom of the skillet, loosen them with a thin spatula. Poach the eggs for 3–4 minutes, until the whites are firm and the yolks have filmed over. Remove them from the water with a slotted spoon and transfer them to buttered toast or onto a paper towel to drain.

If you want to poach the eggs in advance, you can keep them in a bowl of cold water in the fridge for up to 2 days, and reheat them by dipping them into a pan of simmering water for about 30 seconds.

How to bake an egg

Baked eggs have fallen out of fashion, but I personally think they need to make a comeback. To bake an egg (or eggs), break them into individually buttered custard cups or ramekins. If you like, line the cups with a thin slice of ham or Canadian bacon first. Drizzle the eggs with a little cream or dot them with butter and sprinkle them with salt and pepper. If you have some, add a sprinkle of chopped fresh herbs, too. Place the ramekins on a baking sheet and bake them at 350°F (175°C) for 10–15 minutes, until the eggs are set and the whites are firm. If you're a cheese fan, top them with some grated cheese for the last few minutes of baking.

How to fry an egg

It's easy to fry an egg, but making a good fried egg requires a little know-how. When frying an egg, the key to keeping the yolk soft without overcooking the whites and making them rubbery is low heat. Start with a heavy pan, preferably non-stick, set over medium heat, and add a little oil, butter, or bacon drippings. Swirl the fat around to coat the pan and, if you're using butter, wait for it to foam up and then subside. Gently crack the eggs into the pan. They shouldn't sputter or bubble, but should start to set up instantly. As soon as the egg whites are no longer translucent, turn the heat down and sprinkle the eggs with salt and pepper. To finish cooking them you have a few options—for sunny-side up eggs, cover the pan and cook them for 2–4 minutes, until the whites are firm and the yolks are done to your liking. (Two minutes will produce still-runny yolks; 4 minutes will cook them through.) For over-easy eggs, gently flip

them after about 3 minutes and cook them for about 30 seconds on the other side. For basted eggs, spoon any butter or oil in the pan over the yolk until it films over.

How to scramble an egg

Scrambling eggs isn't difficult, and there are no hard and fast rules. You can scramble eggs straight, or add milk or water to make them light and airy. Adding liquid creates steam, which helps produce fluffy curds. Because milk contains protein, fat, and sugars, adding it will create the fluffiest eggs. Use about a tablespoon (15 mL) of liquid per large egg you use. When you stir the eggs, be gentle; over-beating could make them tough and stringy. Thirty seconds with a fork is just fine, and don't forget to add salt and pepper.

Heat some oil, butter or a little of each in a heavy pan, preferably non-stick, set over medium-high heat. Pour in your beaten eggs and push them around in the pan, lifting and folding them, keeping them in constant, gentle motion. Stop for a few seconds once in a while to allow the eggs to puff a little. The whole process is very fast—two eggs should only take about 30 seconds to cook. Scrambled eggs take well to a multitude of ingredients—try adding chopped fresh herbs, grated cheese, chopped cooked bacon, ham or salmon, or sautéed vegetables as your eggs cook. When they're just barely (but not completely) set, remove them from the heat and transfer them to a plate—they'll finish cooking with their own heat.

For the absolute creamiest scrambled eggs imaginable, cook them in a double boiler set over simmering water, stirring or whisking them almost constantly. (This takes about 20 minutes, so it's a good thing to do while talking on the phone.) The resulting eggs are almost custard-like.

Omelet

Ingredients

Oil, butter, or non-stick spray

3 large eggs

1 Tbsp (15 mL) water

Salt and pepper

Any additions you like: chopped fresh herbs, grated cheese, sautéed veggies, chopped cooked meat, or a combination of any of these

Omelets are notoriously intimidating to novice cooks, but they're a cinch to make. An omelet makes the ultimate fast and easy breakfast, lunch, or dinner, especially when all you have are bits of ingredients and leftovers in the fridge. When your kitchen seems empty, you can probably still throw together a decent omelet, and it's perfect to make if you're cooking only for yourself. Stuff it with anything you like: grated or crumbled cheese, cream cheese, chopped fresh herbs, raw or sautéed veggies, cooked potatoes, and cooked meat such as bacon, ham, smoked salmon, or sausage all work well.

To make an omelet you'll need a non-stick skillet with sloped sides that's the right size for the number of eggs you want to cook. If it's too big, the eggs will spread out too thin; if it's too small, they'll be too thick and may not cook through properly. An 8-inch (20 cm) or 9-inch (23 cm) skillet is perfect for 2–3 eggs.

Method

1 Place the skillet over medium heat and a small drizzle of oil, a blob of butter, or a combination of the two, or spray it with non-stick spray. (You'll need a little more if your skillet isn't non-stick.)

2 Stir the eggs, water, and a bit of salt and pepper together in a small bowl with a fork until the whites and yolks are combined. Don't beat them too much, or they could get tough. If you are using fresh herbs or grated hard cheese, you could stir a small amount into the egg mixture.

3 Pour the eggs into the skillet—they should begin to cook immediately. Some people like to stir the eggs with a fork at this point until they thicken. It's not necessary, but it helps to create an even texture. Let the eggs cook for about 30 seconds, then help the omelet cook by gently lifting the edges with a thin spatula and allowing the uncooked egg to run underneath. (This works particularly well with a heatproof spatula.) Cook until the bottom is set and the omelet is still moist and almost (but not completely) set on top.

4 Sprinkle your choice of fillings along the middle and slightly onto one side of the omelet. Fold the opposite side over with a spatula and, if you like, keep it on the heat for another minute to allow the filling to heat through. Then slide the whole thing onto a plate.

5 Repeat as necessary to feed everyone you want to feed.

Serves 1

 What to do with the leftovers

* Keep them covered in the fridge for up to 2 days and reheat them in the microwave or eat them cold. Leftovers make great sandwiches. Put a wedge between two slices of buttered toast.

 Other things to do with it

* Mexican Omelets: Sauté about 1 lb (500 g) ground beef or chicken with a finely chopped onion and a couple crushed cloves of garlic until the meat is no longer pink; stir in 1 tsp (5 mL) chili powder, ½ tsp (2.5 mL) cumin, and salt and pepper. Stir in 1 chopped red bell pepper and ½ cup (125 mL) salsa. Fill omelets with the meat mixture (this should make enough for 4) and shredded cheddar or Monterey Jack cheese, and serve with guacamole or sour cream.

Frittata

Ingredients

1 Tbsp (15 mL) canola oil or butter

5 large eggs

½ cup (125 mL) grated cheddar, Monterey Jack, Gouda, Parmesan, crumbled feta, or goat cheese

Salt and pepper

1–1 ½ cups (250–375 mL) filling: cooked and chopped asparagus, broccoli, mushrooms, potatoes, red peppers, zucchini or spinach, sun-dried tomatoes, caramelized onions, leftover roasted veggies, chopped raw or canned tomatoes, green onion, fresh herbs, cooked spaghetti, cooked crumbled sausage, ham or bacon, or a combination of any of these

A frittata is a baked Italian egg pie, much like a quiche but without a crust. It has the same characteristics as an omelet, but is much less finicky since you cook everything together at once in the pan. Anything that goes well in an omelet makes a great frittata, and it's a perfect way to use up leftovers. The basic proportions are 1 to 1 ½ cups (250–375 mL) of filling for every 5–6 eggs.

Method

1 Preheat the oven to 350°F (175°C).

2 Heat the oil in an ovenproof skillet (non-stick if you have it; 10-inch (25 cm) would be ideal) set over medium heat. If you have any ingredients that need to be precooked, sauté them for a few minutes, until they're tender or cooked through. Stir together the eggs, cheese, and salt and pepper in a medium bowl.

3 Stir any other ingredients you're using into the eggs and pour them into the skillet. Turn the heat down to medium-low and cook the frittata for 5–8 minutes, until the bottom is set.

4 Transfer the skillet to the oven, sprinkling the top of the frittata with extra cheese first, if you like. Bake for about 10 more minutes, until the top is set and golden or the cheese melts. Serve it hot, at room temperature, or cold.

Serves 2–4

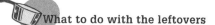

What to do with the leftovers

* Keep them covered in the fridge for up to 2 days. Reheat them in the microwave or eat them cold. Leftovers make great sandwiches. Put a wedge between two slices of buttered toast.

Other things to do with it

* Cut chilled frittata into squares or wedges and serve them as an appetizer.

* Strata: Spread day-old cubes of sturdy bread over the bottom of a greased baking pan and pour the egg mixture on top. Cover and refrigerate it overnight, so that the bread has a chance to fully absorb the egg. If you like, sprinkle cheese over top before you bake it for 20–30 minutes at 350°F (175°C), until the strata is golden and cooked through. (This is a great brunch dish to prepare the night before and pop in the oven in the morning.)

Home Fries

Ingredients

2 medium Yukon Gold or russet
   potatoes, scrubbed but unpeeled

1–2 Tbsp (15–30 mL) canola, corn or
   olive oil

1 onion, peeled and chopped
   (optional)

1 Tbsp (15 mL) butter

Salt and pepper

Paprika (optional)

What to do with the leftovers

* You probably won't have any,
  which is a good thing because they
  don't reheat very well.

Other things to do with it

* Toss them with 1 Tbsp (15 mL)
  chopped fresh parsley and/or grated
  Parmesan while they're still hot.

* Spicy Cheese Home Fries:
  Combine ¼ cup (60 mL) grated
  Parmesan, 1 tsp (5 mL) chili
  powder, and ¼ tsp (1 mL) each
  garlic powder, and salt and pepper.
  Sprinkle the potatoes with the mixture as you cook them in the skillet.

I debated whether to include this in the potato or breakfast section, but since home fries are generally served at breakfast, here they are. Parboiling (see page 41) the potatoes before pan-frying them ensures they're fluffy on the inside, crispy and golden on the outside. Use any kind of potatoes you like. (Yukon Gold are my favorite). Double the recipe as needed, but make sure you either use a large enough skillet or sauté the potatoes in batches. If they're too crowded they'll steam rather than brown properly.

Method

1 Dice the potatoes and place them in a large pot. Add enough water to cover them, and a generous pinch of salt. Place the pot over high heat and as soon as the water comes to a full boil, remove it from the heat and drain the potatoes well.

2 Heat half the oil in a large, heavy skillet set over medium-high heat and sauté the onion for 5–8 minutes, or until golden. Transfer it to a bowl and set aside.

3 Heat the remaining oil and the butter in the skillet and add the potatoes. Shake them around to coat them with the butter and oil. Leave them in a single layer and cook without stirring for about 4 minutes, or until golden on the bottom. Make sure the skillet isn't too crowded, or the potatoes will steam rather than brown properly.

4 Stir the potatoes up, spread them out in a single layer again (make sure they're all flipped over), and cook for a few more minutes. Keep stirring and cooking the potatoes until they're golden all over. Add the onion, salt and pepper to taste, and a sprinkle of paprika and serve them immediately.

Serves 2 (doubles or triples easily)

Pancakes

Ingredients

2 cups (500 mL) buttermilk or 2 cups
(500 mL) milk plus 1 Tbsp (15 mL)
lemon juice or vinegar

2 cups (500 mL) all-purpose flour (or
half whole wheat, half
all-purpose)

2 Tbsp (30 mL) sugar

2 tsp (10 mL) baking powder

½ tsp (2.5 mL) baking soda

¼ tsp (1 mL) salt

1 large egg

2 Tbsp (30 mL) melted butter or oil

Any additions you like: fresh or
frozen (unthawed) berries, sliced
banana, or chopped or ground
nuts

Packaged pancake mix usually contains little more than flour, sugar, and baking powder. Making them from scratch is just as fast and easy, and you can't make a cheaper breakfast. If you want to flavor your pancakes, stir grated lemon or orange zest or a teaspoon (5 mL) of flavored extract into the milk mixture. Of course, pancakes can always be studded with berries, banana slices, nuts, or any additions you like.

Method

1 If you are using regular milk, pour it into a small bowl or measuring cup and stir in the lemon juice; set the mixture aside for a few minutes.

2 In a large bowl, stir together the flour, sugar, baking powder, baking soda, and salt. Stir the egg and melted butter or oil into the buttermilk or milk mixture with a fork or whisk.

3 Make a well in the dry ingredients and pour in the milk mixture; stir just until the two are combined. Don't worry about getting all the lumps out—overmixing may result in tough pancakes.

4 Set a large non-stick skillet over medium heat. When the skillet is hot (you can test it by flicking some drops of water on it—they should bounce) spray it with non-stick spray or drizzle it with oil and swirl to coat it. Ladle the batter onto the skillet, making the pancakes any size you like. If you want to add berries, slices of banana, or anything else, scatter them directly onto the pancakes as they cook.

5 Turn the heat down and cook the pancakes for a few minutes, until the bottoms are golden and bubbles begin to appear on the surface. When the surface appears almost dry with lots of bubbles breaking through, use a thin, flat spatula to flip the pancakes over and cook them for another minute, until they're golden on the other side.

6 Repeat with the remaining batter. If you need to keep the finished pancakes warm, keep them uncovered on a plate in a 200°F (110°C) oven. If you don't want to cook them all at once, the leftover batter can be covered and kept in the fridge for several days.

7 Serve the pancakes with maple syrup, or thaw a package of frozen berries in syrup to top them with.

Serves 4

 What to do with the leftovers

* Wrap extra pancakes in plastic wrap and freeze them to pop in the toaster or microwave on mornings when you don't have time to cook. Toast them from frozen.

 Other things to do with it

* Corn Pancakes: Replace ½ cup (125 mL) of the flour with cornmeal. Stir about 1 cup (250 mL) canned, frozen, or fresh corn kernels and/or a few crumbled pieces of cooked bacon into the batter.

* Multigrain Pecan Pancakes: Use half whole wheat and half all-purpose flour, and add ½ cup (125 mL) oats and ½ cup (125 mL) chopped pecans to the dry ingredients. A few spoonfuls of ground flaxseed make a healthy addition too.

* Apple Pancakes: Add a pinch of cinnamon to the dry ingredients, and stir in a grated apple along with the wet ingredients.

* Gingerbread Pancakes: Use ½ cup (125 mL) molasses in place of the sugar, and add 1 tsp (5 mL) cinnamon and 1 tsp (5 mL) ground ginger to the dry ingredients.

* Pumpkin Pancakes: Use brown sugar, add 1 tsp (5 mL) cinnamon to the dry ingredients, and stir ½ cup (125 mL) canned pumpkin purée into the wet ingredients before you blend the two together.

Puffy Apple Pancake

Ingredients

1–2 apples (tart ones like Granny Smith and McIntosh are the most flavorful and will hold their shape best)

1 Tbsp (15 mL) butter

1–2 Tbsp (15–30 mL) sugar

Pinch cinnamon

3 large eggs

¾ cup (175 mL) all-purpose flour

¾ cup (175 mL) milk

Maple syrup or vanilla yogurt for serving (optional)

What to do with the leftovers

* Keep leftovers covered in the fridge for a day, and reheat them in the microwave. The pancake will sink a little, but will still taste good.

Other things to do with it

* Puffed Berry Pancake: Omit the apples altogether. Drizzle the oven-proof skillet with a little oil or spray it with non-stick spray, and pop it in the oven for a few minutes to heat up. Pour the batter into the hot skillet and bake as directed. Fill the puffed pancake with fresh berries or other sliced fruit, and serve with syrup or yogurt for breakfast or for dessert with vanilla ice cream or whipped cream.

This spectacular looking pancake is similar to a big Yorkshire pudding or popover—baked in the oven with or without sautéed fruit, it rises up all puffed and crunchy around the edges. Although it's traditionally made with apples, a puffy pancake is also perfect made with pears, bananas, peaches, berries, or plums. Sturdier fruits can be sautéed first and baked right into the pancake or set aside to be served on top. Fragile fruits like berries or bananas are better served in the hollow of the finished pancake, which rises even more dramatically when the batter is baked alone.

Method

1 Preheat the oven to 450°F (230°C).

2 Peel, core, and slice the apples. In a large skillet (if you have an ovenproof one, use it), sauté the apples in the butter over medium heat for a minute or two. Sprinkle them with the sugar and cinnamon and cook until they start to turn golden. Remove them from the heat.

3 Whisk together the eggs, flour, and milk. Don't worry about getting all the lumps out. Now you can proceed one of two ways:

   • Pour the batter over the apples in the skillet and put it in the oven. (If you don't have an ovenproof skillet, pour the sautéed apples into a pie plate and pour the batter over them.) The apples will bake straight into the pancake, but it won't rise quite as high with the fruit inside; or

   • Remove the apples and set them aside to serve on top, then pour the batter into the hot skillet. This way the pancake will rise even higher and look more dramatic.

4 Bake for 20–25 minutes, until the pancake is puffed and golden. Cut it into wedges and serve warm with the fruit and a drizzle of maple syrup or dollop of vanilla yogurt.

Serves 2–4

French Toast

Ingredients

2 large eggs

½ cup (125 mL) milk

1 tsp (5 mL) vanilla (optional)

Butter, canola oil, or non-stick spray, for cooking

4 slices stale (or at least day-old) bread

Cinnamon (optional)

French toast is the best way to use up stale bread, and you can use any kind—sourdough, multigrain, challah, and raisin bread are all delicious. Cinnamon buns or croissants, cut in half crosswise, make particularly decadent French toast. Whichever bread you choose, it should be at least a day old—fresh bread tends to turn mushy.

Method

1 In a shallow bowl, stir the eggs, milk, and vanilla together with a fork.

2 Set a large non-stick skillet over medium heat. Add a small amount of butter or oil and swirl to coat it, or spray it with non-stick spray. Dip each slice of bread in the egg mixture, coating both sides well and letting it soak in. Pick up the slices, let the excess egg drip off, and place them on the hot skillet. Sprinkle them with cinnamon if you like.

3 Cook the French toast until it's golden on both sides, about 2 minutes on the first side and 1 minute on the second, flipping them as necessary. Serve immediately, or keep them warm in a 200°F (110°C) oven while you cook the rest.

Serves 4

What to do with the leftovers

* Keep them in the fridge for a few days. Reheat in the microwave or on a baking sheet in the oven.

Other things to do with it

* Crunchy French Toast: Dredge the egg-dipped bread in crushed Corn Flakes or Frosted Flakes before cooking them.

* Stuffed French Toast: Start with thick slices of bread, and slice them almost in half widthwise, creating a pocket. Mix equal amounts of cream cheese and marmalade or jam and spread the mixture inside each pocket, or stuff the pockets with thinly sliced ham and slices of Gouda, Brie, or other cheese. Close them and dip them in the egg mixture; cook as directed, allowing a little extra time to make up for the added thickness.

* Banana French Toast: Make the French toast using raisin bread. Before serving it, melt 2 Tbsp (30 mL) butter in a skillet; add 2 Tbsp (30 mL) sugar and 2 Tbsp (30 mL) water and stir until the sugar dissolves. Continue stirring over medium heat for a few minutes, until the mixture is foamy. Add 1 or 2 sliced bananas and cook for about 5 minutes, until they're starting to turn golden. Serve over the raisin French toast.

* Multigrain French Toast: Make your French toast using multigrain bread. Replace half the milk with orange juice, and add a little grated orange zest to the egg mixture as well.

Waffles

Ingredients

1 cup (250 mL) all-purpose flour
(or half whole wheat, half
all-purpose)

1 tsp (5 mL) baking powder

1 tsp (5 mL) sugar (optional)

¼ tsp (1 mL) salt

¾ cup (175 mL) milk

1 large egg

2 Tbsp (30 mL) canola oil or
melted butter

The only catch to making waffles is that you need a waffle iron. But at around $20, they're well worth the investment—think of the expense as waffles for life for about the same price as going out for breakfast once! This recipe makes enough for two big Belgian-style waffles, but it doubles or triples easily if you're cooking for a crowd. To fancy them up, try stirring some grated orange or lemon zest, a sprinkle of cinnamon, a few slices of cooked and crumbled bacon, or a handful of chopped nuts, finely chopped fruit, granola, or grated cheese into the batter along with the wet ingredients.

Method

1 Plug in the waffle iron to preheat it while you mix up the batter.

2 In a medium bowl, stir together the flour, baking powder, sugar (if using) and salt. In a small bowl, whisk together the milk, egg, and oil or melted butter. Add the wet ingredients all at once to the dry ingredients and stir just until combined—don't worry about getting all the lumps out. Overmixing could make your waffles tough.

3 Spoon an appropriate amount of batter onto the waffle iron, using your best judgment or according to the manufacturer's directions. Close the lid and cook for 2–5 minutes, until the waffles are golden. Usually the steam will subside when the waffles are close to being done. Serve them right away or keep them warm in a 200°F (110°C) oven while you cook the rest. (If you do this, place them in a single layer or they will steam and become soggy on the bottom. If you have one, put them on a rack set on a cookie sheet.)

Serves 2 (doubles or triples easily)

What to do with the leftovers

* Wrap cooled waffles in plastic wrap and freeze for up to 3 months. Reheat them in the toaster, toaster oven, or microwave.

Other things to do with it

* Eat waffles for dessert with a scoop of ice cream or whipped cream and fresh fruit or chocolate sauce.

* For lighter waffles, separate the egg, add the yolk to the batter, and beat the white in a separate (clean) bowl until stiff peaks form. Gently fold the beaten egg white into the batter after combining the wet and dry ingredients, and bake as directed.

* Pecan Waffles with Caramelized Bananas: Add ¼–½ cup (60–125 mL) finely chopped or ground pecans to the dry ingredients. Heat a small blob of butter in a medium non-stick skillet. Add 2 sliced bananas, sprinkle them with about 2 Tbsp (30 mL) white or brown sugar and sauté them for a few minutes, until the sugar begins to melt and the bananas turn golden. Serve them over the waffles, drizzled with maple syrup.

* Power Waffles: Use half whole wheat and half all-purpose flour. Stir 2 Tbsp (30 mL) ground flaxseed and ¼ cup (60 mL) finely chopped walnuts or pecans into the dry ingredients. If you have some, use flax oil in place of the canola oil. Top the waffles with sliced bananas, fresh berries, or other fruit, a dollop of vanilla yogurt, and/or a drizzle of maple syrup.

Breakfast

Granola

Ingredients

6 cups (1.5 L) old-fashioned (large flake) oats

½–1 cup (125–250 mL) chopped nuts (pecans, walnuts, hazelnuts, or sliced or slivered almonds)

¼–½ cup (60–125 mL) seeds (pumpkin seeds, sunflower seeds, sesame seeds, or ground flaxseed)

Pinch cinnamon (optional)

¼ tsp (1 mL) salt

½ cup (125 mL) honey

½ cup (125 mL) maple syrup

1 tsp (5 mL) vanilla

1 cup (250 mL) dried fruit (raisins, cranberries, cherries, chopped dates, apricots, apples, berries and/or pears)

Homemade granola is a virtuous thing. It's cheap (compared to the store-bought variety), easy to make, low in saturated fat, and you can add any combination of fruit, nuts, and seeds to make it your own. Dried fruits, nuts, and seeds make delicious additions and add protein, fiber, vitamins, and minerals. If you're a molasses fan, replace some of the honey or maple syrup with it. If you like coconut but not the saturated fat it contains, add coconut extract instead of vanilla. Many recipes call for up to a cup of butter or oil, but you don't need it, and you won't miss it.

Method

1 Preheat the oven to 350°F (175°C).

2 Spread the oats and nuts on a large rimmed baking sheet and toast them for about 10 minutes, until they're just beginning to turn golden and fragrant. Take them out of the oven and transfer to a large bowl. Stir in the seeds, cinnamon, and salt. Turn the oven down to 300°F (150°C).

3 In a small bowl, stir together the honey, maple syrup, and vanilla. Pour over the oat mixture and stir to coat it well.

4 Spread the mixture on the baking sheet you used to toast the oats, and bake for about half an hour, stirring once or twice, until the granola is golden. Remove from the oven and stir in the dried fruit. Let the granola cool completely on the baking sheet before storing in a tightly sealed container.

Makes about 8 cups

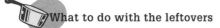 **What to do with the leftovers**

* Keep your granola in a tightly sealed container or jar on the countertop, or store individual portions in zip-lock baggies to stash in your car, desk, or gym bag, or to pack in lunches.

 Other things to do with it

* Make breakfast parfaits by layering granola, yogurt, and berries or chopped fresh fruit in glass bowls or champagne glasses.

* Maple Hazelnut Granola: Use maple syrup in place of the honey or maple extract instead of the vanilla. Add sliced hazelnuts and dried cranberries or cherries.

Muesli

Ingredients

1 cup (250 mL) old-fashioned (large flake) oats

1 cup (250 mL) yogurt (any kind)

A handful of chopped dried fruit (raisins, cranberries, dates, figs, apricots, and/or mango)

A handful of chopped toasted nuts (almonds, pecans, and/or hazelnuts)

1 apple, coarsely grated (peeled or not)

1 Tbsp (15 mL) honey (according to taste and whether or not you used sweetened yogurt)

1 Tbsp (15 mL) lemon juice

The Swiss really have breakfast down pat. This is a great fast and healthy recipe that requires no more than a bowl and spoon. The idea is that you keep a batch in the fridge to dip into whenever you need breakfast or a snack in a rush. It's particularly handy when you need something you can balance in a bowl on the sink. Muesli generally contains everything that makes a healthy breakfast—calcium, fiber, protein, vitamins, and minerals—in the form of raw or toasted cereals (such as oats, wheat, millet, and barley), fruits (such as raisins, apricots, and apples), nuts, and yogurt. Experiment using any combination of grains, fruits and nuts you like. To fancy it up, serve the muesli drizzled with honey or maple syrup and topped with berries.

Method

1 Stir everything together in a large bowl. Refrigerate it overnight.

Serves 6

 What to do with the leftovers

* This recipe is designed to make leftovers—keep them in the fridge to dip into all week long.

 Other things to do with it

* Maple Muesli: Use maple syrup instead of honey, or stir in a teaspoon (5 mL) of maple extract.

Smoothies

The best reason to own a blender is so that you can make smoothies. They make healthy snacks or meals in a pinch, and if you pour one into your travel mug it makes a perfect breakfast on the way to wherever you need to be. If you add yogurt or tofu (I promise you won't taste it), it also delivers a good dose of protein.

Smoothies can be made with any type of soft fruit you have on hand, and they make particularly good use of frozen and overripe fruit you might otherwise toss out. All these measurements are approximate. Feel free to throw in whatever fruit and yogurt combinations you think would taste good, and thin it down with juice or milk until you have something that resembles a smoothie.

Ingredients

Berry-Kiwi Smoothie

1 banana, peeled and broken into chunks

1 cup (250 mL) fresh or frozen strawberries, blackberries, raspberries, or a combination

2 kiwi, peeled and sliced

1 cup (250 mL) yogurt, any flavor

½ cup (125 mL) orange juice

1 cup (250 mL) ice cubes

Honey to taste

Blueberry-Banana Smoothie

1 banana, peeled and broken into chunks

½ cup (125 mL) orange juice or milk

2 cups (500 mL) blueberries (fresh or frozen)

1 cup (250 mL) soft tofu or yogurt

1 cup (250 mL) ice cubes

Honey to taste

Peanut Butter and Banana Smoothie

1 banana, peeled and broken into chunks

2 heaping Tbsp (30 mL) peanut butter (any kind)

2 Tbsp (30 mL) honey (or to taste)

1 cup (250 mL) plain or vanilla yogurt

1 cup (250 mL) ice cubes

Pineapple-Bananaberry Smoothie

1 cup (250 mL) fresh or frozen strawberries

1 cup (250 mL) fresh or frozen blueberries

1 banana, peeled and broken into chunks

1 cup (250 mL) pineapple chunks

1 cup (250 mL) yogurt, any flavor, or plain soft tofu

2 cups (500 mL) ice cubes

Method

1 Put everything in a blender and pulse until smooth, adding a little extra milk or juice if necessary to achieve the consistency of a smoothie.

Serves 2

Soup

Soup is real fast food. Contrary to popular belief,
it doesn't need to simmer for hours to taste wonderful.
Because soup is simply broth to which other elements
(meat, vegetables, and/or starch such as noodles, rice, or potatoes)
are added, it can be made using virtually any ingredients you have in the kitchen.
Impromptu soups are a cinch to throw together.
You don't really need a recipe, just a general guide—recipes for soup
are the least precise of any I know.

Soups are ideal for those who live alone, are always broke, or have limited culinary skills (or think they do). Little is required of the cook beyond chopping ingredients and throwing them into the pot. It's a great way to use up leftovers or small quantities of ingredients you don't know what else to do with. And it's infinitely cheaper and healthier than hitting a drive-thru or ordering pizza.

The stock you use need not be homemade, but the flavor really is far better and making it from scratch is easy. Chicken and vegetable stocks are the ones most commonly called for in recipes, so they're the best to know how to make. Beef stock is very expensive to make well from scratch (you need a lot of meat to produce a rich, meaty stock) so I suggest buying good quality canned beef stock instead when you need it.

Chicken Stock

Chicken carcasses, wings, legs, backs, and necks all make great stock, and you'll find many recipes that call for an entire chicken, usually simmered with onions, carrots, and celery. The problem with this method is 1) it's expensive (you need a whole chicken) and 2) it takes forever to extract the flavor from the chicken, which then must be thrown out after being boiled for hours.

My favorite way to make chicken stock is to use the leftover carcass of a roasted chicken. Roasting or browning any type of meat improves its flavor, so roasting the chicken parts or even the bones before you make stock intensifies the flavor and produces a deeper, richer color. To make a quick and easy stock with your chicken carcass, put it in a pot and cover it with water. Add a small quartered onion and a chopped carrot if you like, and simmer the mixture for about half an hour. Remove it from the heat and set it aside until it's cool enough that you can shred whatever meat is left off the bones (if you want meaty stock); otherwise you can simply strain it through a fine sieve and discard the bones and vegetables.

If you're starting from scratch, you'll need:

Ingredients

Canola or olive oil

2–3 lb (1–1.3 kg) chicken pieces—backs, wings or legs

8 cups (2 L) water

1 onion, unpeeled and cut into quarters

1 carrot, cut into chunks (optional)

A handful of fresh parsley, chopped (optional)

Salt and pepper

Method

1 Heat a drizzle of oil in a large pot or Dutch oven set over medium heat. Sauté the chicken in batches, cooking until the pieces are browned all over. Make sure the pot isn't crowded, or the chicken will steam instead of browning properly. Alternatively, you can toss the chicken pieces with a little oil and roast them in the oven at about 400°F (200°C) for half an hour or so, until they're golden.

2 Return the chicken to the pot and add the water, onion, carrot, parsley, and salt and pepper. Bring to a boil, reduce the heat to low, cover and simmer for 20–30 minutes. Strain the stock through a fine sieve into a container and cool. To remove the fat, skim

it off the top with a spoon, or refrigerate the stock until the fat solidifies—then you can simply lift it off the surface. Don't be alarmed if your stock turns into a sort of chicken gel—this is a result of the naturally occurring gelatin in the bone marrow.

3 Freeze the stock in tightly sealed containers or zip-lock freezer bags. For smaller or pre-measured quantities, fill muffin pans with stock, freeze them, and pop out the frozen stock like ice cubes. Store the frozen cubes in a plastic bag in the freezer.

Vegetable Stock

The quantities listed below are approximate. Some people like to keep scraps of vegetables (the trimmings and ends of carrots, onions, and celery, potato peelings, etc.) in the freezer and pull them out when it's time to make stock, but you can always start with fresh veggies. The onion skins will add a richer color to vegetable stock. If garlic or cilantro isn't your thing, leave it out.

Ingredients

5 carrots, sliced

2 stalks celery, sliced

2 large onions, unpeeled and quartered

1 head garlic, unpeeled and cut in half horizontally (optional)

Peelings from 1–2 potatoes

Small handful cilantro (optional)

Small handful flat leaf parsley

2 bay leaves

1 tsp (5 mL) salt

1 tsp (5 mL) black peppercorns

16 cups (4 L) water

Method

1 Set a large pot or Dutch oven over medium heat, and add all the ingredients. Bring to a boil, reduce the heat, and simmer for about 45 minutes. Strain the stock through a fine sieve and cool.

2 Freeze the stock in tightly sealed containers or zip-lock freezer bags, or fill muffin pans with stock, freeze them, and pop out the frozen stock like ice cubes. Store the frozen cubes in a plastic bag in the freezer.

Roasted Vegetable Stock

Ingredients

½ lb (250 g) portobello mushrooms, chopped

2 large onions, unpeeled and quartered

4 carrots, sliced

1 red, yellow, or orange bell pepper, chopped

4 cloves garlic, peeled

A small handful of fresh parsley

4 sprigs of fresh thyme

2 Tbsp (30 mL) olive oil

1 cup (250 mL) dry white wine or water

½ 14 oz (398 mL) can crushed tomatoes

8 cups (2 L) water

Salt and pepper (whole peppercorns if you have them)

Method

1 Preheat oven to 450°F (230°C).

2 Toss all the vegetables and garlic with the olive oil in a large roasting pan. Sprinkle with parsley and thyme. Roast in the oven, stirring once or twice, for about 45 minutes or until the vegetables are golden.

3 Set the roasting pan over two of the burners on your stovetop and add a little of the wine or water to deglaze the pan, scraping up all the flavorful browned bits that have stuck to the bottom. Pour the rest of the wine or water into the pot and add the tomatoes, the 8 cups (2 L) of water, and salt and pepper to taste. Bring it to a boil, then reduce the heat and simmer for about 45 minutes. Strain it through a fine sieve and cool.

4 Freeze the stock in tightly sealed containers or zip-lock freezer bags, or fill muffin pans with stock, freeze them, and pop out the frozen stock like ice cubes. Store the frozen cubes in a plastic bag in the freezer.

Shrimp stock

Shrimp stock is easy to make using only raw shrimp shells. Next time you peel shrimp, toss the shells into a small pot and cover them with water. Simmer them for about 20 minutes, and add a chopped stalk of lemongrass if you're making something Asian-inspired. Strain it through a sieve, collander, or cheesecloth and you'll have beautiful pink stock.

Mulligatawny (Curried Chicken Soup)

Ingredients

½ cup (125 mL) uncooked long-grain white rice

1 Tbsp (15 mL) canola oil

1 onion, chopped

1–2 carrots, peeled and chopped

1 stalk celery, chopped

1 tart apple, peeled and chopped

1 small red bell pepper, seeded and chopped

1 Tbsp (15 mL) grated fresh ginger

2 Tbsp (30 mL) flour

1 Tbsp (15 mL) curry powder or paste, or to taste

Salt and pepper

2 ½ cups (625 mL) chicken stock, or 2 cans chicken broth plus 2 cans water

¼ cup (60 mL) mango or peach chutney (optional)

2 Tbsp (30 mL) tomato paste

½–1 cup (125–250 mL) chopped cooked chicken

What to do with the leftovers

* Keep them in a sealed container in the fridge for up to 3 days or freeze for up to 4 months. Reheat on the stovetop or in the microwave, adding a little extra liquid if necessary.

This spicy flavorful soup is a perfect example of what you can do to liven up a basic chicken soup. It's a great way to use up meaty chicken stock that you've made by simmering the leftover carcass of a roasted chicken (see page 68).

Method

1 Bring 1 cup (250 mL) of water to a boil in a small pot. Add the rice, turn down the heat to low and cover with a tight-fitting lid. Cook for 20 minutes, until all the water has been absorbed. Remove from the heat and set aside.

2 Heat the oil in a large pot set over medium-high heat. Add the onion, carrots, celery, apple, red pepper, and ginger and cook for about 5 minutes, until the vegetables are soft.

3 Add the flour and cook, stirring, for another minute. Add the curry powder, salt, pepper, chicken stock, chutney, and tomato paste and bring to a simmer. Turn the heat down to low and simmer for about 8 minutes. Stir in the chicken and cook until heated through.

4 Divide the rice among your individual soup bowls and ladle the soup on top.

Serves 3–4

Other things to do with it

* Chicken Noodle Soup: Boil ½ cup (125 mL) egg noodles according to the package directions, instead of the rice. Omit the apple, red pepper, flour, curry powder, chutney, and tomato paste. You can omit the ginger as well, or leave it in if you like gingery chicken noodle soup. If you like, add a small handful of chopped fresh parsley or dill.

* Chicken Soup with Rice: Follow the directions for Chicken Noodle Soup, but cook long-grain white, brown, or wild rice instead of noodles. (Cooking the rice or noodles separately and then adding them to the finished soup will keep the broth from getting too starchy.)

Spinach, Bean, and Pasta Soup

Ingredients

1 Tbsp (15 mL) olive or canola oil

1 spicy or mild Italian or chorizo
   sausage, crumbled (optional)

1 onion, diced

3 cloves garlic, crushed

2 cups (500 mL) water

¾–1 cup (185–250 mL) uncooked
   fusilli or other small pasta

1 14 oz (398 mL) can tomato sauce
   (any kind of spaghetti sauce
   works well)

1 can or 1 ½ cups (375 mL) chicken or
   vegetable stock

1 tsp (5 mL) dried oregano or basil

Salt and pepper

8 cups (2 L) fresh spinach, washed
   and coarsely torn or chopped

1 14 oz (398 mL) or 19 oz (540 mL)
   can white or red kidney beans
   or cannellini beans, rinsed and
   drained

Freshly grated Parmesan

This wonderful, hearty soup is a meal in itself—the combination of beans and pasta produces a complete protein. Omit the sausage for an equally delicious vegetarian soup. Either way, make sure you serve it with a loaf of fresh crusty bread to mop up the broth.

Method

1 In a large pot set over medium heat, heat the oil and sauté the sausage until it's no longer pink. Add the onion and garlic and cook for 2–3 minutes, until soft.

2 Add the water, pasta, tomato sauce, stock, oregano, and salt and pepper to taste. Bring to a boil, reduce the heat, and simmer for about 15 minutes, until the pasta is tender. Add the spinach and beans and cook the soup for another 3–5 minutes. If it seems too thick, thin it with a little extra stock, tomato juice, or water.

3 Ladle into bowls and sprinkle each serving with Parmesan while it's still hot.

Serves 4–6

What to do with the leftovers

* Keep them covered in the fridge for up to 3 days. Reheat in the microwave or on the stovetop, adding a little extra liquid if necessary.

Other things to do with it

* White Bean and Greens Soup: Omit the sausage, cook a chopped carrot along with the onion, and use white kidney or navy beans. Use chopped fresh chard, escarole, kale, spinach, or a combination of greens.

Roasted Tomato Soup

Ingredients

4 lb (2 kg) ripe tomatoes (about 10)

2 Tbsp (30 mL) olive oil

Salt and pepper

1 head garlic

2 cups (500 mL) chicken or vegetable
stock

2 tsp (10 mL) sugar

½ cup (125 mL) half and half or
whipping cream (optional)

Chopped fresh basil or pesto
(optional)

It's important to use ripe, flavorful tomatoes for this soup, since their flavor is paramount. If you have overripe, wrinkled, or squishy tomatoes around, use them up, so long as they don't have any bad spots. Roasting them transforms their flavor, making them sweet and smoky. It's a great way to make tomato sauce for pasta, too.

Method

1 Preheat the oven to 450°F (230°C).

2 Cut the tomatoes in half widthwise and place them on a large rimmed baking sheet or in a roasting pan. Drizzle them with olive oil and sprinkle with salt and pepper. Add the whole unpeeled head of garlic to the pan and roast for about an hour, until the tomatoes are golden and the garlic is very soft. Set it aside to cool for a bit.

3 Transfer the tomatoes and all the juices that have collected in the pan into a food processor or blender. Squeeze the garlic cloves from their skins into the blender and process until it's as smooth or chunky as you like.

4 Transfer to a medium pot and set it over medium heat. Add the chicken stock and sugar. Bring to a simmer and cook for about 10 minutes. If you're going to add cream, turn the heat down to low and add it at the last minute, stirring just until the soup is heated through. If you like, stir in a small handful of chopped fresh basil or a spoonful of pesto just before serving.

Serves 4

What to do with the leftovers

* Keep them in a sealed container in the fridge for several days or freeze for up to 4 months. Reheat on the stovetop or in the microwave, adding a little extra liquid if necessary.

Other things to do with it

* Omit the chicken stock and serve the puréed roasted tomatoes and garlic on pasta, topped with freshly grated Parmesan or crumbled feta cheese.

* Italian Bread Soup: Tear a small loaf of good quality, sturdy, day-old bread into chunks and stir it into the soup along with the basil. Toast the chunks of bread on a baking sheet first, if you like, to boost flavor.

Curried Squash Soup
with Apples or Pears

Ingredients

1 medium butternut or acorn squash

1–2 Tbsp (15–30 mL) canola or olive oil or butter

1 onion, chopped

1 Tbsp (15 mL) curry powder or paste, or to taste

1 tart apple or ripe pear, peeled and chopped

1 Tbsp (15 mL) grated fresh ginger

2 cloves garlic, crushed

3 cups (750 mL) chicken or vegetable stock

1 cup (250 mL) milk, evaporated milk or half and half (optional)

Salt and pepper

 **What to do with the leftovers**

* Keep them in a sealed container in the fridge for up to 4 days or freeze for up to 4 months. Reheat on the stovetop or in the microwave, adding a little extra liquid if necessary.

Other things to do with it

Cooked squash is much easier to peel than raw squash. If you don't have time to roast it, cut it in half, place both halves on a plate or baking dish, and cover them with plastic wrap. Pop them in the microwave for about 10 minutes, then peel them with your fingers once they're cool enough to handle. Squash is an excellent source of beta carotene and other vitamins and minerals, and contains very few calories. This soup freezes really well, so double the batch if you want a stash tucked away for the next few months.

Method

1 Preheat the oven to 375°F (190°C).

2 Cut the squash in half lengthwise and scoop out the seeds. Place it cut side down in a roasting pan that has been sprayed with non-stick spray and bake for 40–45 minutes or until very tender. Set aside until it's cool enough to handle. (You can cook the squash up to 2 days in advance; keep it covered in the fridge until you need it.)

3 Heat the oil in a large pot set over medium heat and sauté the onion until soft. Add the curry powder, apple, ginger, and garlic and cook for a few more minutes, until the apples start to soften. Peel the skin off the cooked squash using a vegetable peeler or your fingers, and cut it into chunks. Add it to the soup with the chicken stock and bring it to a simmer. Reduce the heat and cook for about 10 minutes.

4 Purée the soup in a blender, or use a hand-held immersion blender to purée it right in the pot until it's as chunky or as smooth as you like. Return the soup to the stovetop, add the milk or cream (if using), season with salt and pepper, and stir until it's heated through. Make sure you don't boil it at this point, or the milk may curdle.

Serves 4

* Squash Soup with Cheesy Croutons: Make plain squash soup by omitting the apple and curry powder. Add 1 tsp (5 mL) each of chopped fresh thyme and sage. Toast thin slices of baguette on a baking sheet in a 350°F (175°C) oven until golden. Top each piece with a slice of Brie or Gruyère cheese, or spread each one with goat cheese. Divide the soup among individual ovenproof bowls and top each bowl with a crouton. Place the bowls on the baking sheet and pop back in the oven for a few minutes, until the cheese melts.

Potato and Leek Soup

Ingredients

2 medium leeks

1 Tbsp (15 mL) butter or canola oil

1 small onion, chopped

2–4 cloves garlic, crushed (optional)

2–3 potatoes (russet, Yukon Gold, and red potatoes all work well), peeled and chopped

3 cups (750 mL) chicken stock

Salt and pepper

½ cup (125 mL) milk, half and half, or cream

There are few foods more consoling than soup and potatoes, and chances are you have a sack of potatoes and some chicken stock somewhere in the house. Leek and potato soup gets a fancy name, vichyssoise, when it's served chilled—it's a cheap luxury. If you have some fresh tarragon, adding about a tablespoon to the soup (or sprinkling it on top) would be delicious, too.

Method

... lengthwise before you wash them—sand and grit tend to ... be very thorough. Thinly ... out the green tops.

... dd the butter or oil. ... ntil soft and translu- ... Reduce the heat and ... ender. Season with salt

... a hand-held immersion ... urn the soup to the ... cream. Heat it through

... dge and serve it chilled.

What to do with the leftov...

* Keep them in a sealed conta... the fridge for up to 4 days ... for up to 4 months. Serve t... cold or reheat on the stove ... the microwave, adding a li... liquid if necessary.

... Instead of using fresh cloves ... e page 26). Squeeze the cloves

... ntil crispy. Remove the bacon ... leeks in about 1 Tbsp (15 mL) ... pe, and top the bowls of soup

Minestrone

Ingredients

2 Tbsp (30 mL) olive or canola oil

¼ lb (125 g) pancetta or 2 slices
   bacon, chopped (optional)

1 onion, chopped, or 1 large leek,
   washed well and chopped

1 large carrot, peeled and chopped

1 stalk celery, chopped

2–3 cloves garlic, crushed

1 zucchini, halved lengthwise
   and sliced

¼ lb (125 g) green beans, trimmed, or
   asparagus, cut into 2 or 3 pieces
   (snap off the tough ends first)

1 potato, cubed (peeled or not) or
   ¼–½ cup (60–125 mL) small pasta
   (such as shells, orzo, or broken
   spaghetti)

3 cups (750 mL) chicken or
   vegetable stock

1 14 oz (398 mL) can whole, stewed
   or diced tomatoes

1 14 oz (398 mL) can red or white
   kidney, navy, or Great Northern
   beans, rinsed and drained

2–4 cups (500 mL–1 L) shredded
   kale, green cabbage, or spinach

Salt and pepper

Grated Parmesan to sprinkle
   on top

Your mom would be so proud of you for making such a substantial vegetable soup. This is one of the most nutritious meals you can eat! Because minestrone is an Italian soup, pancetta is more authentic (and also leaner) than bacon. But either is fine, or leave it out altogether to make vegetarian minestrone. Make sure you have lots of crusty bread to mop up the broth.

Method

1 In a large pot or Dutch oven set over medium-high heat, cook the pancetta in the oil until pale golden and crisp. Add the onion and cook for a few minutes, until it softens. Add the carrot, celery, and garlic and cook, stirring often, for a few more minutes. Add the zucchini, green beans, and potatoes and cook for a few more minutes. If you're using asparagus or pasta, save them to add at the end.

2 Add the chicken stock and tomatoes. Bring to a simmer, reduce the heat, cover the pot and let the soup cook for 15–20 minutes, until the vegetables are tender. If you're using asparagus or pasta, add it during the last 10 minutes of cooking time, and cook until it's tender. Add the kidney beans and greens and cook just until the greens wilt. Season with salt and pepper.

3 Serve the soup hot, with grated Parmesan sprinkled on top of each bowl.

Serves 4

 What to do with the leftovers

* Keep them in a sealed container in the fridge for up to 2 days or freeze for up to 4 months. Reheat on the stovetop or in the microwave, adding a little extra liquid if necessary. (This soup doesn't freeze as well as others in this book.)

 Other things to do with it

* Add or substitute any kind of vegetables or herbs you like. Fresh basil, squash, and corn are all good choices.

* Swirl a spoonful of pesto into each bowl of soup.

Corn, Chicken, and Cheddar Chowder

Ingredients

3 slices bacon, chopped, or 1 Tbsp (15 mL) oil and 1 Tbsp (15 mL) butter

1 large onion, finely chopped

1 stalk celery, chopped

2 Tbsp (30 mL) flour

1–2 tsp (5–10 mL) cumin or 1 tsp (5 mL) dried thyme

3 cups (750 mL) chicken stock

1–2 potatoes, peeled (or not) and diced

1–2 cups (250–500 mL) fresh, canned, or frozen corn kernels

1 cup (250 mL) chopped cooked chicken (optional)

1 cup (500 mL) milk or ½ cup (125 mL) cream

1 cup (250 mL) grated old cheddar cheese

Salt and pepper

This hearty chowder is perfect to make with the meaty stock you get from simmering a roasted chicken carcass (see page 68). If there's still a lot of meat clinging to the bones, it will fall off into the stock, and you won't need to add any extra.

Method

1 In a medium pot set over medium-high heat, cook the bacon (if using) until crisp. Transfer it to paper towels to drain and cool, then crumble and set it aside. If you're not using bacon, heat the oil and butter in the pot over medium heat.

2 Sauté the onion and celery in the bacon fat or oil and butter mixture for about 5 minutes, until softened. Add the flour and cumin and cook, stirring, for another minute. Stir in the stock and potatoes and bring to a simmer. Reduce heat, cover, and cook for 8–10 minutes, until the potatoes are tender.

3 Stir in the corn, chicken, and milk or cream and allow the chowder to return to a gentle simmer. Don't let it boil, or the milk may curdle. Add the cheese and stir just until it melts. Season to taste with salt and pepper.

4 Serve hot topped with the crumbled bacon, if you used it.

Serves 4–6

 What to do with the leftovers

* Keep them in a sealed container in the fridge for up to 4 days or freeze for up to 4 months. Reheat on the stovetop or in the microwave, adding a little extra liquid if necessary.

 Other things to do with it

* Corn, Potato, and Crab Chowder: Omit the bacon and use thyme instead of cumin. Replace the chicken with ½ lb (250 g) crabmeat. Stir in a small handful of chopped fresh parsley before serving.

Soup

Cream of Mushroom Soup

Ingredients

¾ lb (340 g) mushrooms (button, shiitake, cremini, oyster, portobello, or a combination)

1 Tbsp (15 mL) canola oil

1 Tbsp (15 mL) butter

1 onion or 3 shallots, peeled and finely chopped

1–2 cloves garlic, crushed

½ cup (125 mL) ham, diced (optional)

3 Tbsp (45 mL) sherry or brandy (optional)

2 Tbsp (30 mL) flour

3 cups (750 mL) chicken, beef, or vegetable stock

½ cup (125 mL) sour cream, half and half, or whipping cream

Salt and pepper

Button mushrooms are fine to use in cream of mushroom soup, or try meatier portobello mushrooms and exotic varieties such as shiitake, oyster, and cremini to give it more substance and intense flavor.

Method

1 Clean the mushrooms and slice half of them. Finely chop the other half. Heat the oil and butter in a medium pot set over medium-high heat, and sauté the onion, garlic, and mushrooms until the moisture evaporates and the mushrooms begin to turn golden.

2 Add the ham and cook for a minute. Add the sherry and cook until it evaporates, then add the flour and cook, stirring, for another 2 minutes. Add the stock and bring to a simmer. Reduce the heat to low and simmer for about 15 minutes.

3 Remove the soup from the heat and stir in the sour cream or cream. Season to taste with salt and pepper.

Serves 4

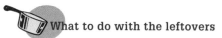 What to do with the leftovers

* Keep them in a sealed container in the fridge for up to 4 days or freeze for up to 4 months. Reheat on the stovetop or in the microwave, adding a little extra liquid if necessary.

 Other things to do with it

* Wild Rice or Barley Mushroom Soup: Sauté 1 chopped carrot and 1 chopped stalk of celery along with the onion. Cook ½ cup (125 mL) wild rice or barley according to the package directions, and stir it into the soup at the very end.

* Wild Rice, Turkey, and Mushroom Soup: Replace the ham with chopped cooked turkey or chicken and add ½ tsp (2.5 mL) thyme. Cook ½ cup (125 mL) wild rice according to the package directions, and stir it into the soup at the very end.

* Baked Mushroom Soup with Brie Croutons: Toast thin slices of baguette on a baking sheet in a 350°F (180°C) oven until golden. Top each piece with a slice of Brie or Gruyère. Divide the soup among individual ovenproof bowls and top each serving with a cheese crouton. Place the bowls on the baking sheet and pop back in the oven for a few minutes, until the cheese melts.

Black Bean Soup

Ingredients

1 Tbsp (15 mL) olive or canola oil

1 onion, peeled and chopped

1 carrot, peeled and chopped

1–2 jalapeño peppers, or 1 Tbsp (15 mL) chopped canned chipotle chilies

4 cloves garlic, crushed

1 small red bell pepper, seeded and chopped (optional)

2 tsp (10 mL) ground cumin

1 19 oz (540 mL) can black beans, undrained

1 14 oz (398 mL) can diced or stewed tomatoes

1 cup (250 mL) chicken or vegetable stock (or more or less according to your taste)

Salt and pepper

Sour cream, chopped cilantro, chopped green onions, and/or crumbled feta cheese (optional)

On its own, a steaming bowl of black bean soup will feed you well. To make it more substantial, put a scoop of rice into each bowl and ladle the soup over it. Or add a wineglass of red wine and some sliced kielbasa sausage. It's good with the cornbread on page 247.

Method

1 Heat the oil in a large pot set over medium-high heat and sauté the onion and carrot for about 5 minutes, until they begin to soften. Finely chop the jalapeño, removing the seeds first if you don't want your soup to be too hot—the seeds contain the most heat. Add them to the pot along with the garlic, red pepper, and cumin and cook for another minute. Add the beans and tomatoes, without draining either of them, and the chicken stock. Bring the soup to a boil, reduce the heat to low, cover and cook for 15–20 minutes, until the carrot is tender.

2 Using a blender, food processor, or hand-held immersion blender, process about half of the soup until smooth, and return it to the pot. (Process as much or as little of the soup as you want to make the consistency as chunky or smooth as you like.) Simmer the soup uncovered for another 15 minutes to allow it to thicken slightly. Season to taste with salt and pepper.

3 Serve hot or chilled, with a dollop of sour cream and a sprinkle of cilantro, green onions, and/or feta cheese on top.

Serves 4–6

What to do with the leftovers

* This soup gets even better with age. Keep it in a sealed container in the fridge for up to a week, or freeze for up to 4 months. Reheat on the stovetop or in the microwave, adding a little extra liquid if necessary.

Other things to do with it

* Chop a few strips of bacon or squeeze a couple of chorizo sausages out of their casings and cook the sausage until it's no longer pink, or the bacon until crispy. Set them aside and sauté the onion in 1 Tbsp (15 mL) of the drippings. Proceed with the recipe, adding a large diced potato along with the carrot. Stir in the bacon or sausage at the end.

* Lentil Soup: Add an extra carrot and replace the red pepper with a few stalks of chopped celery. Omit the jalapeño and cumin and replace the can of black beans with a can of lentils.

Thai Coconut Soup
with Chicken or Seafood

Ingredients

1 stalk fresh lemongrass

4 cups (1 L) chicken or vegetable stock

1 14 oz (398 mL) can light or regular coconut milk

½ cup (125 mL) water

¼ cup (60 mL) fish sauce (nam pla)

1 cup (250 mL) thinly sliced mushrooms

2 Tbsp (30 mL) grated fresh ginger

1 Tbsp (15 mL) sugar

2–3 tsp (10–15 mL) red chili paste, chili-garlic sauce, or 1 small Serrano or jalapeño chili, minced

1–2 skinless, boneless chicken breasts, cut into small strips, or ½–1 lb (250–500 g) raw shrimp, peeled and deveined

¼ cup (60 mL) lime juice

2 green onions, thinly sliced

¼ cup (60 mL) fresh basil or cilantro, thinly sliced

This ingredient list may seem exotic, but everything can be easily located in most grocery stores. If there's something you can't find, a trip to an Asian market is always worthwhile. This recipe easily halves or doubles, or you can make the whole batch of stock, freeze half, and add chicken or seafood to the rest for dinner.

Method

1 Remove the tough outer leaves from the lemongrass and cut the stalk into two or three pieces. In a large pot set over medium heat, combine the lemongrass, chicken stock, coconut milk, water, fish sauce, mushrooms, ginger, sugar, and chili paste. Bring to a simmer, cover, and cook for 10–15 minutes.

2 Add the chicken or seafood and simmer for 3–5 minutes, until cooked through. Fish out the chunks of lemongrass, which will flavor the broth but aren't meant to be eaten. Stir in the lime juice, green onions, and basil or cilantro and serve immediately.

Serves 4

 What to do with the leftovers

  * Keep them in a sealed container in the fridge for a day or two. Reheat on the stovetop or in the microwave.

 Other things to do with it

  * Use raw scallops in place of the shrimp.

  * Curried Coconut Noodle Soup: Add 1 tsp–1 Tbsp (5–15 mL) curry paste or curry powder to the broth. Cook enough rice noodles to satisfy your appetite according to the package directions, and put a small pile of them into each bowl. Ladle soup over top.

Big Noodle Bowl

Ingredients

Chicken, vegetable or shrimp
stock (about 1 ½ cups/375 mL
per person)

Rice noodles, fresh or dried Asian
noodles, or any other type of
noodles (a handful per person)

Shredded cooked chicken, chopped
cooked pork, or cooked or raw
peeled shrimp (as much as you
like)

Baby bok choy or spinach (about
a handful per person), coarsely
chopped or left whole

Sesame oil, chili sauce, soy sauce,
and/or fish sauce to taste

When you're cooking for one, a noodle bowl makes a quick, nourishing, and warming yet light dinner and a great alternative to cereal.

This recipe is just a guideline—as long as you have some stock you can use whatever leftover chicken, pork, or shrimp you might have in the fridge. Bags of frozen shrimp are fairly inexpensive and are great to stash in the freezer to throw into this kind of dish. Dried noodles keep indefinitely, so you're likely to have a bag of some sort in the pantry. Add some greens and you'll have yourself a noodle bowl comparable to take-out.

Method

1　Heat the stock to a simmer in a pot appropriate for the amount you have. In a separate pot or bowl, boil or soak the noodles according to the package directions and drain them well. Divide the noodles among your serving bowls.

2　Season the stock with sesame oil, chili sauce, soy sauce, and/or fish sauce, or put the bottles out on the table so that people can season their own. Add the meat or seafood and bok choy to the stock and simmer just until the greens wilt. If you are using raw shrimp, make sure they have turned pink—this indicates they're cooked. Shrimp typically only need a minute or two to cook, depending on their size, so take them off the heat as soon as they turn pink; otherwise they will overcook and become rubbery.

3　Ladle the soup over the noodles and serve.

Serves as many as you want to feed.

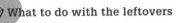 **What to do with the leftovers**

  * Eat them. They're good for you.

Other things to do with it

  * Beef Noodle Bowl: Use beef stock and add paper-thin slices of raw beef that will cook quickly in the hot broth.

  * Miso Soup: Add about 1 Tbsp (15 mL) miso paste, mixed with 2 Tbsp (30 mL) boiling water, for every cup of broth. Simmer a few sliced shiitake mushrooms in the broth, and add cubed tofu instead of the meat or shrimp. Add a small handful of bean sprouts to each bowl along with the noodles, and season your soup with soy sauce immediately before ladling it over the noodles.

Salads

Salads are among the easiest and most versatile dishes to prepare since they can be
made out of anything and don't really require a recipe. They're typically
built on greens, but are also often based on other vegetables, fruit, beans, meat,
or starches such as pasta, noodles, grains, bread, or potatoes.
The common denominator is that the combination of ingredients you choose
is typically dressed with vinaigrette or another type of dressing.

To build a salad, first decide how involved an affair you want it to be, and what ingredients you want to include. Start with greens, vegetables, fruit, or a starch, and build on that. Using meat, fish, cheese, eggs, nuts, or seeds in your salad adds protein, as does a combination of legumes and grains such as rice or couscous, so you could easily turn a salad into a balanced meal. Vegetables don't have to be raw—roasted or grilled veggies add a unique flavor and texture to salads. Roasted beets are especially good, and they will keep in the fridge for a few days after you roast them (see page 201).

When choosing greens, pick one variety (for example, romaine for a Caesar salad) or mix and match; combinations of textures, colors, and flavors make for an interesting salad on their own or a great base for anything else you want to add. Separate and wash greens well, spin them dry in a salad spinner or gently wrap them in a clean tea towel to dry them, and then tear them into a bowl or bag. It's a good idea to throw a sheet of paper towel in the bag to absorb any excess water. Greens can be prepared up to 24 hours ahead of time and stored, washed and dried, in the fridge.

A guide to choosing greens

Lettuces

Butter or Butterhead: Boston and Bibb lettuce are the most common butter lettuces. Loose heads with round, soft, pale green leaves. Very mild flavor and tender, almost buttery, texture.

Green or Red Leaf: comes in a very loose head with ruffled leaves that are either green or red-tipped. Crisp and slightly sweet flavor.

Iceberg: round, pale green, tight head with thick, watery but sturdy leaves that don't wilt easily. Mild flavor, very crunchy, watery texture but not a lot of nutritional value.

Romaine: long, loose heads with sturdy dark green leaves. Crunchy, mild flavor. Traditionally used in Caesar salads.

Salad greens

Arugula: also known as rocket. Has tender, dark green leaves on stems and varies in flavor from mildly peppery to spicy.

Chicory: also known as curly endive. Has a loose head with curly, ragged bright green leaves. Bitter flavor; the inner leaves are usually more tender.

Endive: small, cigar-shaped heads with pale, yellow-tipped leaves. Mild flavor and crisp, crunchy flavor.

Escarole: loose head with smooth, broad leaves with ruffled edges. Slightly bitter flavor.

Radicchio: tight, round purple heads that resemble a small cabbage, with leaves that have white ribs. Flavorful and slightly bitter.

Spinach: flat, dark green leaves on stems that should be removed if they're too big. Mild flavor; the smaller leaves are more tender— sometimes bags of prewashed baby spinach are available. Excellent source of vitamins, minerals, and fiber.

Watercress: small, delicate leaves with long stems. Delicate, slightly peppery flavor.

Great salad additions you may not have thought of

Avocado

Boiled or roasted potatoes

Candied or spiced nuts

Canned artichoke hearts

Canned, steamed, or grilled corn

Cooked bacon or pancetta

Cooked chicken, ham, pork, thinly sliced steak, or any other type of meat

Cooked grains such as quinoa or bulgur

Cooked long-grain white, brown, or wild rice

Cooked pasta or noodles

Cooked shrimp, salmon, tuna, crab, or any other seafood

Dried fruit, such as cherries, cranberries, or figs

Fresh herbs

Fruit, such as mango, berries, grapes, oranges, apples, peaches, or pineapple

Grated or crumbled cheeses

Grilled portobello mushrooms

Hard- or soft-boiled egg

Legumes such as chickpeas, lentils, kidney beans, and black beans

Nuts or seeds (to boost flavor, toast them first in a dry skillet set over medium heat for a few minutes, until golden and fragrant)

Olives

Poached egg (place it on top of the salad; when the yolk breaks, it mingles with the dressing)

Roasted or grilled vegetables

Roasted red, yellow, or orange peppers

Shredded cabbage

Torn bread or croutons

Vinaigrettes and Dressings

Broken down to its components, vinaigrette is no more than oil and an acid, usually in the form of vinegar or lemon juice. Olive oil and red or white wine vinegars are most commonly used, but any other kind of oil or vinegar can be substituted to change the flavor of your vinaigrette.

Choosing a type of olive oil can be confusing. Cold-pressed olive oil is your best choice—cold pressing is a chemical-free process that involves only pressure. "Extra-virgin" olive oil is the result of the first pressing, and is the fruitiest and most expensive kind of oil you can buy. It's best for drizzling on breads and salads—anytime flavor is really important. Generally, the greener an olive oil is, the more intense the olive flavor. "Virgin" olive oil also comes from the first pressing, but has a slightly higher level of acidity. Anything simply labeled "olive oil" contains a combination of olive and virgin or extra-virgin oils and is much cheaper and more appropriate for cooking with. "Light" olive oil doesn't refer to calories, but to the oil's color and flavor.

When making a vinaigrette, the traditional ratio is two parts oil to one part vinegar, but it's really something you can adjust according to your taste. After that, it's a free-for-all: try adding other types of vinegar and oil (nut oils are healthy and delicious, but their strong flavor may overpower greens—use half nut oil and half olive or canola), citrus juices, garlic, herbs, or other flavorings. Often honey, maple syrup, or sugar is added to vinaigrettes, but that, too, is a matter of taste. Because oil and vinegar don't combine well, an emulsifying ingredient like mustard or puréed roasted garlic will allow your dressing to blend more smoothly and stay that way for a longer time without separating.

Basic Vinaigrette

Ingredients

½ cup (125 mL) olive oil

¼ cup (60 mL) wine, balsamic, sherry, rice or any other kind of vinegar, or lemon juice

1 tsp (5 mL) honey or sugar

½ tsp (2.5 mL) Dijon or grainy mustard

Salt and pepper

Any other additions you like: a clove of crushed garlic; roasted garlic cloves, mashed until smooth; dried or fresh minced herbs such as basil, chives, tarragon, marjoram, or parsley; ¼ cup (60 mL) whipping cream; a minced shallot; maple syrup instead of honey; more mustard or flavored mustard; finely grated fresh ginger; soy sauce; sesame oil; Worcestershire sauce; grated Parmesan; a squeeze of anchovy or olive paste; a chopped canned chipotle in adobo or a squeeze of chipotle purée; a few capers; a blob of wasabi; some poppyseeds; ¼ cup (60 mL) chopped toasted hazelnuts or almonds (if you use nuts, add them to the vinaigrette just before serving it, or they'll get soggy)

Method

Whisk all the ingredients together in a bowl or shake in a jar until well blended. Store in the fridge for up to a week.

Makes ¾ cup (185 mL)

 **What to do with the leftovers**

* Keep vinaigrette in the fridge for up to a week, or for only a few days if it contains more perishable ingredients. Many vinaigrettes will separate as they sit in the fridge—shake them up to blend the ingredients again before you use them.

* Vinaigrette can be used on more than just salads; try tossing cold cooked pasta, potatoes, beans, or leftover roasted vegetables with vinaigrette, or using it as a marinade for chicken or vegetables.

* Marinate portobello mushrooms, which will soak up a lot of the flavor from the vinaigrette, before grilling them on the barbecue.

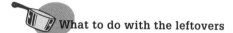

Asian Vinaigrette

Ingredients

¼ cup (60 mL) lime juice

1 Tbsp (15 mL) sesame oil (optional)

1 Tbsp (15 mL) brown sugar

1 Tbsp (15 mL) soy sauce

1 Tbsp (15 mL) fish sauce (nam pla)

1 Tbsp (15 mL) water

1 small hot red chili, seeded and finely chopped

1 tsp (5 mL) finely chopped cilantro

Method

Whisk all the ingredients together in a bowl or shake in a jar until well blended. Store in the fridge for up to a week.

Makes about ⅔ cup (150 mL)

Buttermilk Dressing

Ingredients

¼ cup (60 mL) buttermilk

¼ cup (60 mL) light sour cream

2 tsp (10 mL) white wine vinegar

1 tsp (5 mL) Dijon mustard

Salt and pepper

1 Tbsp (15 mL) chopped chives

1 Tbsp (15 mL) chopped fresh basil or parsley (optional)

2 Tbsp (30 mL) grated Parmesan or crumbled blue cheese (optional)

Method

Whisk all the ingredients together in a bowl or shake in a jar until well blended. Store in the fridge for up to a week.

Makes about ½ cup (125 mL)

Caesar Dressing

Ingredients

1 oil-packed anchovy fillet, finely chopped and mashed, or a squeeze of anchovy paste (optional)

3 Tbsp (45 mL) grated Parmesan

2 Tbsp (30 mL) mayonnaise, regular or light

1 Tbsp (15 mL) lemon juice

½ tsp (2.5 mL) Dijon mustard

1 small clove garlic, crushed

¼ tsp (1 mL) Worcestershire sauce (optional)

2–4 Tbsp (30–60 mL) extra-virgin olive or canola oil

Method

Whisk all the ingredients together in a bowl or shake in a jar until well blended. Store in the fridge for up to a week.

Makes about ⅔ cup (150 mL)

Creamy Garlic Dressing

Ingredients

3 Tbsp (45 mL) olive oil

2 Tbsp (30 mL) sour cream or plain yogurt

1 Tbsp (15 mL) white wine vinegar

1 Tbsp (15 mL) lemon juice

2 tsp (10 mL) Dijon mustard

1 small clove garlic, finely crushed

Salt and pepper

Method

Whisk all the ingredients together in a bowl or shake in a jar until well blended. Store in the fridge for up to a week.

Makes about ½ cup (125 mL)

Honey Roasted Garlic Dressing

Ingredients

1 head garlic, cloves separated and peeled

¼ cup (60 mL) olive oil

2 Tbsp (30 mL) honey

2 Tbsp (30 mL) white wine vinegar

1 Tbsp (15 mL) Dijon mustard

Salt and pepper

Method

1 Preheat the oven to 350°F (175°C).

2 In a small ovenproof dish, toss the garlic in the oil and cover the dish tightly with foil. Bake for about 45 minutes, until the garlic is tender. Set the oil and garlic aside to cool.

3 Put the garlic cloves in a blender or food processor, reserving the oil. Add the honey, vinegar, mustard, and salt and pepper and blend until puréed. With the motor running, gradually add the reserved oil in a steady, thin stream, blending until the mixture has emulsified and thickened.

4 Store in a jar or tightly sealed container in the fridge for up to a week.

Makes about ¾ cup (185 mL)

Roasted Tomato Dressing

Ingredients

1 pint cherry or grape tomatoes, or 4 Roma tomatoes, cut in half lengthwise

¼ cup (60 mL) olive oil

Salt and pepper

1 Tbsp (15 mL) red wine or sherry vinegar

2 tsp (10 mL) honey or brown sugar

2 tsp (10 mL) lemon juice

¼ cup (60 mL) vegetable or chicken stock

Method

1 Preheat oven to 450°F (230°C).

2 Place the tomatoes (cut side up if you're using large ones) in a baking dish and drizzle with the olive oil, salt and pepper. Roast for 45 minutes, until soft and golden. Set aside to cool slightly.

3 Scrape the tomatoes and oil into a blender or food processor and add the remaining ingredients. Purée until smooth. Store in the fridge for up to a week.

Makes about 1 cup (250 mL)

Salads

Greek Salad

Ingredients

½ small head romaine lettuce

2 ripe tomatoes, diced, or 1 pint (500 mL) cherry or grape tomatoes

½ long English cucumber, quartered lengthwise and sliced

½ cup (125 mL) black olives (preferably kalamata), whole or sliced

½ small purple onion, peeled and chopped or thinly sliced

¼ lb (125 g) feta cheese, crumbled

Basic vinaigrette, made with red wine or balsamic vinegar, a squeeze of lemon and a shake of oregano (see page 86)

As with most salad recipes, this is just a basic guideline for you to follow—adjust proportions to suit your taste and how many people you'd like to feed.

Method

1 Wash and dry the lettuce and chop or tear it into a bowl. Add the tomatoes, cucumber, olives, onion, and feta cheese. Drizzle with dressing and toss well to coat just before serving.

Serves 2–4

What to do with the leftovers

* Store the salad covered in the fridge for up to a day. Lettuce tends to get soggy from the dressing, but the other veggies hold up pretty well.

Other things to do with it

* Add a small jar of marinated artichoke hearts, drained and chopped, a roasted red pepper, cut into strips, and/or a drained can of tuna.

* Stuff a pita with Greek salad to make a sandwich. Add grilled chicken and/or hummus too, if you like.

* Greek Pasta Salad: Cook a cup of rotini or penne pasta according to the package directions, then run it under cold water and drain it well. Add it to the salad.

Potato Salad

Ingredients

2 lb (1 kg) potatoes, peeled or not, cut into chunks of similar size

2 Tbsp (30 mL) red wine vinegar (optional)

3 green onions, chopped, or ½ small onion, finely chopped or grated

2–3 eggs, hard-boiled, peeled, and chopped (see page 51)

1–2 stalks celery, diced

4 radishes, halved and thinly sliced (optional)

2 Tbsp (30 mL) sweet pickles, finely chopped

½ cup (125 mL) regular or light mayonnaise

2–4 Tbsp (30–60 mL) sweet pickle juice or milk

1–2 tsp (5–10 mL) yellow or Dijon mustard

Salt and pepper

Potato salad has that nostalgic charm of recipes that came into their own in the 1950s, like ambrosia and deviled eggs. It became popular to bring to potlucks and picnics because of its portability.

Classic potato salad is little more than potatoes moistened with mayonnaise and spiked with vinegar, maybe with some onion, celery, or egg thrown in as well. The measurements are approximate; let your taste dictate the quantity of each ingredient. You can use any kind of potato you like, but the variety you choose does make a difference: russets are mealier, so they absorb more dressing than waxier Yukon Gold, red, or baby new potatoes. Most people boil their potatoes to make potato salad, but you can also roast the potatoes instead to give them a crunchy, flavorful exterior. As a bonus, roasted potatoes won't absorb as much dressing, so you can get away with using less.

Method

1 Cook the potatoes in a large pot of boiling water until they're tender but still firm. Drain well, transfer to a large bowl, and toss with the red wine vinegar, if using. Set them aside to cool.

2 Add the onion, eggs, celery, radishes, and pickles. In a small bowl, stir together the mayonnaise, pickle juice, and mustard. Pour over the potato mixture and toss gently to coat. Season with salt and pepper to taste. Refrigerate until you're ready to eat.

Serves 4–6

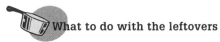 What to do with the leftovers

* Keep them covered in the fridge for up to 3 days.

 Other things to do with it

* Roasted Potato Salad with Bacon: Cook a few slices of bacon over medium-high heat until crispy and set them aside, reserving the drippings. Toss the chunks of potato with enough of the bacon fat to coat them well. Roast the potatoes in a single layer on a baking sheet at 450°F (230°C) until tender. Let them cool completely before tossing with the dressing. Crumble the bacon and add it at the end so that it doesn't get soggy.

* Salad Niçoise: Omit the celery, radishes, and dressing. Toss the potatoes with ½ lb (250 g) steamed and cooled green beans, 1 lb (500 g) roasted and cooled sliced beets (see page 201), 2 cups (500 mL) cherry or grape tomatoes, 1 Tbsp (15 mL) capers, and ½–1 cup (125–250 mL) roasted beets Niçoise olives, along with the eggs and green onions. Toss with a vinaigrette made with white wine vinegar, Dijon, and a bit of honey.

Ginger-Sesame Noodle Salad

Ingredients

8 oz (250 g) spaghetti, buckwheat or rice noodles (or about enough for 2–4)

1 cup (250 mL) sugar snap peas

1 cup (250 mL) asparagus, tough ends snapped off and cut into pieces, or broccoli florets

2 cups (500 mL) bean sprouts

1 small red bell pepper, cored and sliced

1 carrot, peeled and coarsely grated

1 cup (250 mL) cooked shrimp, peeled and deveined, or shredded cooked chicken

3 Tbsp (45 mL) rice vinegar

2 Tbsp (30 mL) soy sauce

1–2 Tbsp (15–30 mL) sesame or canola oil

1 tsp (5 mL) grated fresh ginger

½ tsp (2.5 mL) sugar

Salt and pepper

2 Tbsp (30 mL) sesame seeds, toasted (see page 111)

This salad is substantial enough to make a meal on its own, and is perfect during the summer when you don't feel like turning on the oven. Feel free to add tofu in place of the shrimp or chicken, or experiment with different kinds of veggies. Jicama, bok choy, blanched green beans, and even sliced mango are all good choices for this salad.

Method

1 Cook the pasta according to the package directions until tender. Throw the peas and asparagus into the water with the pasta for about 20 seconds at the very end to blanch them, then drain the pot into a colander and rinse the pasta and vegetables with cold water to stop them from cooking. Drain them well and transfer to a large bowl. Add the bean sprouts, red pepper, carrot, and shrimp or chicken.

2 In a small bowl or jar, whisk or shake together the vinegar, soy sauce, oil, ginger, sugar, and salt and pepper to taste. Pour over the salad and sprinkle with sesame seeds; toss to coat.

Serves 4

 What to do with the leftovers

* Keep them covered in the fridge for a day or two.

 Other things to do with it

* Add pan-seared scallops: sprinkle fresh, raw scallops with a pinch of sugar, and salt and pepper. Heat some canola or sesame oil in large skillet over medium-high heat and sauté the scallops for about 3 minutes, flipping them once, until they're just opaque in the middle.

* Peanut-Sesame Noodle Salad: Add ¼ cup (60 mL) peanut butter and 1 Tbsp (15 mL) honey or brown sugar to the dressing. Sprinkle with chopped peanuts instead of sesame seeds.

Salads

Coleslaw

Ingredients

¼ cup (60 mL) white vinegar

3 Tbsp (45 mL) sugar

3 Tbsp (45 mL) canola oil

1 tsp (5 mL) mustard

1 tsp (5 mL) celery seed

Salt and pepper

½ medium cabbage, thinly sliced

1 small sweet or purple onion, halved
    and thinly sliced

1 carrot, grated

1 small green, red, or yellow bell
    pepper, cored and thinly sliced

Most people don't take coleslaw seriously; it's usually little more than an afterthought, sitting sadly in a small paper cup alongside fish and chips or a smoked meat sandwich. It's a shame, since cabbage is so good for you. If you don't have celery seed, this coleslaw is still delicious without. If plain coleslaw bores you, try one of the variations below.

Method

1 In a small pot set over medium heat, combine the vinegar, sugar, oil, mustard, and celery seed. Bring the mixture to a boil, then immediately remove it from the heat and stir in the salt and pepper. Set it aside to cool.

2 In a large bowl, combine the cabbage, onion, carrot, and green pepper. Add the vinaigrette and toss to coat the vegetables. Refrigerate the coleslaw for about an hour, or until it's well chilled.

Serves 4

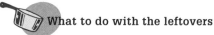 **What to do with the leftovers**

*   Keep them covered in the fridge for up to a day; coleslaw tends to get soggy as it sits.

 **Other things to do with it**

*   Asian Slaw: Add a handful of sugar snap or snow peas and thinly sliced radicchio instead of the green pepper and onion. When making the vinaigrette, use rice vinegar, replace half the canola oil with sesame oil, replace the celery seed with freshly grated ginger, and add 1 tsp (5 mL) soy sauce.

*   Ichiban Salad: Crush a package of dry Ichiban noodles and toss it into the salad. Make the dressing by mixing 2 Tbsp (30 mL) canola oil, 2 Tbsp (30 mL) rice vinegar, and the contents of the Ichiban seasoning pouch. Top the salad with toasted sliced or slivered almonds.

Spinach and Feta Rice or Orzo Salad

Ingredients

1 ½ cups (375 mL) uncooked long-grain white rice or orzo

1 small bunch fresh spinach or half a bag of prewashed spinach

1 small purple onion, finely chopped

½–1 cup (125–250 mL) crumbled feta cheese

Grated zest and juice of 1 lemon

2 Tbsp (30 mL) rice vinegar

2 Tbsp (30 mL) canola or olive oil

Salt and pepper

This salad keeps well in the fridge, so you can mix up a big batch and be well fed all week. It's delicious made with rice or orzo (small rice-shaped pasta), or try using brown rice for added fiber.

Method

1 Cook the rice or orzo according to package directions (or the directions on page 182) and cool it in the fridge until it's room temperature or cold. Transfer to a large bowl.

2 If you're using unwashed spinach, fill the sink with cold water and put the bunch of spinach in it, then swish the leaves around well to get rid of all the grit. Spin the leaves dry in a salad spinner or wrap them in a tea towel and blot them dry. Stack a bunch of leaves, roll them up tightly, and thinly slice the whole bunch. This is the fastest way to slice large quantities of spinach. Add the sliced spinach to the rice along with the onion, feta, and lemon zest. Toss everything well.

3 Squeeze the lemon juice over the salad, and drizzle with the rice vinegar, oil, and salt and pepper to taste. Toss to coat well. Taste and adjust the seasonings if necessary. Serve immediately or refrigerate until you're ready for it.

Serves 6–8

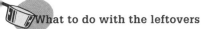 **What to do with the leftovers**

* Keep them covered in the fridge for up to 4 days.

 Other things to do with it

* Orzo, Basil, and Parmesan Salad: Use orzo instead of rice, ½ cup (125 mL) freshly grated Parmesan instead of feta, balsamic vinegar instead of rice vinegar, ½ cup (125 mL) fresh basil instead of the spinach, and omit the lemon. Add ½ cup (125 mL) kalamata olives, ¼ cup (60 mL) chopped oil-packed sun-dried tomatoes, and a crushed clove of garlic.

Rice Salad

Ingredients

3 cups (750 mL) steamed brown, basmati, or wild rice, or a combination (about 1 cup/250 mL) uncooked, see page 182)

1 red, orange, or yellow bell pepper, cored and diced

2 stalks celery, diced

½ purple onion, peeled and finely chopped

½ long English cucumber, halved lengthwise and sliced

1 cup (250 mL) cherry or grape tomatoes, halved

¼ cup (60 mL) chopped fresh parsley or cilantro (optional)

3 Tbsp (45 mL) olive oil

3 Tbsp (45 mL) balsamic vinegar

½ tsp (2.5 mL) Dijon or grainy mustard

Salt and pepper

Rice salads have staying power, which makes them perfect to stash in the fridge and dip into all week. This is a great way to use up leftover rice from dinner, but if you cook rice especially for salad, you could boost the flavor by cooking it in chicken or vegetable stock instead of water.

Method

1 Toss the cooled rice, vegetables, and parsley together in a large bowl. In a small bowl or jar, whisk or shake together the oil, vinegar, mustard, and salt and pepper to taste. Pour the dressing over the salad and toss to coat.

Serves 6

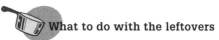

What to do with the leftovers

* Keep them covered in the fridge for up to 5 days.

Other things to do with it

* Add cooked shrimp, shredded cooked chicken, or rinsed and drained black beans, chickpeas or lentils.

* Add ½ cup (125 mL) crumbled feta cheese and fresh mint instead of cilantro.

* Black Bean and Rice Salad: Add a 14 oz (398 mL) can black beans, rinsed and drained, and omit the cucumber and celery. Use red wine vinegar in place of the balsamic vinegar and add 2 Tbsp (30 mL) orange juice, ½ tsp (2.5 mL) cumin, and ¼ tsp (1 mL) chili powder. An ear of corn, steamed or grilled and scraped off the cob, is good too.

Couscous Salad

Ingredients

1 ¼ cups (310 mL) chicken or
vegetable stock or water

1 cup (250 mL) uncooked couscous

2 tomatoes, chopped

1 cup (250 mL) diced mozzarella or
Gouda cheese

3 green onions, thinly sliced

¼ cup (60 mL) thinly sliced fresh
basil

2 Tbsp (60 mL) olive oil

2 Tbsp (60 mL) balsamic vinegar

1 small clove garlic, crushed
(optional)

Salt and pepper to taste

Couscous is great for soaking up flavors, so it makes for a very intensely
flavored yet light salad.

Method

1 Bring the stock or water to a boil in a medium pot and stir in the couscous.
Remove from the heat, cover, and let stand for 5 minutes. Fluff it with a fork
and set aside to cool. Transfer to a large bowl and add the tomatoes, cheese,
onions, and basil.

2 Stir together the oil, vinegar, and garlic and pour over the salad. Season to
taste with salt and pepper and toss gently to coat.

Serves 4

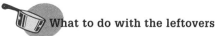 **What to do with the leftovers**

* Keep them covered in the fridge for up to 3 days.

 **Other things to do with it**

* Couscous Salad with Red Pepper and Corn: Replace the
tomatoes and cheese with a small chopped red bell pepper and
2 ears of corn, grilled or scraped off the cob and sautéed in a little
oil until golden. Replace the basil with cilantro and the balsamic
vinegar with red wine vinegar. Add ¼ tsp (1 mL) ground cumin
to the dressing.

* Couscous Salad with Shrimp: Replace the mozzarella with
½ lb (250 g) peeled cooked shrimp, and the balsamic vinegar
with lemon juice. Add a small handful of fresh mint if you like.

Salads

Tabbouleh

Ingredients

½ cup (125 mL) fine grain bulgur, rinsed and drained

2 cups (500 mL) fresh parsley, chopped

2 tomatoes, seeded and finely chopped

1 small red or white onion or 4 green onions, finely chopped

¼–½ cup (60–125 mL) chopped fresh mint (optional)

⅓ cup (80 mL) extra-virgin olive oil

¼ cup (60 mL) fresh lemon juice

This is one of the few times you'll see fresh parsley (an excellent source of vitamins A and C) used as a main ingredient rather than a garnish, mixed with bulgur (otherwise known as cracked or bulgur wheat) and tossed with a lemony dressing. Serve it with wedges of pita bread.

Method

1 Pour 1 ½ cups (375 mL) of hot water over the bulgur in a large bowl and let it stand for 20–30 minutes, until tender. Drain well and squeeze out as much liquid as possible.

2 Add the parsley, tomatoes, onion, and mint. In a small bowl, whisk together the olive oil and lemon juice and pour over the salad. Toss well and refrigerate for an hour to allow the flavors to blend.

Serves 4–6

 What to do with the leftovers

* Keep them covered in the fridge for up to 2 days.

 Other things to do with it

* Add crumbled feta cheese and/or chopped fresh avocado.

* Bulgur Salad with Chickpeas and Roasted Peppers: Double the amount of bulgur and cut the parsley down to ¼ cup (60 mL). Add a can of chickpeas, rinsed and drained, and 1 or 2 roasted red peppers, thinly sliced, instead of the tomatoes and onion. Add 1 tsp (5 mL) each honey and ground cumin and ¼ tsp (1 mL) cayenne pepper to the dressing.

Salads

Stew

We eat for so many reasons other than to satisfy ourselves nutritionally.
Stews are all about sustenance and warmth and the comfort
that comes from a pot of something good for you bubbling on the stove,
especially when it didn't come from a can. And there's nothing more consoling
than food that requires something starchy to mop up
the extra sauce from your bowl.

Stew Basics

Stews are the best way to use tough (i.e., cheap) cuts of meat, are very difficult to screw up, and can keep you fed for weeks or months if you have room in your freezer.

Stews are very similar to soups, the difference being they're heartier, contain less liquid, and are usually cooked over low heat for a long period of time to tenderize tough cuts of meat. Most stews could more accurately be called braises, since stewing is essentially the same method of cooking (see page 41) but stews do contain more liquid than most other braised dishes.

Braising and stewing tenderizes tough cuts of meat by breaking down their connective tissues, so stews are perfect for using more inexpensive (but often more flavorful) cuts of beef, pork, and lamb, and stretching them further. When it comes to beef, chuck, brisket, round, and rump are generally the best choices for making stew. Stay away from any of the leaner cuts of meat, which tend to dry out when cooked for long periods of time. Packaged "stewing meat" is usually fine, although supermarkets tend to package up scraps from different cuts, so you never know for sure what you're getting.

When you make a stew, begin by browning your meat, which caramelizes its exterior, adding flavor and depth to the finished dish. When browning meat, it's essential that your pan isn't crowded, or the meat will steam rather than brown properly. Browning and searing merely add flavor; they don't "seal in" the juices as is commonly believed. This is a good thing because it's important for stewing meat to release its juices into the sauce.

Because the flavor of the stock takes on so much of the flavor of the meat, using canned broth is perfectly fine. Once you bring your stew to a simmer, keep it over low heat so that the meat braises rather than boils. This can be done on the lowest setting of your stovetop, or in a 300°F (150°C) oven. Make sure you cover the pot tightly so that the moisture doesn't evaporate as it cooks.

Stew

Beef Stew

Ingredients

2 Tbsp (30 mL) flour

Salt and pepper

1–1 ½ lb (500–750 g) beef stew meat or chuck, trimmed of fat and cut into 1-inch (2.5 cm) cubes

2–3 Tbsp (30–45 mL) olive or canola oil

1–2 onions, chopped

3 cloves garlic, crushed

1 cup (250 mL) red wine (optional)

1 10-oz (284-mL) can beef, vegetable or chicken broth, plus 1 can of water

1 28-oz (796-mL) can diced tomatoes, undrained

1 tsp (5 mL) thyme

1–2 bay leaves

2 medium potatoes, cut into 1-inch (2.5-cm) cubes (peeled or not)

2 carrots, peeled and sliced

½ cup (125 mL) frozen peas

The best beef stew is made with beef chuck, commonly labeled "boneless chuck-eye," "cross-rib roast," "blade steak/roast," or "shoulder steak/roast." Buy a steak or roast and cube it yourself, or pick up a package of pre-cubed "stewing beef," which you may need to trim into more uniform pieces so that they cook evenly. Tossing the pieces in flour before you brown them helps them to caramelize and then thickens the liquid as your stew simmers. Feel free to adjust the types and quantities of the vegetables to make it your own.

Method

1 Season the flour with salt and pepper in a medium bowl. Add the beef cubes and toss them with the flour until well coated. In a large pot or Dutch oven, heat about a tablespoon of oil over medium-high heat, until it's hot but not smoking. Brown the beef in batches, cooking for a few minutes on each side, until browned all over. Add a little more oil to the pot if you need it as you add more beef. Remember that browning is only to add flavor—it's not necessary to cook the meat all the way through. Remove the meat from the pot and set aside.

2 Add another tablespoon of oil to the pot and cook the onions for about 5 minutes, until they have softened. Add the garlic and cook for another minute. Add the wine, broth, and tomatoes with their juice, scraping the bottom of the pot to loosen any flavorful browned bits that have stuck to the bottom.

3 Return the beef to the pot and add the thyme and bay leaves. Bring to a simmer. Turn the heat down to low, cover the pot, and let it simmer for about an hour. Add the potatoes and carrots and cook the stew uncovered for another 45 minutes. Add the peas for the last 5 minutes. Fish out the bay leaves, season to taste with salt and pepper, and serve it hot.

Serves 4–6

Beef Stew (continued)

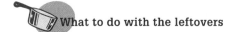

What to do with the leftovers

* Keep them covered in the fridge for up to 3 days, or divide into containers and freeze for up to 3 months. Reheat in the microwave or on the stovetop, adding a little extra liquid if necessary.

Other things to do with it

* Use peeled and diced sweet potatoes, rutabaga, or parsnips instead of the potatoes and/or carrots.

* Omit the beef broth, double the wine, and add ½ cup (125 mL) hoisin sauce.

* Mushroom Beef Stew: Use 2 cans of beef broth and 2 cups (500 mL) of wine omit the tomatoes. Instead of the peas, add 1 lb (500 g) fresh shiitake or portobello mushrooms, stemmed and thickly sliced, during the last 5 minutes of cooking.

Beef Carbonnade

Ingredients

2 slices bacon, chopped (optional)

2 ½ lb (1.25 kg) chuck roast or blade steak, cut into 1-inch (2.5 cm) cubes

Salt and pepper

4 onions, peeled and thinly sliced

1–2 cloves garlic, crushed

3 Tbsp (45 mL) flour

1 can (10 oz/284 mL) beef broth

1 can or bottle beer (dark beer is especially good)

1 Tbsp (15 mL) brown sugar

½ tsp (2.5 mL) thyme

1 bay leaf

12 oz (300 g) egg noodles

What to do with the leftovers

* Keep them covered in the fridge for up to 3 days or freeze in a sealed container for up to 4 months. Reheat in the microwave.

Beef carbonnade is a Belgian stew in which not-so-tender cuts of beef are braised slowly in beer and broth, creating an intensely flavorful sauce. A carbonnade is very beefy, with fewer vegetables and less liquid than most stews. Traditionally it's served over buttered egg noodles, but mashed potatoes are delicious too—you'll just need something to catch all the sauce.

Method

1 Preheat the oven to 300°F (150°C).

2 In a large pot or Dutch oven, cook the bacon over medium-high heat until crisp. Remove it from the pot and set it aside, leaving the drippings. If you're not using bacon, heat a drizzle of oil in the pot over medium-high heat.

3 Pat the beef dry with paper towels and season it with salt and pepper. Cook in the bacon drippings or oil for 5 minutes, browning the pieces well on all sides. Do this in batches if the pot is too crowded for them to brown properly. Transfer the meat to a plate or bowl with the bacon.

4 Add the onions to the pot, with a little extra oil if you need it, and sauté for about 10 minutes, until softened and starting to turn golden. Add the garlic and cook for another minute. Add the flour and cook for 2 minutes. Stir in the broth, scraping up any brown bits that have stuck to the bottom of the pot. Add the beer, brown sugar, thyme, and bay leaf. Return the bacon and beef to the pot and bring the mixture to a simmer. Cover it and place it in the oven.

5 Bake the carbonnade for 2 hours, until the beef is very tender. Meanwhile, cook the egg noodles according to package directions, timing it so that they're done at roughly the same time as the carbonnade. Discard the bay leaf, and season to taste with salt and pepper. Serve the beef carbonnade hot over buttered noodles.

Serves 4–6

Pork Cassoulet

Ingredients

2 19-oz (540-mL) cans white beans, such as kidney or navy beans, or 1 lb (500 g) dried

3 slices bacon, chopped

3 lb (1.5 kg) boneless pork shoulder or boneless pork loin, trimmed of excess fat and cut into 1-inch (2.5 cm) pieces

1 lb (500 g) kielbasa (preferably lean turkey kielbasa), cut into ½-inch slices

2 large onions, chopped

2–3 stalks celery, sliced

2–3 carrots, peeled and sliced

1 red bell pepper, seeded and chopped

4 cloves garlic, crushed

2 tsp (10 mL) thyme

1 10 oz (284 mL) can chicken broth

1 14 oz (398 mL) can diced tomatoes

2 Tbsp (30 mL) tomato paste

½ cup (125 mL) dry white wine (optional)

Salt and pepper

1–2 cups (250–500 mL) fresh bread crumbs

½ cup (125 mL) grated Parmesan

Putting together a cassoulet (kind of a fancy French pork & beans) may seem complicated, but it requires more patience than skill. Most of the time it takes is spent simmering or baking, so this is a great recipe to make on days when you're just going to be hanging around the house. It makes a large batch, so it's perfect if you're having friends around for dinner, and it freezes well, so even if you're making it for yourself, you'll end up with a freezer stashed with leftovers for lunches and dinners down the road.

Method

1 If you're using dried beans, place them in a large pot or Dutch oven and add enough water to cover them by about 2 inches. Bring to a boil over medium-high heat and cook for a few minutes; remove the pot from the heat, and let it stand for an hour. Drain the beans, cover them with fresh water, and bring them to a boil again. Reduce the heat to low, cover and simmer for 20–30 minutes, until the beans are almost tender. Drain and set aside.

2 Preheat the oven to 300°F (150°C).

3 In the same pot, cook the bacon over medium-high heat until crisp. Remove it from the pot, set it aside, and add the pork to the drippings in the pot. Cook the pork for about 5 minutes, until it's browned all over. Set the pork aside with the bacon and add the kielbasa to the pot. Cook for 5 minutes, until browned. Remove it from the pot and add it to the pork and bacon. Add the onions, celery, carrots, red pepper, garlic, and thyme to the pot and cook for about 5 minutes, until the vegetables are tender.

4 Add the can of broth to the onion mixture, fill the empty can with water and add that too, then add the diced tomatoes with their juices and the tomato paste and bring the mixture to a boil. Add the bacon, pork, and kielbasa, along with any juices that have accumulated in the bottom of the bowl, and the beans. Cover the pot (make sure the lid is ovenproof, or use foil) and put it in the oven for an hour.

5 Take the pot out of the oven. Scoop out a cup or two of the cassoulet and purée it in a food processor or blender, or use a hand-held immersion blender to purée some of the mixture while it's in the pot. Return the puréed cassoulet to the pot and stir in the wine, then season it with salt and pepper.

6 Combine the bread crumbs and Parmesan and sprinkle it over the whole thing. Return the pot to the oven for another 45 minutes, until the topping is golden.

Serves 8–10

What to do with the leftovers

* Keep them covered in the fridge for up to 3 days, or divide into containers and freeze for up to 4 months. Reheat on the stovetop or in the microwave, adding a little extra liquid if necessary.

Other things to do with it

* Omit the bread crumb and Parmesan topping altogether, and bake the mixture for an extra half hour before puréeing a portion of it. Serve it as is, with crusty bread to mop up the broth.

* Omit the bacon and pork and use 3 lb (1.5 kg) kielbasa instead. Replace the carrots with a peeled, chopped apple and use sage instead of thyme.

Stew

Irish Lamb Stew

Ingredients

1 Tbsp (15 mL) olive or canola oil

1 Tbsp (15 mL) butter

2 Tbsp (30 mL) flour

Salt and pepper

1–1 ½ lb (500–750 g) lamb stew meat
   or shoulder lamb chops, cut into
   1-inch (2.5-cm) cubes

2 medium onions, coarsely chopped,
   or 12 small boiling onions, peeled
   but left whole

2 medium potatoes, peeled (or not)
   and cut into 1-inch (2.5 cm)
   chunks (Yukon Gold are the best)

2 carrots, peeled and cut into
   1-inch (2.5 cm) chunks

1 tsp (5 mL) dried thyme

2 bay leaves

2 cups (500 mL) beef or chicken stock

¼ cup (60 mL) frozen peas, thawed
   (optional)

¼ cup (60 mL) chopped fresh parsley

True Irish stew contains only meat, potatoes, and onions, but I've added a few peas and carrots as well. Other root vegetables are also delicious and authentic—replace half the potatoes with peeled and diced turnips if you like, or use pork shoulder instead of lamb.

Method

1   Heat the oil and butter in a large saucepan or Dutch oven set over medium-high heat. Season the flour generously with salt and pepper in a medium bowl, and toss the chunks of lamb in it to coat them well. Add the lamb to the pot in batches and sauté for about 5 minutes, until the pieces are golden all over. Remove the lamb from the pot as you cook it—if your pot is too crowded, the meat will steam instead of browning properly. After the last of the lamb has been browned, remove it from the pot and sauté the onion for a few minutes, until tender.

2   Return the cooked lamb to the pot and add any leftover flour. Cook for another minute. Add the potatoes, carrots, thyme, and bay leaves. Add the stock and bring the stew to a boil. Reduce the heat to low, cover the pot, and simmer for about an hour.

3   Uncover the pot, add the peas and simmer for another 15 minutes, until the gravy thickens and the meat is very tender. Season to taste with salt and pepper, fish out the bay leaves, and stir in the parsley. Serve immediately.

Serves 4

Stew

What to do with the leftovers

* Keep them covered in the fridge for up to 3 days, or divide them into containers and freeze for up to 4 months. Reheat on the stovetop or in the microwave, adding a little extra liquid if necessary.

 Other things to do with it

* Moroccan Lamb Stew: Replace the potatoes with 2 cups (500 mL) cubed butternut squash. Add 4 crushed cloves of garlic, the grated zest of an orange, 1 tsp (5 mL) each chili powder and cumin, and ½ tsp (2.5 mL) cinnamon with the vegetables. Add 2 chopped roasted red peppers and ⅓ cup (80 mL) slivered dry apricots during the final 15 minutes of cooking, and stir in some cilantro instead of parsley. Serve over couscous (see page 187).

* Pork and Mushroom Stew: Use pork shoulder instead of lamb. Add ½ tsp (2.5 mL) Italian seasoning to the flour with the salt and pepper. Omit the potatoes, and sauté 4 cloves of crushed garlic along with the onions. Stir 2 cups (500 mL) sliced mushrooms and ¼ cup (60 mL) frozen peas into the stew when you uncover the pot; simmer for 15–20 minutes, until the mushrooms are tender and the gravy has thickened.

Seafood Stew

Ingredients

2 Tbsp (30 mL) olive oil

1 large onion, chopped

3 cloves garlic, crushed or chopped

1 Tbsp (15 mL) dried oregano

1 tsp (5 mL) fennel seeds, crushed

1 28 oz (796 mL) can diced or crushed
tomatoes

2 cups (500 mL) clam juice

1 cup (250 mL) dry white wine

2 142 g cans clams, drained (reserve
the liquid)

1 lb (500 g) uncooked large shrimp,
peeled and deveined

1 lb (500 g) cod, haddock, or other
whitefish fillets, cut into 2-inch
(5 cm) pieces

1 120 g can crabmeat, drained

½ cup (125 mL) chopped fresh basil
or parsley

Salt and pepper

Cayenne pepper

Known on Italian restaurant menus as cioppino, seafood stew can be made with any assortment of fresh, frozen, or canned seafood you can get your hands on. It needs crusty bread to mop up the broth.

Method

1 Heat the oil in a large pot or Dutch oven set over medium heat. Sauté the onion, garlic, oregano, and fennel seeds for about 8 minutes, until the onion is tender. Add the tomatoes, clam juice, wine, and the reserved liquid from the clams. Bring to a boil, then reduce the heat, and simmer for 20–30 minutes, until slightly thickened.

2 Add the clams, shrimp, fish, and crabmeat and simmer for 5 minutes, until the shrimp and fish are opaque. Stir in the basil and season to taste with salt, pepper, and cayenne pepper. Serve immediately.

Serves 4

 What to do with the leftovers

* Keep them covered in the fridge for up to 2 days, or divide them into containers and freeze for up to 4 months. Gently reheat on the stovetop or in the microwave, adding a little extra liquid if necessary.

* Serve reheated leftovers over hot pasta with crumbled feta cheese or grated Parmesan.

 Other things to do with it

* Add ½ lb (250 g) bay scallops along with the seafood or instead of the fish.

* Add the grated zest of an orange and a generous pinch of dried red pepper flakes.

* Use fresh clams or mussels instead of the canned clams. After the broth has simmered, add 12 fresh, well-scrubbed littleneck clams or mussels to the pot, cover with a lid and cook for 10 minutes, until the shells open. Discard any that don't open. Add the shrimp, fish, and crabmeat as directed.

Meals
in a bowl

Sometimes it's nice to eat your entire meal out of one bowl,
without bothering with knives and serving dishes
and coordinating several elements to create a full meal.
Maybe you own only one bowl, or maybe you love to curl up
and eat on the couch. There are many ways
to consolidate your meat, veg, and grain
into one comforting dish,
and most are adaptable to make use
of any type of meat and veg.

Meals
in a
bowl

Pad Thai

Ingredients

½–1 lb (250–500 g) package rice noodles, thin or thick

Sesame, peanut, or canola oil, for cooking

¼ cup (60 mL) tomato sauce or ketchup

¼ cup (60 mL) fish sauce (nam pla)

¼ cup (60 mL) lime juice or 2 Tbsp (30 mL) rice vinegar

2–4 Tbsp (30–60 mL) brown sugar

1 tsp (5 mL) chili sauce or sambal oelek (optional)

1 tsp (5 mL) tamarind concentrate (optional)

2 chicken breasts, thinly sliced, or 1 cup (250 mL) chopped cooked chicken (optional)

Up to ½ lb (250 g) cooked or uncooked shrimp, shelled and deveined (optional)

½–1 cup (125–250 mL) firm tofu, drained and diced (optional)

1–3 small red chilies (optional)

2 eggs, lightly beaten

2 cloves garlic, crushed (optional)

3 green onions, cut into 1-inch (2.5 cm) pieces

2 cups (500 mL) bean sprouts

¼ cup (60 mL) chopped peanuts or cashews, salted or unsalted

Lime wedges (optional)

Pad Thai is a perfect way to use up leftover roasted chicken, tofu, or even pork, and if you keep a bag of shrimp in the freezer it's easy to add a handful. Tamarind concentrate, fish sauce, and chili sauce can be found in the ethnic section of grocery stores or in Asian markets. All will keep in the fridge for a long time, so don't worry about buying a whole jar just to use a few spoonfuls.

Method

1 Soak the rice noodles according to package directions. Rinse them with cold water and drain well. Drizzle with a little oil and toss to coat.

2 In a small bowl, stir together the tomato sauce, fish sauce, lime juice, brown sugar, chili sauce, and tamarind concentrate (if using).

3 Heat a good drizzle of oil in a large non-stick skillet set over medium-high heat. Add the meat or shrimp if they're uncooked (if your meat is cooked, set it aside for now), along with the tofu and the chilies if you're using them. Cook for a few minutes, until the meat is cooked through or the tofu is golden. Push the mixture aside or remove it from the skillet. If you are using shrimp, remove them so they don't overcook and become tough. Add the eggs and cook them as if you were making scrambled eggs, breaking them up with a spatula. Push them aside.

4 Add a little more oil if you need it and stir-fry the garlic and green onions for about a minute. Add the noodles and cook, tossing them with tongs, for another minute. Return any reserved cooked meat to the skillet, pour as much of the sauce as you want over it all, and cook for 2–3 minutes, tossing the mixture with tongs to coat everything with sauce and heat it through. Add the bean sprouts at the very end.

5 Serve in large shallow bowls, sprinkled with chopped peanuts, with lime wedges to squeeze over top.

Serves 4 (Doubles and halves easily)

 What to do with the leftovers

* You can store them in the fridge for up to a day, but pad Thai doesn't keep very well.

 Other things to do with it

* Coconut Pad Thai: Use coconut cream in place of the tomato sauce.

Chicken, Shrimp, and Sausage
Jambalaya

Ingredients

1 Tbsp (15 mL) olive or canola oil

4 chicken thighs, with skin and bones

½ lb (250 g) kielbasa, andouille, or hot Italian sausage, sliced or coarsely chopped

1 onion, coarsely chopped

1 red bell pepper, seeded and coarsely chopped

1 stalk celery, coarsely chopped

2–5 cloves garlic, crushed

1 ½ cups (375 mL) long-grain white rice

1 bay leaf

1 tsp (5 mL) chili powder

½ tsp (2.5 mL) salt

½ tsp (2.5 mL) dried thyme

A few shakes of Tabasco sauce

2 ½ cups (625 mL) chicken stock (or 1 can plus a can of water)

1 14-oz (398-mL) can diced or stewed tomatoes, undrained

Salt and pepper

½ lb (250 g) large shrimp, peeled and deveined, with or without the tails on

Jambalaya is a Creole dish that combines rice with vegetables and a variety of meats, most often sausage, ham, chicken and seafood. You can make it as gutsy or mild-mannered as you like with (or without) hot Italian sausage, spices and hot sauce.

Method

1 Heat the oil in a large pot or Dutch oven set over medium-high heat. Cook the chicken thighs for a few minutes, turning as necessary until browned on all sides. Remove them from the pot and set aside. Reduce the heat to medium. Add the sausage to the pot and cook, stirring frequently, for a few minutes or until browned. Remove from the pot and set aside.

2 Add the onion, pepper, celery, and garlic to the pot and sauté for about 5 minutes, until tender. Add the rice and cook for a minute, stirring well. Add the cooked sausage, bay leaf, chili powder, salt, thyme, and Tabasco.

3 Add the stock and diced tomatoes and stir everything together. Bring the mixture to a boil. Pull the skin off the chicken thighs and add them to the pot, meat side down, on top of the rice. Reduce the heat to low, cover, and simmer for about 15 minutes.

4 Remove the lid and stir the jambalaya, keeping the chicken pieces more or less on top. Replace the lid and cook for another 15–20 minutes, until the liquid is absorbed, the rice is tender, and the chicken is cooked through. Remove the bay leaf and season with salt and pepper to taste. Scatter the shrimp over the jambalaya, cover, and cook for 5–10 minutes, just until the shrimp are pink and opaque. Serve immediately.

Serves 6

 What to do with the leftovers

* Keep them covered in the fridge for up to 3 days and reheat in the microwave. Jambalaya doesn't freeze very well—it tends to get watery as it thaws.

 Other things to do with it

* Substitute 1–2 cups (250–500 mL) diced cooked ham for the sausage; add it at the point you would add the cooked sausage.

Chicken, Pork, or Shrimp Stir-fry

Ingredients

1 lb (500 g) skinless, boneless
chicken breasts, pork
tenderloin, or uncooked
shrimp, shelled and deveined

Marinade

2 Tbsp (30 mL) soy sauce

2 Tbsp (30 mL) water

2 cloves garlic, crushed

1 Tbsp (15 mL) cornstarch (optional,
if using chicken)

1 Tbsp (15 mL) flour (optional,
if using chicken)

2–4 Tbsp (30–60 mL) sesame,
peanut or canola oil

Sauce

¼ cup (60 mL) chicken broth

1 Tbsp (15 mL) soy sauce

1 Tbsp (15 mL) oyster sauce

2 tsp (10 mL) grated fresh ginger

1 tsp (5 mL) cornstarch

2 stalks celery, cut diagonally into
thick slices

1 cup (250 mL) snow peas, cut in half
crosswise on a slight diagonal

Ingredients continue on next page

It's not easy to replicate an authentic stir-fry from a good Chinese restaurant, but it's fun to try. Stir-frying is a lot like sautéing; its purpose is to cook food quickly at a very high temperature. You don't need a wok, but a large non-stick skillet will allow you to toss the meat and veggies around easily without having them stick to the pan.

When making stir-fries, your goal is to not overcook your vegetables so that they stay crisp. Cooking them separately ensures all the vegetables are cooked perfectly. This may seem like an enormous hassle, but if you have all your ingredients ready to go before you start cooking, a stir-fry will only take a few minutes from beginning to end.

If you are stir-frying chicken, a traditional Chinese process called "velveting" that involves coating the chicken in a cornstarch mixture after marinating and before cooking will make it even more tender and juicy, but it's not a required step.

Method

1 Cut the chicken or pork into ¼- × 1-inch slices (5 mm × 2.5 cm). To make the marinade, stir together the soy sauce, water, and garlic and pour it over the meat. Put it in the fridge to marinate while you prepare the vegetables.

2 If you're using chicken and want to use the velveting process, stir together the 1 Tbsp (15 mL) cornstarch, flour and 2 Tbsp (30 mL) of the oil. Drain the marinade off the chicken and toss the chicken with the cornstarch mixture to coat it well.

3 To make the sauce, stir together the chicken broth, soy sauce, oyster sauce, ginger, and 1 tsp (5 mL) cornstarch in a small bowl. When everything is ready to go, heat a large non-stick skillet over medium-high heat until it's hot but not smoking—a drop of water should evaporate immediately when it hits the surface.

4 Drizzle about a teaspoon (5 mL) of oil in the skillet and stir-fry the celery for about a minute, until tender-crisp. Transfer it to a large bowl. Working in the same manner, stir-fry each vegetable (except the bean sprouts) separately just until tender-crisp and transfer to the same bowl. Use a small drizzle of oil for each vegetable if you need it.

Meals
in a
bowl

½ lb (250 g) bok choy, washed, leaves separated and cut diagonally into ¼-inch (5 mm) strips

1 small onion, halved and thinly sliced, or 4 green onions, cut into 1-inch (2.5 cm) pieces

1 red bell pepper, cored, seeded and cut into strips

¼ lb (125 g) mushrooms, sliced

¼ lb (125 g) bean sprouts

Salt

Steamed rice (see page 182) or Asian noodles, cooked according to package directions

5 Remove the chicken, shrimp, or pork from the marinade or cornstarch mixture, and stir-fry it for a few minutes, until the chicken or pork are golden or the shrimp are pink and opaque. Return all the vegetables, including the bean sprouts, to the skillet, and make a well in the center. Pour in the chicken broth mixture and bring it to a boil without stirring. Once it has come to a boil, toss it around with the meat and vegetables, and serve your stir-fry immediately over steamed rice or noodles.

Serves 4

What to do with the leftovers

* You could store them in your fridge for up to a day, but leftover stir-fries don't generally keep very well.

Other things to do with it

* Add fresh asparagus or green beans, cut into 1-inch (2.5 cm) slices, thinly sliced carrot, or a small can of sliced water chestnuts.

* Add 1–3 tsp (5–15 mL) Asian chili sauce to the sauce mixture to give it a spicy kick.

* Sprinkle the stir-fry with toasted sesame seeds. You can buy them toasted, or toast your own in a small, dry skillet set over medium heat until they turn golden and fragrant. Watch them carefully—they burn fast!

Basic Curry
with Chicken, Shrimp, Fish, or Just Veg

Ingredients

2 tsp (10 mL) olive or canola oil

2 onions, peeled and thinly sliced or chopped

4 cloves garlic, minced

2 Tbsp (30 mL) grated fresh ginger (or use bottled)

1 red, orange or yellow bell pepper, seeded and chopped

1–2 cups (250–500 mL) zucchini, green beans, cauliflower, or eggplant, chopped into bite-sized pieces, or ½ cup (125 mL) cooked lentils (optional)

2–3 tsp (30–45 mL) curry paste

½ tsp (2.5 mL) ground cumin or cumin seed (optional)

¼ tsp (1 mL) salt

1 14-oz (398-mL) can diced tomatoes, drained, or 2 chopped fresh tomatoes

1 14-oz (398-mL) can regular or light coconut milk

1 tart apple, such as Granny Smith or McIntosh, peeled and sliced or chopped (optional)

Ingredients continue on next page

This is a great cupboard cleaner—you can make a curry out of chicken, pork, shrimp or fish, or make a vegetarian curry with potatoes, zucchini, spinach, onions, lentils, beans, peppers, kale, and/or cauliflower. Bottled curry paste and canned coconut milk make the sauce easy. If you're using light coconut milk and want to boost the coconut flavor even further without adding extra fat, add a teaspoon (5 mL) of coconut extract. Serve the curry over steamed jasmine or basmati rice (see page 182).

Method

1 In a large skillet set over medium-high heat, sauté the onions in the oil for 2–3 minutes, until soft. Add the garlic and ginger and cook for another minute. If you are using raw chicken or pork, add it and cook until opaque.

2 Add the pepper and any other veggies you've chosen. Sauté them for a few minutes, just until the vegetables start to release their juices and soften.

3 Add the curry paste, cumin, salt, tomatoes, and coconut milk and bring the mixture to a simmer. Add the apple along with any uncooked shrimp or fish you are using, and cook for about 5 minutes, until the apple is tender-crisp, the sauce is thickened and the shrimp or fish are cooked through. If you are using leftover cooked chicken or pork, add it now.

4 Season with salt and pepper. Stir in the spinach and cook for a minute, just until it wilts. Serve immediately over rice with chopped peanuts sprinkled on top.

Serves 4

Meals in a bowl

1 cup (250 mL) raw or cooked chopped chicken or pork, uncooked shrimp, peeled and deveined, or chunks of raw whitefish (such as haddock, flounder, sole, cod, pickerel, snapper, perch, sea bass, halibut, or Boston bluefish)

Salt and pepper

A couple handfuls of fresh spinach, chopped

Chopped peanuts, salted or unsalted, to sprinkle on top (optional)

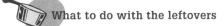

What to do with the leftovers

* Keep them covered in the fridge for up to 2 days. Reheat in the microwave.

Other things to do with it

* Chunky Curry Soup: Leave the tomatoes undrained and add some chicken or vegetable stock or extra coconut milk to turn it into soup.

* Red Thai Curry: Use Thai red curry paste and add 1 tsp (5 mL) paprika and 3 Tbsp (45 mL) tomato paste instead of the can of tomatoes.

Meals
in a
bowl

Beef

Choosing a cut of beef can be confusing if you don't know the difference between them, or which cut is the best choice for the recipe you want to make. Fortunately, grocery stores know this, and often label their meat with basic grilling or roasting instructions. If you forget what you're looking for, read the packages or go by price. The most tender cuts of meat make up a small proportion of the cow, so they're in the highest demand and are therefore the most expensive. Cuts from the less-used muscles along the back, such as the rib and loin, will always be more tender than cuts of meat from the more active muscles such as the shoulder, flank, and leg. Tender cuts are the best choice for grilling or pan-frying; tougher cuts require slower cooking methods such as braising, stewing, or slow-roasting to break down their tough connective tissues.

Buying beef

Choose cuts of beef, roasts, and steaks that are firm, not soft or squishy, and bright red without any gray spots—beef changes color when it has been exposed to air. Make sure that the meat is cold and well wrapped, that the package hasn't been damaged, and that there isn't any excess liquid in the tray. Excess liquid is usually moisture that has leaked out of the meat—an indication that the beef has been above 38°F–40°F (3°C–4°C) and will probably not taste as good as properly chilled beef.

Store beef in the coldest part of the fridge for up to 2 days for ground beef or 3 days for other cuts. It can also be frozen, well wrapped, for up to 6 months.

Ground beef contains varying quantities of fat: regular ground beef has the most, lean ground beef not as much, extra-lean ground beef contains the least, and they're priced accordingly. Lean and extra-lean ground beef are the best choices nutritionally, and are more expensive because you aren't paying for fat, which mostly gets cooked and drained off anyway. The other option is to grind your own beef using cubes of chuck or round that you have trimmed of excess fat; pulse them in the food processor until they're as coarsely or finely ground as you like.

Cuts of beef

Brisket: cuts from the chest region, used to make corned beef and often smoked for barbecue.

Chuck: cuts from the shoulder or front end, usually used to roast and commonly referred to as pot roasts. Cuts include chuck roast, blade roast, and arm roast; also used to make ground beef.

Flank: cuts usually labeled as flank steaks, which are lean and usually very stringy in texture.

Loin or short loin: very tender cuts from the middle of the back, usually cut into steaks. Cuts include club steak, T-bone, porterhouse, tenderloin, New York strip, and filet mignon.

Rib: steaks and roasts cut from the back just below the shoulder. Cuts include rib roast, rib steaks, and rib eye.

Round: cuts from the back end region, usually used when making roasts. Cuts include rump roast, top round, bottom round, inside round, and eye of round.

Sirloin: steaks and roasts cut from the small back region. Cuts include sirloin steaks, pin-bone, flat-bone, and wedge-bone.

Pan-Seared Steak

Ingredients

4 beef steaks, such as porterhouse,
   sirloin, rib eye, tenderloin, or filet
   mignon, about ½ lb/250 g each,
   and ¾–1 inch (2–2.5 cm) thick

Salt and pepper

To deglaze the pan (optional)

Red wine, butter, or beef, vegetable
   or chicken stock

2 shallots, finely minced (optional)

A good squeeze of lemon juice

You don't need a grill to produce a fantastic steak. This basic formula can be used no matter how many steaks you're cooking, but it's important to measure the thickness of the steaks before you start cooking so you can accurately gauge the cooking time. If you do have a grill, these cooking times still apply.

Method

1 Make small incisions with a sharp knife about 1 ½ inches (4 cm) apart in the fat around the outside of each steak, if there is some. Pat them dry with a paper towel and season with salt and pepper.

2 Set a heavy skillet over high heat until it's very hot but not smoking. Add the steaks, making sure there's at least ¼ inch between them. Cook for 4 minutes, until they're crusty and brown on one side. Flip them over and cook for another 4 minutes for rare, 6 minutes for medium, or 8 minutes for well done. Transfer them to a plate, cover loosely with foil, and let them rest for 5–10 minutes.

3 If you want to, you can deglaze the pan to make an intensely flavored sauce for your steaks while they rest. If you do plan to deglaze your pan, don't clean it out after cooking the steaks! The whole idea is to make the most of those flavorful browned bits stuck to the bottom. Add a splash of red wine or stock (as much as you want, keeping in mind it will reduce as it cooks) or about 2 tablespoons (30 mL) of butter to the hot pan and let it simmer for a minute, scraping up the bits on the bottom. If you're using butter, you can also add a couple of finely chopped shallots and a squeeze of lemon juice—cook the mixture for a minute until the shallots have softened. You won't have a lot of sauce, but what there is will be very intensely flavored. Drizzle it over your steaks and serve them immediately.

Serves 4

What to do with the leftovers

* Keep them well wrapped in the fridge for up to 3 days. Reheat them gently in the microwave or wrapped in foil in the oven, or eat them cold.

* Thinly slice leftover steak and make sandwiches on a bun with some thinly sliced purple onion, fresh arugula, and mayonnaise spiked with horseradish (about 1 part horseradish to 2 parts mayo).

* Serve warm or cold sliced steak on mixed greens with thinly sliced purple onion, crumbled blue cheese, and vinaigrette made with red wine or balsamic vinegar and Dijon mustard (see page 86).

Other things to do with it

* Pepper-Crusted Steak: Crush about 3 Tbsp (45 mL) black peppercorns with a mallet or mortar and pestle; coat both sides of the steaks with the pepper before you cook them.

* Spice-Rubbed Steak: To make a spicy steak rub, toast 2 tsp (10 mL) cumin seeds and 2 tsp (10 mL) coriander seeds in a small dry skillet for a few minutes, until they're fragrant. Crush them in a spice mill or with a mortar and pestle along with 1 tsp (5 mL) peppercorns (or start with ground spices). Add 2 Tbsp (30 mL) chili powder, 2 tsp (10 mL) sugar, and 1 tsp (5 mL) salt and blend well. Rub the mixture generously over both sides the steaks and put them in the fridge for at least half an hour before you cook them.

Pot Roast

Ingredients

3 Tbsp (45 mL) all-purpose flour

Salt and pepper

3–4 lb (1.5–2 kg) chuck roast, rump roast, boneless bottom, or eye of round or brisket

2 Tbsp (30 mL) canola or olive oil

1 onion, peeled and chopped

1 carrot, peeled and chopped (optional)

2 cloves garlic, crushed or chopped

1–2 cups (250–500 mL) liquid (beef or vegetable broth, wine, tomato sauce or juice, water, or a combination)

1 Tbsp (15 mL) Worcestershire sauce, soy sauce, balsamic vinegar, sherry, or chili sauce (optional)

For generations pot roasts have been a way to make tough (i.e., cheap) cuts of beef tender and edible by way of braising (see page 41). There are two ways to cook a pot roast: on the stovetop or in the oven, and the choice of liquid and flavorings you use are largely up to you. Any kind of broth, wine, tomato juice, and water all work well, and I have even heard of people using coffee.

Method

1 Season the flour with salt and pepper and pound it all over the surface of the roast with a meat mallet, your knuckles, or the bottom of a sturdy glass. Throw out any leftover flour. In a large pot or Dutch oven set over medium-high heat, heat the oil until hot but not smoking. Brown the roast on all sides, turning it with tongs or a fork. This caramelizes the outside of the meat, adding flavor. The flour will also help thicken the liquid the beef simmers in.

2 Remove the roast from the pot and set it aside on a plate. Add the onion, carrot, and garlic to the pot and cook for a few minutes, until they start to brown. (If you want to skip this step, just throw the veggies in with the roast. Cooking them first caramelizes them a bit, adding more flavor.) Return the roast to the pot and add the liquid and any seasonings you like.

3 Cover the pot tightly and simmer the roast on low heat on the stovetop or in a 275°F (140°C) oven for 2–4 hours (depending on the size and thickness of your roast), turning the meat about every half an hour. Don't worry about cooking it for too long.

4 Remove the roast from the juices and set it aside. Tent it with foil to keep it warm. Let the juices settle for a few minutes, then scoop any excess fat off the surface with a wide spoon. Strain the solids out by pouring the juices through a sieve or using a slotted spoon, or purée them with a hand-held immersion blender or in a regular blender or food processor. Return the strained or puréed liquid to the pot, set it over medium heat, and bring it to a boil. Simmer for about 10 minutes to reduce and concentrate the juices, adding salt and pepper to taste.

5 Slice or shred the beef and serve it with the sauce poured overtop, preferably with mashed potatoes to catch the drips.

Serves 6–8

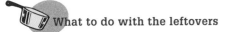 **What to do with the leftovers**

* Keep them covered in the fridge for up to 5 days. Reheat in the microwave.

* Make fajitas—shred the beef and wrap it in warmed flour tortillas with sautéed bell peppers and sliced onions, salsa, shredded cheese, and sour cream.

* Shred the beef and moisten it with barbecue sauce; heat it up on the stovetop or in the micro-wave and serve it on soft buns. Top the BBQ beef with creamy coleslaw, if you like.

 Other things to do with it

* Cut several peeled cloves of garlic lengthwise in half or into quarters. Cut about 10 small slits all over the roast before searing it, and push a sliver of garlic into each cut.

* After the sauce has reduced, take it off the heat and stir in ½ cup (125 mL) sour cream to make a rich, creamy gravy.

* Add two peeled and chopped potatoes or a cou-ple of handfuls of baby new potatoes to the pot during the final 20–30 minutes of cooking time. Make sure there's enough liquid to submerge the vegetables. If not, add more.

Beef

Meatloaf

Ingredients

1 tsp (5 mL) canola or olive oil

1 onion, peeled and finely chopped

2 cloves garlic, crushed (optional)

1 ½–2 lb (750 g–1 kg) lean ground
 beef, or a combination of beef
 and pork

1 cup (250 mL) bread crumbs or
 ½ cup (125 mL) crushed saltine
 crackers or quick oats

½ cup (125 mL) milk or plain yogurt

½ cup (125 mL) tomato sauce, or half
 tomato sauce and half ketchup

1 large egg

¼ cup (60 mL) chopped fresh parsley
 (optional)

2 tsp (10 mL) Worcestershire sauce

½ tsp (2.5 mL) salt

½ tsp (2.5 mL) pepper

Glaze (optional)

½ cup (125 mL) ketchup, tomato
 sauce, or chili sauce

2 Tbsp (30 mL) packed brown sugar

2 Tbsp (30 mL) cider or white vinegar

1 Tbsp (15 mL) mustard (optional)

Meatloaf is becoming trendy again, and for good reason—there are few people who don't love it. It should be mandatory to serve meatloaf with mashed potatoes (or another potato product) to create the ultimate combination of comfort foods.

Classic meatloaf is made with a mixture of 50% ground chuck (beef), 25% ground pork, and 25% ground veal, but it's not necessary to use that precise combination. Adding some pork to your beef will add flavor but also more fat. You could substitute half ground chicken or turkey instead for a leaner meatloaf.

Method

1 Preheat the oven to 350°F (175°C). Line a rimmed baking sheet with foil.

2 Heat the oil in a medium skillet set over medium heat and sauté the onion and garlic for about 5 minutes, until the onion is translucent. Set aside to cool slightly.

3 In a large bowl, combine the meat, sautéed onion and garlic, bread crumbs, milk, tomato sauce, egg, parsley, Worcestershire sauce, and salt and pepper. Mix everything together with your hands until it's well blended. Shape the meat mixture into a loaf that's roughly 9 × 5 inches (23 × 12 cm) on the baking sheet or press it into a 9- × 5-inch loaf pan.

4 To make the glaze, stir together all the ingredients in a small bowl. Brush the loaf with half the glaze and bake for 30 minutes. Brush with the remaining glaze and bake for another 30–45 minutes. (If you have a meat thermometer, the internal temperature should read 160°F (71°C).) Let the meatloaf rest for about 15 minutes before you cut it.

Serves 6

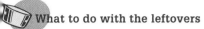

What to do with the leftovers

* Keep them covered in the fridge for up to 3 days, or wrap them well in plastic wrap and freeze for up to 4 months. Eat them cold, or reheat them in the microwave or wrapped in foil in the oven.

* Meatloaf sandwiches are the best reason to make a meatloaf in the first place! Stuff thick slabs between two slices of buttered bread, with or without ketchup.

* Crumble leftover meatloaf into tomato sauce to serve over spaghetti or other pasta.

Other things to do with it

* Meatballs: Add ¼ cup (60 mL) grated Parmesan to the meatloaf mixture and shape it into walnut-sized balls. Cook as many as you like in a skillet with a little olive or canola oil, rolling them around until they brown on all sides and cook through. It should take about 15 minutes. If you're making spaghetti sauce, pour it over the meatballs after they've browned, and simmer them in the sauce until they've cooked through. Raw meatballs can be frozen on a cookie sheet, then transferred to freezer bags to store for up to 4 months. Cook as directed straight from the freezer—there's no need to thaw them first.

* Mushroom Meatloaf: Omit the glaze. Add half a can of condensed cream of mushroom soup to the meat mixture in place of the ½ cup (125 mL) tomato sauce. Heat up the rest of the soup in a small pot with ⅓ cup (80 mL) milk and serve the sauce drizzled over slices of meatloaf.

* Meatzza: Sauté 1 thinly sliced onion and 1 sliced red bell pepper in a little olive or canola oil for about 10 minutes, until softened and starting to turn golden. Pat the meatloaf mixture into a 10-inch (25 cm) circle on a pizza pan or pie plate. Top it with about ½ cup (125 mL) spaghetti or pizza sauce and the sautéed vegetables. Sprinkle the whole thing with grated mozzarella or cheddar cheese and bake for about 30 minutes, or until the meat is cooked through and the cheese has melted. Pour off any excess fat before serving.

Roast Beef

There's a certain sentimental quality to a good old roast beef, particularly when it's served with crusty mile-high Yorkshire puddings, roast potatoes, and gravy. It may seem like a splurge, but unless you break the bank on a beef tenderloin, roast beef isn't really that expensive, especially when you compare it to eating out. You can feed a crowd with one roast, and if you don't have a crowd to feed, you'll have leftovers that can be transformed into all kinds of meals.

The problem with most roast recipes is that the roasting time is based on weight, when shape usually has more to do with it. A very thick roast will take longer to cook than a thin one, since the distance from the outside to the interior is further. So a basic rule of thumb is: the greater the surface area, the faster the cooking time. It makes sense that a round roast will take longer to cook than a long thin one, even if they weigh the same. Oven thermometers have made our lives easier when it comes to roasting meat, but if you don't have one you can still get by just fine.

There are two methods of roasting: fast or slow, and the method you choose depends on the type and cut of beef you have and how you want it to turn out. When roasting is done quickly at a higher heat—450°F (230°C) or so—it caramelizes the exterior of foods while slowly cooking the interior. The outside, having been exposed to high heat for a much longer time, will be considerably more well done than the inside. On the other hand, slow roasting won't produce a crusty exterior, but the roast will be more evenly cooked throughout. Slow roasts are also very tender, since the longer cooking time enables any tough connective tissues to break down. The good news is, you can have the best of both worlds: start the roast at a high heat to produce a flavorful crust, and then drop the temperature down and cook it until it's done to your liking, or do it the other way around. (Contrary to popular belief, searing the exterior of the meat at high heat doesn't "seal" the juices in, but rather creates flavor by caramelizing the exterior.)

Ingredients

3–4 lb (1.5–2 kg) boneless sirloin or eye of round roast (top and bottom round are good choices too)

Salt and pepper

1 Tbsp (15 mL) canola oil

Method

1 Let the meat stand at room temperature for half an hour before you cook it. Preheat the oven to 450°F (230°C), making sure the rack is in the lower-middle position.

2 Put the roast on a rack in a roasting pan—leave the string on and put the fat side up, if there's a fattier side. Pat the meat dry with a paper towel and season well with salt and pepper. Add about ¼ inch (5 mm) of water to the bottom of the pan, put it in the oven, and immediately turn the temperature down to 350°F (175°C).

3 Cook the roast until a meat thermometer inserted in the center registers 120°F (49°C) for rare, 125°F (52°C) for medium-rare or 130°F (55°C) for medium. (If you have a meat thermometer, stick it in at a 45° angle so that the end is right in the middle of the roast.) The cooking time will vary from 10 to 20 minutes per pound, depending on the size and shape of your roast.

4 Remove the roast from the oven and transfer it to a chopping board or serving platter. Tent it with foil and let it rest for 15–20 minutes before slicing. The resting period is important—it allows the meat to relax (it tenses up as it cooks) and the juices to redistribute throughout the meat. If you were to cut into the roast right away, a lot of the juices would still be moving around and would pour out onto the plate, leaving your roast dry. Slice as thinly or as thickly as you like.

Serves 6–8

Roast Beef (continued)

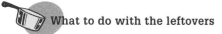

What to do with the leftovers

* Keep them well wrapped in the fridge for up to 3 days. Eat them cold or gently reheat them in the microwave.

* Leftover roast beef makes the best sandwiches. Serve it cold or reheated on bread or crusty rolls with tomato and horseradish-spiked mayonnaise, or with crumbled blue cheese and caramelized onions (see page 146).

* Roast Beef Hash: Mix 2 cups (500 mL) of chopped leftover roast beef, 2 cups (500 mL) cubed cooked potatoes, 1 chopped onion, and about ½ cup (125 mL) gravy, beef stock, tomato sauce, or milk—just enough liquid to moisten it. Heat some oil or butter in a heavy skillet and press the hash into it, forming a big patty. Cook for about 10 minutes, until the bottom is golden. Slide it out onto a plate and invert it back into the skillet to cook it on the other side, or leave it in the skillet and run it under the broiler for a few minutes to crisp it up on top. Serve the hash in wedges with ketchup.

Other things to do with it

* Make a paste with 2 Tbsp (30 mL) horseradish, 1 tsp (5 mL) Worcestershire sauce, and ½ tsp (2.5 mL) pepper; rub the mixture all over the roast before putting it in the oven.

* Honey Mustard Roast with Garlic: Cut several peeled cloves of garlic lengthwise in half or into quarters. Cut small slits all over the roast and press a sliver of garlic into each cut. Rub the surface of the roast with a mixture of 2 Tbsp (30 mL) each honey and Dijon mustard before roasting it.

* Slow-Roast Beef: If you're cooking for a crowd and have all day to hang around while dinner cooks, start with an 8–14 lb (3.5–6.5 kg) boneless rolled roast of beef. When it's time to turn the oven down, turn it to the lowest possible setting and leave it for 8 hours. Make sure you don't open the oven door during those 8 hours. (Tape it closed so you don't forget.) After 8 hours have passed, turn the oven up to 350°F (175°C) for 20 minutes to heat the roast through.

* Yorkshire Pudding: To make Yorkies to go with your beef, whisk together 1 cup (250 mL) flour, 1 tsp (5 mL) salt, 2 large eggs, and 1 cup (250 mL) milk. Set the mixture aside for about half an hour while the roast cooks. When the roast comes out, turn the oven up to 425°F (220°C) and move the rack to the middle. Take a 12 cup muffin tin and pour about a teaspoon (5 mL) of beef fat from the roast (or canola oil) into the bottom of each cup. Put the pan into the oven until it's really hot. Whisk the batter again and quickly divide it among the hot cups (use about 2 Tbsp/30 mL per cup). Return the pan to the oven for 20 minutes, until the puddings are puffed and golden. Serve them immediately with the roast beef.

Sloppy Joes

Ingredients

1 Tbsp (15 mL) olive or canola oil

1 onion, peeled and chopped

1 stalk celery, chopped (optional)

1 red bell pepper, seeded and
chopped

2 cloves garlic, crushed

1 ½ lb (750 g) lean ground beef or
ground turkey or chicken, or a
combination

1 28-oz (796-mL) can diced, whole, or
stewed tomatoes

½ cup (125 mL) ketchup or half
ketchup, half barbecue sauce

2 Tbsp (30 mL) cider vinegar

1 Tbsp (15 mL) brown sugar

1 Tbsp (15 mL) Worcestershire sauce

A few shots of Tabasco (optional)

Salt and pepper

6 plain soft buns, cheese buns, plain
or cheese biscuits (see page 251)
or thick slices of Sour Cream
Cheese Bread (see page 246).

I get excited about any food that's sloppy, particularly any that are so much so
it's specified in the name.

If you use ground turkey or chicken, keep in mind that supermarkets generally don't trim the fat from poultry before they grind it. If you're concerned about fat, it's best to trim the skin and fat from turkey or chicken breasts or thighs yourself, then pulse it in your food processor. Dark thigh meat is much more flavorful than white meat because of its slightly higher fat content, but it still contains far less fat than ground beef.

Method

1 Heat the oil in a large pot set over medium-high heat and sauté the onion, celery, red pepper, and garlic for about 10 minutes, until the onions are starting to turn golden. Add the meat and cook for about 5 minutes, breaking it up as you cook, until the meat is no longer pink.

2 Add the tomatoes, ketchup, vinegar, brown sugar, Worcestershire sauce, Tabasco, and salt and pepper to taste and simmer for 20–30 minutes, until the sauce has thickened. Split the buns or biscuits in half and ladle the sloppy joe mixture on top.

Serves 6

 What to do with the leftovers

* Leftovers keep really well in the fridge for several days. Reheat them in the microwave or on the stovetop, adding a little extra liquid if necessary.

 Other things to do with it

* Turn it into chili: Add a can of drained kidney beans, a can of brown beans, chili powder to suit your taste, and a glug of salsa to turn the mixture into chili.

Burgers

Ingredients

1 ½ lb (750 g) lean ground beef or diced chuck or sirloin steaks (if you really want to go all out), ground in the food processor

¼ cup (60 mL) bottled barbecue sauce (optional)

½ tsp (2.5 mL) garlic powder (optional)

½ tsp (2.5 mL) salt

½ tsp (2.5 mL) pepper

Sliced or grated cheddar, havarti, Brie, or any other cheese you like

4 hamburger buns, toasted or not

Any toppings you like: thinly sliced or caramelized onions (see page 146), sautéed mushrooms, cooked slices of bacon, a fried egg, slices of tomato, shredded lettuce, mayo, ketchup, mustard, pickles

Burgers are most often consumed out of a box or paper bag, which is a shame; homemade burgers are fantastic and can be made as sloppy as you please. When you make them yourself, burgers tend to dome in the middle as they cook, resulting in a rounder burger than you would eat at a restaurant. The way around this is to press a gradual indent into the middle after you shape your burgers, so that the edges are thicker than the center. This way when the middle puffs up (a result of the collagen in the meat shrinking) the patty will be more level. You can cook your burgers on a grill or in a skillet on the stove.

Method

1   In a medium bowl, gently blend the meat, barbecue sauce, garlic powder, and salt and pepper with your hands. Don't overmix, or the burgers may be tough.

2   Shape the meat mixture into 4 patties that are 4–5 inches (10–12 cm) across. Press the middle of each patty with your fingers to create a bit of an indent, so that they don't bulge in the middle when you cook them.

3   To cook burgers on the grill: spray the cold grill rack with non-stick spray to keep the meat from sticking, and preheat the barbecue to medium-high heat. Grill the burgers for 3–5 minutes per side, depending on the thickness of the patties and how well you want them done. Don't press down on them as they cook, or you'll squeeze all the juices out. For cheeseburgers, top the patties with cheese for the final minute of cooking so that it has a chance to melt on top.

4   For pan-seared burgers: heat a heavy skillet over medium-high heat. When the skillet is hot, add the patties. Cook them, turning once, for 3–5 minutes per side, depending on the thickness of the patties and how well you want them done. Don't press down on them as they cook, or you'll squeeze all the juices out. For cheeseburgers, top the patties with cheese for the final minute of cooking so that it melts on top.

5   Serve the burgers hot on buns, topped with whatever extras you like.

Makes 4 burgers (doubles or triples easily)

What to do with the leftovers

* Keep them covered in the fridge for up to 3 days. Reheat them in the microwave or eat them cold.

* If you want to freeze your burger patties uncooked, separate them with small pieces of waxed paper, place them in freezer bags or wrap well in plastic wrap and freeze them for up to 4 months. Patties can be cooked from frozen—allow some extra cooking time, and cook them over medium-low heat, otherwise the exterior will cook before the middle gets a chance to thaw and cook properly.

* Crumble burgers into tomato sauce and serve over spaghetti or other pasta.

Other things to do with it

* Beef and Andouille Sausage Burgers: Replace ½ lb (250 g) of the beef with ½ lb (250 g) of finely chopped andouille or kielbasa sausage. Omit the barbecue sauce. Top the burgers with Asiago cheese, strips of roasted red pepper, and thinly sliced purple onion.

* Mushroom Brie Burgers: Top the burgers with thin slices of Brie as they finish cooking, and then top them with sautéed mushrooms. To sauté mushrooms, slice them and cook over medium-high heat in a combination of butter and oil until they soften, start to turn golden, and the moisture has evaporated.

* Turkey Burgers: Use ground turkey instead of beef, then add ½ cup (125 mL) fresh bread crumbs, 2 Tbsp (30 mL) Worcestershire or soy sauce, and 2 crushed cloves of garlic.

Pork
and lamb

Most of the pork we buy comes cured (like ham and bacon),
or made into sausage, and the rest is referred to as "fresh
pork." Today's pork is much leaner and higher in protein
than it was 10 years ago, and trichinosis (a nasty illness
caused by eating raw or undercooked pork) is rarely an
issue these days. Many of us have memories of dried-out
pork chops—a result of overcooking due to paranoia
about trichinosis. Lots of cookbooks recommend
cooking pork to 170°F–185°F (77°C–85°C), but
today experts recommend an internal temperature of 150°F–165°F (65.5°C–76°C), which will
ensure your pork stays juicy and tender.

Buying pork

Pork is available year-round, but it's usually cheaper and more plentiful between October and February. Buy pork that is pale pink with a small amount of marbling and white, not yellow, fat. The darker the flesh, the older the pig. Make sure it's cold, tightly wrapped, and firm to the touch, without too much moisture in the packaging. Store pork in the coldest part of the refrigerator for up to 2 days, or wrap it well and freeze it for up to 6 months. Larger cuts (such as roasts) will keep in the freezer better than thinner cuts (such as chops).

Cuts of pork

Bacon: comes in the familiar strips and also as much leaner Canadian back bacon.

Ham: hams are sold in many forms, but most are cured and already fully cooked. Dry cured hams include prosciutto and Parma ham. When it comes to roasting hams, the most popular shapes and sizes are whole, halves (shank or butt ends), shank, butt, and center-cut slices and steaks. They come with their bone, or boneless. Boneless hams tend to have a "pressed" texture, and it's a general rule that any meat roasted with its bone has more flavor. When buying a ham to roast, shank ends and butt ends are both good choices, but shank ends tend to be easier to carve because of their shape. Most hams have water added: "ham with natural juices" has some water added; "ham with water added" contains even more water. Obviously the more water a ham contains, the cheaper it is per pound. Spiral-sliced hams are pre-cut, so you don't have to worry about carving them. "Fresh ham" is not as common. It isn't cooked or cured, and must be fully roasted before eating.

Loin: cuts from the back region; they can be thin or thick. Cuts include back ribs, center cut, loin chops, tenderloin, and sirloin.

Picnic shoulder: cut from the lower region of the shoulder; usually used when cooking roasts.

Ribs: pork ribs come in full racks and in a smaller "sweet and sour" cut, in which the butcher cuts the ribs crosswise down the entire rack to make finger-sized pieces.

Shoulder butt: cut from the top of the shoulder region just behind the neck; usually used in cooking roasts. This is where Boston butt comes from.

Oven-Roasted Pork Chops

Ingredients

4–6 pork chops, about ¾ inch (2 cm) thick, with or without bone

Milk—enough to cover the pork chops (optional)

1 clove garlic, crushed (optional)

2 cups (250–500 mL) breadcrumbs, fresh or dry

1 Tbsp (15 mL) chopped fresh rosemary, thyme, sage or parsley, or ½ tsp (2.5 mL) dried

Salt and pepper

1–2 Tbsp (15–30 mL) canola or olive oil

1–2 Tbsp (15–30 mL) butter

Pork chops are far too often tough and leathery—a result of overcooking, which was common in the past, when pork was often cooked to temperatures as high as 190°F (88°C) for fear of trichinosis. Today, the risk of trichinosis is nearly nonexistent and you'll find pork cooked to varying degrees of doneness (including medium-rare) on restaurant menus. Buy chops that are of even thickness, so that both ends cook through at the same speed.

Method

1   If you want to soak the pork chops in milk (which will tenderize them), put them in a shallow dish and pour enough milk overtop to cover them. Stir in the garlic and refrigerate for at least an hour. Turn them once or twice, if you think of it. (It won't matter if you don't turn them, but it will help the milk penetrate the surface of the meat.)

2   Preheat the oven to 375°F (190°C). In a shallow bowl, stir together the bread crumbs, rosemary, and salt and pepper. Heat about half the oil and butter in a large skillet set over medium heat.

3   Lift the pork chops out of the milk, letting the excess drip off, and dredge them in the bread crumbs, pressing to help them adhere. Sauté the pork chops, turning them over once, for about 3 minutes per side. Add more oil and butter to the pan as you need it.

4   Slide the skillet into the oven and bake for 7–9 minutes, until the pork chops are just cooked through. (Chops with bone will take slightly longer to cook than those without.)

5   If you have a meat thermometer, it should read 145°F (63°C); if you don't have a thermometer, poke one of the pork chops with a knife to see if it's done inside. Alternatively, cover the pan, turn the heat down to low, and cook the pork chops for 7–9 minutes. Serve immediately, with applesauce or cranberry sauce if you like.

Serves 4–6

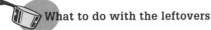

What to do with the leftovers

* Keep them covered in the fridge for up to 2 days; reheat in the microwave.

Other things to do with it

* Mustard-Crusted Pork Chops: Don't bother to soak the pork chops in milk. Instead, pat them dry and spread both sides with grainy mustard. Mix the bread crumbs with fresh parsley instead of the herbs, and dredge the mustard-coated chops. Cook as directed.

* Spice-rubbed Pork Chops: Don't bother to soak the pork chops in milk. Instead, combine 1 Tbsp (15 mL) cumin, 1 Tbsp (15 mL) chili powder, 1 tsp (5 mL) curry powder, 1 tsp.(5 mL) brown sugar and 1 tsp (5 mL) pepper, and rub the mixture all over the pork chops. (Omit the remaining ingredients.) If you have time, cover and refrigerate them for an hour to allow the flavor to penetrate the meat, then cook as directed.

* Pork Chops with Caramelized Onions and Apples: After cooking the pork chops (any of the ways described above), keep them warm in a 200°F (95°C) oven and sauté 2 large, thinly sliced onions in a drizzle of oil in the skillet for about 10 minutes, until they start to turn golden. Add a peeled, sliced tart apple and cook for another 10 minutes, until the apples are golden and the onions are caramelized. Pour ½–1 cup (125–250 mL) apple juice or chicken stock into the pan and scrape up all the browned bits from the bottom. Serve the onions and apples over the pork chops.

Oven-Roasted Barbecue Ribs

Ingredients

2 racks spareribs (about 6 lb/2.7 kg) trimmed of excess fat

1–2 cups (250–500 mL) barbecue sauce

Dry Rub (enough for about 4 big racks of ribs)

2 Tbsp (30 mL) paprika

1 Tbsp (15 mL) chili powder

1 Tbsp (15 mL) ground cumin

1 Tbsp (15 mL) brown sugar

1 Tbsp (15 mL) salt

2 tsp (10 mL) black pepper

1 tsp (5 mL) oregano

½ tsp (2.5 mL) cayenne pepper (optional)

Here's a recipe for sticky, finger-licking ribs with meat that falls off the bone. The secret to tender ribs is slow roasting, which also cooks away any excess fat. If you want to grill your ribs, you can do the initial cooking in the oven and then finish them off on the grill.

Use any bottled sauce you like in place of the barbecue sauce, which isn't added until halfway through the cooking time because its high sugar content makes it burn easily. The dry rub is optional but penetrates the meat to add depth to its flavor. If you make the full amount, you'll have a large enough batch to put some away for next time. There isn't really much work involved here—the reward far outweighs any effort!

Method

1 If you want to use the dry rub, combine all the ingredients for it and rub the ribs all over with the mixture, covering both sides. Let them stand at room temperature for an hour, or wrap them well in plastic and refrigerate them for up to 24 hours to intensify the flavors. If you aren't using the rub, just sprinkle the ribs with salt and pepper. Keep any extra rub in a zip-lock baggie or other container—it will last for about a year before it starts to lose its punch.

2 Preheat the oven to 300°F (150°C).

3 Place the ribs meat side up on a rimmed baking sheet, and cover the pan completely with foil. Bake them for 2 hours. Remove the foil and slather the ribs generously with barbecue sauce. Roast for another hour, until the meat is very tender and falling off the bone.

4 If you want to grill your ribs, bake them in the foil for 2 ½ hours. (They can be made ahead up to this point, and then refrigerated for up to a day before you need them.) Brush the ribs with sauce and grill over medium-low heat for about 15 minutes.

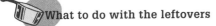
What to do with the leftovers

* Don't worry about it; there won't be any.

Other things to do with it

* Maple Ribs: Simmer ⅔ cup (160 mL) maple syrup (grade B is cheaper and works just as well), 1 grated onion, 1 Tbsp (15 mL) chili sauce, 1 Tbsp (15 mL) Worcestershire sauce, and 1 Tbsp (15 mL) red wine vinegar in a small pot for 5 minutes. Use this instead of the barbecue sauce, basting the ribs frequently during the final hour of baking.

* Sweet and Sticky Ginger-Soy Ribs: Sauté a couple cloves of crushed garlic and about 1 Tbsp (15 mL) grated fresh ginger in a drizzle of oil in a fairly large pot—one that will accommodate the ribs. For about 2 racks of ribs' worth of sauce, add ¾ cup (185 mL) packed brown sugar, ¾ cup (185 mL) rice vinegar, and ½ cup (125 mL) soy sauce to the garlic and ginger. After baking the ribs in the foil, let them cool slightly, cut them into individual ribs, then add them to the pot. Simmer for 45 minutes, until the ribs are very tender. Dissolve 2 tsp (10 mL) cornstarch in about a tablespoon (15 mL) of cold water and add it to the sauce; cook until it bubbles and thickens slightly. Add more cornstarch and water if you want the sauce even thicker. Serve the ribs and sauce over steamed rice (see page 182).

Baked Ham

Pork and Lamb

Ingredients

1 5–8 lb (2.5–3.75 kg) fully cooked ham half (shank or butt end)

½ cup (125 mL) packed brown sugar

3 Tbsp (45 mL) balsamic vinegar

2 Tbsp (30 mL) Dijon mustard

I've always wondered why it's said that hams are baked and turkeys are roasted, when they're both cooked in the oven the exact same way. Most hams come cured and are already fully cooked, which makes baking them a no-brainer. You're basically heating up the ham with a nice sticky glaze brushed on top. There are a million formulas for ham glazes, and most are based on a combination of mustard and brown sugar.

If you think baking a ham without a crowd to feed is a waste, think again: ham makes for the best leftovers. From one meal comes many, so to speak. If you don't like your ham too salty, soak it in water in the fridge for 24 hours before you bake it; this will draw out some of the sodium.

Method

1   Preheat the oven to 350°F (175°C). Line a roasting pan with foil to avoid spending an hour scrubbing it later.

2   Place the ham in the roasting pan. If there's a layer of fat on top, score the surface into 1-inch (2.5 cm) diamonds by cutting slits an inch apart, running parallel to each other, and do the same thing in the opposite direction. (Traditionally, cloves are used to stud the skin of the ham before you bake it. If you want, push a whole clove into the middle of each diamond after you score the skin.) Roast the ham uncovered for 1 hour (for a 5-lb/2.2 kg ham) to 1 ½ hours (for a 8-lb/3.75 kg ham). Remember that the hams are already cooked through, so the cooking time doesn't need to be exact.

3   Meanwhile, combine the brown sugar, balsamic vinegar, and mustard in a small bowl. Brush the ham all over with the glaze and continue roasting it for another 30 minutes, basting with more glaze every 10 minutes. Remove it from the oven and let it stand for 15 minutes before carving.

Serves 10–12

What to do with the leftovers

* Keep the cooked ham covered in the fridge for up to 5 days, or slice it, wrap it well in plastic, and freeze it for up to 4 months.

* Cut thick slices of ham to make ham steaks, and marinate them in a mixture of ¼ cup (60 mL) brown sugar and 2 Tbsp (30 mL) lime juice for at least an hour. Heat up the steaks in a skillet with the glaze until golden and heated through.

* Stir diced ham into omelets, pasta or potato salad, or brown beans, slice it thinly and add it to grilled cheese sandwiches, or use it to make Cream of Mushroom Soup with Ham (page 78) or in Corn, Chicken, and Cheddar Chowder (page 77) in place of the chicken.

 Other things to do with it

* If you're in a hurry, instead of baking the whole ham, slice it into ½-inch (1 cm) thick slices and lay them, slightly overlapping, in a 9- × 13-inch baking dish. Pour the glaze (you'll only need about half of it) over the meat, cover it with foil and bake for about 30 minutes, until heated through.

* Maple or Honey Mustard Ham: Make a glaze by combining ¼ cup (60 mL) Dijon mustard, and ⅓ cup (80 mL) maple syrup or honey.

* Ham with Cranberry Glaze: Make a glaze by combining ½ cup (125 mL) whole berry cranberry sauce, 3 Tbsp (45 mL) brown sugar, and 1 Tbsp (15 mL) Dijon mustard.

* Sticky Orange Glazed Ham: Make a glaze by combining ¼ cup (60 mL) orange juice concentrate, 3 Tbsp (45 mL) brown sugar, 3 Tbsp (45 mL) honey, and 2 Tbsp (30 mL) Dijon mustard.

Maple Roast Pork Tenderloin
with Apples

Ingredients

½ cup (125 mL) maple syrup

2 Tbsp (30 mL) Dijon or grainy mustard

2 Tbsp (30 mL) chopped fresh rosemary (optional)

2 Tbsp (30 mL) lemon juice

2 Tbsp (30 mL) soy sauce

2 ¾ lb (375 g) pork tenderloins

1 Tbsp (15 mL) canola oil

1 Tbsp (15 mL) butter

3 large Granny Smith, McIntosh, or other tart apples, peeled, cored and sliced

1 ½ cups (375 mL) apple cider or juice

1 tsp (5 mL) cornstarch

What to do with the leftovers

* Keep them covered in the fridge for up to 2 days. Reheat in the microwave or eat them cold.

* Dice the pork and stir it (along with any leftover apples and sauce) into a can of brown beans. Heat the whole thing up and serve it with mashed potatoes or oven fries.

This is the ultimate cold weather comfort food, served with mashed potatoes to catch all the sauce. Cheaper grade B maple syrup is great for cooking with.

Method

1 In a small bowl, whisk together the maple syrup, mustard, rosemary, lemon juice, and soy sauce. Pour over the pork and marinate for at least 2 hours, or overnight. Preheat the oven to 450°F (230°C).

2 Heat the oil in a large skillet set over medium-high heat. Remove the pork from the marinade, reserving the marinade, and brown the tenderloins on all sides, turning as necessary. This should take about 5 minutes.

3 Transfer the pork to a baking dish and bake for 12–15 minutes. (If you have a meat thermometer, it should register 155°F/68°C). Transfer the pork to a cutting board, cover it with foil, and let it stand until you're ready for it.

4 Meanwhile, add the butter to the skillet (don't wash it out!) and sauté the apples for 5–7 minutes, until the apples are tender and golden. Transfer the apples to a plate. Add the marinade and apple cider to the pan and bring to a simmer, scraping up any flavourful browned bits stuck to the bottom of the pan.

5 Pour a small amount of the sauce (about ¼ cup/60 mL) into a small dish, whisk in the cornstarch until you get rid of all the lumps (this is called a slurry), and return the mixture to the pan. Simmer for about 5 minutes, until the sauce is slightly thickened. Return the apples to the sauce along with any juices that have collected on the plate.

6 Slice the pork and serve it topped with the apples and sauce.

Serves 4

Other things to do with it

* Honey Mustard Pork Tenderloin: Omit the apples. Marinate the pork in a mixture of ¼ cup (60 mL) grainy mustard, 2 Tbsp (30 mL) honey, and 1 Tbsp (15 mL) sherry or white wine vinegar. Follow the instructions to drain and cook the pork. To make the sauce, combine the saved marinade with ½ cup (125 mL) chicken stock, 2 Tbsp (30 mL) honey, 1 Tbsp (15 mL) sherry or white wine vinegar, and 1 Tbsp (15 mL) grainy mustard in a small pot. Bring it to a boil, then simmer for 15 minutes and serve it with the pork.

Roast Pork Loin

Ingredients

3 cloves garlic, crushed

1 tsp (5 mL) salt

1 tsp (5 mL) sage

1 tsp (5 mL) thyme

1 bay leaf, crumbled

½ tsp (2.5 mL) pepper

1 3 lb (1.5 kg) pork loin roast

When you buy a pork loin that's not tied, it often lies flat. A tied pork loin has a round shape that will cook more evenly. To do it yourself, tie the pork up at even intervals along the length of the roast using any kind of string that won't melt in the oven.

Method

1 Combine the garlic, salt, sage, thyme, bay leaf, and pepper in a small bowl, and rub it evenly over the entire roast. Cover and refrigerate it for a few hours, all day, or overnight to allow the flavors to penetrate the meat.

2 Preheat the oven to 350°F (175°C). Place the pork on a rack in a roasting pan and roast for about an hour and 15 minutes, until a meat thermometer registers 150°F (75°C). Remove the roast from the oven and transfer it to a cutting board; tent it with foil and let it rest for 15 minutes before slicing.

Serves 4–6

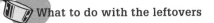

What to do with the leftovers

* Keep them covered in the fridge for up to a few days, sliced or unsliced, or wrap well and freeze for up to 4 months.

* Sliced leftover roast pork is great in noodle bowls (see page 81), stirred into a can of brown beans, or added to chili (page 125) or fried rice (page 185).

Other things to do with it

* Cranberry Pork Loin Roast: Pour 2 cups (500 mL) cranberry juice (and ¼ cup/60 mL red wine, if you want) around the roast before you cook it. After 30 minutes, add 1 cup (250 mL) fresh or frozen cranberries to the liquid and continue to roast. When the roast is done, pour the cranberry sauce into a saucepan, add 3 Tbsp (45 mL) sugar and cook it over medium-high heat until it has reduced to about a cup. Serve the sauce along with the pork.

* Chinese Barbecue Pork: Whisk together 1 Tbsp (15 mL) each hoisin sauce, ketchup, and soy sauce. Add a couple cloves of crushed garlic and ½ tsp (2.5 mL) sugar; coat the pork and allow it to marinate for at least an hour or overnight, and then roast as directed. This is also good made with roast pork tenderloin, which should cook in 35–40 minutes.

Buying lamb

Cuts of lamb are similar to pork; they're generally categorized as legs, loins, racks (ribs), and shoulders. You can often find it ground, or cubed as stew meat. When shopping, look for lamb that's light to dark pink in color, with a firm and fine-grained texture. Many large cuts of lamb will have a smooth covering of fat, and there may be a thin paper-like covering on the fat. This is called the "fell" and should be left on roasts to seal in juices while cooking but removed from other cuts to prevent them from curling when cooked.

Store fresh lamb in the coolest part of your refrigerator for up to 3 days, or wrap it well and freeze for up to 4 months. Larger cuts (such as roasts) will keep in the freezer better than thinner cuts (such as chops).

Cuts of lamb

Foreshank & breast: cuts include shanks and spareribs. Most cuts from this area can be tough, so are best for braising.

Leg: cuts include whole leg and boneless leg roasts, sirloin chops, and sirloin roasts.

Loin: tender cuts include the loin roast, loin chop, and double loin chop. These are great for roasting, pan-frying, or grilling.

Rib: cuts with ribs include the rack (as in rack of lamb), rib chops (regular and Frenched, meaning they leave a little bit of bone sticking out), crown roast (the circle of ribs you may have seen with those little paper hats on the end of each rib), and rib roast.

Greek Lamb Kebabs
with Tzatziki

Ingredients

Marinade

¼ cup (60 mL) olive oil

¼ cup (60 mL) lemon juice

2 cloves garlic, crushed

1 Tbsp (15 mL) chopped fresh mint (optional)

2 tsp (10 mL) dried oregano

1 tsp (5 mL) salt

1 tsp (5 mL) freshly ground pepper

½ tsp (2.5 mL) cumin

Kebabs

1 ½ lb (750 g) boneless leg of lamb, cut into 2-inch (5 cm) cubes

2 yellow, orange or red bell peppers, seeded and cut into 1-inch (2.5 cm) chunks

2 red onions, each cut into wedges or chunks

16 cherry tomatoes

Tzatziki

2 cucumbers, coarsely grated

1 Tbsp (15 mL) lemon juice

1 cup (250 mL) good quality (preferably Balkan-style) plain yogurt

1–2 cloves garlic, crushed

Kebabs are a great way to stretch a small amount of lamb into several servings, and perfect to bring to a barbecue.

Method

1 In a small bowl or jar, stir or shake together the olive oil, lemon juice, garlic, mint (if using), oregano, cumin, and salt and pepper. Pour over the lamb in a container or plastic bag and refrigerate it for at least 2 hours, or overnight. Turn the bag or shake the container whenever you think of it.

2 Get out some metal skewers, or soak some bamboo skewers in water for at least 10 minutes so that the ends don't burn on the grill. Remove the lamb from the marinade and thread the meat, peppers, onion, and tomatoes alternately onto the skewers. Set them aside on a plate or baking sheet.

3 To grill the kebabs, spray the grill rack with non-stick spray and heat the barbecue to medium. Grill the kebabs for about 8 minutes, rotating them often, until the lamb is medium rare and lightly charred. To cook the kebabs in the oven, preheat the broiler, place them on a baking sheet, and broil for 6–8 minutes, rotating them until they're evenly browned.

4 To make the tzatziki, stir together all the ingredients in a bowl. If you want to do this a day ahead, extra time in the fridge will allow the flavors to blend.

5 Serve immediately over rice (see page 182) or couscous (see page 187) or stuff the lamb and veg into fresh pitas and top with tzatziki.

Serves 4–6

 What to do with the leftovers

* Keep them covered in the fridge for up to 2 days. Reheat them in the microwave.

* Pull the meat and veggies off the skewers onto a bowl of hot or cold rice or couscous, and toss with a red wine vinaigrette.

Other things to do with it

* Use chicken or pork instead of lamb.

Braised Lamb Shanks

Ingredients

2 Tbsp (30 mL) all-purpose flour

Salt and pepper

4–6 lamb shanks, trimmed of any excess fat

2 Tbsp (30 mL) olive or canola oil

2 onions, peeled and chopped

2 carrots, peeled and chopped

4–5 cloves garlic, crushed or left whole

1 Tbsp (15 mL) chopped fresh rosemary or thyme, or a few whole sprigs

1 bay leaf (optional)

Freshly ground black pepper

2 cups (500 mL) red wine

1 small can tomato paste

¼ cup (60 mL) red or white wine vinegar

1 tsp (5 mL) sugar

3 cups (750 mL) chicken, beef or vegetable stock

Lamb shanks are one of the most richly flavored cuts of meat you can buy. Choose the largest shanks you can find—about a pound or so each—because the smaller ones are mostly bone. Lamb shanks have a lot of connective tissue, so braising is the best cooking method. Serve them with mashed potatoes or polenta to catch all the richly flavored sauce.

Method

1 Season the flour with salt and pepper, and toss the lamb shanks in it to coat them well. Heat a drizzle of oil in a large skillet set over medium-high heat and brown the lamb on all sides, working in batches so the pan isn't crowded. As you brown the shanks, place them in a roasting pan. If you have whole sprigs of rosemary or thyme, lay them overtop the shanks. Preheat the oven to 325°F (170°C).

2 Add the remaining oil to the skillet and sauté the onions and carrots for about 5 minutes, until soft. Add the garlic, rosemary (if you're using chopped rosemary), bay leaf, and pepper and cook for another minute or two.

3 Add the wine, tomato paste, vinegar, and sugar and bring to a simmer. Add the stock and bring it to a boil. Pour the mixture over the lamb shanks in the roasting pan and cover tightly with a lid or with foil.

4 Bake for an hour, then remove the lid and cook for another 2–2 ½ hours, turning the lamb shanks every half hour or so, until the meat is fall-off-the-bone tender.

5 Remove the lamb from the sauce and skim as much fat from the surface as you can. Leave the vegetables or strain them out and purée them in a blender or food processor, then return the purée to the pot. Season with salt and pepper. Serve the lamb shanks over mashed potatoes, topped with the sauce.

Serves 4–6

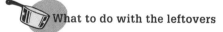 **What to do with the leftovers**

* Keep them covered in the fridge for up to 3 days. Reheat them in the microwave or covered with foil in the oven.

 **Other things to do with it**

* Add 2 chopped anchovy fillets or a squeeze of anchovy paste along with the garlic.

Chicken

Chicken is the staple of every non-vegetarian North American home,
and can be prepared in about as many ways as there are people.
The best chicken dishes are simple and uncluttered, like roast chicken.
It's ironic that roast chicken (and turkey) is a dish most often associated
with meals that are a production, when it really is one of the simplest things
in the world to make. If you can roast a chicken, you can make yourself
a wonderful dinner with very little effort. If you have a pan and an oven,
there's no need for those pre-roasted supermarket chickens.

Buying chicken

Shopping for chicken is easier than shopping for cuts of beef or pork, because the parts are much easier to identify. Free-range and organic chickens tend to be much tastier than those typically found in the supermarket, but the downside is they usually cost almost twice as much. When you're buying fresh chicken, make sure it's plump, the packaging doesn't leak, and there's no odor. Store chicken in the fridge as soon as you get it home, and use it within 2 days or freeze it for up to 4 months.

Whole chickens come labelled as broilers or fryers. They typically weigh 3–4 ½ lb (1.3–2 kg), and are packaged with or without the giblets. The only difference between them is that fryers are slightly smaller than roasters, so you can buy either if you're looking for a chicken to roast.

Cut-up chickens are whole chickens cut into pieces; you should get 2 breast halves, 2 thighs, 2 drumsticks, and 2 wings.

Skinless, boneless chicken breasts are typically the most expensive part of the chicken, because they're all white meat with no skin or bones. Chicken breasts also come with the bone in and skin on, and are almost always cut in half along the breast bone.

Chicken tenderloins (or "tenders") are the long, narrow pieces of meat attached to each chicken breast. Sometimes they're removed and sold separately. They're very tender and at least as expensive as skinless, boneless chicken breasts. They make great chicken fingers and are perfect for stir-fries.

Wings come whole or separated at the joint into two pieces: wing tips and drumettes, which resemble tiny drumsticks and contain the meatiest first section of the wing.

Legs come packaged as drumsticks, the portion of the leg just below the knee joint, or whole legs with the thigh and sometimes the back attached. They're all dark meat.

Thighs are the portion of the leg above the knee joint, and come with the bone in and skin on, or boneless and skinless. The meat is dark, which is more flavorful than white meat. Because it also contains more fat than white meat, thighs tend not to dry out as easily as chicken breasts can. Chicken thighs are a good choice economically; you get more meat and less skin and bone than you do when you buy drumsticks.

Chicken is also available ground in packages, but if you look closely you can see that most supermarkets don't bother to remove the fat before grinding it. A better option is to buy skinless, boneless chicken breasts or thighs (or a combination of the two), trim them of any excess fat, and grind them yourself in your food processor until they're as coarsely or finely ground as you like.

Sticky Honey-Garlic
or Buffalo Chicken Wings

Ingredients

2 lb (about 1 kg) chicken wings

Sticky Honey-Garlic

½ cup (125 mL) soy sauce

½ cup (125 mL) honey

1 Tbsp (15 mL) sesame or canola oil

2–3 cloves garlic, crushed

1 Tbsp (15 mL) grated fresh ginger
(optional)

¼ cup (60 mL) chili sauce (optional)

Sesame seeds for sprinkling
(optional)

Hot Buffalo

½ cup (125 mL) hot sauce, such as
Tabasco

¼ cup (60 mL) melted butter or
canola oil

2 Tbsp (30 mL) white wine or red
wine vinegar

¼ tsp (1 mL) salt

¼ tsp (1 mL) garlic powder or 1
crushed clove of garlic (optional)

What to do with the leftovers

* Leftover chicken wings? Seriously?

You can usually buy fresh chicken wings and "drumettes" (chicken wings with the tips removed) at the grocery store, packaged and ready to go. It's easy to stir together your own sauce to marinate and bake them in, or you could buy a bottle of teriyaki, sweet garlic, or barbecue sauce.

Method

1 Rinse the chicken wings and pat them dry with paper towels. If you want, cut off the tips with a sharp knife and throw them out, then separate each wing at the joint into 2 pieces if it hasn't already been done. (To do this, use your fingers to find the joint, and then use a sharp knife to cut through it to separate the wing into 2 pieces.)

2 Stir together the ingredients for the marinade you have chosen (leaving out the sesame seeds if you're making honey-garlic wings) and pour it over the wings in a large bowl or plastic bag. Stir to coat them well. Cover and refrigerate for at least an hour, or overnight. (The chicken wings can be frozen in the sauce at this point for up to 4 months—let them thaw before baking.)

3 Preheat your broiler and cover a roasting pan or rimmed baking sheet with foil to avoid having to scrub it afterward.

4 Place the wings in a single layer on the pan and broil for 8–10 minutes. Turn them over and broil for another 8–10 minutes, or until the juices run clear. If you're making honey-garlic wings, sprinkle them with sesame seeds when you turn them over. Serve while they're hot, with plenty of napkins.

Serves 4

Other things to do with it

* After patting the wings dry, toss them with a little oil to coat, and then a packaged shake-n-bake mix or coarse salt and freshly ground black pepper instead of using a sauce.

* Five-Spice Wings: After patting the wings dry, toss them with a combination of 1 ½ tsp (7.5 mL) Chinese five-spice powder, 1 tsp (5 mL) salt, 1 tsp (5 mL) soy sauce, and 2 cloves of crushed garlic before baking them.

Sautéed, Grilled,
or Broiled Chicken Breasts

Ingredients

2 Tbsp (30 mL) olive or
 canola oil

4 skinless, boneless
 chicken breast halves

Salt and pepper

Skinless, boneless chicken breasts are one of the most commonly purchased cuts of meat, and for good reason: they're easy to cook in a variety of ways, take on the flavor of virtually any seasoning, and can be cooked with any number of ingredients. They're also a very lean source of protein, and are low in calories.

Because chicken breasts have little flavor of their own, they always benefit from marinating. Typically, a marinade is made using oil and juice as a carrier and tenderizer, with herbs, spices, and other ingredients added for flavor. A marinade need not be fancy—even a vinaigrette will do. The longer you marinate your chicken, the more the flavors will penetrate the meat, but even 10 minutes will help boost flavor. Raw chicken can also be frozen in its marinade for up to 4 months.

Curry or Tandoori Marinade

¼ cup (60 mL) plain yogurt

2 cloves of garlic, crushed

1 Tbsp (15 mL) curry or tandoori
 paste

½ tsp (2.5 mL) cumin and ½ tsp
 (2.5 mL) salt

Garlic, Ginger, and Soy Marinade

¼ cup (60 mL) soy sauce

1 tsp (5 mL) chili paste

3 green onions, chopped

3 cloves of garlic, crushed

1 Tbsp (15 mL) grated fresh ginger

Garlic Salt and Pepper Rub

2 cloves of garlic, crushed

2 Tbsp (30 mL) coarsely ground
 black pepper

1 tsp (5 mL) coarse salt

Herb Marinade

¼ cup (60 mL) olive oil

¼ cup (60 mL) lemon juice

1 Tbsp (15 mL) dried herbs or ¼ cup
 (60 mL) chopped fresh herbs

2 cloves of garlic, crushed

Teriyaki Marinade

¼ cup (60 mL) soy sauce

1 Tbsp (15 mL) honey or brown sugar

1 Tbsp (15 mL) sherry, orange juice,
 or water

1 Tbsp (15 mL) grated fresh ginger

3 green onions, chopped

2 cloves of garlic, crushed

1 tsp (5 mL) sesame oil

Jamaican Jerk Marinade

¼ cup (60 mL) lime juice

2 Tbsp (30 mL) soy sauce

2 Tbsp (30 mL) olive oil

1 Tbsp (15 mL) brown sugar

1 tsp (5 mL) salt

2 tsp (10 mL) thyme

1 tsp (5 mL) allspice

1 tsp (5 mL) pepper

½ tsp (2.5 mL) cinnamon

3 green onions, chopped

3 cloves of garlic, crushed

2 jalapeño peppers, minced

Method

1 If you like, put them between two sheets of waxed paper and pound your chicken breasts with a can or mallet until they're of uniform thickness; this ensures they will cook more evenly.

2 Combine your marinade or rub ingredients of choice and pour them over or rub them into the chicken. Cover and refrigerate it for as much time as you have, or overnight.

3 To sauté the chicken, heat the oil in a large, heavy skillet set over medium-high heat. Remove the chicken from its marinade and cook it for 3–4 minutes per side, just until it's cooked through and the juices run clear. Cover the cooked chicken loosely with foil and let it rest for 5 minutes before cutting.

4 To grill or broil the chicken, brush the grill rack with a little oil or spray it with non-stick spray, and then preheat the grill or broiler. If you're broiling, line a baking sheet with foil. Remove the chicken from its marinade and grill or broil it for 3–4 minutes per side, just until it's cooked through. If you decide to brush it with reserved marinade, you must do so early on so that the marinade also cooks—remember that it has had raw chicken in it. Cover the cooked chicken loosely with foil and let it rest for 5 minutes before cutting into it.

Serves 4

 What to do with the leftovers

* Keep them covered in the fridge for up to 4 days. Reheat in the microwave.

* Warm leftover chicken in the microwave, slice it, and serve it over hot spaghetti with marinara sauce (see pages 170–71) and grated Parmesan, or stuff it into a sandwich or toss into a salad.

* Chop cold cooked chicken breasts and moisten them with a little mayonnaise to make chicken salad, which is particularly flavorful when the chicken has been marinated.

 Other things to do with it

* Instead of using a marinade, rub the chicken breasts with homemade or bottled pesto, olive paste, or a blended spice rub.

Chicken Stuffed with Brie,
Caramelized Onions, and Garlic

Ingredients

Olive or canola oil, for cooking with

2 onions, cut in half lengthwise and
thinly sliced

4 cloves garlic, crushed

¼ cup (60 mL) white wine or
1 Tbsp (15 mL) balsamic vinegar
(optional)

4 skinless, boneless chicken breasts,
trimmed of fat

4 oz (125 g) Brie, sliced or cut into
chunks

½ cup (125 mL) dry bread crumbs or
panko (Japanese breadcrumbs)

2 Tbsp (30 mL) grated Parmesan

2 Tbsp (30 mL) chopped fresh
parsley (optional)

Salt and pepper

1 egg or ¼ cup (60 mL) buttermilk

Stuffing chicken breasts isn't difficult if you don't let yourself get intimidated by the process. It requires much less skill than you might expect—stuffed chicken breasts hold their shape even when you expect them not to. They're best stuffed with flavorful ingredients such as cheese, olives, herbs, and intensely flavored meats—ingredients that are already cooked are your best choices so you don't have to worry about the chicken becoming overcooked and tough by the time the middle is properly cooked through.

Method

1 In a large skillet set over medium heat, heat a drizzle of oil and sauté the onions for about 20 minutes, stirring often, until they turn deep golden. Add the garlic and wine and cook for a few more minutes, until the liquid evaporates. Set the onions aside to cool.

2 Preheat the oven to 400°F (200°C).

3 Place the chicken on a cutting board, and cut a slit horizontally along one edge of the breast, cutting nearly to the opposite side but not all the way through. Open it so it forms two flaps, attached at the center, like a butterfly. Stuff each breast with about a quarter of the caramelized onions and a quarter of the Brie; close the flap, press it down firmly, and set them aside on a baking sheet. Don't worry that they aren't sealed around the edges.

4 In a shallow dish, combine the bread crumbs, Parmesan, parsley, and salt and pepper to taste. In another dish, lightly beat the egg with a fork, or pour in the buttermilk.

5 Holding a chicken breast together, dip it in the beaten egg or buttermilk, coating it on both sides, then in the bread crumb mixture, turning it over to coat it well. Repeat with each chicken breast.

6 Drizzle a little oil into a large ovenproof skillet set over medium-high heat. Cook the chicken breasts until browned on one side, then turn them over and place the skillet in the oven. If you don't have an ovenproof skillet, brown the chicken breasts on the other side, then transfer them to a baking sheet or dish and put them in the oven.

7 Bake the chicken for 15–20 minutes, until no longer pink inside. (Poke them with a sharp knife to peek if you can't tell.) Serve immediately.

Serves 4

What to do with the leftovers

* Keep them covered in the fridge for 2–3 days, or wrap them well and freeze for up to 3 months. Reheat them in the microwave or covered with foil in the oven.

* Slice leftover chicken breasts and serve them over hot pasta with marinara sauce (see pages 170–71) and grated Parmesan.

Other things to do with it

* Stuff the chicken breasts with sliced Black Forest ham and Brie, grated cheddar, or Monterey Jack.

* Sauté a thinly sliced apple along with the onions for the last 5 minutes of cooking time; stuff the chicken with the apple-onion mixture and some thinly sliced smoked Gouda.

* Stuff the chicken breasts with chopped canned artichoke hearts, crumbled goat cheese, a sprinkle of chopped fresh thyme, and some grated lemon zest.

* Sauté a handful of fresh spinach in a little oil until it wilts. Add a few chopped sun-dried tomatoes, a few chopped olives, and some crumbled feta cheese and use the mixture to stuff the chicken breasts.

Sticky Oven-Roasted
Chicken Pieces

Ingredients

Chicken pieces, bone-in, with or without skin (such as breasts, thighs, and legs)

Canola or olive oil, for cooking

Your choice of sauce

Chicken pieces roast considerably faster than a whole chicken, can be done in the oven or on the grill, and can be brushed with any number of sauces to add flavor. These will make enough for 4–6 pieces of chicken. Sugary glazes can burn easily, so if you're grilling brush them onto the chicken toward the end of the cooking time. If you don't feel like making your own sauce, use your choice of bottled sauce instead.

Chili-Teriyaki

¼ cup (60 mL) bottled teriyaki sauce

1 Tbsp (15 mL) chili sauce

1 clove of garlic, crushed

Honey-Garlic

¼ cup (60 mL) soy sauce

¼ cup (60 mL) honey

2–3 cloves of garlic, crushed

2 tsp (10 mL) grated fresh ginger

Honey-Lime

1 small onion, grated or finely chopped

¼ cup (60 mL) honey

2 Tbsp (30 mL) soy sauce

Grated zest and juice of 1 lime

1 clove of garlic, crushed

1 tsp (5 mL) ground cumin

Honey-Mustard

3 Tbsp (45 mL) honey

3 Tbsp (45 mL) regular, Dijon, or grainy mustard

1 tsp (5 mL) canola oil

1 tsp (5 mL) curry powder or paste

¼ tsp (1 mL) each salt and pepper

Olive Oil and Herb

3 Tbsp (45 mL) olive oil

½ cup (125 mL) finely chopped fresh green herbs (basil, thyme, sage, rosemary, parsley, and/or chives)

Sticky Peach or Orange

¼ cup (60 mL) peach or apricot jam or orange marmalade

1 Tbsp (15 mL) mustard

1 Tbsp (15 mL) soy sauce

2 tsp (10 mL) lemon juice

Pinch red pepper flakes

Spicy Plum

½ cup (125 mL) plum sauce

2 cloves of garlic, crushed

1 tsp (5 mL) grated fresh ginger

A few shakes of Tabasco sauce

¼ tsp (1 mL) salt

Method

1 Preheat the oven to 425°F (220°C).

2 In a medium bowl, combine all the ingredients for whichever sauce you choose.

3 Drizzle some oil into a large non-stick skillet set over medium heat, and brown the chicken pieces on all sides. It should take about 5 minutes to do this—you don't need to cook them all the way through. Do them in batches if necessary so that the pan isn't crowded.

4 Place the chicken pieces in a baking dish and pour the sauce on top, making sure you coat the chicken well. Bake it uncovered for 35–45 minutes, basting with the sauce once or twice. When the chicken is cooked through, it will be springy to the touch and the juices will run clear.

Serves as many as you want to feed

What to do with the leftovers

* Keep them covered in the fridge for up to 3 days. Reheat them in the microwave or eat them cold.

Other things to do with it

* Marinate the chicken in your choice of sauce for at least an hour, or overnight if possible. Remove the chicken pieces from the sauce and grill them over medium heat until they're cooked through.

* If you like your chicken saucy, prepare double the amount of sauce and, after you take the chicken out of the oven, simmer the sauce in a small pot on the stovetop for a few minutes. Pour the sauce over the cooked chicken.

Crunchy Chicken Fingers
with Honey Mustard

Ingredients

½ cup (125 mL) buttermilk

3 skinless, boneless chicken breast halves, cut into strips (about 1 lb/500 g)

1–2 cups (250–500 mL) panko, dry breadcrumbs, crushed crackers, or corn flake crumbs

¼ cup (60 mL) grated Parmesan or ground pecans (optional)

Salt and pepper

¼–½ cup (60–125 mL) canola oil (optional, if you want to cook them on the stovetop)

Equal parts honey or maple syrup and mustard, or bottled plum sauce, for dipping

All you need to make chicken fingers on par with something you'd get at a restaurant is chicken (or turkey) and some sort of crunchy crumbs to coat it with. If you can find panko—extra-crunchy Japanese crumbs that create a wonderful crust—get some. Otherwise dry bread crumbs, crushed crackers, or corn flakes will work just fine. Letting the chicken strips sit in buttermilk for a day will do a lot to tenderize them.

Method

1 Pour the buttermilk over the chicken in a bowl or plastic bag and refrigerate it for an hour, or up to a day.

2 Preheat the oven to 375°F (190°C). Line a baking sheet with foil or spray it with non-stick spray. Or if you want to cook them on the stovetop, heat the canola oil in a wide skillet over medium heat.

3 Combine the crumbs, Parmesan, and salt and pepper in a shallow dish.

4 Take the chicken strips out of the buttermilk, letting the excess drip off, and roll them in the crumbs to coat them well, pressing with your fingers to help the crumbs adhere. To bake them, place the strips about an inch apart on the prepared baking sheet. If you like, lightly drizzle the chicken strips with oil or lightly spray them with cooking spray—this will help them brown nicely. Bake for 15–20 minutes, until golden and cooked through.

5 To fry them, place the chicken strips into the skillet once the oil is hot but not smoking. Cook until golden on each side, flipping with tongs as necessary. Transfer to a paper towel to drain any excess fat.

6 Mix equal amounts of honey or maple syrup and mustard for dipping.

Serves 4

What to do with the leftovers

* Leftovers can be kept covered in the fridge for up to 2 days, but won't be as crispy the second time around. Reheat them in the microwave or on a baking sheet in the oven.

Other things to do with it

* Add chopped parsley, chili powder, sesame seeds, or any other seasonings you like to the crumb mixture.

* Curried Almond Chicken Fingers: Coat chicken strips in a mixture of 1 ½ cups (375 mL) bread crumbs, ½ cup (125 mL) finely chopped almonds, and 1 tsp (5 mL) curry powder.

* Pecan-Crusted Chicken Fingers: Coat the chicken strips in equal amounts of finely chopped pecans and crumbs, seasoned with salt and pepper to taste.

* Crunchy Buffalo Chicken Fingers: Dip the raw chicken strips in ½ cup (125 mL) low fat creamy ranch dressing spiked with 1 tsp (5 mL) Tabasco sauce instead of the buttermilk before coating them with crumbs.

* Crispy Sesame Chicken Fingers: Coat the chicken strips in equal amounts of sesame seeds and crumbs, seasoned with salt and pepper to taste. Serve with sweet and sour or sweet garlic dipping sauce.

* Oven-Fried Chicken: Use chicken pieces instead of strips and bake them at 350°F (175°C) for about an hour, until they're cooked through.

Chicken Satay

Chicken

Ingredients

1 ½ lb (750 g) skinless, boneless
  chicken breasts

Curry Marinade

2 Tbsp (30 mL) soy sauce

2 Tbsp (30 mL) lemon juice

1 Tbsp (15 mL) honey

1 tsp (5 mL) sesame oil

2 cloves garlic, crushed

1–2 tsp (5–10 mL) curry paste

1 tsp (5 mL) grated fresh ginger

Ginger-Orange Marinade

⅓ cup (80 mL) soy sauce

2–3 cloves garlic, crushed

2 Tbsp (30 mL) packed brown sugar

Juice of 1 orange (grate the zest in
  too, if you want)

1 tsp (5 mL) grated fresh ginger
  (or use bottled)

Satay are flavorful strips of chicken, pork, or shrimp that have been marinated, threaded onto a bamboo skewer and then broiled or grilled. They're perfect for parties, for dinner, or for snacking, and can be eaten hot, cold, or at room temperature. Try serving satay on their own with peanut sauce (see page 179) for dipping, or serve a few skewers over rice or rice pilaf (see pages 182–83) and any vegetables you're in the mood for to make a complete meal.

Method

1   Cut the chicken lengthwise into ½- to 1-inch (1–2.5 cm) thick strips and put them in a bowl or zip-lock bag. Combine all the ingredients for the marinade you have chosen and pour them over the chicken. Stir to coat the chicken well, cover the bowl or seal the bag, and put it in the fridge for a few hours, or overnight. The longer the chicken marinates, the more intense the flavors will be. (You can freeze the raw chicken in the marinade at this point for up to 4 months, or grill only what you want, and freeze the rest. Thaw the frozen chicken before continuing with the next step.)

2   Preheat the grill or broiler and soak about 20 bamboo skewers in water for at least 10 minutes, so that the ends won't burn when you cook them. If you are using the broiler, line a baking sheet with foil to make cleanup easier.

3   Remove the chicken strips from the marinade and thread them onto the skewers, weaving back and forth in an "S" shape. Leave some room at the blunt end so that you have something to hold on to. Put the satays directly onto the grill or onto the prepared baking sheet and grill or broil them for about 5 minutes, turning once or twice, just until they're cooked through. Serve them warm, at room temperature, or cold.

Makes about 20 satay

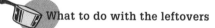 **What to do with the leftovers**

*   Keep them covered in the fridge for 2–3 days. Gently reheat them in the microwave or eat them cold. Overcooking can make them tough.

*   Cut the satay into pieces and add them to Ginger-Sesame Noodle Salad (see pate 91) or fried rice (see page 185).

 **Other things to do with it**

*   Use strips of pork or raw, peeled shrimp instead of (or along with) the chicken.

*   Tandoori Chicken Satay: Marinate the chicken strips in a mixture of ½ cup (125 mL) bottled tandoori paste and ½ cup (125 mL) plain yogurt.

How to Roast a Chicken

Ingredients

1 chicken, a roaster or fryer (any size)

Half a lemon (optional)

A few cloves of garlic, peeled or
   unpeeled, or half a head of garlic,
   cut in half widthwise (optional)

Oil or butter, any kind

Salt and pepper

There are thousands of recipes out there for roast chicken, some trussed and fancy, some plain. Before roasting, a chicken can be rubbed with herbs and spices, basted with a glaze, stuffed with any number of ingredients, or you can use absolutely nothing but a little oil, and salt and pepper and it will still be perfect. Roast chicken can be dressed up or dressed down, but even the plainest roast chicken is virtually effortless and makes a great meal regardless of the occasion. Throwing half a lemon and a few garlic cloves inside the chicken is easy and will add flavor.

Roasting a chicken is virtually foolproof: it can be cooked for a long time at a low temperature or for a short time at a high temperature. There's no right or wrong way, although cooks around the world are convinced their method is best. If you flip through several cookbooks, no two will give you the same instructions for roasting a chicken—cooking times and temperatures will vary greatly. Basting has also been a subject of great debate—some will tell you it's essential, while others believe you should never baste a chicken as it roasts. So if you forget to, don't worry about it.

Roasting a turkey is essentially the same as roasting a chicken—see the end of the recipe for more detailed instructions for a bigger bird.

Method

1 Preheat the oven to 400°F (200°C). Let the chicken stand at room temperature for about half an hour so it isn't cold when you put it in the oven. It isn't necessary to wash it, but rinse it inside and out with cold water if you like, removing any giblets from inside its cavity. Dry it well with paper towels—this ensures a crispy crust.

2 Throw the lemon half and garlic inside the chicken cavity. Trussing the chicken is unnecessary, and in fact the insides of the drumsticks don't brown as well on a trussed chicken, but you can tie the legs together with some kitchen string if you really want to. Trussing is really done only for aesthetic purposes.

Roast Chicken (continued)

3 Put the chicken in a roasting pan or baking dish (usually an 8- × 8-inch pan will do the trick). Rub the chicken all over with oil or butter—the fat helps produce a golden, crispy crust—and sprinkle it with salt and pepper. If you want to get fancy, mash some fresh herbs or garlic into the butter to make a paste before you rub it over the skin. Some people like to loosen the skin and rub the butter pomade underneath the skin, directly on the meat, as well.

4 Roast the chicken for about 1 ½ hours—20 minutes per pound plus half an hour. If you want to baste it you can—whenever you think of it—but it's not really necessary. When the chicken is done it will be deep golden, the drumsticks will wiggle in their sockets, and the juices will run clear when pierced. Tip the pan to let the juices from the cavity run out—if they're red, it needs to be cooked longer. If you have an oven thermometer, it should read 170°F (76°C) when poked into the thickest part of the thigh. Make sure your thermometer isn't touching bone, which conducts heat better than meat does and will give you an inaccurate reading. If the chicken needs to be cooked longer, leave it in and check it every 10 minutes or so, until it's done.

5 Tent the chicken with foil and let it stand for 10 minutes before carving it. While it's resting, in the pan or on a platter, pour the pan juices out and spoon off as much of the fat as you can. Use the juices to make gravy (see below—you may need extra chicken stock) or just serve them as is, drizzled over the chicken.

Serves 4

 What to do with the leftovers

* Leftover roasted chicken makes great sandwiches. Slice it, shred it, or chop it and add a little mayonnaise or peanut sauce, a few drops of lemon juice, a chopped green onion, and some salt and pepper to make chicken salad.

* Any meat that has been roasted on the bone is more flavorful, so leftover roasted chicken is perfect for any recipe that calls for cooked chicken. Add it to salads, curries, soups, fried rice, frittatas, pad Thai, pizzas, noodle dishes, or pasta dishes.

* Cover the chicken carcass with water and simmer it to make a great chicken stock (see page 68).

Other things to do with it

* Before roasting the chicken, slide your fingers under the skin to create a pocket, and rub the meat with flavorful ingredients such as pesto, garlic butter, or olive tapenade, or tuck in a few whole sprigs of fresh rosemary or other herbs of your choice.

* To make gravy, first remove as much fat as you can from the pan juices, and set it aside. Drain the juices into another container. Place the roasting pan or a pot over medium-high heat while the chicken is resting. Add 1–2 Tbsp (15–30 mL) of the reserved chicken fat (or use canola or olive oil if you prefer) to the pan, whisk in 2–4 Tbsp (30–60 mL) of flour and cook the mixture, whisking constantly and scraping up any flavorful browned bits that have stuck to the bottom of the pan, until it turns golden. Whisk in the reserved juices plus enough chicken stock to make about 2 cups (500 mL) and cook, whisking constantly, until the gravy bubbles and thickens. If you roasted any garlic cloves with the chicken, mash them into the gravy as well. Season with salt and pepper.

* Roasted Chicken with Potatoes: If you want to roast potatoes along with the chicken, peel (or not) as many potatoes as you would like, cut them into similar sized chunks and boil them for about 10 minutes. Drain well and shake them around a little in the empty pan to crush the edges a bit, which will make them crispier. Scatter them around the chicken about halfway through the roasting time, and stir them once or twice to coat with the pan juices. If the chicken has finished cooking but the potatoes haven't, leave them in the oven while the chicken rests.

* Chicken with 40 Cloves of Garlic: Separate and peel the cloves from 3–4 heads of garlic, and scatter them over the bottom of your roasting pan. Place the chicken on top and roast as directed. When you take the chicken out of the oven mash the garlic cloves into a paste to add them to the gravy, stir them into mashed potatoes, or spread them onto fresh crusty bread. The garlic mellows as it cooks, so it won't be as intense as it sounds.

* Spiced Roasted Chicken: Make a paste by stirring together 2 Tbsp (30 mL) olive or canola oil, 1 tsp (5 mL) each cumin, garlic powder, onion powder, allspice, and paprika and ½ tsp (2.5 mL) each salt and pepper. Rub the chicken all over with the mixture before you roast it.

* Roasted Turkey: Roasting a turkey is essentially the same as roasting a chicken. Prepare it in the same way, and stuff the cavity with a bunch of fresh thyme, a whole lemon cut in half, an onion cut in quarters, and a head of garlic cut in half widthwise or separated into cloves. Or, use your favorite stuffing. Roast the bird at 325°F (170°C) for 10–12 minutes per pound if it's not stuffed, 12–15 minutes per pound if it is. When it's cooked, the drumstick should move easily in its socket and the juices from the thigh will run clear. If you have a meat thermometer, the temperature in the thickest part of the thigh should register 175°F (76°C). If the turkey is done before the stuffing inside is cooked through (it should read 165°F/73°C), pull the stuffing out and bake it in a casserole dish until it reaches a safe temperature. Let the turkey rest, tented with foil, for 20 minutes before carving.

Fish and shellfish

Fish is the fastest of fast food, requiring little more than a turn
in a hot pan or run under the broiler to cook a fillet through.
And the less you muck about with fish before cooking it, the better.

Fish is also one of the healthiest foods—a great source of protein, B vitamins, and minerals such as calcium, iron, potassium, and phosphorus. It ranges from lean to oily, but the fat that fish contains is primarily in the form of omega-3 fatty acids, a healthy type that we want to include in our diets. White fish such as sole, pike, haddock, halibut, red snapper, cod, sea bass, flounder, carp, pollock, perch, and hake are all very lean—their fat stores are mainly in the liver, which isn't consumed. Striped bass, swordfish, trout, tuna, and whiting have a moderate amount of fat, and herring, salmon, mackerel, sardine, smelt, and sturgeon are fattier, averaging about 12% fat in their flesh.

Buying fish and shellfish

When you buy whole fish, their eyes should be bright and clear—cloudy eyes indicate stale fish. The skin should be brightly colored and firm to the touch, with no missing scales and with pink or red gills that are free from residue. Fish should have a mild, fresh odor that reminds you of the ocean. Fillets are usually boneless and cut lengthwise from the sides of a fish, and steaks are cross-sections that usually contain some backbone. Both should have a firm texture and moist appearance. White fish should have no pink or brown spots, which could be bruises or indicate spoilage. Any fresh fish needs to be well wrapped and refrigerated immediately, and used within a day or two. If you've been fishing, clean and gut your fish immediately before you store it—the innards deteriorate faster than the flesh.

Make sure frozen fish is solid with no damage to the packaging and has no dark, white, icy or dry spots, or odor. Don't buy fish that has been thawed and refrozen, which can affect its flavor and texture. Keep frozen fish frozen for up to 6 months, and when you're ready to use it, thaw it in the fridge or in a bowl of cold water.

Salmon

Fresh salmon is typically sold whole or in fillets and steaks, and you can sometimes find it ground. It also comes smoked, candied, barbecued, and canned. Wild salmon is much more flavorful and has a deeper color and nicer texture than farmed salmon, which is more abundant and less expensive. Pacific and Atlantic salmon are by far the most widely available, and come in many varieties, with flesh ranging from pale pink to bright red. Chinook and king salmon are the largest and often regarded as best, followed by coho, silver, sockeye, red, and pink salmon, which are the smallest and have the lowest fat content. Red, pink, and sockeye salmon are the varieties that are most often canned.

Shellfish

Shellfish are separated into two categories: mollusks and crustaceans. Mollusks include clams, mussels, scallops, oysters, snails, octopus, and squid. Crab, lobster, and shrimp are crustaceans. Lobster, crab, clams in their shells, oysters, and mussels are often sold live. Live lobster and crab should seem lively—if they appear sluggish, don't buy them. If mollusks are alive and healthy, their muscles should make it difficult to pry them apart. If they have been shucked (removed from their shells) they will have a longer shelf life. No shellfish should have an "off" odor.

You can buy shrimp in a wide variety of sizes, generally labeled small (51–60 shrimp per pound), medium (40–50 shrimp per pound), large (31–40 shrimp per pound), and jumbo (21–25 shrimp per pound). Cocktail shrimp are tiny, come fresh and canned, and are best used for shrimp salad and recipes that call for chopped shrimp meat. Fresh shrimp come cooked (pink) or uncooked (gray), shelled and deveined, with the tails on, or in their shells. Shrimp are usually shipped frozen and then thawed before they're sold, so you're not doing yourself a disservice by buying frozen shrimp, which are usually cheaper. Frozen shrimp can be thawed in a colander under cool running water.

Bagged shrimp in their shells have often already been deveined. If so, it will say so on the package. If not, removing the vein is easy: use the tip of a small paring knife to make a shallow slit along the length of the back, and remove the vein by rinsing under cold water. Simply peel the shells off if you want them shelled, leaving the tails intact if you want something to hold on to when you eat them.

Sautéed (or Pan-fried)
Whitefish Fillets

Ingredients

Flour for dredging

Salt and pepper

1 Tbsp (15 mL) canola or olive oil

1 Tbsp (15 mL) butter

½–¾ lb (250–350 g) whitefish
fillets, cut about ¼ inch (5 mm)
thick

Haddock, flounder, sole, cod, pike, pickerel, snapper, perch, catfish, sea bass, halibut, pollock, Boston bluefish, orange roughy, carp, striped bass, grouper, whiting, and monkfish are all mild-flavored white fish. Some are firmer and some more delicate, but all can be baked, broiled, sautéed, fried, grilled, poached, or steamed. Sautéeing (or pan-frying) works especially well with thin fish fillets.

Method

1 Season the flour with salt and pepper in a shallow bowl.

2 Heat a large, preferably non-stick skillet over medium-high heat until it's hot but not smoking. Add the oil and butter and, while it's heating up, dredge the fillets in the seasoned flour, shaking off any excess. When the foam from the butter subsides, add the fillets to the pan and cook them for 2–4 minutes per side, until golden. Serve them immediately.

Serves 2 (doubles or triples easily)

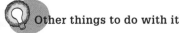 **Other things to do with it**

* Add 1–2 Tbsp (15–30 mL) butter to the pan after you remove the fish, and when the foam subsides, squeeze in the juice of a lemon. Cook for about half a minute, scraping down the pan, and pour the sauce over the fish.

* Extra-Crispy Fish Fillets: Use thicker fillets of cod, snapper, Boston bluefish, grouper, or orange roughy. After dredging the fillets in flour, dip them into 2 beaten eggs, then back in the flour or in crushed dry breadcrumbs or panko (crunchy Japanese breadcrumbs); cook them as directed, but the total cooking time will be closer to 10 minutes.

* Sautéed Whitefish with Moroccan Sauce: In a food processor or blender purée ¼ cup (60 mL) cilantro, ¼ cup (60 mL) fresh parsley, 1 clove of garlic, 2 Tbsp (30 mL) lemon juice, 2 Tbsp (30 mL) olive or canola oil, ½ tsp (2.5 mL) paprika, and ½ tsp (2.5 mL) cumin. Drizzle the sauce over the fish right before you serve it.

* Mediterranean Whitefish Fillets: As soon as you remove the fish from the pan, add ¼ cup (60 mL) chopped fresh parsley and a generous pinch of dried red pepper flakes to the pan and sauté them for about a minute. Add 2 cups (500 mL) halved cherry tomatoes, ¼ to ½ cup (60–125 mL) chopped kalamata olives and 2–3 crushed cloves of garlic to the pan and cook for a few more minutes, until the tomatoes are soft and have released their juices. Pour the mixture over the fish and serve it immediately.

* Whitefish Fillets with Mushrooms and Soy: After removing the fish from the pan, add 2 Tbsp (30 mL) soy sauce, ¼ cup (60 mL) mirin (Japanese rice wine), and ¼ cup (60 mL) water to the pan. Add 1 cup (250 mL) sliced mushrooms and 2–3 chopped green onions, and simmer for 6–7 minutes, until the sauce thickens. Serve the sauce over the fish.

Broiled Whitefish

Ingredients

1 ½ lb (750 g) whitefish fillets

1 Tbsp (15 mL) olive oil or butter

Salt and pepper

To gauge cooking time, measure the fish at its thickest point—it needs to cook for 8–10 minutes per inch. How do you tell when it's cooked? By the time the outside of thinner fillets is opaque, the inside should be done, or close to it. When properly cooked, fish will be opaque and flake without falling apart when prodded with a fork. Undercooked fish is translucent. If you are second-guessing yourself, cooked fish should register 145°F (63°C) when a meat thermometer is inserted into the middle of the flesh. Remember that the fish will continue to cook between the oven and table, so if it's just barely translucent in the middle, it should be perfectly cooked by the time you sit down to eat it.

Method

1 Preheat the broiler. Spray a rimmed baking sheet, broiling pan, or pie plate with non-stick spray or rub it with oil.

2 Lay the fish fillets on the prepared pan, brush them with oil and sprinkle them with salt and pepper. Broil them for 2–4 minutes (without turning) for ¼-inch (5 mm) thick fillets, longer if the fish is thicker, until it's firm and opaque and the edges flake with a fork. Remove them from the sheet with a thin spatula.

Serves 4

 Other things to do with it

* Broiled Whitefish with Basil Butter: Sprinkle the fish fillets with salt and pepper. Combine ¼ cup (60 mL) softened butter, 1 Tbsp (15 mL) chopped fresh basil and a clove of crushed garlic and spread the mixture over the fillets before broiling.

* Broiled Whitefish with Ginger and Soy: Marinate the fillets with a mixture of ¼ cup (60 mL) soy sauce, a few chopped green onions, 1 Tbsp (15 mL) brown sugar or honey, 2 tsp (10 mL) grated fresh ginger, a clove of crushed garlic, and 1 tsp (5 mL) sesame oil for about 20 minutes. Place the fillets on the baking sheet and pour the marinade over the fish before broiling it as directed above.

* Mustard Broiled Whitefish: Spread your fish fillets with a mixture of ¼ cup (60 mL) grainy or Dijon mustard, 1 Tbsp (15 mL) white or brown sugar, and 1 Tbsp (15 mL) lemon juice. Sprinkle them with 1 Tbsp (15 mL) chopped fresh rosemary, parsley or basil before or after broiling.

* Whitefish with Browned Butter and Balsamic Vinegar: Bring ¼ cup (60 mL) butter to a simmer in a small pot set over medium heat, swirling the pan until the butter turns a deep golden brown. Remove it from the heat and whisk in 2 Tbsp (30 mL) balsamic vinegar, 2 tsp (10 mL) honey, and 2 tsp (10 mL) mustard. Serve the sauce over the broiled fish.

Fish Cakes

Ingredients

1 lb (500 g) cooked cod, halibut or salmon, flaked (about 1 ½ cups/375 mL), or canned salmon, drained

1–2 largish peeled, cubed potatoes, or 1 ½ cups (375 mL) leftover mashed or boiled potatoes

2–4 green onions, thinly sliced (optional)

2 Tbsp (30 mL) chopped fresh parsley (optional)

½ tsp (2.5 mL) salt

½ tsp (2.5 mL) pepper

Bread crumbs, panko (Japanese breadcrumbs), or flour for dredging

Canola oil or butter for cooking with

Tartar Sauce (optional)

½ cup (125 mL) light mayonnaise

3 Tbsp (45 mL) relish or finely chopped sweet pickles

2 Tbsp (30 mL) finely chopped or grated onion

2 tsp (10 mL) Dijon or grainy mustard

2 tsp (10 mL) lemon juice

Fish cakes are best made with equal parts mashed potato and fish—if you remember that, the rest is pretty much up to you. If you don't want to bother making tartar sauce from scratch, dip the cakes in bottled tartar sauce or creamy cucumber salad dressing.

Method

1 If you're starting with raw potato, put it in a small pot or microwave-safe bowl with some water and cook until it's tender. Mash it with a fork or potato masher and set it aside to cool.

2 In a large bowl, roughly mash together the fish, potato, onions, parsley, and salt and pepper. Shape the mixture into patties any size you like. Dredge the patties in bread crumbs or flour to coat them well.

3 Drizzle a little oil or butter in a skillet set over medium-high heat, and cook the patties in batches until they're golden brown and crispy. It should take about 5 minutes per side.

4 To make the tartar sauce, stir together the mayonnaise, relish, onion, mustard, and lemon juice in a small bowl. Put it in the fridge until you need it. Serve the fish cakes warm or at room temperature, plain or with the tartar sauce.

Serves 4–6

 What to do with the leftovers

* Keep them covered in the fridge for up to 3 days. Reheat them in the microwave or in a drizzle of oil in a hot skillet.

* Serve the patties warm or cold on a bed of greens, drizzled with any salad dressing or vinaigrette.

 Other things to do with it

* Add some chopped cooked shrimp, thinly sliced smoked salmon, a few capers, and/or a small handful of chopped fresh dill.

Poached Salmon

Ingredients

½ cup (125 mL) dry white wine (optional)

½ cup (125 mL) water

1 shallot, thinly sliced

A few sprigs of fresh parsley

2 ½ lb (1.25 kg) salmon fillet or six 6-oz (150-g) salmon fillets

Salt

Poaching salmon is easy, and the process doesn't add any extra fat or calories. It's a great way to cook salmon ahead of time if you're having people over, especially during the spring or summertime when cold poached salmon tastes best.

Method

1   In a large skillet, combine the wine and water, or use 1 cup (250 mL) water if you don't want to use wine. Add the shallot and parsley, and place the salmon skin side down in the skillet. Sprinkle it with salt.

2   Cover the skillet tightly (use foil if it doesn't have a lid) and bring the mixture to a simmer over medium-low heat. Simmer the salmon for about 10 minutes, until it's barely opaque in the middle. Remove it from the heat and let it stand, covered, for 5 minutes. Transfer the fish to a plate, draining off the liquid. Cover with plastic wrap and refrigerate for at least 2 hours, or for up to 24 hours.

3   Serve poached salmon plain, or with any of the sauces below.

Serves 6

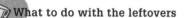

What to do with the leftovers

*   Keep them covered in the fridge for up to a few days. Leftover poached salmon is great in salads, stirred into Corn, Potato, and Crab Chowder (page 77), or moistened with mayonnaise to make salmon salad for a sandwich.

Other things to do with it

Serve it with a sauce drizzled overtop:

*   Creamy Dijon-Lime: Whisk together ¾ cup (185 mL) light sour cream, ¼ cup (60 mL) Dijon mustard, 1 Tbsp (15 mL) honey, 1 Tbsp (15 mL) lime juice, and a little grated lime zest.

*   Ginger-Lime: Whisk together ¼ cup (60 mL) lime juice, 2 Tbsp (30 mL) sesame oil, 2 Tbsp (30 mL) soy sauce, 2 Tbsp (30 mL) finely chopped fresh basil, and 1 tsp (5 mL) finely grated fresh ginger.

*   Lemon-Herb Mayo: Whisk together ½ cup (125 mL) light mayonnaise, the grated zest of 1 lemon, 2 Tbsp (30 mL) lemon juice, 2 Tbsp (30 mL) chopped fresh chives, 2 Tbsp (30 mL) chopped fresh parsley, and 1 Tbsp (15 mL) grainy mustard.

Oven-Roasted Salmon

Ingredients

4 serving-size salmon fillets or steaks

Roasting is one of the fastest and easiest ways to prepare salmon, and you can flavor it however you like. Stir up one of these sauces, buy a bottled sauce, or rub the salmon with a little oil, sprinkle it with salt and pepper, and roast it as is. Use fillets or steaks of similar thickness so that they cook evenly.

What to do with the leftovers

* Keep them covered in the fridge for up to 2 days. Eat them cold or reheat them in the microwave.

* Flake cold leftover salmon into salads, or add a little mayonnaise and a few drops of lemon juice to make salmon salad for a sandwich.

Method

1 Preheat the oven to 450°F (230°C). Line a baking sheet or shallow baking dish with foil.

2 Place the salmon fillets or steaks skin side down on the prepared baking sheet. Stir together the sauce ingredients of your choice and spoon or rub the mixture over the salmon.

3 Bake for 11–12 minutes (about 10 minutes per inch), until the fish flakes with a fork. Use a thin spatula to remove the fish from the pan, and try to leave the skin behind on the foil. Serve immediately.

Serves 4

Balsamic Sauce

2 Tbsp (30 mL) balsamic vinegar

2 Tbsp (30 mL) honey or packed brown sugar

1 Tbsp (15 mL) grainy or Dijon mustard

2 tsp (10 mL) sesame or olive oil

1 tsp (5 mL) sesame seeds (optional)

Chili-Barbecue Rub

2 Tbsp (30 mL) packed brown sugar

1 Tbsp (15 mL) chili powder

½ tsp (2.5 mL) ground cumin

½ tsp (2.5 mL) salt

Grated zest of 1 lemon

Pinch cinnamon

Honey-Mustard Sauce

2 Tbsp (30 mL) honey

1 Tbsp (15 mL) Dijon mustard

Grated zest of half a lime or 1 tsp (5 mL) chopped fresh thyme

Honey-Soy Sauce

2 Tbsp (30 mL) soy sauce

2 Tbsp (30 mL) honey or maple syrup

1 Tbsp (15 mL) lime juice

1 tsp (5 mL) Dijon mustard

Miso Glaze

¼ cup (60 mL) packed brown sugar

2 Tbsp (30 mL) miso (soybean paste)

2 Tbsp (30 mL) soy sauce

2 Tbsp (30 mL) water

Hoisin Sauce

2 Tbsp (30 mL) soy sauce

2 Tbsp (30 mL) hoisin sauce

1 Tbsp (15 mL) lemon juice

1 Tbsp (15 mL) sesame or olive oil

1 tsp (15 mL) grated fresh ginger

1 green onion, finely chopped

2 cloves garlic, crushed

¼ tsp (1 mL) pepper

Spice Rub

1 Tbsp (15 mL) fennel seeds, coarsely ground

1 Tbsp (15 mL) finely chopped fresh rosemary

Grated orange zest of 1 orange

Salt and freshly ground pepper

Salmon Burgers

Ingredients

1 lb (500 g) skinless salmon fillet

1 cup (250 mL) fresh breadcrumbs

2–3 green onions, finely chopped

1 egg, lightly beaten

1 Tbsp (15 mL) mayonnaise or
tartar sauce (optional)

1 Tbsp (15 mL) lemon juice

1 Tbsp (15 mL) capers, drained
(optional)

1 Tbsp (15 mL) chopped fresh
tarragon or dill

1 tsp (5 mL) Dijon mustard

Salt and pepper

1 Tbsp (15 mL) butter or canola oil

4 hamburger buns, toasted or not

Mayonnaise or tartar sauce, sliced
tomato, and lettuce (optional)

Salmon burgers are a nutritious alternative to beef burgers, with less fat, fewer calories and the added benefit of omega-3 fatty acids. You can often find ground salmon at the grocery store. Otherwise, pulse fillets in your food processor.

Method

1 Finely chop the salmon fillet by hand, or cut it into chunks and pulse it in a food processor until the salmon is as coarsely or finely ground as you like. In a medium bowl, combine the salmon, bread crumbs, onions, egg, mayonnaise, lemon juice, capers, tarragon, mustard, and salt and pepper to taste.

2 Shape the mixture into four 1-inch (2.5 cm) thick patties. In a heavy skillet, heat the butter or oil over medium-high heat. Add the patties and cook them for about 3 minutes per side, until golden and crusty and just firm to the touch.

3 Serve the salmon burgers on buns with mayo or tartar sauce, tomato and lettuce, or whatever condiments you like.

Serves 4

 What to do with the leftovers

* Keep them well wrapped in the fridge for up to a day. Eat them cold or reheat them in the microwave or in a drizzle of oil in a hot skillet.

 **Other things to do with it**

* Asian Salmon Burgers: Add 1 Tbsp (15 mL) Dijon mustard, 2 tsp (10 mL) grated fresh ginger, and 1 tsp (5 mL) soy sauce to the salmon mixture. Top the burgers with peanut sauce or mayonnaise spiked with a little Dijon and soy sauce.

Shrimp with Orzo and Feta

Ingredients

1 cup (250 mL) orzo

2–4 Tbsp (30–60 mL) olive oil

¼ cup (60 mL) grated Parmesan

1 lb (500 g) uncooked jumbo shrimp, peeled and deveined, with the tails on

2–3 cloves garlic, crushed

1 14-oz (398-mL) can diced tomatoes

½ cup (125 mL) dry white wine or shrimp or vegetable stock

1 tsp (5 mL) oregano

Small handful fresh basil, chopped (optional)

Salt and pepper

½–1 cup (125–250 mL) crumbled feta cheese

This is a classic Greek baked shrimp dish, made with rice-shaped pasta called orzo. Because it has shrimp, rice, and veg all in one dish, you don't need to make anything else for dinner. But it's good with fresh bread and a green salad.

Method

1 Preheat the oven to 400°F (200°C). Spray a baking dish with non-stick spray, or brush it with some olive oil.

2 Cook the orzo according to the package directions and drain it well. Pour it into the prepared pan, drizzle with a little bit of the olive oil, and stir in the Parmesan.

3 Heat about a tablespoon (15 mL) of oil in a large skillet set over medium-high heat and sauté the shrimp for a minute or two, until they're just turning pink. Spread them over the orzo.

4 Add the rest of the oil to the skillet and sauté the garlic for about a minute. Add the tomatoes with their juice, wine, oregano, and basil. Simmer the mixture for a few minutes, until it thickens slightly. Season it with salt and pepper and pour the sauce over the shrimp.

5 Sprinkle the feta cheese overtop and bake for 10–15 minutes, until heated through and bubbly around the edges.

Serves 4–6

 **What to do with the leftovers**

* Keep them covered in the fridge for up to 2 days. Gently reheat in the microwave.

 **Other things to do with it**

* Add a small jar or can of artichoke hearts, chopped and drained, with the shrimp.

Spicy Garlic
Pan-Seared Shrimp

Ingredients

2–3 Tbsp (30–45 mL) olive oil, or half olive oil and half butter

5–6 cloves garlic, crushed or chopped

Generous pinch dried red pepper flakes

1–1 ½ lb (500–750 g) large uncooked shrimp, peeled and deveined with the tail on

¼ tsp (2.5 mL) salt

1–2 Tbsp (15–30 mL) lemon juice

Sautéing or pan-searing is a quick and easy way to cook shrimp, but you must be careful not to overcook them or they'll become rubbery. You can tell that shrimp are cooked as soon as they turn from a watery gray color to opaque and pink. After that, the longer they cook, the tougher they get.

Peeled shrimp are easiest to eat. They also absorb more flavor from the other ingredients you cook them with, which tends to be lost if you cook the shrimp in their shells and then peel them. Leaving the tail on is a good idea—it provides a convenient handle.

Method

1 In a large skillet set over low heat, heat the oil and cook the garlic and red pepper flakes for a few minutes, until the garlic turns pale golden. Turn the heat up to medium-high and add half the shrimp. (Don't crowd the skillet by cooking them all at once, or they'll steam instead of caramelizing properly.) Sauté the shrimp for 1–2 minutes, flipping them as required, just until they're cooked—you will know they're cooked when they turn pink and opaque. Remove them from the skillet and repeat with the remaining shrimp.

2 Remove the skillet from the heat, return all the shrimp to the pan, sprinkle them with salt and lemon juice and serve immediately.

Serves 4–6

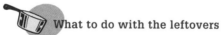

What to do with the leftovers

* Keep them covered in the fridge for up to 2 days. Eat them cold or gently reheat in the microwave or in a little oil in a hot skillet.

Fish and shellfish

Other things to do with it

* Add a splash of dry white wine as the shrimp cook.

* Serve the shrimp over rice, couscous, or angel hair pasta with stir-fried or roasted vegetables.

* Creole Shrimp: Toss the shrimp with a mixture of 1 tsp (5 mL) paprika, ½ tsp (2.5 mL) pepper, ½ tsp (2.5 mL) salt, ½ tsp (2.5 mL) garlic powder, ¼ tsp (1 mL) oregano, a pinch of cayenne pepper, and a pinch of thyme. Use half butter and half olive or canola oil and don't bother cooking the garlic first—cook the seasoned shrimp along with 2 crushed cloves of garlic, the lemon juice, and 1 Tbsp (15 mL) Worcestershire sauce.

* Ginger-Hoisin Shrimp: Use only a clove or two of garlic. Stir together 2 Tbsp (30 mL) hoisin sauce, 1 Tbsp (15 mL) rice vinegar, 2 tsp (10 mL) grated fresh ginger, 2 tsp (10 mL) water, 1 tsp (5 mL) soy sauce, and 2 sliced green onions. When you remove the skillet of shrimp from the heat, toss them with this sauce instead of sprinkling them with salt and lemon juice.

* Orange-Rosemary Shrimp: Sauté 1 Tbsp (15 mL) chopped fresh rosemary in the oil instead of the garlic and red pepper flakes until it starts to sizzle. Cook the shrimp along with the grated zest of an orange, and finish them with a squeeze of orange juice instead of lemon.

* Rosemary Garlic Shrimp: Marinate the shrimp in a mixture of 2 Tbsp (30 mL) olive oil, 1 Tbsp (15 mL) Dijon mustard, and 1 Tbsp (15 mL) chopped fresh rosemary overnight before cooking them. Omit the red pepper flakes.

* Shrimp Scampi: Use 2 Tbsp (30 mL) each olive oil and butter and omit the red pepper flakes. Cook the shrimp in the oil, remove them from the skillet, and add the butter to the pan. When the foaming subsides, add the lemon juice, 1 Tbsp (15 mL) vermouth, and 2 Tbsp (30 mL) chopped fresh parsley. Return the shrimp to the skillet, season them with salt and pepper and toss them quickly to coat them with sauce. Serve them immediately, with bread to mop up the extra sauce.

Pasta
and noodles

There's no dish as versatile as pasta, speaking from a culinary as well as an emotional point of view. It comes big and small, long and chunky, can be turned into an elegant dinner and yet is always devoured by children. It can act as the main event or as ballast to your meat and veg. You can toss it with sauces, vegetables, meat, fish, or cheese, stuff it, layer it, smother it, bake it, stir-fry it, simmer it in soup, toss it into a salad, or use it as a base to catch the richly flavored drippings of braised meat or stews. Even pasta lubricated with olive oil or butter and tossed with Parmesan makes dinner in a pinch. And depending on what you do with it, a bowl of pasta or noodles can be invigorating, healing, comforting, or downright soporific.

Learning to cook pasta and a few sauces will ensure you are well fed for little money with whatever ingredients you have knocking around the house. Most kitchens have a bag or two of dried pasta in the pantry that can be quickly turned into a meal, even on days when you think there's nothing in the house to eat.

Pasta Basics

Dried pasta is used far more often than fresh because of its low cost and virtually indefinite shelf life. Fresh pasta is wonderful, but it costs more and won't last as long in the fridge.

When you cook pasta, use a big pot and lots of water—at least a gallon (about 4 L) per pound (500 g) of pasta. It needs room to move around. If your pasta is crowded it may stick together. Some people believe that adding oil to the water will prevent pasta from sticking but this is not so—it's the quantity of water that's important, and making sure you stir it regularly.

Salt the water generously—this improves the flavor of the pasta itself. Although it seems like a lot, the general consensus of most chefs is to use a ratio of 2 tsp (10 mL) of salt per gallon (about 4 L) of water. Most of the salt won't make it into the pasta, so don't worry about adding so much.

When you're cooking pasta or noodles, bring the water to a full rolling boil before you add the pasta, and keep it boiling. Adding the pasta will cool the water down, so you may have to bring it back up to a boil. You can lower the heat once it's boiling vigorously, but make sure you keep the water boiling. (If you cover the pot, keep an eye on it or it will inevitably boil over.) Stir the pasta frequently once it's in the water to keep it from clumping and sticking together.

Fresh pasta will cook in about half the time it takes to cook dried pasta. Taste it to tell if it's done, starting about 2 minutes before the package says it will be done. Aim for about 9 minutes for dried pasta—more for thicker shapes such as rigatoni. Pasta can go from just right to mushy in no time at all, so check it often and as soon as it's al dente—tender but firm to the bite—take it off the heat and drain it right away in a colander. Its retained heat will allow it to cook a little more as you drain and sauce it. Put the drained pasta back into the pot, or directly into a serving bowl, and save a little of the pasta water in case you need it to thin your sauce—this will help the sauce to coat the pasta more evenly. Never rinse pasta; it will cool the noodles and rinse off the starch that helps sauces adhere. (If your plan is to make pasta salad, however, rinsing it is a good idea.)

You can mix and match any pasta shape with any type of sauce, although there are some traditional combinations you may want to stick with, such as macaroni and cheese or fettuccine Alfredo. Generally, long, thin pastas (such as spaghetti, fettuccine, and linguini) are better suited to smooth sauces, and stocky, shaped pastas (such as fusilli, penne, shells, farfalle, and rigatoni) work well with chunky, heartier sauces.

Spaghetti with Bolognese
(Meaty Tomato) Sauce

Ingredients

1 Tbsp (15 mL) olive oil

1 small onion, finely chopped

1 small carrot, peeled and finely
chopped (optional)

1 stalk celery, finely chopped

3 cloves garlic, crushed

3 slices bacon or pancetta, finely
chopped (optional)

1 lb (500 g) lean ground beef, or half
ground beef and half ground pork

½ cup (125 mL) red or dry white wine
(optional)

1 28 oz (798 mL) can diced or whole
plum tomatoes, drained

2 Tbsp (30 mL) balsamic vinegar

1 tsp (5 mL) dried oregano or basil

Salt and pepper

½–1 cup (125–250 mL) milk or half
and half (optional)

1 lb (500 g) spaghetti

This is a basic thick and meaty tomato sauce that goes really well with spaghetti but can also be used with fettuccine, linguine, penne, or rotini, or used for lasagna. For a vegetarian sauce, omit the meat and add more vegetables—chopped red bell pepper and zucchini are good. For a basic marinara sauce, check the variation opposite.

Method

1 Heat the olive oil in a large, deep skillet set over medium-high heat, and sauté the onion, carrot, celery, garlic, and bacon (if using) for about 10 minutes, until the vegetables are tender. Add the ground beef and cook, stirring and breaking up the lumps of meat until no traces of pink remain. Add the wine (if using) and cook until the liquid evaporates.

2 Crush the tomatoes with a fork and add them to the skillet with the balsamic vinegar and oregano. Reduce the heat to a simmer and cook for half an hour to an hour, stirring occasionally, until the sauce has thickened to your liking. Add salt and pepper to taste and stir in the milk. Simmer for another 15 minutes.

3 Meanwhile, bring a large pot of salted water to a boil. Cook the pasta until tender but still firm and drain it well. Return the pasta to the pot and toss it with the sauce, or divide it among individual serving dishes and top it with sauce. Serve immediately, and pass the grated Parmesan.

Serves 4

What to do with the leftovers

* Keep them in a covered container in the fridge for up to 3 days and reheat in the microwave. Any extra sauce can be frozen in plastic containers or zip-lock bags for up to 4 months, then reheated in the microwave or on the stovetop.

Other things to do with it

* Replace the beef with Italian sausage, squeezed out of its casing and crumbled into the skillet.

* Marinara Sauce: Omit the meat, carrot, and celery and sauté 1 lb (500 g) of sliced fresh mushrooms along with the onion and garlic. Add a 14 oz (398 mL) can of tomato sauce along with the tomatoes, and omit the milk or cream.

* Spaghetti and Meatballs: Omit the meat and add sautéed meatballs (page 121) to the sauce; simmer for 15 minutes (with the meatballs in the sauce) before serving.

* Pasta with Ribs: Omit the meat. Brown about 8 spare ribs (separate the ribs first) in the pot for about 10 minutes before you cook the vegetables; drain the fat and set aside. Add the ribs to the sauce along with the tomatoes and simmer the sauce for an hour, until the ribs are very tender. Serve over pasta, allowing a couple of ribs per person.

Pasta and Noodles

Rigatoni
with Mushroom Sauce

Ingredients

1–2 Tbsp (15–30 mL) olive oil

1 onion or 5 shallots, peeled and quartered

5 cloves garlic, peeled

1 lb (500 g) assorted mushrooms (button, portobello, cremini, shiitake, oyster, chanterelle, porcini, and/or morel), sliced

1 Tbsp (15 mL) chopped fresh rosemary or thyme, or 1 tsp (5 mL) dried

1 Tbsp (15 mL) flour

½ cup (125 mL) dry sherry, red wine, or port (optional)

1 lb (500 g) rigatoni

1 ½ cups (375 mL) chicken or vegetable stock or beef broth

1 cup (250 mL) half and half or whipping cream

Salt and pepper

This sauce works well with big chunky pasta shapes such as rigatoni, penne or rotini, which has a spiral shape that traps lots of sauce. Using an assortment of mushrooms beyond the usual button mushrooms will give this sauce the most flavor. To lighten it, use 2% evaporated milk in place of the cream.

Method

1 Preheat the oven to 350°F (175°C). Combine the oil, onion, and garlic in a small baking dish, cover with foil and bake for about an hour, until they're pale golden and tender. (You can do this a few days in advance and keep it in the fridge until you're ready for it.) Put a big pot of salted water on to boil for the rigatoni.

2 Chop the onion and mash the garlic when it's cool enough to handle. Pour the whole thing, including the oil, into a heavy skillet set over medium-high heat. Add the mushrooms, rosemary, and thyme and sauté for about 5 minutes, until the mushrooms are tender and the liquid has evaporated. Sprinkle the flour over the mushrooms and cook for about a minute.

3 Add the sherry or wine and cook until the sauce is bubbly and starts to thicken. Add the stock and simmer for about 10 minutes, until the liquid reduces and thickens. As it cooks, cook the rigatoni noodles according to the package directions. Add the cream to the mushroom mixture and cook over low heat until it thickens to the consistency of a sauce. If it's too thick, add a little extra liquid. If it isn't thick enough, simmer until it thickens. Season with salt and pepper.

4 When the pasta is tender but still firm, drain it well. Return the pasta to the pot and toss it with the sauce, or divide it among individual serving dishes and top it with sauce. Serve immediately.

Serves 4–6

What to do with the leftovers

* Keep them covered in the fridge for up to 3 days and reheat in the microwave.

Other things to do with it

* Add a spoonful of light cream cheese or sour cream to the sauce instead of, or along with, the cream to make it even creamier.

* Omit the flour and add more liquid, if you need it, for a vegetarian mushroom gravy.

* Serve the mushroom sauce with other types of pasta, or use it in place of the tomato sauce to make vegetarian lasagna (see page 175).

Easy Ravioli

Ingredients

About 24 wonton wrappers, thawed if frozen

Ricotta and Basil Filling

1 cup (250 g) part-skim ricotta cheese

½ cup (125 mL) chopped fresh basil or spinach

¼ cup (60 mL) grated Parmesan

1 large egg

Salt and pepper

Bacon and Chard Filling

2 slices bacon

1 clove garlic, crushed

2 cups (500 mL) chopped chard or kale, coarse stems removed

½ cup (125 mL) part-skim ricotta cheese

Salt and pepper

Other things to do with it

* Chop up leftover roasted vegetables and mix them with ricotta cheese to fill the ravioli.

* Sauté a few handfuls of arugula in a little olive oil until wilted. Chop it and mix it with crumbled goat cheese to fill the ravioli.

* Mash leftover roasted squash and mix it with ricotta and Parmesan cheeses; use it to fill the ravioli.

Wonton wrappers are small, thin squares of dough made from flour, egg and water, essentially the same as sheets of fresh pasta. They make ravioli from scratch easy, and much cheaper than buying fresh pasta. Wonton wrappers can be found fresh or frozen at most grocery stores (look for them with the Asian noodles) and at Asian markets. Freeze whatever filled ravioli you don't use for quick meals later on.

Method

1   To make the ricotta and basil filling: Stir together all the ingredients.

2   To make the bacon and chard filling: Cook the bacon in a skillet set over medium-high heat until crispy. Remove the bacon from the pan, crumble, and set it aside.

3   Add the garlic and chard to the bacon drippings in the pan and cook them for a few minutes, until the chard wilts. Transfer it to a bowl and set aside to cool slightly, then stir in the bacon, ricotta, and salt and pepper to taste.

4   To assemble the ravioli, first fill a small dish with water. Lay the wonton wrappers on a clean, dry work surface. Working with one or two at a time and keeping the rest in the package so that they don't dry out, place a spoonful of filling onto the middle of each wrapper, then dip your finger into the water and use it to moisten the edge. Fold the wonton over, pressing out any air bubbles, and press to seal the edges. Repeat with the remaining wonton wrappers and filling. (You can freeze the uncooked ravioli at this point in a single layer on a cookie sheet, then transfer them to freezer bags to store for up to 3 months. Boil them from frozen.)

5   To cook the ravioli, bring a large pot of salted water to a boil. Gently drop in the ravioli, making sure not to crowd the pot, and boil for 5–6 minutes, until they float to the surface. Remove them from the water with a slotted spoon and drain them well before dividing them among plates. Top with any kind of sauce you like.

Serves 4

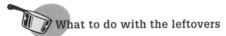

What to do with the leftovers

* Keep them covered in the fridge for up to 2 days, and reheat them in the microwave.

Lasagna

Ingredients

1 box no-bake lasagna noodles (you'll only need about half the box)

Sauce

1 Tbsp (15 mL) olive or canola oil

1 large onion, chopped

½–1 cup (125–250 mL) sliced mushrooms

2 cloves garlic, crushed

1 lb (500 g) lean ground beef, or ½ lb (250 g) lean ground beef and ½ lb (250 g) spicy Italian sausage, squeezed out of their casings

2 28 oz (796 mL) cans diced or crushed tomatoes

1 small can tomato paste (about ¼ cup/60 mL)

1 Tbsp (15 mL) brown sugar

1 tsp (5 mL) oregano

1 bay leaf (optional)

¼ tsp (1 mL) dried red pepper flakes

Salt and pepper

Ingredients continue on next page

Lasagna seems impressive and time-consuming, but it's really a snap to make. Lasagna can be made with any combination of meat, veggies, and sauces—once you get the hang of it, try using chicken, seafood or sausage, roasted vegetables, creamy sauces, and different cheeses. No-bake lasagna noodles are infinitely faster and easier to work with, but it's important to use enough sauce so that they're able to cook through without drying out the whole dish. You can, of course, use regular lasagna noodles and cook them first according to the package directions. If you don't have time to make the sauce from scratch (or don't feel like it), use bottled pasta sauce and add your own cooked meat and veggies.

Method

1 To make the sauce, heat the oil in a large, preferably non-stick, skillet set over medium heat. Sauté the onion, mushrooms, and garlic for about 8 minutes, until softened. Add the beef and sausage (if using) to the pan and cook, crumbling it with a spoon, until the meat is no longer pink. Drain any excess fat out of the pan.

2 Add the tomatoes, tomato paste, brown sugar, oregano, bay leaf, red pepper flakes, and salt and pepper to taste. Simmer for about 20 minutes, until the sauce thickens. Discard the bay leaf and set the sauce aside to cool slightly.

3 Preheat the oven to 350°F (175°C).

4 To make the cheese layer, stir together the ricotta, ¼ cup (60 mL) of the Parmesan, spinach, egg, and some salt and pepper. Now you're ready to assemble the lasagna. Take a 9- × 13-inch baking dish (glass if you have it), and spread about ½ cup (125 mL) of the tomato sauce over the bottom.

Cheese layer

1 500 mL container part-skim ricotta
cheese or cottage cheese

½ cup (125 mL) grated Parmesan

1 10 oz (300 g) package frozen
chopped spinach, thawed and
squeezed dry

1 large egg

4–5 cups (1–1.25 L) grated part-skim
or regular mozzarella

5 Lay 3 or 4 noodles over the bottom of the pan—you may need to break one of them to get it to fit. I usually place 3 noodles parallel and then break the end off a fourth to fit it across at the end. Spread half the ricotta mixture over the noodles, and then sprinkle with 1–2 cups (250–500 mL) of mozzarella cheese. Spoon about 1 ½ cups (375 mL) of the tomato sauce over the cheese, then repeat with more noodles, the rest of the ricotta mixture, more mozzarella, and another 1 ½ cups (375 mL) of tomato sauce. Place another layer of noodles on top of the sauce, and pour the remaining sauce on top. Sprinkle with what's left of the mozzarella and Parmesan.

6 Cover the lasagna with foil and bake for half an hour, then uncover it and bake for another 45 minutes, until it's golden and bubbly around the edges. Let it sit for at least 15 minutes to allow it to set before cutting into it.

Serves 8

 What to do with the leftovers

* Keep them covered in the fridge for up to 5 days, or wrap individual servings and freeze for up to 4 months. Reheat leftovers in the microwave or cover with foil and reheat in the oven.

 Other things to do with it

* Add a small handful of chopped fresh basil to the sauce.

* Use half ground chicken and half ground beef.

* Use roasted or sautéed vegetables in place of the meat for vegetarian lasagna.

Macaroni & Cheese

Ingredients

½ lb (250 g) dry macaroni

Salt

2 Tbsp (30 mL) butter or margarine

3 Tbsp (45 mL) flour

½ tsp (2.5 mL) dry mustard (optional)

2 ½ cups (625 mL) milk

2 cups (500 mL) grated old cheddar
  cheese, or half cheddar and half
  Monterey Jack

Bread Crumb Topping (optional)

2–3 slices sandwich bread, torn into
  pieces

1–2 Tbsp (15–30 mL) butter

¼ cup (60 mL) grated Parmesan
  (optional)

Mac and cheese that doesn't come out of a box is something everyone should be able to make. It doesn't require much more time or effort than KD, and is the ultimate in comfort food. Experiment by adding different cheeses—intensely flavored ones such as Gruyère or blue cheese are best. It's a great way to get rid of leftover cheese bits you might have lurking in the fridge.

Method

1 In a large pot of boiling salted water, cook the pasta until it's tender but not mushy. Drain well in a colander and set aside.

2 Preheat the oven to 350°F (175°C).

3 In the empty pot (no need to wash it out), melt the butter over medium heat. Add the flour and mustard and stir well with a whisk, cooking for a minute or so until the mixture starts to turn golden. Stir in the milk and bring the sauce to a boil, whisking constantly. The sauce must reach a full boil in order for the flour to reach its full thickening potential. Reduce the heat and simmer for a few minutes, until the mixture is nice and thick.

4 Remove the sauce from the heat and stir in the cheese until it melts. Add salt to taste, then stir in the drained pasta.

5 If you want a bread crumb topping, pulse the bread, butter, and Parmesan in a food processor until the bread turns to crumbs and the mixture is well blended. Pour the macaroni and cheese into an appropriately sized baking dish and top with the bread crumbs or additional cheese. (It can be made up to 24 hours ahead and refrigerated in the baking dish; sprinkle with the crumb mixture or cheese right before you bake it.) Bake for 15–20 minutes, until the topping is golden and it's bubbly around the edges.

Serves 4–6

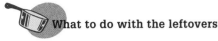

What to do with the leftovers

* Keep them covered in the fridge for up to 4 days or seal tightly with plastic wrap and freeze for up to 3 months. Reheat in the microwave.

Other things to do with it

* Stir in some chopped cooked ham or a can of drained stewed tomatoes before pouring the macaroni into the baking dish.

* Add up to a cup of grated Parmesan along with or instead of some of the grated cheddar.

* Garlic Chipotle Mac & Cheese: Stir 2–3 finely chopped chipotle chilies in adobo sauce into the cheese sauce, and pulse a crushed clove of garlic along with the bread crumbs.

* Mac & Cheese with Bacon, Mushrooms, and Onion: Cook 4 pieces of bacon until crisp; crumble them and set aside. Sauté a finely chopped onion and ½ lb (250 g) sliced mushrooms in the remaining bacon fat (omit the butter) for about 5 minutes, until the onion is tender. Add the flour and mustard and proceed with the recipe as directed, stirring in the reserved bacon before baking.

Stir-Fried Noodles
with Shrimp, Chicken, or Tofu

Pasta and Noodles

Ingredients

3 Tbsp (45 mL) soy sauce

1 tsp (5 mL) rice vinegar

1 clove garlic, crushed

½–1 lb (250–500 g) flat rice noodles or fresh thin Chinese noodles

1 tsp (5 mL) chili sauce

½ lb (250 g) medium or large uncooked shrimp, shelled and deveined, skinless, boneless chicken breasts or thighs, cut into small strips, or diced firm tofu

½ tsp (2.5 mL) white or brown sugar

1 Tbsp (15 mL) sesame, peanut or canola oil

1 small onion, cut in half and thinly sliced, or 3 green onions, sliced

1 tsp (5 mL) grated fresh ginger (or use bottled)

2 cups (500 mL) bean sprouts

½ cup (125 mL) chopped roasted peanuts or cashews, salted or unsalted

If you want to add veggies to this dish, stir-fry some fresh asparagus, chopped bok choy, sliced celery, sliced red or yellow bell peppers, or sugar snap peas in between cooking the noodles and meat. Add them to the bowl with the noodles. If you can't find Asian noodles, substitute cooked spaghetti or linguine, rinsed and drained well.

Method

1 Stir together 1 Tbsp (15 mL) of the soy sauce, the rice vinegar, and garlic and pour over the shrimp, chicken, or tofu. Toss to coat well and let it stand while you prepare the rest of the ingredients.

2 Soak or cook the noodles in water according to the package directions and drain them well. Stir together the remaining 2 Tbsp (30 mL) soy sauce, the chili sauce, and sugar in a small dish and set aside.

3 Heat a large non-stick skillet over medium-high heat until it's hot but not smoking. Add the oil and when it's hot, add the cooked noodles. Stir-fry the noodles, using tongs to lift and separate them, for 2–3 minutes. Transfer them to a bowl and set aside.

4 Add the shrimp, chicken, or tofu to the pan and cook just until the meat is cooked through or the tofu is starting to brown. If you used shrimp, remove them from the pan as soon as they're cooked so that they don't overcook and become tough. Add the onion and ginger and cook for another minute. Return the noodles to the skillet, add the bean sprouts, and pour the soy sauce mixture over the whole thing. Return the shrimp to the skillet if you're using them. Toss to heat the noodles through and coat everything with sauce.

5 Serve immediately in bowls, sprinkled with chopped peanuts.

Serves 4

What to do with the leftovers

* Keep them covered in the fridge for up to a day. Eat them cold or reheat in the microwave. Stir-fries don't freeze very well.

Other things to do with it

* Szechuan Pork Noodles: Use raw ground pork in place of the shrimp and substitute sherry for the vinegar in the marinade. Whisk 2 Tbsp (30 mL) oyster sauce, ¼ cup (60 mL) peanut butter or tahini (sesame seed paste), and 1 Tbsp (15 mL) rice vinegar into the soy sauce-chili mixture.

Peanut Noodles
with Chicken and Veggies

Ingredients

½ lb (250 g) steamed Chinese noodles or spaghetti

¼ cup (60 mL) chicken or vegetable stock

3 Tbsp (45 mL) peanut butter

3 Tbsp (45 mL) soy sauce

2 Tbsp (30 mL) brown sugar or honey

2 Tbsp (30 mL) rice vinegar

2 cloves garlic, crushed

1–2 tsp (5–10 mL) grated fresh ginger

½ tsp (2.5 mL) curry paste (optional)

2 cups (500 mL) chopped cooked chicken, pork, shrimp, or tofu

1 carrot, peeled and grated

1 red bell pepper, sliced

1–2 green onions, chopped

½ cup (125 mL) chopped peanuts (optional)

Fresh cilantro for sprinkling (optional)

Peanut noodles are best eaten cold, which makes leftovers perfect to keep in the fridge and take to work for lunch. You can add all sorts of fresh veggies to this dish. Peppers, zucchini, bok choy, bean sprouts, broccoli, asparagus, and pea pods are all good choices. Cut the recipe in half if you're only cooking for two, but if you want to make a full batch of peanut sauce it keeps well in the fridge and makes a perfect dip for the chicken satay on page 152.

Method

1 Cook the noodles according to the package directions. Rinse with cold water in a colander and drain well. Set aside.

2 In a small bowl, whisk together the chicken stock, peanut butter, soy sauce, brown sugar, vinegar, garlic, ginger, and curry paste (if using) until smooth. Or instead of whisking it, shake it all up in a jar.

3 In a large bowl, toss the noodles, chicken, carrot, pepper, green onions, and peanut sauce. Serve in bowls sprinkled with chopped peanuts and/or cilantro.

Serves 4–6

 What to do with the leftovers

* Keep them covered in the fridge for up to 2 days.

 Other things to do with it

* Mix and match any kind of meat and veggies you have in the fridge.

* Use coconut milk in place of the chicken stock.

Rice and grains

Fortunately, our fear of carbs is morphing into an understanding that they're an essential part of any diet—particularly complex carbs such as whole grains. Rice is the most commonly prepared grain in North American households, but couscous (not actually a grain but treated as such), quinoa, bulgur, barley, polenta, wheat, and oats are quickly gaining popularity as well. If you can cook a pot of rice you can cook other grains too, and they're worth experimenting with.

Because all grains are dried, they must be rehydrated before you eat them. Grains with an outer hull, such as brown rice, take longer to cook than those without, such as white rice. When in doubt, read the package directions, unless you bought them in bulk.

Rice Basics

There are essentially two kinds of rice: long-grain and short- (or medium-) grain. Short-grain rice is soft and sticky and absorbs more liquid, which makes it ideal for risotto and rice puddings, or when you want sticky rice you can easily pick up with chopsticks. Arborio is a widely available variety of short-grain rice. Long-grain rice is more common, and when cooked the grains are firmer and separate. Basmati, jasmine, and other aromatic varieties are long-grain.

Most rice is white, meaning the outer layer has been stripped and the grains polished. Some is parboiled or "converted," which means it has already been steamed so it doesn't take as long to cook. Instant rice is precooked and only needs to be reconstituted, but it also has the consistency of glue.

Brown rice, with its bran layer intact, is considerably more nutritious than white rice, containing more potassium, protein, vitamins, and fiber. It also takes twice as long to cook because of its outer hull, so plan ahead a little if you intend to make some.

Wild rice isn't really rice at all: it's the seed of wild grasses native to the Great Lakes region. It's very high in fiber, protein, and vitamin B.

Rice and grains

Basic Steamed Rice

Ingredients

3 cups (750 mL) water

1 ½ cups (375 mL) long-grain white
or brown rice or wild rice

½ tsp (2.5 mL) salt

There are three simple things to remember when you're making rice: 1) use 1 part rice to 2 parts water; 2) turn the heat down as low as it will go as soon as the water returns to a boil with the rice in it; and 3) put a tight-fitting lid (or plate) on top and don't peek until the time is up. To boost flavor, feel free to cook your rice in stock, vegetable juice, or even coconut milk instead of (or combined with) water.

Method

1 Bring the water to a boil in a medium pot set over medium-high heat. Add the rice and salt and wait until the water begins boiling again—adding the rice will bring the temperature down a little. Immediately turn the heat down to low and cover with a tight-fitting lid.

2 Set the timer for 20 minutes if you're making white rice, or 50 minutes if it's brown or wild. Don't peek! When the time is up, remove the pot from the heat and set it aside for 5 minutes. The water should be absorbed and there should be tunnels through the rice. Fluff it with a fork before serving.

Serves 4

 What to do with the leftovers

* Keep them in the fridge for up to 4 days, and reheat in the microwave or on the stovetop, adding a tablespoon of water for each cup of cooked rice.

* Leftover rice is perfect for making fried rice (see page 185), because the cold grains are separate and won't clump together when you stir-fry them.

* Stir leftovers into soup—adding precooked rice (instead of adding it raw) will ensure soup doesn't get too starchy.

* Turn them into rice pudding—add about ¾ cup (185 mL) milk and 2-3 Tbsp. (30-45 mL) sugar per cup of cooked rice and cook over medium heat until creamy, adding more milk if you need to. Flavor it with a few drops of vanilla or a shake of cinnamon, and stir in some raisins if you want them.

Basic Rice Pilaf

Ingredients

2 Tbsp (30 mL) butter or oil

1 onion, peeled and finely chopped

1 ½ cups (375 mL) long-grain rice

Salt and pepper

2 ½ cups (625 mL) chicken, beef, or veggie stock or water

In a pilaf, rice is briefly sautéed in butter or oil before cooking, which adds flavor and separates the grains. To infuse the rice with even more flavor, stir about a teaspoon (5 mL) of sturdy spices (such as cumin or curry) into the oil at the beginning as you sauté it, or add more fragile fresh herbs (such as basil, cilantro, parsley, mint, or chives), which don't take as well to long cooking times, at the end.

Method

1   Heat the butter or oil in a large skillet set over medium-high heat. Sauté the onion for about 5 minutes, until soft.

2   Add the rice and cook for a few minutes, stirring to coat the grains with the butter or oil. Season to taste with salt and pepper, add the stock, and turn the heat down to low. Cover and cook for 15 minutes, until the rice is tender and the liquid has been absorbed.

Serves 4

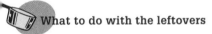 **What to do with the leftovers**

*   Keep them in the fridge for up to 4 days, and reheat in the microwave or on the stovetop, adding a tablespoon (15 mL) of water for each cup (250 mL) of cooked rice.

*   Stir leftovers into soup. Adding precooked rice (instead of adding it raw) will ensure soup doesn't get too starchy.

 **Other things to do with it**

*   Curried Basmati Rice with Fruit: Add a crushed clove of garlic and 1 Tbsp (15 mL) grated fresh ginger to the onion as you sauté it, and use basmati rice. Add a small chopped apple, ¼ cup (60 mL) chopped raisins or dried apricots, 1 tsp (5 mL) curry powder, and a cinnamon stick along with the rice and cook as directed. Sprinkle the finished rice with toasted sliced or slivered almonds.

    (To toast almonds, cook them in a single layer in a dry pan set over medium heat until they turn golden and fragrant. Watch them carefully and shake the pan often—nuts burn quickly!)

Baked Wild Rice Pilaf
with Pecans

Ingredients

1 Tbsp (15 mL) olive oil, or half oil and half butter

1 small onion, cut in half and thinly sliced

1 small red, orange, or yellow bell pepper, chopped

1 ¼ cups (310 mL) wild rice

2 ¼ cups (560 mL) chicken or veggie stock or water

¼ tsp (1 mL) thyme

Salt and pepper

½ cup (125 mL) chopped pecans, or sliced or slivered almonds, toasted

Baked rice is a snap to cook while you're roasting any kind of meat—you can pop it in alongside as it roasts. Leftovers keep well, and will turn a can of mushroom soup into a good lunch the next day.

Method

1 Preheat the oven to 375°F (190°C).

2 Heat the oil in a medium ovenproof pot set over medium heat. Sauté the onion and pepper for a few minutes, until softened, and transfer to a bowl.

3 Add the rice to the pan and cook it, stirring constantly, for about a minute. Add the broth, thyme, and salt and pepper to taste and bring it to a simmer. If you aren't using an ovenproof pot, transfer the whole thing to a baking dish.

4 Cover the pot or dish of rice and put it into the oven. Bake for 40 minutes, then stir in the onion mixture and bake for another 30 minutes, until the rice is tender and the liquid has been absorbed. Stir in the pecans and serve.

Serves 6

 What to do with the leftovers

* Keep them in the fridge for up to 4 days, and reheat in the microwave or in a hot skillet set over medium heat.

* Stir them into a can of cream of mushroom, chicken, or asparagus soup.

 Other things to do with it

* Bulgur Pilaf: Use 1 ½ cups (375 mL) bulgur and 2 cups (500 mL) chicken stock. Instead of baking it, cook the mixture over low heat on the stovetop, covered, for 12 minutes or until the liquid is absorbed. Remove the pan from the heat and let it stand, covered, for 5 minutes.

Fried Rice

Ingredients

1–2 Tbsp (15–30 mL) sesame, peanut, or canola oil

2–3 eggs, lightly beaten

3 green onions, chopped

1–2 cloves garlic, crushed

1 tsp (5 mL) grated fresh ginger

2–4 cups (500 mL–1 L) cooked cold rice, white or brown

2–3 Tbsp (30–45 mL) soy sauce

½ cup (125 mL) shredded cooked chicken, chopped cooked pork, diced tofu, and/or 1 cup (250 mL) cooked shrimp

½ cup (125 mL) frozen peas, thawed

Salt and pepper

Fried rice is the best reason I can think of to have leftovers. Whenever I make a pot of rice, I make sure there's a surplus so that I can make fried rice later on. Cold leftover rice works better than fresh rice because the grains become separate, making it easier to stir-fry without ending up in clumps.

The quantities here are approximate; scale it up or down according to how many you're cooking for, and adjust proportions to suit your taste.

Method

1 Heat about half of the oil in a large skillet set over medium-high heat. Add the eggs and scramble them until they're cooked through. Remove them from the pan and set aside.

2 Heat the remaining oil and add the onions, garlic, and ginger, and sauté for about 30 seconds. Add the rice and stir-fry for 2–3 minutes. Add the soy sauce, meat, tofu or seafood, peas, cooked eggs, and salt and pepper to taste. Cook for another minute, stirring well to mix it all up and heat everything through. Serve right away, while it's still hot.

Serves 2–4

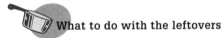 **What to do with the leftovers**

* Keep them covered in the fridge for up to 2 days. Reheat leftovers in the microwave or by stir-frying in a skillet with a little oil.

Other things to do with it

* Bacon Fried Rice: Omit the garlic, ginger, chicken, and peas. Chop 3 slices of bacon and cook until crisp. Add 1 chopped carrot and 1 chopped celery stalk and sauté for a few minutes, and then add the onions, rice, eggs, and half a small can of drained water chestnuts.

* Mushroom Fried Rice: Sauté ½–1 cup (125–250 mL) chopped fresh mushrooms in a drizzle of oil until they start to turn brown and most of the liquid has evaporated. Remove them from the pan and proceed with the recipe as directed, adding the mushrooms in place of the meat.

* Jambalaya Fried Rice: Omit the eggs, ginger, and soy sauce. Sauté a chopped onion and red bell pepper in the oil with the garlic and ½ tsp (2.5 mL) each chili powder and cumin until the onion softens. Add 1 or 2 chorizo or Italian sausages, squeezed out of their casings, and cook, crumbling them up until they're no longer pink. Add the rice and cook until the grains begin to turn golden, then add the chicken, (shrimp, too, if you have some), peas, and salt and pepper and stir to heat through.

Basic Lemon-Parmesan Risotto

Ingredients

6 cups (1.5 L) chicken stock

2–4 Tbsp (30–60 mL) butter, or half butter and half olive oil

1 onion or 2 shallots, finely chopped

2 cups (500 mL) arborio rice

½ cup (125 mL) dry white wine

½–1 cup (125–250 mL) grated Parmesan

2 Tbsp (30 mL) lemon juice

2 Tbsp (30 mL) chopped fresh parsley (optional)

Salt and pepper

Risotto may sound like a very chi-chi dish that only those who consider themselves knowledgeable cooks would dream of attempting. In truth, this creamy Italian rice dish (made by stirring hot stock into rice that has been sautéed in butter, creating a creamy consistency as it cooks) really doesn't require any skill beyond stirring. Just remember to use arborio or other short-grained rice, which is stickier and absorbs more liquid, and to stir it often.

Method

1 Bring the stock to a simmer in a pot set over medium heat. Reduce the heat to low and cover it—you just need to keep it warm.

2 Heat half the butter or oil in a heavy pot set over medium heat. Add the onion and sauté for about 7 minutes, until it's very soft and translucent. Add the rice and cook for about 3 minutes, until the edges of the rice begin to turn translucent.

3 Add the wine and cook it for a minute, until it has been absorbed. Add half of the warmed stock and simmer until it has been absorbed, stirring every few minutes. Add the rest of the stock half a cup (125 mL) at a time, stirring for a few minutes after each addition, until the liquid is absorbed. Keep adding stock, cooking and stirring until the rice is creamy and tender, about 30 minutes. Stir in the Parmesan, lemon juice, and parsley and season to taste with salt and pepper. Serve immediately.

Serves 4–6

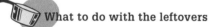 **What to do with the leftovers**

* Keep them covered in the fridge for up to 4 days. Reheat in the microwave.

* Make risotto cakes by forming chilled risotto into small (½-inch thick) patties. Dredge them first in a beaten egg, then in fresh bread crumbs or panko (Japanese bread crumbs) to coat, and sauté them in olive or canola oil over medium-high heat until they're golden on both sides.

 **Other things to do with it**

* Italian Sausage Risotto: Cook a spicy Italian sausage along with the onion, crumbling it and cooking until it's no longer pink.

* Asparagus Risotto: Snap the tough ends off ½–1 lb (250–500 g) asparagus stalks and cut them on a slight diagonal into ½–inch pieces. Add the asparagus to the risotto toward the end, along with the last addition of broth, so that it cooks without getting mushy.

Couscous

Ingredients

1 cup (250 mL) water or chicken or
vegetable stock

1 tsp (5 mL) olive or canola oil

Pinch salt

¾ cup (175 mL) couscous (regular or
whole wheat)

Couscous isn't actually a grain but a semolina product made with tiny particles of durum wheat, which makes it a type of pasta. Like pasta, it comes in whole wheat varieties, which take slightly longer to absorb the liquid than regular couscous. Unlike pasta, it also comes in "quick-cooking" varieties, which isn't really necessary because traditional couscous already cooks very quickly. Like rice, you can cook couscous in stock or juice instead of water, and add any number of ingredients—chopped nuts, fresh herbs, cheese, or cooked vegetables or meat. Or make sweet couscous by adding a little sugar to the water along with a pinch of cinnamon, grated orange or lemon zest, or chopped dried fruit.

What to do with the leftovers

* Keep them covered in the fridge for up to 5 days. Reheat them in the microwave or turn them into a cold salad.

Method

1 Bring the water, oil, and salt to a boil in a medium pot. Add the couscous, remove the pot from the heat, and cover it with a tight-fitting lid or plate. Let it stand for 10 minutes, or until all the liquid is absorbed. Fluff with a fork before serving.

Makes about 2 cups

Other things to do with it

* Couscous with Beets and Goat Cheese: Chop 2 peeled roasted beets (see page 201) and stir them into the finished couscous with about 4 oz (120 g) crumbled goat cheese.

* Couscous with Veggies: Toss couscous with leftover roasted vegetables (see page 217), or sauté 1 small chopped onion, ½ small chopped zucchini, ½ cup (125 mL) corn kernels, and ½ chopped red bell pepper in a drizzle of olive or canola oil for 3–5 minutes, until tender. Season with salt and pepper and stir into the finished couscous. This is delicious with some crumbled feta cheese stirred in as well.

* Couscous Salad: Prepare couscous with chicken broth instead of water. Toss cooled couscous with 2 cups (500 mL) halved cherry tomatoes, 2 cups (500 mL) chopped fresh spinach, 1 14 oz (398 mL) can lentils, rinsed and drained, and ½ cup (125 mL) crumbled feta cheese. Drizzle with a vinaigrette made with balsamic or red wine vinegar and a finely crushed clove of garlic (see page 86).

* Sweet Breakfast Couscous: Cook 1 cup (250 mL) couscous with 1 cup (250 mL) water and ½ cup (125 mL) orange juice according to the directions above. Fluff it with a fork and stir in ½ cup (125 mL) chopped toasted nuts (such as walnuts, almonds, hazelnuts, pecans, or pistachios) and ½ cup (125 mL) chopped dried fruit (such as dates, raisins, cranberries, or apricots). Serve like you would oatmeal, with milk and brown sugar.

Rice and grains

Polenta

Ingredients

4 cups (1 L) water or milk

1 tsp (5 mL) salt

1 cup (250 mL) yellow cornmeal

If you let polenta stand longer than about half an hour, it will solidify—if you like it this way, pour it into a loaf pan and put it in the fridge. The next day you can cut it into slices and fry the slices in a little butter or oil, grill or roast them in the oven. Use milk for creamier polenta.

Method

1 Bring the water and salt to a boil in a pot set over medium heat. Pour in the polenta in a thin stream, whisking constantly.

2 Cook for 2 minutes, whisking constantly. Cover the polenta; reduce the heat to low and simmer, stirring for about a minute every 10 minutes, for 45 minutes.

3 Remove from the heat and serve warm.

Serves 4

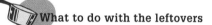

What to do with the leftovers

* Keep them covered in the fridge for up to 4 days. Cut into slices and sauté in a little oil in a hot pan until golden and heated through.

Other things to do with it

* Use chicken or vegetable stock (see pages 68–69) instead of water.

* Parmesan Polenta: Stir ½ cup (125 mL) grated Parmesan into the polenta during the last 5 minutes of cooking. To make it even fancier, stir in about 5 oz (150 g) Brie (rind removed), cut into pieces, a sautéed onion, a handful of sautéed mushrooms, and/or a few cloves of roasted garlic as well.

* Polenta "Fries": Increase the amount of cornmeal to 2 cups (500 mL). Stir ½ cup (125 mL) grated Parmesan or 1 cup (250 mL) grated mozzarella, smoked Gouda or old cheddar into the polenta as soon as it's finished cooking, and pour it into a 9- × 13-inch pan that has been sprayed with non-stick spray. Spread it evenly and refrigerate for an hour, or up to a day. Cut the polenta into 1-inch (2.5 cm) strips. You can cook them one of two ways: brush them with oil on a baking sheet and broil them for 5–7 minutes, turning once, until golden, or dredge the "fries" in flour and cook them in about ½ cup (125 mL) canola oil in a heavy skillet set over medium-high heat until they're golden on all sides.

Quinoa

Ingredients

1 cup (250 mL) quinoa

½ tsp (2.5 mL) salt

Quinoa (pronounced KEEN-wah) is a nutty grain that's gaining popularity because of its high protein content. It contains 20% protein, more than any other grain. Quinoa is coated in saponin, a naturally occurring substance that acts as a pesticide and tastes bitter if you don't wash the grains thoroughly before you cook them. Quinoa is as easy to cook as rice or couscous, and can be used much as you'd use either one. Like rice, you can cook quinoa in stock, vegetable juice, or even coconut milk instead of (or combined with) the water.

Method

1 Wash the quinoa in 3 changes of cold water, rubbing the grains and letting them settle again before pouring off the water, until the water runs clear. Drain the grains in a large fine sieve.

2 Put the quinoa in a medium saucepan. If you like, toast it for five minutes over medium-high heat to give it a nutty flavor. Add 2 cups (500 mL) of water and bring it to a boil. Reduce the heat to a simmer, cover, and cook for about 15 minutes, until the liquid is absorbed, the grains are translucent, and the germ has spiraled out from each grain. Fluff with a fork before serving.

Serves 4

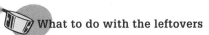

What to do with the leftovers

* Keep them covered in the fridge for up to 4 days. Reheat in the microwave.

* Stir leftover quinoa into your bowl of oatmeal to boost protein.

Other things to do with it

* Stir chopped fresh herbs or toasted chopped nuts into the quinoa.

* Use cooled quinoa as a base for a salad, as you would use rice.

* Quinoa Pilaf: Sauté a small chopped onion and a clove of garlic in a drizzle of olive or canola oil until starting to soften. Add the washed quinoa and cook for a few minutes, until the grains are separate and golden. Stir in 2 cups (500 mL) of water or chicken or vegetable stock, bring to a boil, cover and simmer for 15 minutes, or until the liquid is absorbed. Fluff with a fork.

* Steamed Quinoa: Cook the quinoa in a large saucepan of boiling salted water for 10 minutes, as if you were cooking pasta. Drain the quinoa in the sieve and rinse under cold water. Bring an inch or two of water to boil in the same saucepan, and set the sieve of quinoa over it, making sure the grains don't touch the water. Cover the pot with a tea towel and lid and steam the quinoa for 10–12 more minutes, until fluffy and dry.

Beans
(legumes)

You may have heard on TV, read in books or magazines, or (as in my case) been repeatedly reminded by your parents that beans are good for you. It's true—they're quite possibly the world's most perfect food. Legumes are nutritionally outstanding—they're high in protein, fiber, vitamins and minerals, low in fat and calories, and you don't have to be rich to buy them.

People who say it's too expensive to eat healthily have never cooked with beans. Canned or dried they keep indefinitely on the shelf, and get along well with other ingredients. Glamorous they aren't, but sometimes nutrition and convenience take precedence over aesthetics.

Beans typically come canned or dried, and either is fine. The benefits of dried beans are that they're cheaper, have a virtually infinite shelf life, are a little firmer and more toothsome than the canned variety, and contain no sodium. But they do require some planning—dried beans require soaking, usually for several hours or overnight, before they're cooked. To soak beans, cover them with enough cold water to come about 2 inches (5 cm) above them and let them sit on the countertop for about 6 hours. This may seem like a long time, but they can soak overnight or while you're at work during the day.

If you haven't planned that far ahead, you can speed up the soaking process. Bring the beans and water to a boil, cook them for 2 minutes, then remove the pot from the heat and let them stand for an hour. Whichever way you soak them, beans still need to be simmered for about 20 minutes to tenderize them afterward. The great thing about this last step is that you can add garlic or other seasonings to the water if you like, or simmer the beans in broth instead to add flavor.

Beans (legumes)

Chili

Ingredients

2 Tbsp (30 mL) canola or olive oil

1 large onion, peeled and chopped

1 red bell pepper, seeded and
    chopped (optional)

1 carrot, peeled and diced (optional)

2 cloves garlic, crushed

1 ½ lb (750 g) boneless beef chuck,
    coarsely ground in a food proces-
    sor, or 1 ½ lb (750 g) lean ground
    beef

2 Tbsp (30 mL) chili powder

1 Tbsp (15 mL) paprika

1–2 tsp (5–10 mL) cumin

1 tsp (5 mL) oregano (optional)

1 tsp (5 mL) dried red pepper flakes,
    or to taste

1 19-oz (540-mL) can diced tomatoes,
    undrained

1 19-oz (540-mL) can kidney beans,
    rinsed and drained

1 14-oz (398-mL) can brown beans,
    with pork or in tomato sauce
    (optional)

1 can (10 oz/284 mL) beef broth

½ cup (125 mL) salsa

Salt and pepper

Because it tastes even better the next day, chili is perfect to make ahead if you're having people over, or if you like to have lunches and dinners waiting in the fridge or freezer. It's also an easy way to serve a crowd since you don't have to worry about timing different elements of a meal. Serve it with the cornbread on page 247.

If you want to cut back on fat, use a combination of half beef and half ground chicken or turkey. But remember that supermarkets tend not to trim the fat from the poultry they grind so it's best to buy skinless, boneless chicken breasts or thighs and grind them yourself in your food processor.

Method

1 Heat the oil in a large pot or Dutch oven set over medium heat. Sauté the onion for a few minutes, until it softens. Add the red bell pepper, carrot, and garlic and cook for another minute. Add the beef and cook it, stirring and breaking up any lumps, until it's no longer pink.

2 Add the chili powder, paprika, cumin, oregano, and red pepper flakes and cook for another minute. Add the tomatoes, beans, beef broth, and salsa and bring the mixture to a simmer. Turn the heat down to low and simmer the chili for about an hour. Keep it covered if it's thick enough for your taste; if it seems thin, leave the lid off so that the excess liquid can evaporate.

3 Serve your chili hot, topped with sour cream and grated cheese, or cool it down and refrigerate it for a day or two.

Serves 6 (Doubles easily)

Beans
(legumes)

 **What to do with the leftovers**

*   Keep them covered in the fridge for up to 4 days, or freeze them in plastic containers or freezer bags for up to 4 months. Reheat in the microwave or on the stovetop, adding a little extra liquid if necessary.

*   Serve reheated chili over a split baked potato (see page 220), topped with grated cheese.

 **Other things to do with it**

*   Vegetarian Chili: Omit the beef and add a 14 oz (398 mL) can of chickpeas (garbanzo beans) and a 19 oz (540 mL) can of black beans, navy beans, or white kidney beans, both drained.

*   Chili Pie with Cornbread Crust: Pour the cooked chili into a casserole dish and gently spread a batch of cornbread batter (see page 247) over top. Bake at 350°F (175°C) for 30–45 minutes, or until the cornbread is golden and cooked through.

Baked Beans

Ingredients

2 slices bacon, chopped (optional)

1 onion, chopped

¾ cup (185 mL) ketchup, barbecue sauce, or tomato sauce mixed with ¼ cup (60 mL) packed brown sugar

½ cup (125 mL) water

2 Tbsp (30 mL) cider vinegar

2 Tbsp (30 mL) molasses

2 Tbsp (30 mL) Dijon, yellow, or grainy mustard or 2 tsp (10 mL) dry mustard

1 19 oz (540 mL) can red kidney beans, rinsed and drained

1 19 oz (540 mL) can Great Northern, navy, white kidney or cannellini beans, rinsed and drained

Salt and pepper

A few shakes of Tabasco sauce (optional)

True baked beans start out with dried beans, soaked and then slow simmered in the oven or on the stovetop in a sweet, savory sauce. This recipe calls for canned beans, but you can replace them with ¾–1 cup (185–250 mL) of each kind of dried beans, soaked (see page 191) and then simmered for 20 minutes before you add them to the recipe. (Use more if you like drier beans; less if you like them saucy.) Dried beans are a little firmer than canned beans. If you're lucky enough to have a slow cooker, you can let them simmer all day long while you work or play or sleep.

Method

1 Preheat the oven to 350°F (190°C).

2 In a medium ovenproof pot, sauté the bacon over medium heat until crisp. Remove it from the pot, crumble, and set it aside. If you're not using bacon, heat a drizzle of canola or olive oil in the pan and sauté the onion in the oil or bacon drippings for about 5 minutes, until tender and beginning to turn golden.

3 Add the ketchup, water, vinegar, molasses, mustard, beans, and salt and pepper to taste and bring the mixture to a simmer. Put the pot in the oven for an hour, stirring once or twice, until it's thickened and bubbly. (If you aren't using an ovenproof pot, transfer the mixture to a baking dish.) Stir the bacon back into the beans after about 45 minutes. Add a few shots of Tabasco sauce if you like, and serve the beans hot.

Serves 4–6

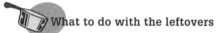 What to do with the leftovers

* Keep them covered in the fridge for up to a week, and reheat in the microwave or on the stovetop. Baked beans don't freeze very well.

* Stir in some chopped leftover roasted pork, warm it up in the microwave or on the stovetop, and serve over a split baked potato (see page 220).

 Other things to do with it

* Add 1–2 canned chipotle peppers, finely chopped, along with the beans.

* Use ¾ cup (185 mL) dark beer instead of the water.

* Add leftover diced roast pork or ham to the pot instead of the bacon.

Red Beans and Rice

Ingredients

Olive or canola oil

1 lb (500 g) andouille or other smoked
    sausage or ham, cut into ½-inch
    (1-cm) thick slices (optional)

1 onion, peeled and chopped

4 cloves garlic, crushed

2 19 oz (540 mL) cans red kidney
    beans, undrained

1 14 oz (398 mL) can of diced or
    stewed tomatoes or 1 cup
    (250 mL) chicken or veggie stock,
    tomato juice or water

2 bay leaves

1 Tbsp (15 mL) thyme

2 tsp (10 mL) oregano

1 tsp (5 mL) salt

½–1 tsp (2.5–5 mL) pepper

½ tsp (2.5 mL) garlic powder

¼ tsp (1 mL) allspice

¼ tsp (1 mL) ground cloves

1 tsp (5 mL) Tabasco sauce

2–3 cups (500–750 mL) steamed rice
    (see page 182)

Beans and rice are one of the earliest known culinary combinations, one that is found in cuisines all over the world. The reason it's so popular is because the combination of beans and rice creates one of the healthiest and most inexpensive sources of a complete protein. Adding flavorful kielbasa or other smoked sausage adds flavor, but you can leave it out entirely to make it vegetarian. Cut the recipe in half if you only need to feed two.

Method

1   Heat the oil in a large pot or Dutch oven set over medium heat. Add the sausage, onion, and garlic and sauté for about 10 minutes, until the onion starts to turn golden. Add the beans, water, herbs and spices and simmer for 30–45 minutes, until the mixture is thick. (Add a little extra water if it's too thick.) Scoop out the bay leaves and serve the hot beans over rice.

Serves 4–6 (halves easily)

 What to do with the leftovers

* Keep them covered in the fridge for up to 4 days and reheat them in the microwave or on the stovetop, adding a little extra liquid if necessary. Make some fresh rice to serve them with.

 Other things to do with it

* Use 1 tsp (5 mL) Cajun seasoning in place of the other herbs and spices.

Beans
(legumes)

Mushroom Lentil Burgers

Ingredients

¾ cup (185 mL) chopped pecans or walnuts

1 Tbsp (15 mL) olive or canola oil

3 cups (750 mL) sliced mushrooms

1 onion, peeled and chopped

2 cloves garlic, crushed

1 19 oz (540 mL) can lentils, rinsed and drained

1 tsp (5 mL) Worcestershire sauce

½ tsp (2.5 mL) thyme

Salt and pepper

½ cup (125 mL) fresh bread crumbs

¼ cup (60 mL) chopped fresh parsley (optional)

These are veggie burgers for meat lovers. They're burly and substantial, thanks to the lentils, pecans, and mushrooms, which also deliver protein, vitamins, minerals, and only the heart-healthy kinds of fat. If you want to score extra nutritional points, serve these on soft grainy buns with greens, sliced tomato, sprouts, and light mayo.

Method

1 In a large dry skillet, toast the nuts over medium heat for 5–7 minutes, until golden and fragrant. Set them aside. Add the oil to the skillet and sauté the mushrooms and onion for about 5 minutes, until soft. Add the garlic and cook for a few more minutes, until all the moisture has evaporated.

2 Put the mushrooms and onion in the bowl of a food processor along with the lentils, Worcestershire, thyme, and salt and pepper to taste. Pulse until the mixture is well blended. Transfer it to a bowl and stir in the bread crumbs and parsley (if using).

3 Shape the mixture into patties and fry them in a little oil in the same skillet set over medium heat. Cook until they're golden and crusty on both sides, flipping them as you need to.

4 Serve the burgers on buns with lettuce, tomato, sprouts, and mayo, or whatever condiments you like.

Makes 4 burgers

What to do with the leftovers

* Keep leftover cooked patties covered in the fridge for up to 4 days. Reheat them in the microwave or in a little oil in a skillet. Freeze uncooked burgers with squares of waxed paper between the patties to make them easier to pull apart, and let them thaw on the countertop before you cook them.

Other things to do with it

* Wilt a handful or two of chopped fresh spinach along with the mushrooms and onions, cooking until all the moisture has evaporated.

* Use black beans instead of the lentils, or add a raw grated carrot or beet to the mixture.

White Beans with Tomatoes,
Spinach, and Pancetta

Ingredients

2 oz (50 g) thinly sliced pancetta, chopped, or 2 slices bacon

1 onion, peeled and chopped

2 carrots, peeled and chopped

2 stalks celery, chopped

3 cloves garlic, crushed

1 19 oz (540 mL) can white kidney or navy beans, rinsed and drained

1 14 oz (398 mL) can diced or stewed tomatoes

½ cup (125 mL) chicken or vegetable stock or water

Handful of chopped or torn fresh spinach, chard, or kale

Salt and pepper

How many dishes do you make that contain six different kinds of veggies? This recipe will help fulfill your daily quota. And it's got protein, too. Pancetta is a fancy kind of Italian bacon that is cured with salt and spices, but use regular bacon if that's what you have.

Method

1 In a medium pot set over medium-high heat, sauté the bacon, onion, carrots, celery, and garlic for about 10 minutes, until the carrots are tender.

2 Add the beans, tomatoes with their juices, and chicken stock. Bring the mixture to a simmer and cook for about 10 more minutes. Add the spinach, chard, or kale and cook until it wilts. Season with salt and pepper to taste and serve it while it's hot.

Serves 4

 What to do with the leftovers

*   Keep them covered in the fridge for up to a week, and reheat on the stovetop or in the microwave.

 Other things to do with it

*   Black Beans with Tomatoes, Garlic, and Cumin: Add 1 tsp (5 mL) cumin and ½ tsp (2.5 mL) chili powder to the vegetables as you cook them. Use black beans instead of kidney beans and omit the stock and spinach; cook until the mixture is thick. If you like, stir in some chopped fresh cilantro after you take it off the heat, and serve with a dollop of sour cream.

*   Cook a hot Italian sausage, squeezed out of its casing and crumbled, instead of the pancetta.

*   Add extra stock to turn it into soup.

Beans (legumes)

Bean Salad

Ingredients

1 14 oz (398 mL) can cut green beans, drained

1 14 oz (398 mL) can cut yellow wax beans, drained

1 14 oz (398 mL) can kidney beans, rinsed and drained

1 19 oz (540 mL) can chickpeas (garbanzo beans), rinsed and drained

1 red, yellow, or green bell pepper, seeded and chopped

2 stalks celery, chopped

1 small purple onion, finely chopped

A small handful of fresh parsley, chopped

½ cup (125 mL) red wine vinegar or white vinegar

⅓ cup (80 mL) sugar

¼ cup (60 mL) canola oil

1 clove garlic, crushed (optional)

Salt and pepper

The great thing about bean salad, besides the fact that it's incredibly good for you, is that it keeps in the fridge for ages and its flavor actually improves over time as the vinaigrette marinates the beans. Because you need a wide variety of beans, this recipe makes a large batch, but large batches are great if you like having something prepared in the fridge to dip into all week, or if you've been asked to bring something to a party. If you want to use fresh green and yellow beans, trim off the ends and boil them for about 5 minutes, until they're tender-crisp, then plunge them into cold water to stop them from cooking, and drain them well.

Method

1 Combine all the beans, vegetables, and parsley in a large bowl.

2 In a small pot, combine the vinegar, sugar, oil, garlic, and salt and pepper to taste. Set it over medium heat and bring the mixture to a simmer. Cook for a few minutes, until the sugar dissolves completely. Set the vinaigrette aside to cool for a few minutes before pouring it over the salad. Toss gently to coat all the beans well.

3 Cover and refrigerate overnight to allow the beans to marinate, and serve the salad cold.

Serves 8–10

 What to do with the leftovers

* This recipe is made for leftovers—they keep well in a covered container in the fridge for at least a week. Bean salad doesn't freeze well.

Other things to do with it

* Add a 14 oz (398 mL) can of black beans and/or drained corn, or substitute them for the chickpeas.

* Marinated Lentil Salad: Use two 19-oz (540-mL) cans of lentils instead of the beans, and omit the red pepper and celery. To make the vinaigrette, use balsamic vinegar and olive oil, and 2 tsp (10 mL) Dijon or grainy mustard instead of the sugar. If you like, add ½ cup (125 mL) crumbled feta and a pint (500 mL) of grape tomatoes.

Beans (legumes)

Vegetables

Even when your mom isn't cooking for you, you really should eat your veggies. They provide fiber, vitamins, and minerals you need even after you've grown up. And they can be much tastier than the frozen mixed veg you may have grown up with. Shop for vegetables in season, at a farmer's market if there's one close by, for the absolute best quality, most flavorful produce you can get. Then you're halfway there. Good produce requires very little in the way of preparation to make it taste wonderful.

Roasted Asparagus

Ingredients

Asparagus (1 lb/500 g will feed 4)

Olive oil

Salt and pepper

Freshly grated Parmesan (optional)

Asparagus isn't to be missed in the springtime when the small, pencil-thin stalks hit the produce stands. They can be steamed in a little water until tender, or if you want to grill them, wrap them in foil, making a little packet, and drizzle them with oil and season with salt and pepper. Throw them on the grill until they're fork-tender.

Method

1 Preheat the oven to 450°F (230°C).

2 To prepare asparagus, you'll need to snap about an inch (2.5 cm) off the ends. If you bend them they'll break naturally wherever the tender part ends and woody part begins.

3 Place the stalks in a shallow baking pan or on a rimmed baking sheet. Drizzle them with olive oil to coat, sprinkle with and salt and pepper to taste, and toss with your fingers to coat them well. Roast for 8–10 minutes, depending on their thickness, until they're tender and golden. Shake the pan occasionally to make sure they brown evenly.

4 Remove the asparagus from the oven and immediately sprinkle them with Parmesan. Shake them around on the pan so that the cheese melts a little and distributes evenly over the asparagus.

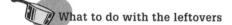

What to do with the leftovers

* Keep them covered in the fridge for up to 3 days; reheat them in the microwave.

Other things to do with it

* Asparagus with Balsamic Glaze: Simmer ½ cup (125 mL) balsamic vinegar in a small pot set over medium heat for 15–20 minutes, until it's reduced by half.Drizzle the cooked asparagus with the reduced vinegar and another drizzle of olive oil, along with the Parmesan.

* Asparagus with Lemon-Anchovy Sauce: Stir 1 Tbsp (15 mL) lemon juice, 2–3 tsp (10–15 mL) anchovy paste (or 2 chopped fillets), and 2 Tbsp (30 mL) capers into the olive oil and pour it over the asparagus, coating them well, before you roast them.

* Asparagus with Sesame-Ginger Vinaigrette: Whisk together 2 Tbsp (30 mL) sesame oil, 2 Tbsp (30 mL) soy sauce, 2 Tbsp (30 mL) lime juice, 1 Tbsp (15 mL) honey, 1 chopped green onion, 1 tsp (5 mL) grated fresh ginger, and 1 crushed clove of garlic and drizzle over the roasted asparagus. Omit the Parmesan.

* Roasted Asparagus with Bacon: Chop 2–3 slices of bacon and cook them until they're crisp. Remove the bacon from the pan and drizzle some of the bacon drippings over the asparagus instead of using the oil. Roast as directed. Squeeze some lemon juice over the roasted asparagus and sprinkle them with the crispy bacon and Parmesan or about 2 oz (50 g) crumbled goat cheese.

Roasted Beets

Ingredients

Beets, it doesn't matter how many

Roasting is the best method for cooking beets—because they're wrapped in foil you won't stain anything pink, and you can store cooked beets in the foil in the fridge for a few days until you need them.

What to do with the leftovers

* Keep them wrapped in foil in the fridge for up to 5 days. Reheat them in the microwave or slice them and sauté in butter (see below) or use them in a recipe.

* Slice them and add to a green salad with goat cheese and toasted walnuts.

Method

1 Preheat oven to 400°F (200°C).

2 Scrub the beets and trim the greens off their tops, if they have them. Wrap the beets individually (or a few at a time, if they're small) in foil and put them directly on the oven rack for 45 minutes to 1 ½ hours (depending on their size), until they're tender when pierced with a knife.

3 Peel and slice the roasted beets or cut them into wedges and serve them right away with butter, vinaigrette, or a squeeze of lemon juice. Refrigerate leftover roasted beets in their foil until you need them.

Other things to do with it

* Buttered Beets: Slice the roasted beets or cut them into chunks. Heat as much butter or oil as you like in a large skillet or pot and sauté the beets for 5 minutes, stirring to coat them well. Season with salt and pepper.

* Orange Beets: Cut 4 roasted beets into wedges or slices. Put them in a medium pot with 1 cup (250 mL) orange juice, 2 Tbsp (30 mL) butter, 2 Tbsp (30 mL) sugar, 2 tsp (10 mL) red wine vinegar, and the grated zest of an orange. Simmer the mixture for about 10 minutes, until the sauce thickens and turns syrupy. Season them with salt and pepper to taste.

* Beets with Caramelized Onions and Feta Cheese: As the beets roast, cook 2 thinly sliced onions in 1 Tbsp (15 mL) oil in a large skillet for about 20 minutes, until golden. Cut the roasted beets into chunks and toss them with the onions and about ½ cup (125 mL) crumbled feta cheese. Whisk together ¼ cup (60 mL) olive oil, 2 Tbsp (30 mL) red wine or cider vinegar, 1 tsp (5 mL) Dijon or grainy mustard, and salt and pepper, and pour the vinaigrette over the warm beets.

Steamed Broccoli
with Olive Oil and Parmesan

Ingredients

1 large bunch broccoli (about
1 ½ lb/750 g)

2 Tbsp (30 mL) olive oil or butter

¼–½ cup (60–125 mL) grated
Parmesan (optional)

Salt and pepper

There's an undeserved stigma to broccoli—it doesn't have to lie limply on the side of your plate. Try it steamed and tossed in salads, noodle bowls, and stir-frys, or steam it and smother it with olive oil and Parmesan.

Method

1   Trim the ends of the broccoli stalks and cut the stems lengthwise into sticks. Separate the head into florets that are roughly the same size, so that they cook evenly.

2   Put a steamer basket into a medium pot and add about an inch of water, keeping it below the basket. Cover the pot and bring the water to a boil over high heat. Add the broccoli to the steamer basket, cover and steam for 4–5 minutes, just until tender. (If you don't have a steamer basket, put the broccoli directly into the boiling water.)

3   Transfer the broccoli to a bowl and toss it with olive oil, Parmesan, and salt and pepper while it's hot.

Serves 4

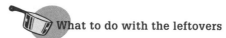 **What to do with the leftovers**

*   Keep them covered in the fridge for up to 3 days. Reheat them in the microwave or add them to a salad cold.

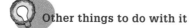 **Other things to do with it**

*   Broccoli with Balsamic Vinaigrette: Omit the Parmesan. Mix the olive oil with 2 Tbsp (30 mL) balsamic vinegar, a crushed clove of garlic, and salt and pepper. Toss the warm broccoli with the vinaigrette.

Vegetables

Roasted Brussels Sprouts
with Bacon

Ingredients

1–1 ½ lb (500–750 g) Brussels sprouts (2–3 cups)

2 slices bacon or pancetta, finely chopped

1 clove garlic, crushed

1–2 tsp (5–10 mL) olive oil

¼ cup (60 mL) chicken or vegetable stock or water

This will tempt even Brussels sprouts haters to have a taste.

Method

1 Preheat oven to 450°F (230°C).

2 Trim the ends off the Brussels sprouts and cut them in half lengthwise. Place them in a baking dish and toss them with the bacon, garlic, and oil.

3 Roast them for 20–30 minutes, until the sprouts are golden and tender. Stir in the stock or water, scraping up any browned bits that have stuck to the bottom of the pan. Serve immediately.

Serves 4

 **What to do with the leftovers**

* Keep them covered in the fridge for up to 3 days. Reheat them in the microwave or in a little butter or oil in a skillet, or add them to a salad cold.

 Other things to do with it

* Cook the Brussels sprouts in a large pot of boiling water for 4–5 minutes, then plunge into cold water to stop them from cooking. Cut in half and sauté in a skillet with the bacon, garlic, and oil until the bacon is crispy and the sprouts are golden. Pour the stock overtop, scraping up any browned bits in the pan, and cook until the moisture has evaporated.

Braised Cabbage with Apples

Ingredients

2 Tbsp (30 mL) butter or canola oil

1 smallish purple cabbage, halved and then thinly sliced

2 apples, peeled, cored, and sliced

¼ cup (60 mL) chicken or vegetable stock, apple cider, white wine, or water

¼ cup (60 mL) red wine vinegar

2 Tbsp (30 mL) honey, brown sugar, or currant or apricot jam

Salt and pepper

Poor cabbage is so often overlooked, which is a shame since it's always a cheap and filling vegetable. Green or Savoy cabbages need no more than to be thinly sliced, blanched (see page 41) and tossed with melted butter. With purple cabbage, you can make this tasty Belgian braised cabbage dish, which goes great with a roasted chicken dinner.

Method

1   In a large skillet, melt the butter over medium heat. Add the cabbage and apples and cook them for about 3 minutes. Add the stock, vinegar, and honey, turn the heat down to low, cover and cook for about 30 minutes, until the cabbage is tender. Season with salt and pepper and serve immediately.

Serves 4

 **What to do with the leftovers**

* Keep them covered in the fridge for up to 3 days. Reheat them in the microwave.

 **Other things to do with it**

* Omit the apples, or use pears instead.

* Add 1 or 2 peeled and grated beets instead of the apples.

Colcannon
(Mashed Potatoes with Cabbage)

Ingredients

3 russet or Yukon Gold potatoes, peeled and diced

Salt and pepper

½ small cabbage, thinly sliced (about 3 cups/750 mL)

½ cup (125 mL) warm milk

2 Tbsp (30 mL) butter, melted

Colcannon is an old Irish recipe—it's a great way to boost the nutritional value of your regular mash.

Method

1 Place the potatoes in a medium pot and add enough water to cover them by about an inch. Salt the water generously. Bring to a boil over high heat, then turn the heat down and simmer for 15–20 minutes, until the potatoes are tender when poked with a knife.

2 In a medium pot, bring about an inch of water to a boil. If you have a steamer basket, place it in the pot and add the cabbage. If not, set the cabbage directly into the water. Cover and steam for about 5 minutes, until it's tender.

3 Drain the potatoes and put them through a potato ricer or mash them with a potato masher. Add the warmed milk, melted butter, and salt and pepper and stir or mash them until you have the consistency you want. Stir in the warm cabbage and serve them right away.

Serves 4

 **What to do with the leftovers**

* Keep them covered in the fridge for up to 3 days. Reheat them in the microwave.

 Other things to do with it

* Colcannon with Bacon and Leeks: Cook 4 slices of bacon until crisp; remove from the pan, crumble, and set aside. Cut 2 leeks in half lengthwise, wash them well (grit tends to work its way between the layers), and thinly slice the white and light green part. Instead of steaming the cabbage, sauté it in the bacon fat with the sliced leeks for about 5 minutes, until both are wilted. Stir them into the potato mixture as directed and sprinkle the crumbled bacon on top.

Braised Carrots
with Butter and Honey

Ingredients

1 lb (500 g) carrots, peeled and
sliced, or a bag of peeled baby
carrots

1–2 Tbsp (15–30 mL) butter

¼ cup (60 mL) water

1 Tbsp (15 mL) honey or maple syrup

Salt and pepper

Braising is an easy way to cook carrots, and allows you to add more flavor than steaming.

Method

1   In a medium pot set over high heat, combine the carrots, butter, water, honey, and salt and pepper. Bring the mixture to a boil, then cover the pot, turn the heat down to medium-low and cook the carrots for 5 minutes.

2   Take the lid off the pot and turn the heat back up to medium-high. Cook the carrots, stirring occasionally, until the liquid has evaporated and the carrots are tender. Serve immediately.

Serves 4

 What to do with the leftovers

*   Keep them covered in the fridge for up to 3 days. Reheat them in the microwave or in a little butter or oil in a skillet, or add them to a salad cold.

Other things to do with it

*   Use another braising liquid in place of the water, such as dry Marsala, orange juice, or chicken or vegetable broth.

*   Orange-Ginger Carrots: Use orange marmalade in place of the honey, and add ½ tsp (2.5 mL) grated fresh ginger.

*   Balsamic Glazed Carrots: Reserve the honey and cook the carrots in the water and butter for 6–8 minutes, until tender but still firm. Drain them well and return to the pot. Add 1 Tbsp (15 mL) balsamic vinegar and 1 Tbsp (15 mL) honey or maple syrup and continue to cook them for about 5 minutes, or until tender.

Roasted Carrots

Ingredients

1 lb (500 g) carrots, peeled and
    sliced, or a bag of peeled baby
    carrots

1 Tbsp (15 mL) olive or canola oil

Salt and pepper

Roasting carrots gives them a sweet smokiness. Try tossing them with other
firm winter vegetables, such as beets, fennel, onions, turnips, and parsnips,
to roast at the same time.

Method

1 Preheat the oven to 450°F (230°C).

2 Spread the carrots on a rimmed baking sheet or shallow baking pan,
drizzle them with oil, and sprinkle with salt and pepper. Toss them with your
fingers to coat them well. Roast the carrots, shaking the pan often, for 20
minutes or until they're golden and tender.

Serves 4

 What to do with the leftovers

* Keep them covered in the fridge for up to 3 days. Reheat them in the
microwave or in a little butter or oil in a skillet, or add them to a salad
cold.

* Mash or purée leftover roasted carrots and stir them into a batch of
hummus along with a good shake of cumin.

 Other things to do with it

* Toss the carrots with 1 Tbsp (15 mL) chopped fresh rosemary with
the oil, and salt and pepper before roasting them.

Steamed or Grilled Corn

Ingredients

corn on the cob (as many as you
want to cook)

Method

1 Steamed corn doesn't really require a recipe. All you need to do is add an inch or two (2.5–5 cm) of water to a pot big enough to accommodate the amount of corn you want to cook (without crowding them too much), add a little salt, and bring it to a boil over high heat. Clean the husks and silk from the cobs of corn and place them in the pot. It's fine if some of the corn is in the water and some is above it. Cover the pot and cook the corn for 5–10 minutes, until it's heated through. Serve steamed corn with butter, and salt and pepper.

2 To grill corn, put whole cobs in their husks on a heated grill for about 15 minutes, until the husks are blackened on all sides, turning occasionally. Wearing oven mitts, remove husks and silk from corn. Alternatively, clean the husks and silk from the corn and brush the cobs with oil, then grill them for 10–12 minutes, turning occasionally, until tender and slightly charred.

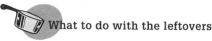 **What to do with the leftovers**

* Keep them covered in the fridge for up to 3 days. Scrape the corn kernels off the cob and reheat them in the microwave or in a little butter or oil in a skillet.

* Scrape the corn kernels off the cob and add them to soup, salad, salsa, or stir them into cornbread batter (see page 247).

 Other things to do with it

* Serve corn with Chili-Lime Butter: Add the grated zest and juice of a lime, 1 small crushed clove of garlic, and 1 tsp (5 mL) minced jalapeño pepper, ½ tsp (2.5 mL) chili powder or 2 tsp (10 mL) finely chopped canned chipotle chile en abodo to ¼ cup (60 mL) softened butter. Serve with the corn.

* Peppery Corn with Feta: Spike ¼ cup (60 mL) mayonnaise with a pinch of cayenne pepper. Grill the corn until it's slightly charred. As soon as the corn comes off the grill, brush it with the peppery mayonnaise and sprinkle with about 1 Tbsp (15 mL) crumbled feta cheese per cob.

Caramelized Corn
with Peppers

Ingredients

2 cups (500 mL) fresh corn kernels
(about 3 ears)

1 Tbsp (15 mL) olive or canola oil

1 small purple onion, finely chopped

1 red bell pepper, seeded and
chopped

1 clove garlic, crushed

½ tsp (2.5 mL) chili powder
(or more if you like it hot)

Salt and pepper

¼ cup (60 mL) chopped cilantro

If you don't like the mess that comes with eating corn on the cob, slice off the kernels and sauté them until tender and golden. This is a fancier way of doing things. If you want to keep it simple, sauté corn kernels in a little butter or oil with salt and pepper.

Method

1 Cut the corn kernels off their cobs with a sharp, serrated knife. (If you have a tube pan, you can stand the ear of corn upright in the hole in the middle of the pan and scrape the kernels off into the surrounding pan.) Set a large skillet (preferably non-stick) over medium-high heat, and fry the corn on its own, without adding any oil, for 8–10 minutes, until it's golden brown and slightly charred. Remove the corn from the skillet and set it aside.

2 Add the oil to the skillet and sauté the onion, red pepper, and garlic for about 5 minutes, until the veggies are tender. Stir in the corn, chili powder, and salt and pepper to taste and cook for another 2 minutes. Remove from heat, stir in the cilantro and serve immediately.

Serves 4

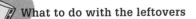

What to do with the leftovers

* Keep them covered in the fridge for up to 3 days. Reheat them in the microwave or in a skillet with a drizzle of oil.

Other things to do with it

* Add 1 cup (250 mL) shredded or chopped leftover roast chicken with the corn and chili powder, and roll the mixture in a soft flour tortilla for lunch or dinner.

* Creamy Charred Corn Dip: Add an 8 oz (250 g) package light cream cheese, ¼ cup water or chicken stock, and ½ tsp (2.5 mL) cumin with the corn and chili powder. Stir until the cheese is melted and smooth. Remove from the heat and stir in 1 cup (250 mL) light sour cream with the cilantro. Serve with tortilla chips.

Marinated Corn and Beans

Ingredients

2 cups (500 mL) fresh corn kernels
(about 3 ears)

1 14 oz (398 mL) can kidney or black
beans, rinsed and drained

1 large tomato, chopped

3 green onions, chopped

¼ cup (60 mL) chopped fresh basil

2 Tbsp (30 mL) olive oil

2 Tbsp (30 mL) lemon juice

1 clove garlic, crushed

Salt and pepper

This is more of a salad, but isn't as bulky as most. It's sturdy and keeps well, so it benefits from time in the fridge to allow the vinaigrette to marinate the vegetables.

Method

1 Clean the husks and silk off the cobs of corn and steam or grill them (see page 208). Cool the corn until it's easy to handle and cut the kernels off the cob (see page 209 for technique).

2 In a large bowl, combine the corn, beans, tomato, onions, and basil. In a small bowl, whisk together the oil, lemon juice, and garlic. Pour the vinaigrette over the corn mixture, season it with salt and pepper and toss well. Cover the corn and chill it for at least an hour, or until you're ready to serve it.

Serves 4

 What to do with the leftovers

* Keep them covered in the fridge for up to 5 days.

 Other things to do with it

* Rice or Quinoa Salad: Substitute red wine vinegar for the lemon juice and add 1 cup (250 mL) steamed long-grain white or wild rice (see page 182) or steamed quinoa (see page 189) to make a grainy salad.

* Pasta Salad: Substitute red wine vinegar for the lemon juice. Add 2 cups (500 mL) cooked small pasta (such as orzo, shells, penne, or farfalle) and ¼–½ cup (60–125 mL) grated Parmesan to the corn mixture.

Vegetables

Eggplant Parmigiana

Ingredients

All-purpose flour for dredging

2 eggs, lightly beaten

1 ½ cups (375 mL) bread crumbs or panko (Japanese breadcrumbs)

¾ cup (185 mL) grated Parmesan

2 small eggplants

Salt and pepper

2 Tbsp (30 mL) olive or canola oil

1 cup (250 mL) ricotta cheese

1–2 cups (250–500 mL) tomato, marinara, or spaghetti sauce

1 cup (250 mL) grated mozzarella cheese

If you don't have the time or inkling to make parmigiana, simply dredge slices of eggplant in flour and fry them in a little oil and butter (or grill them) until they're crispy on the outside, tender on the inside. Serve them plain, or topped with a little tomato sauce or garlic mayo. If you're in the mood for something more elaborate, this is time well spent.

Method

1 Preheat the oven to 350°F (175°C).

2 Take out three shallow bowls and put the flour in one, the eggs in another, and combine the bread crumbs and Parmesan in the third.

3 Slice the eggplants about ½ inch (1 cm) thick and sprinkle with salt and pepper.

4 Drizzle a large rimmed baking sheet with oil or spray it well with non-stick spray. Heat about a tablespoon (15 mL) of oil in a large skillet set over medium-high heat. Dredge the eggplant slices in flour to coat them, and dip them first into the egg, then into the bread crumb mixture, pressing the crumbs to help them adhere. Place the crumbed slices into the hot skillet and cook them for about 5 minutes per side, until golden brown. Cook only a few slices at a time, then transfer them to the oiled sheet when they're done.

5 Spread 2 Tbsp (30 mL) ricotta over each slice of eggplant, then drizzle tomato sauce over the whole thing, and sprinkle with mozzarella. Bake the eggplant parmigiana for about 15 minutes, until the cheese is melted.

Serves 4

What to do with the leftovers

* Keep them covered in the fridge for up to 2 days—the crumbs tend to get soggy. Reheat them in the microwave.

 ### Other things to do with it

* Use the roasted tomatoes on page 216, mashed until chunky, in place of the tomato sauce.

Wilted Kale with Bacon

Ingredients

1 slice bacon, chopped

1 clove garlic, crushed

6 cups (1.5 L) roughly torn kale

½ cup (125 mL) water or chicken stock

Salt and pepper

This is one of those high-reward-for-minimum-effort dishes. You can get a lot of greens into you when they're wilted down to practically nothing.

Method

1   In a heavy skillet set over medium heat, cook the bacon until crisp. Transfer it to a paper towel to drain. Add the garlic to the skillet and cook it in the bacon fat for about 30 seconds, just until it's turning golden.

2   Add the kale and water and cover the skillet. Cook for about 10 minutes, until the kale is wilted and tender. Remove the lid and cook until the liquid has evaporated. Stir in the bacon and season with salt and pepper. Serve immediately.

Serves 2

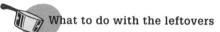 **What to do with the leftovers**

* Eat them, or keep them covered in the fridge for up to a day and stir them into soup or use them to fill an omelet (see page 54).

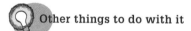 **Other things to do with it**

* Kale with Caramelized Onions: Omit the bacon. Sauté a small, thinly sliced purple onion in 1 Tbsp (15 mL) olive oil for about 15 minutes, until it's golden. Add the garlic, then the kale and water along with 1–2 Tbsp (15–30 mL) red wine vinegar and cook as directed.

Portobello Pizzas

Ingredients

2 portobello mushroom caps

1 clove garlic, crushed

Salt and pepper

1–2 tsp (5–10 mL) olive or canola oil

1 small tomato, chopped

A small handful of fresh basil or spinach, torn into pieces

½–1 cup (125–250 mL) grated mozzarella cheese

Treat the portobello mushrooms as pizza crusts, and experiment with toppings as you would if you were making regular pizza, adjusting ingredients to suit everyone's taste.

Method

1 Preheat the oven to 350°F (175°C).

2 Remove the mushroom stems and scrape the gills out with a spoon. Stir the garlic into the oil and rub it all over the mushroom caps.

3 Place the mushroom caps bowl side up on a baking sheet and bake for 8–10 minutes, until tender. Take them out of the oven and increase the oven temperature to 450°F (230°C).

4 Sprinkle the mushrooms with salt and pepper and top them with the chopped tomato and basil. Sprinkle with grated cheese. Bake for 5–10 minutes, until the cheese melts.

Serves 2 (recipe doubles or triples easily)

 What to do with the leftovers

* Keep them covered in the fridge for up to 2 days. Reheat them in the microwave or on a cookie sheet in a 350°F (175°C) oven.

Other things to do with it

* Sausage Portobello Pizzas: Omit the tomato and basil. Squeeze a sweet or hot Italian sausage out of its casing into a skillet set over medium-high heat. Sauté until it is cooked through, breaking up any lumps as you cook it. Top each cooked mushroom with some sausage, about 2 Tbsp (30 mL) of bottled pizza or spaghetti sauce, and the grated cheese and bake as directed.

Vegetables

Grilled Portobello Burgers

Ingredients

4 portobello mushroom caps

¼ cup (60 mL) balsamic vinegar

2 Tbsp (30 mL) olive or canola oil

1–2 cloves garlic, crushed

1 Tbsp chopped fresh rosemary
  or 1 tsp (5 mL) dried basil or
  oregano (optional)

Salt and pepper

Sliced cheddar, Havarti,
  Monterey Jack, or provolone
  cheese (optional)

4 hamburger buns

Meaty, substantial portobello mushrooms make burgers even carnivores adore. The marinade adds flavor, and the grill adds smokiness. But instead you could also simply roast whole portobello mushroom caps (clean out the stems and gills first) with garlic and butter in the oven until they're tender, then put them on a toasted bun with whatever condiments you like.

Method

1 Remove the mushroom stems and scrape out the gills with a spoon. Place the mushrooms in a shallow dish. Stir together the vinegar, oil, garlic, basil, and salt and pepper to taste and pour the marinade over the mushrooms. Marinate for about 15 minutes.

2 Brush the grill with oil or spray it with non-stick spray, and heat it to medium-high. Grill the mushrooms for 5–8 minutes on each side, brushing them occasionally with the marinade. Lay slices of cheese on them during the final 2 minutes of cooking. If you don't have a grill, you can broil the burgers in your oven on a baking sheet or broiling rack for about 5 minutes per side.

3 Serve the grilled mushrooms on buns with mayo, sliced tomatoes, greens, or whatever condiments you like.

Serves 4

What to do with the leftovers

∗ Keep them covered in the fridge for up to 5 days, and reheat them in the microwave or in a skillet with a drizzle of oil.

Other things to do with it

∗ Process 1 roasted red pepper (see page 29) and ¼ cup (60 mL) low-fat mayonnaise in a food processor until smooth; spread it on the bun lids before you top the burgers with them.

∗ Instead of the balsamic vinaigrette, marinate the mushrooms in a bottled vinaigrette or teriyaki sauce before you grill them.

Wilted Spinach
with Bacon Vinaigrette

Ingredients

4 slices bacon, chopped

1 small onion or 2 shallots, finely chopped

¼ cup (60 mL) balsamic vinegar

2 tsp (10 mL) Dijon mustard

2 Tbsp (30 mL) olive oil

½ lb (250 g) fresh spinach, washed and spun dry, or a bag of washed baby spinach leaves

Salt and pepper

Spinach is fantastic wilted, and because it's less bulky you can get more of it into you that way.

Method

1 In a large skillet set over medium-high heat, cook the bacon until crispy. Transfer it to paper towels. Drain all but 2 Tbsp (30 mL) of the bacon fat from the skillet; add the onion and cook until it's beginning to turn golden. Add the spinach and cook until it begins to wilt. Remove from the heat and add the vinegar, mustard and oil. Toss to coat the greens well.

2 Put the spinach into a bowl, scraping the warm vinaigrette from the pan overtop. Crumble the bacon and sprinkle it over the spinach. Season with salt and pepper and serve immediately.

Serves 4

 What to do with the leftovers

* Eat them. They're good for you, and they don't keep very well in the fridge.

 Other things to do with it

* Wilted Spinach with Bacon and Apples: Cook a small, finely chopped apple along with the onion, until it's soft and beginning to turn golden. Add 1 cup (250 mL) apple cider and the vinegar to the pan and simmer for about 10 minutes, until it reduces by half. Whisk in the mustard and oil and set aside. Add the spinach to the pan and cook for a few minutes, until it wilts. Transfer to a bowl and top with the apple-onion vinaigrette and crumbled bacon.

Roasted Tomatoes

Ingredients

2 lb (1 kg) plum tomatoes, cut in quarters, or cherry tomatoes, cut in half

½ cup (125 mL) chopped fresh basil (optional)

¼ cup (60 mL) freshly grated Parmesan (optional)

¼ cup (60 mL) olive oil

2–3 cloves garlic, crushed

Pinch dried red pepper flakes (optional)

Salt and pepper

This is one of the most indispensable recipes in this book. Not only are roasted tomatoes delicious served alone, over grilled chicken or fish, or atop crostini, they can be mashed with a fork or whizzed in a food processor or blender until chunky or smooth to make a sweet, slightly smoky sauce to spread on pizza or toss with pasta. It's also a great way to use up tomatoes that have gone wrinkly or squishy.

Method

1 Preheat the oven to 400°F (200°C).

2 Combine the tomatoes, basil, Parmesan, oil, garlic, and red pepper flakes (if using) in a shallow baking dish. Season with salt and pepper and bake for 30–40 minutes, until the tomatoes are soft and starting to char on the edges. Serve warm, at room temperature, or cold.

Serves 4

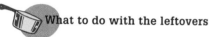

What to do with the leftovers

* Keep them in a tightly sealed container in the fridge for up to 4 days, or freeze them in freezer bags for up to 4 months if you plan to turn them into tomato sauce.

Other things to do with it

* Make Crostini: Slice a baguette into thin slices on a slight diagonal (this makes them easier to bite into). Lay the slices on a baking sheet, brush them with a little olive oil and if you like, rub them with a cut clove of garlic. Toast them in the oven for 5 minutes or until golden, and serve with a spoonful of roasted tomatoes on top.

* Roasted Tomato Soup: Process the roasted tomatoes in a food processor until slightly chunky. Transfer them to a pot and add 4 cups (1 L) chicken or vegetable broth. Bring to a boil, reduce heat and simmer for about 15 minutes, until slightly thickened.

Roasted Winter Vegetables

Ingredients

1 ½–2 lb (750 g –1 kg) winter
vegetables (potatoes, sweet potatoes, carrots, turnips,
parsnips, beets, onions,
butternut squash, fennel,
and/or rutabagas)

¼ cup (60 mL) olive or canola oil, or
half oil and half melted butter

Salt and pepper

1 head garlic

1 Tbsp (15 mL) chopped fresh rosemary, or a few whole sprigs
(optional)

It seems during the winter months we don't get nearly enough vegetables
in our diet, but even uninteresting turnips, carrots and other winter veg can
be delicious when they're roasted, which brings out their natural sweetness.
And roasting them is dead easy. You don't need to be as finicky with the cooking time as you do with more delicate vegetables.

Method

1 Preheat oven to 450°F (230°C).

2 Trim the vegetables and cut them into chunks that are fairly uniform in
size, so that they will roast evenly. Place them in a large roasting pan or on a
rimmed baking sheet, making sure they aren't too crowded or they'll steam
rather than roasting properly. Drizzle the vegetables with oil and sprinkle
with salt and pepper. Toss them with your fingers to coat them well, and put
them in the oven.

3 While the vegetables are roasting, separate and peel the cloves of garlic. After
half an hour, add the garlic and rosemary to the pan and stir up all the vegetables. Continue to roast them for another 30–45 minutes, shaking the pan
often, until the vegetables are tender and golden.

Serves 4

What to do with the leftovers

* Keep them covered in the fridge
for up to 3 days. Reheat them in
the microwave or covered with foil
in the oven.

Other things to do with it

* Drizzle the vegetables with 2 Tbsp (30 mL) maple syrup or honey
along with the oil.

* Toss the roasted vegetables with ¼ cup (60 mL) freshly grated
Parmesan as soon as they come out of the oven.

* Toss the roasted vegetables with a mixture of ¼ cup (60 mL) balsamic
vinegar, 2 Tbsp (30 mL) olive oil, the grated zest of a lemon, and a
squeeze of lemon juice as soon as they come out of the oven.

* Pasta with Roasted Vegetables: Cook 1 lb (500 g) penne or other
small shaped pasta according to the package directions. Toss with
roasted vegetables, 1 or 2 chopped tomatoes, a small handful of torn
fresh basil, ¼ cup (60 mL) olive oil, and 2 Tbsp (30 mL) balsamic
vinegar. Sprinkle generously with grated Parmesan.

Vegetable Steaming Chart

Vegetable	Time (in minutes)	Seasonings that go with it
Asparagus	2–4	Tarragon, dill, garlic, anise, ginger, lemon juice or zest
Beets, tops trimmed	30–45	Garlic, ginger, mint, orange juice or zest
Broccoli florets	4–6	Dill, tarragon, lemon juice or zest
Carrots, sliced or cut into julienne	3–10	Ginger, dill, lemon or orange zest or juice, maple syrup
Cauliflower florets	6–10	Garlic, ginger, curry, fennel seed
Corn on the cob	8–10	Butter, garlic, chili powder
Green Beans	4–6	Basil, dill, thyme, mint, oregano, tarragon
Kale or Swiss Chard	8–10	Basil, chives, oregano, dill, tarragon, nutmeg, rosemary, lemon juice or zest
Peas	3–5	Mint, chervil, marjoram, rosemary, garlic, tarragon
Potatoes, baby new	15–20	Lemon, parsley, rosemary, chives, dill, basil, garlic, thyme, mint
Spinach	3–4	Garlic, nutmeg, rosemary, basil, ginger, lemon juice or zest
Winter squash, sliced	10–12	Curry, maple syrup, garlic, rosemary, dill, thyme, ginger, oregano

Vegetables

Potatoes

Sure, potatoes are cheap and versatile, but there are few foods
that are as pleasurable and reassuring, particularly when it's cold outside.
I don't know anyone who doesn't love buttery mashed potatoes, crispy fries,
crunchy roasted potatoes, or creamy scalloped potatoes.
A baked potato can turn any number of ingredients into supper;
mashed potatoes can turn any supper into an occasion.

How to bake a potato

Russet and baking potatoes make the best baked potatoes, and they need only washing before you bake them. The best, and luckily for us, easiest way to bake a potato is whole (not wrapped in foil), poked with a fork and put directly onto the rack of a 350°F (175°C) oven for 1–1 ¼ hours. The great thing about this method (besides the fact that it's so easy and there's little room for error) is that you can bake as many potatoes as you want, and do it while something else is in the oven.

The best way to open a baked potato is to poke it repeatedly with a fork, making a line of holes lengthwise or in an X, and karate-chopping it with your hand or pressing it with your fingers to open it and expose the flesh. This helps keep the interior fluffy, which cutting it open with a knife won't do.

Stuffed or Twice-Baked
Potatoes

Ingredients

4 russet or baking potatoes

1 head garlic

1 cup (250 mL) shredded cheddar or
   Monterey Jack cheese

½ cup (125 mL) light sour cream

½ cup (125 mL) chopped cooked ham
   (optional)

3 green onions, thinly sliced

Salt and pepper

The flesh of a baked potato can be mashed with virtually any ingredients, stuffed back into its shell, and baked again. Try using any type of cheese, or any spices and seasonings that go well with baked potatoes. If you don't have many people to feed, cut this recipe in half or even by a quarter if you're just cooking for yourself. Roast a few cloves of garlic in a little packet of foil if you don't want to roast the whole head, but keep in mind that roasted garlic keeps very well in the fridge for at least a week.

Method

1 Preheat the oven to 350°F (175°C).

2 Wrap the head of garlic in foil and bake it along with the potatoes for an hour and 15 minutes. Cool the potatoes until they're cool enough to handle, and cut them in half lengthwise. Pay attention to the way the potatoes lie—if they have flatter sides, keep them intact so that your stuffed potatoes will be more stable and won't roll around on the plate.

3 Scoop the flesh from each half into a bowl, leaving a ¼-inch (5 mm) shell. Put the empty shells on a cookie sheet and return them to the oven for about 10 minutes to crisp up while you make the stuffing. Turn the oven up to 400°F (200°C).

4 Add the cheese, sour cream, ham (if using), and onions to the cooked potato, saving a bit of the grated cheese to sprinkle on top. Squeeze as many of the garlic cloves as you want from their skins into the mixture. Mash it all up with a fork, adding salt and pepper to taste.

5 Stuff the shells with the potato mixture, mounding them in the middle, and sprinkle with the remaining cheese. Bake for 15–20 minutes, until golden.

Serves 4–8

What to do with the leftovers

* Keep them covered in the fridge
  for up to 3 days, and reheat them
  in the oven or microwave. Baked
  potatoes don't freeze very well.

Other things to do with it

* Use 4 slices of bacon, cooked until crisp and crumbled,
  instead of the ham.

* Use 12 to 15 baby red-skinned potatoes in place of the
  russet potatoes. Scoop out the flesh with a small spoon
  or melon baller, stuff and bake them as directed. Serve
  them as an appetizer or party snack.

* Potatoes with Rosemary and Blue Cheese: Add
  ½ cup (125 mL) light sour cream, ¼ cup (60 mL)
  crumbled blue cheese, 1 crushed clove of garlic, and
  1 Tbsp (15 mL) chopped fresh rosemary to the cooked
  potato. Stuff and bake the potatoes as directed.

How to make mashed potatoes

Most people don't need a recipe for mashed potatoes; most of us simply boil peeled potatoes and mash them with butter and milk until they're smooth. If that's your method, it's just fine. But if you're clueless about mashed potatoes or feel your technique has room for improvement, there are a few things to know that will improve your chances of producing creamy, fluffy mashed potatoes.

Your first consideration should be your choice of potato. Russets are starchy, mealy, and make fluffy mashed potatoes, but because they're drier than most, they also absorb more liquid. Yukon Golds are waxier and butterier, and are also an excellent choice. Red potatoes tend to turn gummy and gluey when they're mashed, so they don't make the best mashed potatoes.

Second is your cooking method. Most people peel their potatoes, cut them into chunks and boil them, but they can be baked instead. And if you leave the skins on while you boil or bake your potatoes they will retain more potato flavor.

The third factor is what you add and how you add it. Whether you add the butter or milk first makes a difference—adding the butter first allows the fat to coat the starch molecules in the potato, resulting in creamier mashed potatoes. Melting the butter before you add it allows it to do its job even better, and warm butter won't cool down the potatoes. If you're trying to cut back on fat, buttermilk and stock make delicious alternatives to butter and milk or cream.

To do the actual mashing, use a hand-held masher, potato ricer, or food mill. If you want perfectly smooth potatoes, a ricer, which resembles a giant garlic press, is your best bet. If you whip your potatoes with an electric mixer, do it on low speed to avoid overworking the starch in the potatoes, which could make them gummy. Never use a food processor or blender to make mashed potatoes.

Mashed Potatoes

Ingredients

2 lb (about 1 kg) russet or Yukon
   Gold potatoes

2–4 Tbsp (30–60 mL) butter, melted

¾ cup (185 mL) warmed milk or half
   and half

Salt and pepper

Here is a basic recipe to use as a starting point. Adjust quantities according to your taste and how many people you're feeding. If you're not sure of the weight of your potatoes, estimate 1–2 potatoes per person.

Method

1 Peel the potatoes, or leave them unpeeled, and cut them into chunks of roughly the same size so that they will cook evenly. Place the potatoes in a large pot and add enough water to cover them by about an inch. Bring to a boil over high heat, then turn the heat down and simmer for 15–20 minutes, until the potatoes are tender when poked with a knife. Smaller chunks will cook faster, so check them early to make sure they don't become overcooked and mushy.

2 Drain the potatoes well in a colander. If you haven't peeled them yet, spear each potato with a fork or grab it with tongs and use a peeler to peel off the skins. Put the potatoes back into the pot and mash them with a potato masher, or press them through a potato ricer or food mill back into the pot. Stir in the melted butter and then gently stir in the milk or cream and salt and pepper to taste. Serve immediately.

Serves 4–6 (halves or doubles easily)

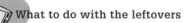
What to do with the leftovers

* Keep them covered in the fridge for up to 4 days. Mashed potatoes generally don't freeze well.

* To make salmon potato cakes, mix equal quantities of drained canned salmon and leftover mashed potato. Stir in an egg and salt and pepper to taste. Shape the mixture into patties and fry them in butter or oil until golden on each side.

Other things to do with it

* Flavor mashed potatoes with a few crushed olives, some grated or crumbled flavorful cheese, a small handful of chopped fresh herbs, a spoonful of pesto, caramelized onions or sautéed mushrooms, or a dab of wasabi.

* Roasted Garlic Mashed Potatoes: Wrap a head of garlic in foil and bake it for about an hour, until it's tender and golden. (You can do this at 350°F/175°C or any temperature your oven happens to be on when you're cooking something else.) Squeeze the roasted garlic cloves out of their skins into the potato mixture along with the butter. Roasted garlic can be made ahead and kept in the fridge for several days, until you need it.

* Leave the skins on and mash them roughly with a hand-held potato masher.

* Mashed Potatoes with Buttermilk and Caramelized Onions: While the potatoes are cooking, sauté a thinly sliced onion or a few shallots in butter or oil in a non-stick skillet over medium-high heat, stirring frequently, for about 15 minutes or until deep golden. Use 2 Tbsp (30 mL) butter and ½ cup (125 mL) buttermilk to make the mashed potatoes, and stir in the caramelized onions at the end. These are also good with some crumbled blue cheese gently stirred in so that it melts slightly into the hot potatoes.

Mashed Sweet Potatoes

Ingredients

2 lb (about 1 kg) sweet potatoes

2–4 Tbsp (30–60 mL) butter or
margarine

¼ cup (60 mL) milk, cream, or orange
juice concentrate

1 Tbsp (15 mL) packed brown sugar

½ tsp (2.5 mL) salt

Sweet potatoes, when they aren't smothered by a tumble of marshmallows, are even better for you than regular potatoes, and can be used in much the same way. Mash them, turn them into fries, or bake them and drizzle them with butter spiked with maple syrup. Sweet potatoes are among the most nutritious of all vegetables—they deliver a healthy dose of fiber and beta carotene, and supply substantial amounts of vitamins C and B6, and manganese.

Method

1 Peel the sweet potatoes and cut them into similar-sized chunks so that they cook evenly. Place them in a large pot and add enough water to cover them by about an inch (2.5 cm). Bring to a boil over high heat, then turn the heat down and simmer for 15–20 minutes, until the potatoes are tender when poked with a knife. Smaller chunks will cook faster, so check them early to make sure they don't become overcooked and mushy.

2 Drain the potatoes well and return them to the pot.

3 Add the butter, milk, brown sugar, and salt and mash them with a potato masher or potato ricer. Serve immediately.

Serves 4–6

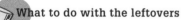 **What to do with the leftovers**

* Keep them covered in the fridge for up to 3 days, and reheat them in the microwave.

 Other things to do with it

* Streusel-Topped Sweet Potatoes: Spread the mashed sweet potatoes into a shallow baking dish. Mix ¼ cup (60 mL) flour, ¼ cup (60 mL) packed brown sugar, 2 Tbsp (30 mL) butter, and ½ cup (125 mL) chopped pecans or almonds until the mixture is well blended and crumbly. Sprinkle the streusel over the mashed sweet potatoes in a shallow baking dish and bake at 350°F (175°C) for 20–30 minutes, until golden.

* Sweet Potato Brûlée: Spread the mashed sweet potatoes into a shallow baking dish. Sprinkle with ½ cup (125 mL) packed brown sugar and place under the broiler for about 2 minutes, until the sugar melts. Let the potatoes stand at room temperature for about 5 minutes to allow the sugar to harden.

Roasted Potatoes

Ingredients

4–5 medium russet or Yukon gold
potatoes, peeled

1 Tbsp (15 mL) flour (optional)

¼–½ cup (60–125 mL) chicken or
turkey fat, or canola or olive oil

What to do with the leftovers

* Keep them covered in the fridge
  for up to 4 days. Reheat them in
  the oven or microwave.

There's nothing quite as satisfying as a perfectly roasted potato. Chicken fat adds depth of flavor and a golden crispy crust to roasted potatoes, but it's not the healthiest choice—use some if you're roasting a bird, otherwise canola or olive oil works just fine. Most classic recipes instruct you to buy a jar of goose fat, and you can certainly do that if you really want to be authentic.

Method

1 Preheat the oven to 450°F (230°C).

2 Cut the potatoes into thirds, cutting them on an angle so that each potato is wedge-shaped to optimize the potential for crunchy edges. Put the potatoes in a large pot, cover them with water, and bring to a boil. Boil them for about 4 minutes, then drain well, and put the potatoes back into the dry pot. (The potatoes can be made ahead up to this point and refrigerated until you're ready for them.)

3 If the pot has a lid, put it on, and shake the pot around to chuff the potatoes up a little. You don't want to break them apart, but roughing up the edges will ensure a crunchy exterior. If you want to help out even more, sprinkle 1 Tbsp (15 mL) of flour over them before you toss them about.

4 Pour the fat or oil into a large roasting pan and put it in the oven to heat up. When it's hot, carefully add the potatoes to the fat and roll them around to coat them. Roast for about 45 minutes, turning them once or twice to make sure they're evenly roasted and deep golden all over.

Serves 4

Other things to do with it

* Parmesan Roasted Potatoes: Use olive or canola oil or melted butter instead of the chicken fat, but don't bother heating it up. Toss the potatoes in enough oil to coat, then toss them in a plastic bag with a mixture of ¼ cup (60 mL) grated Parmesan, ¼ cup (60 mL) flour, and some salt and pepper. Press with your fingers to help the coating adhere to the potatoes. Arrange them in a single layer in a roasting pan, sprinkle with the remaining Parmesan mixture and cook, stirring once or twice, for an hour or until crisp and brown.

* Roasted Baby New Potatoes: Parboil (see page 41) as many new potatoes as you want until they're almost tender. Drain them well, transfer to a baking sheet, and toss with enough olive oil to coat them. Sprinkle with salt and a good grinding of black pepper. Add a few sprigs of chopped fresh rosemary if you like. Roast at 425°F (220°C) for about 20 minutes, or until golden and tender when poked with a fork.

Potatoes

Oven Fries

Ingredients

3 medium russet or Yukon gold
   potatoes, peeled or unpeeled

1 Tbsp (15 mL) canola or olive oil

¼ tsp (1 mL) garlic powder

¼ tsp (1 mL) salt

¼ tsp (1 mL) pepper

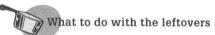

What to do with the leftovers

* Leftover fries don't hold up or
  reheat very well—make only as
  many as you plan to eat.

Other things to do with it

* Sweet Potato Fries: Roast them
  as you would regular potatoes. Try
  adding a crushed clove of garlic to
  the oil and sprinkling them with
  chopped fresh rosemary before you
  bake them.

* Spicy Cheese Fries: Combine
  ¼ cup (60 mL) grated Parmesan
  and 1 tsp (5 mL) chili powder with
  the garlic powder, and salt and
  pepper. Sprinkle the mixture over
  the potatoes and toss with your
  fingers to coat well before you
  bake them.

Oven-baked fries are every bit as good as the deep-fried kind, and they're cheap and easy, too. If you have one of those old baking sheets that are blackened from overuse, use it here—the dark metal will conduct heat more efficiently, helping your fries turn deep golden. If you're in a hurry, skip the soaking step and the foil, and simply roast the oiled potatoes for 30–45 minutes, stirring once or twice, until they're golden and crisp.

Method

1 Preheat the oven to 475°F (245°C).

2 Cut the potatoes into evenly sized wedges or into ¼–½-inch (5 mm–1 cm) sticks. Place them in a large bowl and cover them with water, and let them soak for about 10 minutes. Meanwhile, coat a heavy, rimmed baking sheet with the oil.

3 Drain the potatoes and dry them thoroughly with paper towels or a tea towel. Place them on the prepared baking sheet. Sprinkle the garlic powder, and salt and pepper over the potatoes and toss with your fingers to coat them well with the seasonings and oil, arranging them in a single layer. Make sure they aren't crowded or overlapping or they will steam instead of browning properly.

4 Cover the baking sheet tightly with foil and bake for 5 minutes. Remove the foil and continue to bake for about 20 minutes, turning the fries once or twice with a thin spatula, until they're golden and crisp. Serve immediately.

Serves 2–4

Scalloped Potatoes

Ingredients

1 Tbsp (15 mL) butter

1 Tbsp (15 mL) canola oil

1 onion, finely chopped

1–2 cloves garlic, crushed

2–2 ½ lb (1–1.25 kg) russet or Yukon Gold potatoes (about 5), peeled (or not) and thinly sliced

1 cup (250 mL) chicken or vegetable stock

1 cup (250 mL) cream, milk, half and half, or evaporated 2% milk

1 tsp (5 mL) salt

¼ tsp (1 mL) pepper

1 cup (250 mL) grated old cheddar, Monterey Jack, or Gouda cheese

Scalloped potatoes are traditionally made with copious amounts of butter and heavy cream—the main reason they taste so good! This recipe uses chicken stock in place of half the cream, so even if you choose to use cream instead of milk, it will still be less rich than most recipes. If you want to lighten it even further, go with half and half, evaporated milk, or even plain milk.

Method

1 Preheat the oven to 425°F (220°C).

2 Place a large pot or Dutch oven over medium heat and melt the butter with the oil. Add the onion and cook for about 5 minutes, until soft. Add the garlic and cook for another minute.

3 Add the potatoes, chicken stock, cream, and salt and pepper and bring to a simmer. Cover, reduce the heat to low, and cook for 10–15 minutes, until the potatoes are tender but still firm.

4 Pour the whole lot into a baking dish that will accomodate it and sprinkle with cheese. Bake for 15 minutes, until golden and bubbly around the edges. Let it stand for 15 minutes before serving.

Serves 4–6

What to do with the leftovers

* Keep them covered in the fridge for up to 3 days. Reheat them in the microwave or cover them with a lid or aluminum foil and heat them in the oven.

Other things to do with it

* Use crumbled Gorgonzola or Cambozola in place of the cheddar.

* Sauté a cup of sliced mushrooms along with the onion, cooking until all the moisture has evaporated.

* When you add the potatoes to the baking dish, add about a quarter at a time and scatter some diced cooked ham between each layer.

* Grind a couple of slices of bread in a food processor with a clove of garlic and a tablespoon or two (15–30 mL) of oil or melted butter, and sprinkle the crumbs over the potatoes before you bake them.

Potatoes

Potato Pancakes

Ingredients

2 or 3 medium baking potatoes,
peeled or not

Salt

2–4 Tbsp (30–60 mL) canola oil, or
half oil and half butter

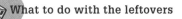

These are those crispy shredded potato pancakes everyone loves—also known as rösti, the Swiss term for "crisp and golden." You can make small individual pancakes or one big pancake to cut into wedges. If you're making breakfast and want to be really indulgent, fry them in a little leftover bacon fat.

Method

1 Grate the potatoes on the coarse side of a box grater onto one or two sheets of paper towel. Pick up handfuls of the shredded potato and squeeze out as much moisture as you can, then put them in a bowl, and toss them with salt to taste.

2 Set a large non-stick skillet over medium heat, add half the oil, and heat until it's hot but not smoking. (You can use a regular skillet, but you may need to use some extra oil.) Drop the potatoes in large spoonfuls onto the skillet and flatten them with a spatula.

3 Cook for 3–4 minutes, until brown and crisp on the bottom. Flip and cook for a few more minutes, until they're golden on the other side as well. To make one big pancake, put all the potatoes into the pan at once; it should take 5–10 minutes to cook on the bottom. Once the bottom is golden and crispy, slide the pancake out or invert it onto a plate and then flip or slide it back into the skillet to cook on the other side. If you need to, keep smaller pancakes in a warm oven while you finish cooking the rest. Serve them hot.

Makes about 8 small potato pancakes, or 1 large one

What to do with the leftovers

* In the unlikely event that there are any, keep them covered in the fridge for no more than a day. Reheat them in the microwave or crisp them up again in a hot skillet.

Other things to do with it

* Grate an onion into the potato mixture, before you squeeze out the excess moisture.

* Ham and Green Onion Rösti with Cheese: Chop about ½ cup (125 mL) of sliced Black Forest ham and add it to the potatoes along with a thinly sliced green onion. Make one large pancake and sprinkle it with ½ cup (125 mL) grated Gruyère or cheddar cheese. Cook for another minute in the skillet or under the broiler until the cheese melts.

Potatoes

Baking
basics

The chemistry involved in baking makes some people nervous.
Baking differs from cooking in that you can't always
experiment and taste your way through it, so knowing a few
basics will increase your chances of success. It really is easy.

Baking
basics

Your oven and baking pans

No matter what you're baking, it won't bake properly if it starts off in a cool oven. Before you even begin mixing your batter or dough, turn your oven on, and make sure it's up to temperature before you put anything in it. If you're unsure of your oven's accuracy, you can buy an oven thermometers at most department stores for around $7. Don't be surprised if you discover your oven is off, even if it's new. If it is, it doesn't necessarily need to be calibrated—just know to adjust the temperature accordingly.

You'll also need to prepare your baking pans. Pans that are lighter in color are generally better for baking with than dark pans, which conduct heat better and can burn the bottoms of your cookies, biscuits, or cakes. Unless a recipe specifies otherwise, spray your pans with non-stick spray (do this outside—the fat is not good for you to breathe in) or rub them with softened butter, margarine, or shortening.

Measuring your ingredients

It's important to be accurate with your measurements when you're baking, particularly when measuring flour. Even though most flour has been pre-sifted, it can settle in its bag or canister and become packed down over time so that when you scoop it out, you're actually getting more flour than you need. Recipes often instruct you to sift your flour or lightly spoon it into a measuring cup, then level it off with a knife—this ensures the flour is aerated rather than packed. The idea is to fill your measuring cup using as little flour as possible. Make sure you use dry measuring cups (the individual ones) to measure flour, rather than liquid measuring cups (glass or plastic cups with the measurements marked on the side), which require you to settle your ingredients down to the line in order to measure them.

When measuring brown sugar, make sure it's soft (see page 43) and firmly packed into the measuring cup. Sticky ingredients like honey or molasses will slide right out of a measuring cup if you grease it or spray it with non-stick spray first.

When measuring butter, remember that individually wrapped sticks and squares are exactly ½ cup (125 mL), so half a stick is ¼ cup (60 mL). Measurements are often printed on the side of butter and shortening wrappers to make it easy for you to slice off an exact amount. My Grandma taught me to measure cold butter using the displacement method—she would add cold water to a glass measuring cup (filling it to the ½ cup line, for example), and then add butter until the water rose accordingly. One-quarter cup of butter would raise the water level to ¾ cup, and so on. If you measure butter this way, make sure the water is cold so that it doesn't melt the butter, and that you drain it all off afterward.

Mixing

Most cookies and cakes and some muffins and quick breads are made using the creaming method, a process by which the butter and sugar are first beaten together until they're light and fluffy. Beating rubs the grains of sugar against the fat, which aerates (incorporates air into) the mixture. These tiny air bubbles later expand in the oven with the help of leavening agents, making whatever it is you're baking rise. Creaming butter and sugar is most easily done with an electric mixer, but you can do it by hand in a pinch, and get a good upper-body workout at the same time. Use room-temperature butter or stick margarine for best results—cold butter is difficult to beat, but if you soften it for too long in the microwave and it starts to melt, it won't beat properly either. In most recipes, stick margarine will give you more consistent results than tub margarine, which has a higher moisture content. Butter or margarine "spreads" are never appropriate for baking, since they have fillers (such as water, yogurt, or even air) added.

If you're adding grated lemon or orange zest, add it at this stage—beating the zest against the granules of sugar will release the maximum amount of citrus oil, giving you the most flavor and distributing it most efficiently throughout the batter.

When you're baking a cake, adding the dry and wet ingredients alternately helps to create a tender crumb. When you're making muffins and quick breads, the wet and dry ingredients are often combined separately and then gently blended together. This is referred to as the "quick bread method." In biscuits and pastries, the fat is "cut in" (meaning it's blended into the dry ingredients) before the liquid is added.

No matter which method you use, in most cases it's very important to be gentle with your mixing once liquid has come into contact with flour. Unless a recipe specifies otherwise, the wet and dry ingredients should be combined gently by hand or on the lowest speed of an electric mixer so as not to overwork the gluten in the flour, which could make your baking tough. This is particularly important when making pastries, biscuits, muffins, and scones. Cake and pastry flour is often used because of its lower gluten content, but it's not necessary—all-purpose flour works just fine for most baked goods.

Beating eggs

Eggs have a binding effect and their protein helps add structure to baked goods. When you're baking a cake, beating them in incorporates even more air bubbles, providing more leavening.

Some recipes require you to separate the eggs, meaning you must separate the whites from the yolks. This is easier to do when eggs are cold—an egg yolk is made up mostly of fat, so it's a little more solid and not as easily broken when it's cold. To separate an egg, tap it gently against the edge of a bowl or on the flat countertop. As soon as it cracks, push your thumbs into the crack and pull it open, separating the shell into two halves. Let the white fall into a bowl, keeping the yolk in one of the shell halves. Pass the yolk back and forth between the two shells, allowing the remaining white to fall into the bowl.

If you plan to beat your egg whites, the key is to keep the yolk intact—the egg whites must remain absolutely uncontaminated in order for them to beat properly. When several eggs need to be separated, many bakers separate each egg into two small dishes, one containing the white and one containing the yolk, and then transfer the white to a clean mixing bowl after each separation. That way if one of the yolks breaks, it doesn't contaminate the entire batch.

Keeping the whites untainted also means the bowl and beaters you use must be immaculate. Even a slight residue on a plastic bowl can keep the whites from reaching their full volume, which is why stainless steel and glass bowls are most often recommended. Egg whites can be beaten by hand, but an electric mixer works best. Start on a low speed and increase the speed as the egg whites become foamy. Beat them for as long as the recipe directs—some call for soft peaks, some for stiff peaks—and use them right away. Beaten egg whites start to deflate if they're set aside for too long, so beat them just before you need them.

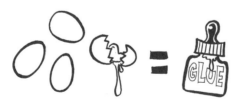

Folding

To incorporate beaten egg whites or other light ingredients into your batter without deflating them, you'll need to fold them in gently using a large rubber spatula. Folding isn't the same as mixing—it's a technique used to combine light, airy mixtures (such as beaten egg whites or whipped cream) with a heavier mixture, or vice versa, without losing any of the volume. To fold two mixtures together, place the lighter mixture on top of the heavier one in a large bowl. Cut down through the middle of the two mixtures using a rubber spatula; pull it across the bottom of the bowl and up the side, turning the underneath batter over on top. Continue these turning motions, rotating the bowl a quarter turn with each gentle stroke, just until the two mixtures are combined. The idea is to blend them together gently, using as few strokes as possible. Some cooks like to lighten the heavier batter first by folding in about a quarter of the lighter mixture, then folding in the rest. Others add the lighter mixture in thirds, folding in each addition before adding the next. Use whichever technique you like, or fold it in all at once. Don't worry if your batter is a little streaky— the two mixtures will bake together just fine.

Baking and storing

Unless you have a convection oven or a recipe specifies otherwise, it's a good idea to bake cookies, cakes, pies, muffins, or any baked goods in a single layer with the rack set in the middle of the oven. When you can smell baked goods baking, it's usually a good indication that they're close to being done. Check on them at the earliest suggested baking time— you can always leave them in the oven longer if you need to. Most cakes, muffins, and quick breads rise, turn golden, and their sides start to pull away from the sides of the pan when they're done. Unless they're meant to be gooey in the middle, the tops will spring back when lightly touched. When you are baking cookies, make sure they're set around the edges but still soft in the middle if you want them to be soft and chewy—remember that they will firm up as they cool. The same thing goes for brownies. If pies or other pastries are browning too quickly, cover them lightly with a piece of foil.

Once your baking is out of the oven, cooling racks allow them to cool without becoming steamy on the bottom or sticking in their pans. Unless a recipe instructs otherwise, always store baked goods at room temperature— bread products actually go stale faster when stored in the fridge. If you plan on freezing loaves, cookies, cakes, or muffins, allow them to cool completely before wrapping in plastic wrap, then in aluminum foil. Most baked goods will freeze well for up to 4 months.

Quick breads

Quick breads are loaves, muffins, biscuits, and scones
that are leavened with baking powder or baking soda and
eggs instead of yeast. Since you don't have to bother waiting
for the dough to rise, punching it down or kneading it, they're pretty
quick to make. In fact, unlike yeast breads, which require
kneading to develop the gluten and build their structure, it's important
not to overwork quick bread dough or batter,
or your loaf/muffins/biscuits will turn out tough.

Quick
breads

Because muffin and quick bread batters are so similar, either can be baked as a loaf or as muffins. Muffins and quick breads are generally made using the "quick bread" method, which requires you to combine the dry ingredients, then the wet ingredients, and then gently stir them together. The "creaming method," most often used for cakes, in which you cream the butter and sugar together first and then add the eggs and dry ingredients, can also be used for muffins, but the results are usually very similar.

The only important thing to remember is not to overmix the batter or the muffins or bread will turn out tough. Once flour comes into contact with liquid and is stirred it creates gluten, which you must minimize in order to keep your bread light and tender. The more you stir, the more you develop the gluten. Blend the batter together by hand as quickly and gently as you can, just until it's combined, and don't worry about getting all the lumps out. A rubber spatula is the best tool for gentle blending—it enables you to scrape the sides and bottom of the bowl as you stir, using a minimum number of strokes to combine your ingredients.

Because baking powder and baking soda are your leaveners, it's essential that they're active—some people don't realize that they lose their punch over time. To test their effectiveness, stir a teaspoon (5 mL) of baking powder into ½ cup (125 mL) of hot water—it should bubble immediately. To test baking soda, stir ¼ teaspoon (1 mL) into 2 teaspoons (10 mL) of vinegar—it should bubble immediately. If they don't react this way, toss them out and buy fresh. Baking powder should last for about 6 months after you open the container; baking soda has a longer shelf life and will last indefinitely if stored in a cool, dry place.

Basic Muffins

Ingredients

2 cups (500 mL) all-purpose flour (or use half all-purpose, half whole wheat)

½ cup (125 mL) sugar

1 Tbsp (15 mL) baking powder

½ tsp (2.5 mL) salt

1 cup (250 mL) milk

¼ cup (60 mL) butter or margarine, melted, or canola oil

1 large egg

Any additional ingredients you like (see the suggestions above)

What to do with the leftovers

* Keep them in an airtight container at room temperature for several days, or wrap them well and freeze. Individually wrapped frozen muffins are ideal to pop into a lunch bag—when it's time to eat they've thawed out.

Since all muffins are more or less the same when you take away the extra ingredients, a basic recipe to play with is the best starting point. You can stir in all kinds of additions to this basic batter to suit your taste—try adding a cup (250 mL) or so of fresh or frozen (unthawed) berries, chopped fruit, grated apple, carrots or zucchini, mashed pumpkin or banana, a handful of dried fruit, chopped nuts, grated cheese, chocolate chips, or oats, and/or flavorings such as cinnamon, citrus zest, and different extracts to create any kind of muffin you like.

Method

1 Preheat the oven to 400°F (200°C). Spray muffin cups with non-stick spray, or line them with paper liners.

2 In a large bowl, combine the flour, sugar, baking powder, and salt.

3 In a medium bowl, stir together the milk, butter, and egg. If you're adding wet ingredients such as pumpkin or mashed banana, add it to the liquid ingredients. If you're adding grated cheese, add it to the dry ingredients and toss to combine.

4 Make a well in the dry ingredients and pour in the wet ingredients. Gently stir a few strokes with a spatula, and then add any extra ingredients you like. Mix the batter just until it's blended. Don't worry about getting all the lumps out—overmixing will make the muffins tough.

5 Fill the prepared muffin cups almost to the top and bake for 20–30 minutes, until the muffins are golden and springy to the touch. Tip them in their cups to help them cool by allowing steam to escape.

Makes 8–12 muffins

Other things to do with it

* Make a streusel by blending together ⅓ cup (80 mL) flour, ¼ cup (60 mL) packed brown sugar, ¼–½ cup (60–125 mL) chopped nuts, 1–2 Tbsp (15–30 mL) butter, and a pinch of cinnamon. Sprinkle on top of the muffins before baking them.

* Sour Cream Muffins: Increase sugar to 1 cup (250 mL). Use 1 ¼ cups (310 mL) light or regular sour cream in place of the milk. These are good with the addition of fresh or frozen berries, chopped fresh, or dried fruit.

* Banana Muffins: Replace ½ cup (125 mL) of the milk with 1 cup (250 mL) of mashed overripe banana. Add a handful of nuts and a pinch of cinnamon to the dry ingredients, if you like.

* Double Chocolate Chip Muffins: Replace ½ cup (125 mL) of the flour with cocoa, and add ½–1 cup (125–250 mL) chocolate chips to the batter.

* Cranberry-Orange or Cranberry-Lemon Muffins: Add the grated zest of an orange or lemon to the wet ingredients, and stir 1 ½ cups (375 mL) of fresh or frozen (unthawed) cranberries into the batter.

* Cheese Muffins: Add 1 cup (250 mL) of grated old cheddar cheese to the dry ingredients, tossing to blend and break up any lumps of cheese.

* Cheddar, Bacon, and Green Onion Muffins: Add 1 cup (250 mL) of grated old cheddar cheese to the dry ingredients, tossing to blend and break up any lumps of cheese. Add a few slices of cooked, crumbled bacon or about ½ cup (125 mL) of chopped ham, and a few chopped green onions to the batter.

Quick breads

Oatmeal Muffins

Ingredients

1 cup (250 mL) oats, old-fashioned or quick-cooking

1 ½ cups (375 mL) buttermilk or sour milk (see page 45)

½ cup (125 mL) packed brown sugar

¼ cup (60 mL) butter or margarine, melted, or canola oil

1 large egg

1 cup (250 mL) all-purpose flour

1 tsp (5 mL) baking powder

½ tsp (2.5 mL) baking soda

½ tsp (2.5 mL) salt

Any additional ingredients you like (see suggestions above)

Oatmeal muffins lend themselves well to a multitude of additions. Try stirring any type of fresh or frozen (unthawed) berries, peeled and chopped peaches, apples or bananas, chocolate chips, chopped nuts, or raisins or other dried fruit into the batter.

Method

1 In a large bowl, stir together the oats and buttermilk and set them aside for half an hour to soak. Spray muffin cups with non-stick spray or line them with paper liners.

2 Preheat the oven to 350°F (175°C).

3 Add the sugar, butter, and egg to the oatmeal mixture and blend well. In a small bowl, stir together the flour, baking powder, baking soda, and salt. Add to the oat mixture and stir a few strokes with a spatula. Add any extra ingredients you like, and mix the batter just until it's combined. Don't worry about getting all the lumps out—overmixing will make the muffins tough.

4 Fill the prepared muffin cups almost to the top and bake in the middle of the oven for 25–30 minutes, until the muffins are golden and the tops are springy to the touch. Tip them in their cups to help them cool by allowing steam to escape.

Makes 10–12 muffins

 What to do with the leftovers

* Keep them in an airtight container at room temperature for up to 3 days, or wrap them well and freeze for up to 4 months.

 Other things to do with it

* Cranberry-White Chocolate Oatmeal Muffins: Add ½ cup (125 mL) each dried cranberries and white chocolate chunks or chips to the batter.

Carrot Apple
Morning Glory Muffins

Ingredients

1 cup (250 mL) all-purpose flour

1 cup (250 mL) whole wheat flour

1 cup (250 mL) sugar (white or
    brown)

1 Tbsp (15 mL) cinnamon

2 tsp (10 mL) baking soda

½ tsp (2.5 mL) salt

2 cups (500 mL) packed grated
    carrots

½ cup (125 mL) chopped pecans
    or walnuts

½ cup (125 mL) raisins

¼ cup (60 mL) flaked coconut, sweet-
    ened or unsweetened (optional)

½ cup (125 mL) canola oil

3 large eggs

¼ cup (60 mL) buttermilk or plain
    yogurt

2 tsp (10 mL) vanilla extract

1 apple, coarsely grated (peeled or
    not)

These muffins have so many good things in them—they make a perfect snack or breakfast on your way out the door. To boost fiber, protein, vitamin, and mineral content, add a few spoonfuls of ground flax seed to the dry ingredients. If you have no whole wheat flour, feel free to substitute all-purpose. To reduce the fat even further, switch the amounts of oil and buttermilk. Keep in mind, though, that canola oil contains healthy fats—the kind we want to include in our diet!

Method

1 Preheat the oven to 350°F (175°C). Spray muffin cups with non-stick spray or line them with paper liners.

2 In a large bowl, stir together the flours, sugar, cinnamon, baking soda, and salt. Add the carrots, pecans, raisins, and coconut and toss to combine well.

3 In a medium bowl, whisk together the oil, eggs, buttermilk, and vanilla. Add to the carrot mixture with the grated apple and stir just until the batter is combined. Don't worry about getting all the lumps out—overmixing will make the muffins tough.

4 Fill the prepared muffin tins almost to the top and bake in the middle of the oven for 25–30 minutes, until the muffins are golden and the tops are springy to the touch. Tip them in their cups to help them cool by allowing steam to escape.

Makes about 1 ½ dozen muffins

 What to do with the leftovers

* Keep them in an airtight container at room temperature for up to 3 days, or wrap them well and freeze for up to 4 months.

 Other things to do with it

* Add the grated zest of an orange to the egg mixture and use dried cranberries instead of raisins.

Banana Bread

Ingredients

¼ cup (60 mL) butter or margarine, softened

¾ cup (185 mL) sugar

1 ½ cups (375 mL) mashed very ripe banana (about 3 bananas)

2 large eggs

⅓ cup (80 mL) plain low fat yogurt, low fat sour cream, or buttermilk

1 tsp (5 mL) vanilla extract

2 cups (500 mL) all-purpose flour, or half whole wheat and half all-purpose

1 tsp (5 mL) baking soda

½ tsp (2.5 mL) salt

⅓ cup (80 mL) chopped walnuts or pecans, or chocolate or butterscotch chips (optional)

Everyone needs a good banana bread recipe in their repertoire. Banana bread makes great peanut butter sandwiches, and toasted slices are delicious spread with cream cheese. To make muffins, divide the batter among 12 muffin tins that have been sprayed with non-stick spray or lined with paper liners, and bake at 400°F (200°C) for 20–25 minutes, until golden and springy to the touch.

Method

1 Preheat the oven to 350°F (175°C). Spray an 8- × 4-inch loaf pan with non-stick spray.

2 In a large bowl, beat the butter and sugar until well combined—the mixture should have the consistency of wet sand. Add the banana, eggs, yogurt, and vanilla and beat until well blended. Don't worry about getting all the lumps of banana out.

3 Add the flour, baking soda, and salt and gently stir with a spatula until just combined. If you are adding nuts or other optional ingredients, throw them in before the batter is completely blended.

4 Pour the batter into the prepared pan and bake in the middle of the oven for 1 hour and 10 minutes, until the top is cracked and springy to the touch. Cool in the pan on a wire rack.

Makes 1 loaf

What to do with the leftovers

* Keep the covered loaf or individually wrapped slices at room temperature for 2 days, or wrap well in plastic and freeze for up to 4 months. If you wrap slices individually before you freeze them, they're easy to grab and take with you.

Other things to do with it

* Blueberry-Lemon Banana Bread: Add the grated zest of a lemon to the butter-sugar mixture, and gently stir in 1 cup (250 mL) fresh or frozen (unthawed) blueberries as you combine the batter.

* Chocolate Swirl Banana Bread: Remove about a cup of the batter and gently stir 2 Tbsp (30 mL) cocoa and ¼ cup (60 mL) chocolate chips into it. Alternate big spoonfuls of plain and chocolate batter in the pan and gently run a knife through both to create a marbled effect.

Quick breads

Cranberry-Orange Bread

Ingredients

2 cups (500 mL) all-purpose flour

1 cup (250 mL) sugar

1 ½ tsp (7 mL) baking powder

½ tsp (2.5 mL) baking soda

½ tsp (2.5 mL) salt

¼ cup (60 mL) butter, chilled

Grated zest of 1 orange

¾ cup (185 mL) orange juice

1 large egg

1 ½ cups (375 mL) fresh or frozen (unthawed) cranberries or blueberries

The dry ingredients and butter blend quickly in a food processor, but you can do it by hand just as easily. Alternatively, soften the butter and beat it with the orange zest, sugar, and egg, then add the dry ingredients and orange juice alternately in two or three batches, mixing by hand just until the batter is combined. To make muffins, divide the batter among 12 muffin tins that have been sprayed with non-stick spray or lined with paper liners, and bake them for 20–25 minutes, until golden and springy to the touch.

Method

1 Preheat oven to 350°F (175°C). Spray an 8- × 4-inch loaf pan with non-stick spray.

2 In the bowl of a food processor, combine the flour, sugar, baking powder, baking soda, and salt. Process until combined. Add the butter and orange zest and pulse until well blended and crumbly; transfer to a large bowl. (If you don't have a food processor, you can mix everything up with a fork until well blended.)

3 In a small bowl, stir together the orange juice and egg. Add to the flour mixture and stir with a spatula until the dough is partially combined; add the berries and stir gently until just blended.

4 Pour the batter into the prepared pan and smooth the top. Bake for 1 hour and 10 minutes, until the loaf is golden and the top is springy to the touch. Cool in the pan on a wire rack.

Makes 1 loaf

What to do with the leftovers

* Keep the covered loaf or individually wrapped slices at room temperature for 2 days, or wrap well in plastic and freeze for up to 4 months.

Other things to do with it

* Replace the cranberries with blueberries, blackberries, or chocolate chunks.

* Cranberry Nut Bread: Add ½ cup (125 mL) coarsely chopped pecans along with the cranberries.

* Blueberry Lemon Bread: Replace the juice with milk, the orange zest with lemon zest, and add 1 Tbsp (15 mL) of lemon juice. Use fresh or frozen (unthawed) blueberries instead of cranberries.

Quick breads

Berry-Lemon Loaf

Ingredients

¼ cup (60 mL) butter or margarine, softened

1 cup (250 mL) sugar

Grated zest of 1–2 lemons

2 large eggs

1 ½ cups (375 mL) all-purpose flour

1 tsp (5 mL) baking powder

¼ tsp (1 mL) salt

½ cup (125 mL) milk

1 ½ cups (375 mL) fresh or frozen (unthawed) blackberries, raspberries, or blueberries

Glaze

3 Tbsp (45 mL) lemon juice

¼ cup (60 mL) confectioners' sugar

This is a great way to use berries when they're in season, but the loaf tastes just as good with frozen berries. Make sure you keep the berries frozen right up until you add them to prevent their juice streaking through your batter and turning it blue. Some cooks toss their berries with a bit of flour first (use some from the recipe rather than adding more) to help absorb any excess juice. Leave the berries out completely for a plain lemon loaf.

Method

1 Preheat the oven to 350°F (175°C). Spray an 8- × 4-inch loaf pan with non-stick spray.

2 In a large bowl, beat the butter, sugar, and lemon zest with an electric mixer for about a minute, until fluffy. Add the eggs one at a time, beating well after each addition.

3 If you want, toss the berries with about a tablespoon of the flour to prevent them from releasing their juices into the batter and turning it blue. Put them back into the freezer until it's time to use them. In a medium bowl, stir together the flour, baking powder, and salt. Add one-third of the flour mixture to the butter mixture and stir by hand just until it's combined. Add half the milk in the same manner. Add another third of the flour mixture, the rest of the milk, and the rest of the flour mixture, along with the berries. Stir by hand just until your batter is blended.

4 Pour the batter into the prepared pan and bake for 1 hour, until it's cracked and golden and the top is springy to the touch. Poke the top of the loaf all over with a bamboo skewer or toothpick. Stir together the lemon juice and confectioners' sugar and brush or drizzle over the loaf while it's still warm. I like to brush half over the top, let it soak in, then brush on the rest. Cool in the pan on a wire rack.

Makes 1 loaf

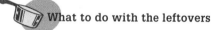 **What to do with the leftovers**

* Keep the covered loaf or individually wrapped slices at room temperature for 2 days, or wrap well in plastic and freeze for up to 4 months.

 Other things to do with it

* Serve thick slices topped with fresh berries and a dollop of whipped cream.

Zucchini-Walnut Loaf

Ingredients

2 cups (500 mL) all-purpose
   flour, or half whole wheat,
   half all-purpose

¾ cup (185 mL) sugar

1 Tbsp (15 mL) baking powder

½ tsp (2.5 mL) baking soda

½ tsp (2.5 mL) cinnamon (optional)

¼ tsp (1 mL) salt

½ cup (125 mL) milk

¼ cup (60 mL) canola oil

2 large eggs

Grated zest of 1 lemon (optional)

2 cups (500 mL) grated unpeeled zucchini (about 1 large zucchini)

½ cup (125 mL) chopped walnuts or
   pecans

This makes a nice dense loaf, and it's a great way to use up zucchini in August when your neighbors are trying to pawn them off on you. To make muffins, divide the batter among 12 muffin tins that have been sprayed with non-stick spray or lined with paper liners, and bake at 400°F (200°C) for 20–25 minutes, until golden and springy to the touch.

Method

1 Preheat the oven to 350°F (175°C). Spray an 8- × 4-inch loaf pan with non-stick spray.

2 In a large bowl, combine the flour, sugar, baking powder, baking soda, cinnamon, and salt.

3 In a small bowl, whisk together the milk, oil, eggs, and lemon zest and add to the flour mixture with the grated zucchini and walnuts. Stir by hand until just combined. Don't worry about getting all the lumps out—overmixing will make the loaf tough.

4 Pour the batter into the prepared pan and bake in the middle of the oven for 1 hour, until the loaf is golden and springy to the touch. Cool in the pan on a wire rack.

Makes 1 loaf

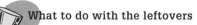 **What to do with the leftovers**

* Keep the covered loaf or individually wrapped slices at room temperature for 2 days, or wrap well in plastic and freeze for up to 4 months.

 Other things to do with it

* Chocolate Zucchini Loaf: Omit the lemon zest and replace ½ cup (125 mL) of the flour with cocoa. Add ½ cup (125 mL) chocolate chips with the walnuts or pecans.

Whole Wheat Nut Bread

Ingredients

2 cups (500 mL) all-purpose flour

1 cup (250 mL) whole wheat flour

¾ cup (185 mL) sugar

1 Tbsp (15 mL) baking powder

¼ tsp (1 mL) baking soda

½ tsp (2.5 mL) salt

1 ½ cups (375 mL) milk

¼ cup (60 mL) canola oil or melted
    butter or margarine

1 large egg

1 cup (250 mL) chopped walnuts,
    pecans, almonds, or a combina-
    tion

This plain whole wheat loaf is quick, easy, good for you, and really delicious toasted and spread with peanut butter or cream cheese. If you freeze individual slices, you can toast them from frozen. Try adding a handful of raisins or chopped dried fruit along with the nuts.

Method

1 Preheat the oven to 350°F (175°C). Spray an 8- × 4-inch or 9- × 5-inch loaf pan with non-stick spray.

2 In a large bowl, combine the flours, sugar, baking powder, baking soda, and salt. In a small bowl, stir together the milk, oil, and egg.

3 Make a well in the middle of the dry ingredients and add the wet ingredients along with the nuts. Stir with a spatula until just combined. Don't worry about getting all the lumps out—overmixing will make your bread tough.

4 Spread the batter into the prepared pan. Bake for 1 hour and 10 minutes, until the loaf is golden and the top is springy to the touch. Cool in the pan on a wire rack.

Makes 1 loaf

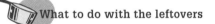

What to do with the leftovers

*   Keep the covered loaf or individually wrapped slices at room temperature for 2 days, or wrap well in plastic and freeze for up to 4 months.

Other things to do with it

*   Cranberry Nut Bread: Add 1 cup (250 mL) of fresh or frozen (unthawed) cranberries and the grated zest of an orange along with the nuts.

*   Cinnamon Raisin Nut Bread: Add ½ cup (125 mL) raisins (or any other chopped dried fruit) and a big pinch of cinnamon along with the nuts.

Quick
breads

Cinnamon Ripple
Streusel Bread

Ingredients

2 cups (500 mL) all-purpose flour

1 cup (250 mL) sugar

2 tsp (10 mL) baking powder

½ tsp (2.5 mL) baking soda

½ tsp (2.5 mL) salt

1 ½ cups (375 mL) buttermilk

2 large eggs

¼ cup (60 mL) canola oil

1 tsp (5 mL) vanilla extract

Ripple and Streusel

¼ cup (60 mL) packed brown sugar

2 tsp (10 mL) cinnamon

2 Tbsp (30 mL) flour

2 tsp (10 mL) butter or margarine

This loaf resembles a loaf-shaped coffee cake. For a cinnamon boost, add an extra teaspoon to the dry ingredients when you make the batter. If you don't have buttermilk, substitute plain yogurt, thinned with a little milk.

Method

1   Preheat oven to 350°F (175°C). Spray an 8- × 4-inch loaf pan with non-stick spray.

2   In a large bowl, combine the flour, sugar, baking powder, baking soda, and salt. In a small bowl, stir together the buttermilk, eggs, oil, and vanilla. Add the wet ingredients to the dry ingredients and stir gently by hand, just until blended. Don't overmix, or the bread will be tough.

3   In a small dish, blend together the brown sugar and cinnamon. Spread one-third of the batter into the prepared pan and sprinkle with about a quarter of the cinnamon sugar. Top with another third of the batter and another quarter of the cinnamon sugar. Add the flour and butter to the remaining cinnamon sugar and blend with a fork or your fingers until well combined and crumbly.

4   Spread the remaining batter over the rest in the pan and sprinkle with the streusel mixture. Bake for 1 hour, until the loaf is golden and the top is springy to the touch. Cool in the pan on a wire rack.

Makes 1 loaf

What to do with the leftovers

*   Keep the covered loaf or individually wrapped slices at room temperature for 2 days, or wrap well in plastic and freeze for up to 4 months.

Other things to do with it

*   Chunky Apple-Cinnamon Bread: Peel and chop a tart apple and stir it into the batter. Add a handful of chopped walnuts, almonds, or pecans to the streusel mixture.

*   Cinnamon Ripple Raisin Bread: Add ½ cup (125 mL) raisins to the batter as you combine the wet and dry ingredients.

Sour Cream Cheese Bread

Ingredients

3 cups (750 mL) all-purpose flour

1 Tbsp (15 mL) baking powder

1 tsp (5 mL) salt

¼ tsp (1 mL) cayenne pepper
(optional)

1 cup (250 mL) grated old
cheddar or other intensely
flavored cheese

½ cup (125 mL) grated Parmesan

1 ¼ cups (310 mL) milk

¾ cup (185 mL) light sour cream

3 Tbsp (45 mL) butter or margarine,
melted

1 large egg

Cheesy bread is easy to mix and bake in a hurry and is perfect for dunking in chili, stews, or soup. It's also a great way to use up any leftover bits of cheese you have in the fridge.

Method

1 Preheat the oven to 350°F (175°C). Spray a 9- × 5-inch loaf pan with non-stick spray.

2 In a large bowl, stir together the flour, baking powder, salt, and cayenne pepper. Stir in the cheeses, tossing to blend and get rid of clumps.

3 In a medium bowl, stir together the milk, sour cream, butter, and egg. Add it to the dry ingredients and stir gently with a spatula until just combined. Don't overmix, or the bread will be tough.

4 Pour the batter into the prepared pan. If you like, sprinkle the top with more grated cheddar or Parmesan.

5 Bake for 45–50 minutes, until the loaf is golden and the top is springy to the touch. Cool in the pan on a wire rack.

Makes 1 loaf

 What to do with the leftovers

* Keep the covered loaf or individually wrapped slices at room temperature for 2 days, or wrap well in plastic and freeze for up to 4 months.

Other things to do with it

* Stir in a handful of chopped fresh herbs, diced ham, or a few slices of crumbled cooked bacon.

* Serve topped with the sloppy Joe mixture on page 125.

* To make muffins, fill 12 greased or paper-lined muffin tins and bake them for 20–25 minutes, until golden and springy to the touch. Makes 12 to 14 muffins.

Corn Bread

Ingredients

1 ½ cups (375 mL) cornmeal

½ cup (125 mL) all-purpose flour

1 Tbsp (15 mL) sugar

1 ½ tsp (7 mL) baking powder

½ tsp (2.5 mL) salt

1 ¼ cups (310 mL) buttermilk, sour
milk (see page 45) or plain yogurt

¼ cup (60 mL) butter, melted, or
canola or olive oil

1 large egg

Corn bread is delicious plain, but you can do all kinds of great things with it. Try stirring in some crumbled cooked bacon, sautéed onions (especially good if you sauté them in a little bacon fat), grated cheese, chopped cilantro, chili powder or cumin, or about a cup of fresh or creamed corn. Or make it sweet by adding an extra spoonful of sugar or maple syrup and some fresh or frozen blueberries or chopped pecans.

Method

1 Preheat the oven to 375°F (190°C). Spray an 8-inch round pan or cast iron skillet with non-stick spray.

2 In a medium bowl, combine the cornmeal, flour, sugar, baking powder, and salt. In a small bowl, stir together the buttermilk, butter, and egg. Add to the flour mixture and stir gently, until just combined.

3 Pour the batter into the prepared pan or skillet. Bake for 25–30 minutes, until golden around the edges and puffed and cracked on top.

Serves 6

 What to do with the leftovers

* Keep wrapped in plastic at room temperature for 2 days or wrap well and freeze.

* Stale corn bread makes great stuffing, or crumble it over soup or chili instead of using croutons.

 Other things to do with it

* Blueberry-Maple Corn Bread: Add 2 Tbsp (30 mL) of maple syrup instead of the sugar, and stir in a handful of fresh or frozen (unthawed) blueberries. Brush the top with maple syrup while it's still warm.

Quick
breads

Pan Bread

Ingredients

1 Tbsp (15 mL) butter

1 Tbsp (15 mL) oil

2 large onions, cut in half and thinly sliced

1 tsp (5 mL) sugar (white or brown)

2 cups (500 mL) all-purpose flour

1 Tbsp (15 mL) baking powder

½ tsp (2.5 mL) salt

1 cup (250 mL) milk

¼ cup (60 mL) canola oil

1 large egg

Pan bread is like a giant biscuit, baked in a round or square pan with caramelized onions underneath to make a loaf similar to an upside-down cake. Try stirring some chopped fresh herbs or crumbled bits of cheese into the batter, or make it sweet by caramelizing apples instead of onions.

Method

1 Preheat the oven to 350°F (175°C). Spray the bottom of a pie plate or an 8-inch round or square pan with non-stick spray.

2 In a large skillet set over medium heat, melt the butter with the oil. Sauté the onions for about 15 minutes, until they're soft and starting to turn golden. Stir in the sugar and spread the onions over the bottom of the prepared pan.

3 In a medium bowl, combine the flour, baking powder, and salt. In a small bowl, stir together the milk, oil, and egg. Add the milk mixture to the flour mixture and stir until just blended.

4 Spread the batter over the onions and bake for 35–40 minutes, until golden around the edges, cracked on top, and springy to the touch.

5 Cut into wedges or squares and serve warm.

Makes 1 round loaf

What to do with the leftovers

* Keep them covered in the fridge for up to 2 days, or wrap well and freeze for up to 4 months.

Other things to do with it

* Add a few crushed cloves of garlic (or if you're a real fan, leave them whole) to the onion mixture.

* Stir a handful of chopped fresh herbs and/or about ½ cup (125 mL) grated cheddar or crumbled feta cheese into the batter.

* Apple Pan Bread: Sauté peeled, sliced apples instead of the onions, adding an extra spoonful of sugar, for a few minutes until they start to soften and turn golden. Add 2 Tbsp (30 mL) sugar and a shake of cinnamon to the batter and bake as directed.

Quick breads

Irish Soda Bread

Ingredients

2 cups (500 mL) all-purpose flour

2 cups (500 mL) whole wheat flour

2 Tbsp (30 mL) packed brown sugar

2 tsp (10 mL) baking powder

1 tsp (5 mL) baking soda

1 tsp (5 mL) salt

2 cups (500 mL) buttermilk or yogurt,
thinned with a little milk

1 large egg

2 Tbsp (30 mL) canola or olive oil

Flour or old-fashioned (large flake)
oats, for rolling

I'm always amazed that people don't make soda bread more often. It's such an easy way to have freshly baked bread in no time at all! Soda bread is ideal for those who are hesitant to attempt yeast bread from scratch—success is all but guaranteed. Add any extras you like, such as a handful of dried fruit, nuts, grated cheese, or fresh herbs.

Method

1 Preheat the oven to 375°F (190°C). Spray a baking sheet with non-stick spray.

2 In a large bowl, combine the flours, sugar, baking powder, baking soda, and salt. In a medium bowl, stir together the buttermilk, egg, and oil, and add all at once to the dry ingredients. Stir by hand just until you have a soft ball of dough.

3 Sprinkle the countertop with a little flour or oats and knead the dough about 10 times, forming it into a ball. (To knead the dough, press down into it using the heels of both hands, and push it away from you. Fold it in half, make a quarter turn and repeat.) Place the ball of dough on the prepared baking sheet and lightly cut an X on the top with a sharp knife.

4 Bake for 45–55 minutes, until the loaf is golden and sounds hollow when you tap it on the bottom.

Makes 1 loaf

 What to do with the leftovers

* Keep it well wrapped at room temperature and freeze whatever you don't eat the same day. It's easiest if you slice the loaf first before freezing, then you can thaw only as many slices as you need or toast them from frozen.

 Other things to do with it

* Raisin Caraway Soda Bread: Add 2 cups (500 mL) raisins and 2 Tbsp (30 mL) caraway seeds to make a traditional Irish soda bread.

* Oatmeal-Walnut Soda Bread: Soak 2 cups (500 mL) of old-fashioned oats in the buttermilk for an hour before you make the bread. Mix and bake the bread as directed, adding the oats and 1 cup (250 mL) chopped, toasted walnuts when it's time to add the extras. (To toast walnuts, put them in a dry pan over medium heat and cook, shaking the pan frequently, until they're golden and fragrant.)

Quick breads

Biscuits

Ingredients

1 cup (250 mL) all-purpose flour

1 cup (250 mL) whole wheat flour

1 Tbsp (15 mL) sugar (optional)

1 Tbsp (15 mL) baking powder

¼ tsp (1 mL) baking soda

pinch salt

¼ cup (60 mL) butter, chilled and cut into pieces

¼ cup (60 mL) olive oil

¾ cup (185 mL) milk or buttermilk

What to do with the leftovers

* Wrap well and freeze whatever you don't eat the same day. They will keep in the freezer for up to 3 months.

Biscuits and scones are the fastest and easiest of all quick breads to make. They take no more than a few minutes to stir up from scratch, and then rise in the oven to about twice their original height. Fresh baking powder is essential for your biscuits to rise—if you are unsure of its age, see page 235.

These are made healthier with the addition of olive oil and whole wheat flour, but you can use all white flour if you like. To flavor the dough, add grated lemon or orange zest, ginger, fresh or dried herbs (such as basil or rosemary) or spices (such as cinnamon, star anise or fennel seed), or stir in a handful of grated cheese or fresh, frozen or dried berries.

Scones are very closely related to biscuits, but are usually made sweeter and richer with the addition of cream and/or an egg. See the variations on the next page to turn your biscuits into scones.

Method

1 Preheat the oven to 400°F (200°C). Spray a baking sheet with non-stick spray.

2 In a large bowl or the bowl of a food processor, combine the flours, sugar, baking powder, baking soda and salt and stir until well blended. Add the butter and oil and pulse or stir with a wire whisk or fork until crumbly. If you're using a food processor, transfer the mixture to a medium bowl.

3 Add the milk and stir gently just until the dough begins to come together. Add any additions (cheese, raisins, nuts, fruit etc.) as you stir the dough together.

4 For round biscuits, pat the dough about 1 inch (2.5 cm) thick and cut it into rounds with a biscuit cutter, glass rim or open end of a can, rerolling the scraps only once to get as many biscuits as possible. For wedge-shaped biscuits, pat the dough into a circle that is about 1 inch (2.5 cm) thick and 8–9 inches (20–23 cm) in diameter on the cookie sheet. (If they are sweet and you want a brown, crunchy top, brush them with a little milk and sprinkle with sugar.) Cut the circle into 8 wedges with a knife or pastry cutter and separate them on the sheet so that they are at least 1 inch (2.5 cm) apart.

5 Bake for 15–20 minutes, until golden. Serve warm. Wrap well and freeze any you don't eat the same day.

Makes 8 (or more) biscuits

Quick breads

Other things to do with it

* Buttery Lemon Scones: Add ¼ cup (60 mL) sugar to the flour mixture, double the amount of butter (or add ¼ cup olive or canola oil with the butter), and add the grated zest of 1 lemon along with it. Add ½ cup (125 mL) finely chopped candied ginger, dried cranberries or cherries, raisins or currants, or 1 cup (250 mL) fresh blueberries when you combine the wet and dry ingredients.

* Cheese Biscuits: Stir 1 cup (250 mL) of grated cheese (a combination of old cheddar and Parmesan is good) into the flour mixture after you blend in the butter.

* Chocolate Biscuits: Replace ½ cup (125 mL) of the flour with cocoa. Chocolate biscuits are great split and filled with berries and vanilla yogurt or whipped cream.

* Cranberry-Orange or Blueberry-Lemon Biscuits: Add 2 Tbsp (30 mL) sugar and the grated zest of an orange or lemon to the dry ingredients, and add a handful of fresh or frozen (unthawed) cranberries or blueberries to the dough as you stir it together.

* Cream Scones: Add ¼ cup (60 mL) sugar to the flour mixture, omit the butter and milk, and stir in 1 ¼ cups (310 mL) of whipping cream instead. These may sound incredibly rich, but because you've removed all the butter, they aren't quite as high-fat as they sound, even with the cream. Flavor the scones with grated orange or lemon zest, or add a handful of currants or raisins. If you like, brush them with a little milk and sprinkle with sugar before they go into the oven.

* Jam-Filled Biscuits: Push your thumb into the middle of the cut biscuits, making a dent that reaches almost to the bottom, and push outward to create a 1-inch (2.5 cm) hole. Dollop a small spoonful of jam into each hole before you bake them. These may need a few extra minutes in the oven.

* Orange or Maple-Pecan Biscuits: Add the grated zest of an orange or 1 tsp (5 mL) maple extract to the milk, and ½ cup (125 mL) chopped toasted pecans to the mixture after you blend in the butter.

* Parmesan, Olive, and Sun-Dried Tomato Biscuits: Stir a few chopped black olives, a few chopped sun-dried tomatoes and 2 Tbsp (30 mL) grated Parmesan into the flour mixture after you blend in the butter.

* Shortcake Biscuits: Add 3 Tbsp (45 mL) sugar to the dry ingredients. Split the baked shortcakes and fill them with fresh berries (or sliced stone fruits) tossed with a little sugar, and a dollop of whipped cream.

Cinnamon Sticky Buns

Ingredients

1 lb (500 g) loaf frozen bread dough, thawed (white or whole wheat)

Syrup

⅓ cup (80 mL) packed brown sugar

⅓ cup (80 mL) corn syrup, honey, or maple syrup

1 Tbsp (15 mL) butter, softened

¼ cup (60 mL) chopped pecans (optional)

Filling

½ cup (125 mL) packed brown sugar

½ tsp (2.5 mL) cinnamon

¼ cup (60 mL) chopped pecans (optional)

¼ cup (60 mL) raisins (optional)

1–2 Tbsp (15–30 mL) butter, softened or melted

There's nothing better than a big, sticky cinnamon bun, fresh out of the oven, and they're easier to make than you might think. If you've made yeast bread before, use your favorite recipe to make the dough yourself. If you're a fan of cream cheese icing, use the recipe on page 284, and spread the frosting thickly over your buns once they've cooled.

Method

1 Spray an 8-inch or 9-inch round or square cake pan with non-stick spray.

2 Combine the ⅓ cup (80 mL) sugar, corn syrup, butter, and pecans in a small microwave-safe bowl and heat for about 30 seconds. Stir until melted and smooth. (Alternatively, combine the ingredients in a small pot set over medium heat, and stir until melted and smooth.) Pour the mixture over the bottom of the prepared pan.

3 In a small bowl, combine the ½ cup (125 mL) brown sugar, cinnamon, pecans (if using), and raisins (if using). Roll the dough out on a lightly floured surface into a rectangle that is roughly 12 ×16 inches (30–40 cm). Brush the dough with the softened or melted butter, leaving about an inch along one short edge bare so that the dough sticks when you roll it up. Sprinkle evenly with the brown sugar and cinnamon mixture, leaving the same end bare.

4 Starting at the side opposite the unbuttered edge, tightly roll the dough up jelly roll style, forming a log. Pinch the edge to seal. Using a sharp, serrated knife or some dental floss, cut the dough into 8 even slices if you're using a round pan, or 9 if you're using a square pan.

Quick breads

5 Place the rolls cut side down in the pan—in a round pan, they fit best if you put one in the middle and then the other 7 around it. In a square pan, arrange them in 3 rows of 3. Cover with a tea towel and let them rise in a warm place for about an hour, until doubled in bulk.

6 Preheat the oven to 350°F (175°C).

7 Place the pan on a cookie sheet to catch any drips and bake for 20–30 minutes, until golden. Immediately invert onto a plate.

Makes 8 or 9 buns

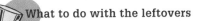

What to do with the leftovers

* Cover them with plastic and keep them at room temperature for a day; wrap and freeze any you intend to keep longer.

Other things to do with it

* Cranberry-Orange Sticky Buns: Grate some orange zest into the filling mixture and sprinkle with fresh or dried cranberries instead of the raisins.

Cookies and bars

Even people who don't bake have likely mixed up a batch of cookies at some point during their lifetime. In fact, it was most likely your first kitchen experience as a child. And for good reason—cookies are among the most rewarding things to make. Freshly baked cookies are infinitely better than the packaged variety, including those made from dough that has been squeezed out of a tube. There are always circumstances—bake sales, rainy weekends, school parties, sad days—that call for homemade cookies, but the best reason to make some is that it will make lots of people very happy.

There aren't many hard and fast rules to cookie baking, but there are a few things to know that may make your cookies even better. Read up on baking basics (page 229), and remember the two cardinal rules of cookie baking: cookies are best when the dough hasn't been overmixed, and don't bake them for too long if you want them to be chewy.

Peanut Butter Cookies

Ingredients

1 ½ cups (375 mL) peanut butter (regular, crunchy, or light)

½ cup (125 mL) sugar

½ cup (125 mL) packed brown sugar

1 large egg white

These are the best (and easiest) peanut butter cookies you'll ever make. Because they have no flour in them, there's nothing to dilute their peanut buttery flavour, and they have a rich melt-in-your-mouth texture. They're also perfect for anyone who has a gluten intolerance and can't eat flour.

Method

1 Preheat the oven to 350°F (175°C).

2 In a large bowl, stir together the peanut butter, sugars, and egg white until well blended.

3 Roll the dough into walnut-sized balls and place them about 2 inches (5 cm) apart on an ungreased cookie sheet. Press down on each cookie once or twice with the back of a fork.

4 Bake them for 12–15 minutes, until they're very pale golden around the edges. Gently transfer to a wire rack to cool.

Makes about 2 dozen cookies

 What to do with the leftovers

* These cookies keep really well. Store them in a tightly sealed container for up to a week, or wrap them well and freeze them for up to 3 months.

 Other things to do with it

* Add ½ cup (125 mL) white chocolate chips or chunks to the dough, or ½ cup (125 mL) raisins.

Ginger Molasses Crinkles

Ingredients

2 Tbsp (30 mL) canola oil

¼ cup (60 mL) butter or
   margarine, at room temperature

⅓ cup (80 mL) dark molasses

1 cup (250 mL) packed brown sugar

1 large egg

1 tsp (5 mL) vanilla extract

2 cups (500 mL) all-purpose flour

2 tsp (10 mL) baking soda

1 tsp (5 mL) cinnamon

½ tsp (2.5 mL) ground ginger

½ tsp (2.5 mL) salt

Sugar, for rolling

Baking these cookies is better than using potpourri—they're worth making just for the aroma. If you have fresh ginger, grate some and add 1–3 tsp (5–15 mL) (depending on your love for ginger) to the butter-molasses mixture, and omit the ground ginger. The gingery dough is rolled into balls and then rolled in sugar before baking them, so the cookies spread and crack as they bake and end up with a wonderfully sugary, crunchy exterior.

Method

1   Preheat the oven to 350°F (175°C). Spray a cookie sheet with non-stick spray.

2   In a large bowl, combine the oil, butter, molasses, brown sugar, egg, and vanilla. Stir until the mixture is well blended.

3   In a medium bowl, stir together the flour, baking soda, cinnamon, ginger, and salt. Add the flour mixture to the molasses mixture and stir by hand just until you have a soft dough.

4   Roll the dough into walnut-sized balls and roll the balls in sugar to coat them well. Place about an inch (2.5 cm) apart on the greased cookie sheet.

5   Bake the cookies for 12–14 minutes, until they're just set around the edges but still soft in the middle. Transfer them to a wire rack to cool.

Makes about 2 dozen cookies

What to do with the leftovers

*   Store extras in a tightly sealed container for a few days or wrap them well and freeze them for up to 3 months.

Other things to do with it

*   Stir ½ cup (125 mL) chopped crystallized ginger into the dough along with the dry ingredients.

*   Ice Cream Sandwiches: Spread softened vanilla ice cream or lemon sherbet on the underside of half of the cooled cookies and top them with a second cookie to make sandwiches. Wrap the ice cream sandwiches individually in plastic wrap and freeze them until firm.

Chewy Oatmeal Raisin Cookies

Ingredients

¼ cup (60 mL) butter or stick margarine, softened

1 cup (250 mL) packed dark or golden brown sugar

2 Tbsp (30 mL) honey or corn syrup

1 large egg

1 tsp (5 mL) vanilla extract

1 cup (250 mL) all-purpose flour

½ tsp (2.5 mL) cinnamon

½ tsp (2.5 mL) baking powder

¼ tsp (1 mL) baking soda

¼ tsp (1 mL) salt

1 ½ cups (375 mL) old-fashioned oats

1 cup (250 mL) raisins

If there was a cookie popularity contest, oatmeal raisin would run a close second to chocolate chip. You could, of course, replace the raisins with chocolate chips for oatmeal-chocolate chip cookies, or use chocolate-covered raisins. I can never stress enough—don't bake your cookies for too long if you want them to be chewy. Check them at the earliest suggested baking time and take them out when they're golden and just set around the edges, but still soft in the middle.

Method

1 Preheat the oven to 350°F (175°C). Spray a cookie sheet with non-stick spray.

2 In a large bowl, beat the butter and brown sugar until well blended—the mixture should have the consistency of wet sand. Add the honey, egg, and vanilla and beat until smooth.

3 In a small bowl, stir together the flour, cinnamon, baking powder, baking soda, and salt. Add the flour mixture to the butter mixture with the oats and stir until the dough starts to come together. Add the raisins and stir just until the dough is combined.

4 Drop spoonfuls of dough, or roll balls of dough and place them 1–2 inches apart on the greased cookie sheet. Flatten each cookie a little with your hand.

5 Bake for 10–12 minutes, until the cookies are golden around the edges but still soft in the middle. Transfer them to a wire rack to cool.

Makes about 1 ½ dozen cookies

What to do with the leftovers

* Keep them in a tightly sealed container for a few days, or wrap them well and freeze for up to 3 months.

Other things to do with it

* Add ½ cup (125 mL) chopped walnuts or pecans with the raisins.

* Use a mixture of chopped dried fruit (such as cranberries and apricots) or chocolate chips in place of the raisins. Omit the c innamon if you're using chocolate chips.

* Oatmeal Marmalade Cookies: Use ¼ cup (60 mL) marmalade instead of the honey.

Chocolate Chip Cookies

Ingredients

¼–½ cup (60–125 mL) butter or stick margarine, softened

1 cup (250 mL) packed brown sugar

1 large egg

2 Tbsp (30 mL) corn syrup or honey

1 tsp (5 mL) vanilla extract

1 ½ cups (375 mL) all-purpose flour

1 tsp (5 mL) baking soda

¼ tsp (1 mL) salt

1 cup (250 mL) chocolate chips

½ cup (125 mL) chopped pecans (optional)

What to do with the leftovers

*   Keep them in a tightly sealed container for up to 2 days, or wrap them well and freeze them for up to 3 months.

Other things to do with them

*   Cranberry-White Chocolate Chunk Oatmeal Cookies: Add ½ cup (125 mL) oats to the flour mixture, and use white chocolate chunks or chips. Add ½ cup (125 mL) dried cranberries with the chocolate.

*   Add butterscotch, white chocolate, or peanut butter chips, chocolate covered raisins, or chopped peanut butter cups instead of the chocolate chips.

Everyone should know how to bake a batch of chocolate chip cookies without having to squeeze the dough out of a tube. These ones are chewy (like chocolate chip cookies ought to be), with a slightly crunchy edge. These cookies contain at least half the butter of traditional recipes. If you prefer buttery cookies, increase the butter to ½ cup (125 mL).

Method

1   Preheat the oven to 350°F (175°C). Spray a cookie sheet with non-stick spray.

2   In a large bowl, beat the butter and brown sugar with an electric mixer or by hand until well blended—the mixture should have the consistency of wet sand. Add the egg, corn syrup, and vanilla and beat until smooth.

3   In a medium bowl, combine the flour, baking soda, and salt. Add the flour mixture to the butter mixture and stir until the dough starts to come together. Add the chocolate chips and pecans (if using) and stir just until the dough is combined.

4   Drop spoonfuls of dough about 2 inches (5 cm) apart on the greased cookie sheet, and flatten each cookie a little with your hand. Bake for 12–15 minutes, until the cookies are barely golden and set around the edges but still soft in the middle. Transfer them to a wire rack to cool.

Makes about 20 cookies

*   Double Chocolate Chip Cookies: Replace ¼ cup (60 mL) of the flour with ¼ cup (60 mL) cocoa. If you like, mix 1 tsp (5 mL) instant coffee into 1 tsp (5 mL) water, and add it along with the vanilla. This coffee "extract" enhances the chocolate flavour without adding fat or calories.

*   Grind ½ cup (125 mL) oats in a food processor until they have the texture of coarse flour, and use it in place of ½ cup (125 mL) of the flour.

Sugar Cookies

Ingredients

¼ cup (60 mL) butter or stick
    margarine, softened

1 Tbsp (15 mL) canola oil

¾ cup (185 mL) sugar

Grated zest of 1 lemon (optional)

1 large egg

1 tsp (5 mL) vanilla extract

1 ⅔ cups (410 mL) all-purpose flour

1 tsp (5 mL) baking powder

¼ tsp (1 mL) salt

Other things to do with it

*   Add the grated zest of an orange
    instead of a lemon, or make spice
    cookies by adding ½ tsp (2.5 mL)
    cinnamon, ¼ tsp (1 mL) nutmeg,
    and ¼ tsp (1 mL) ground ginger to
    the flour mixture.

*   Chocolate Sugar Cookies: Replace
    ⅓ cup (80 mL) of the flour with
    ⅓ cup (80 mL) cocoa.

*   Icebox Cookies: Shape the fin-
    ished dough into a log instead of a
    disk, wrap it well in plastic wrap,
    and freeze for up to 4 months. Roll
    the log in coarse sugar or chopped
    nuts for a sweet or crunchy edge.
    When you want freshly baked
    cookies, slice the frozen dough
    directly onto a cookie sheet and
    bake as directed.

When you feel the need for a festive sort of cookie, these are the kind you roll out, cut into shapes and decorate. If you don't have any cookie cutters, use the open end of a can or the rim of a glass, or cut into shapes with a knife. If you want to hang them with ribbon or string, cut a hole near the top with a straw before baking.

Method

1   In a large bowl, beat the butter, oil, sugar, and lemon zest with an electric mixer until light. Add the egg and vanilla and beat until smooth.

2   In a small bowl, combine the flour, baking powder, and salt. Add the flour mixture to the sugar mixture and stir by hand just until you have a soft dough. Divide the dough in half, shape each piece into a disk, wrap in plastic wrap, and refrigerate for about an hour. (You can make the dough ahead up to this point and keep it in the fridge for a few days or freeze it for up to 4 months.)

3   Preheat the oven to 350°F (175°C); spray a cookie sheet with non-stick spray.

4   Remove one piece of dough from the fridge and roll it out between two sheets of waxed paper or parchment until it's ⅛–¼ inch (3–5 mm) thick. (Rolling it this way minimizes excess flour being absorbed by the dough—if you don't have waxed paper, lightly flour the countertop with a combination of flour and sugar.) Alternatively, you can roll the dough by hand into wal-nut-sized balls and place them on a cookie sheet that has been sprayed with non-stick spray; dip the bottom of a glass into water, then in sugar (add some cinnamon to the sugar if you like), and use it to flatten the cookies.

5   If you've rolled the dough out, cut out the cookies using a cookie cutter, the rim of a glass, or a knife. Re-roll the scraps only once—the more you handle the dough, the tougher it will get. Place the cookies about an inch apart on the greased cookie sheet.

6   Bake for 10–12 minutes, until they're pale golden around the edges. Transfer the cookies to a wire rack to cool. Once they're completely cool, you can dec-orate them with any of the icings or frostings on page 284.

Makes about 3 dozen cookies

What to do with the leftovers

*   Keep them in a tightly sealed container for up to a week, or
    wrap them well in plastic wrap and freeze for up to 3 months.

Shortbread

Ingredients

1 cup (250 mL) butter, at room temperature

¼ cup (60 mL) sugar

¼ cup (60 mL) confectioners' sugar

½ tsp (2.5 mL) vanilla extract

Scant 2 cups (500 mL) all-purpose flour

½ tsp (2.5 mL) baking powder

¼ tsp (1 mL) salt

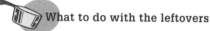

What to do with the leftovers

* Keep them in a tightly sealed container for up to a week, or wrap them well and freeze for up to 3 months.

Other things to do with it

* Coconut Shortbread: Use coconut extract in place of the vanilla, and add ¾ cup (180 mL) toasted shredded coconut to the flour mixture before adding it to the butter mixture. (Toast coconut in a dry pan set over medium heat, shaking it often until the coconut is pale golden and fragrant.)

* Pecan-Praline Shortbread: Use ½ cup (125 mL) packed brown sugar in place of the white and confectioners' sugars, and add ½ cup (125 mL) finely chopped pecans to the dough along with the flour mixture.

Shortbread is high in fat, namely butter. That's just the way it is. Shortbread is made with a precise ratio of butter, sugar, and flour; removing some of the fat and adding wet ingredients such as eggs or milk will cause it to become cakey and lose its melt-in-your-mouth texture. So if you're worried about fat, just enjoy it occasionally without devouring the whole batch.

Never try substituting margarine for the butter—its flavor and texture just won't be the same.

Method

1 Preheat the oven to 300°F (150°C).

2 In a large bowl, beat the butter and sugars with an electric mixer for about 2 minutes, until light and fluffy. Beat in the vanilla.

3 In a medium bowl, stir together the flour, baking powder, and salt. Add the flour mixture to the butter mixture and stir by hand or on the lowest speed of the electric mixer just until the dough comes together. Divide the dough in half and press each half into the bottom of an 8-inch round or square cake pan. If you have only one pan, pop the remaining dough in the fridge or freezer for another time.

4 Prick the dough a few times with a fork and press all around the edge with the fork to make a border. Bake for 30–35 minutes, until it's just barely golden around the edges. Cool it in the pan for 5 minutes before cutting it into wedges or squares while it's still warm.

Makes about 2 dozen cookies

* Lemon Shortbread: Add the grated zest of 1 lemon to the butter and sugar mixture before you beat it.

* Rosemary Shortbread: Add 1 Tbsp (15 mL) chopped fresh rosemary to the dough with the dry ingredients.

* Orange-Chocolate Chip Shortbread: Add the grated zest of an orange to the butter and sugar mixture before you beat it, and add about ½ cup (125 mL) chopped chocolate or mini chocolate chips with the flour mixture.

Brownies

Ingredients

¼ cup (60 mL) butter or stick
   margarine

2 squares (2 oz/50 g) unsweetened
   chocolate

⅔ cup (160 mL) cocoa

1 ½ cups (375 mL) sugar

1 tsp (5 mL) instant coffee granules

2 large eggs

1 tsp (5 mL) vanilla extract

1 cup (250 mL) all-purpose flour

½ tsp (2.5 mL) baking powder

¼ tsp (1 mL) salt

½ cup (125 mL) chopped walnuts
   or pecans, or chocolate or white
   chocolate chips (optional)

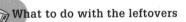

What to do with the leftovers

* Keep them in a tightly sealed container for 2 days, or wrap them
   well in plastic wrap and freeze
   them for up to 4 months.

Other things to do with it

* Caramel Pecan Brownies:
   Coarsely chop 1 Caramilk bar or
   a package of Rolos and scatter the
   pieces on top of the brownie batter along with ¼ cup (60 mL)
   chopped pecans. Drizzle with 2
   Tbsp (30 mL) caramel or butterscotch sundae topping and bake
   as directed.

These brownies are fudgy with a slightly crunchy top. They also contain about half the butter of a traditional brownie—if you miss it, use ½ cup (125 mL) instead.

Make sure you don't overbake them. You'll know brownies are ready to come out of the oven when the sides start to pull from the sides of the pan, but the middle is still soft.

Method

1 Preheat the oven to 325°F (170°C). Spray an 8-inch square pan with non-stick spray.

2 In a medium pot, melt the butter and chocolate over medium heat. Stir in the cocoa and sugar. Mix until well blended—it should have the consistency of very wet sand. Remove the pan from the heat.

3 Stir the instant coffee into 1 tsp (5 mL) water to dissolve it. In a large bowl, stir together the eggs, coffee, and vanilla. Slowly stir in the chocolate mixture, mixing until smooth. In a small bowl, combine the flour, baking powder, and salt. Add the flour mixture to the chocolate mixture and stir until almost combined; if you want to add nuts or chocolate chips, add them and stir just until the batter is blended.

4 Pour the batter into the prepared pan and bake for 25–30 minutes, until the sides are set and just begin to pull away from the sides of the pan, but the mid-dle is still soft. If you want to use the toothpick test, poke a toothpick into the middle; it should come out not gooey but with lots of moist crumbs sticking to it. Check them at the earliest suggested baking time to avoid overbaking them. Cool the brownies in the pan if you can resist eating them warm.

Makes 16 brownies

* Chocolate Mint Brownies: Chop a
   box of Junior Mints or a Pep mint
   pattie and scatter the pieces over
   the unbaked batter after you have
   spread it into the pan. If you have
   mint extract, use it in place of the
   vanilla.

* Oreo Brownies: Chop 6 Oreo
   cookies into quarters and scatter
   the pieces on top of the batter,
   pressing them down into the
   batter slightly before baking.

Lemon Bars

Ingredients

Base

¼ cup (60 mL) butter or stick margarine, softened

¼ cup (60 mL) sugar

1 scant cup (about 225 mL) all-purpose flour

Pinch salt

Topping

1 large lemon

1 cup (250 mL) sugar

2 Tbsp (30 mL) all-purpose flour

¼ tsp (1 mL) baking powder

Pinch salt

1 large egg

1 large egg white

Confectioner's sugar for sprinkling (optional)

Lemon bars are a glorious thing to make—and you will win a lot of friends with a panful of them. This base is a great one to use for any bar recipe that calls for a shortbread crust, and it contains half the fat of a traditional crust. The mixture will be crumbly as you press it into the pan, but will hold its shape once it has been baked. For a traditional shortbread crust, use ½ cup (125 mL) butter.

Method

1 Preheat the oven to 350°F (175°C). Spray an 8-inch square pan with non-stick spray.

2 To make the base, beat the butter and sugar in a medium bowl until it's creamy. Add the flour and salt and stir until the mixture is well blended and crumbly.

3 Press the crumb mixture firmly into the bottom of the prepared pan. Bake for 8-10 minutes, until it's just barely golden around the edges. Don't worry if it cracks a little—you won't be able to tell once the lemon mixture has been poured on top.

4 To make the topping, finely grate the zest from the lemon using a rasp or the rough side of a box grater. Only grate the brightly colored outer skin (this is known as the zest)—the white "pith" underneath is bitter and has no flavour.

5 Roll the lemon back and forth on the counter or zap it in the microwave for 10 seconds—this will help you get more juice out of it. Juice the lemon— you should have about 3 Tbsp (45 mL). You may need to squeeze another lemon or add a little extra lemon juice from your fridge if the first one isn't juicy enough. Using the same bowl (no need to wash it), combine the sugar, flour, baking powder, and salt. Add the egg, egg white, and lemon zest and juice and stir until smooth. Pour the lemon mixture over the base.

6 Bake for 25–30 minutes, until the lemon topping is golden and bubbly around the edges. Cool completely in the pan before cutting it into bars. Sprinkle the cooled bars with confectioners' sugar, shaken through a fine sieve if you have one.

Makes 12 bars

What to do with the leftovers

* Keep them in a tightly sealed container for a few days or wrap them well and freeze for up to 3 months. If you want to freeze the entire batch, line the pan with foil before making the squares. Freeze the whole thing once it's been baked and cooled, and lift the frozen uncut square out of the pan by the edges of foil. Wrap it well in more foil and return it to the freezer for up to 4 months. It's easy to cut into neat bars while it's still frozen; let the bars thaw on a plate at room temperature.

Other things to do with it

* Cream Cheese Lemon Bars: Drop half an 8 oz (250 g) tub of light cream cheese in spoonfuls over the base when it comes out of the oven and is still warm. Let it sit for a minute to soften the cream cheese, then gently spread it over the base. Pour the lemon filling overtop and bake as directed, adding about 10 minutes to the baking time.

Berry Oatmeal Crumble Bars

Ingredients

Crust and crumble topping

1 cup (250 mL) all-purpose flour

1 cup (250 mL) oats, old-fashioned or quick-cooking

⅔ cup (160 mL) packed brown sugar

¼ tsp (1 mL) baking soda

¼ tsp (1 mL) salt

½ cup (125 mL) butter, cut into bits

Filling

2 cups (500 mL) fresh or thawed frozen blueberries or other mixed berries

½ cup (125 mL) raspberry jam

1 Tbsp (15 mL) all-purpose flour

Grated zest of 1 lemon (optional)

These are like a fruit crisp in bar form. You can fill the oatmeal crumble with berries, date filling, or coconut and raspberry jam, or use bottled pie filling or mincemeat during the holidays.

Method

1 Preheat the oven to 375°F (190°C). Spray an 8-inch square pan with non-stick spray.

2 To make the base and topping, combine the flour, oats, brown sugar, baking soda, and salt in a large bowl. Add the butter and blend with a fork or your fingers until the mixture is well combined and crumbly. Press half of the crumble mixture into the prepared pan.

3 In a medium bowl, mix the berries with the jam, flour, and lemon zest. Spread the mixture over the crust and sprinkle the remaining crumble mixture on top.

4 Bake for 35–40 minutes, until the topping is golden and bubbly around the edges. Cool in the pan before cutting into bars.

Makes 12 bars

What to do with the leftovers

* Keep them covered in the fridge for up to 3 days, or wrap them well and freeze them for up to 4 months.

Other things to do with it

* Oatmeal Coconut-Raspberry Bars: Add ½ cup (125 mL) shredded coconut to the crumble mixture. Omit the berries, flour, and lemon zest and spread the base with ½ cup (125 mL) raspberry jam. Top with the remaining crumble and sprinkle another ¼ cup (60 mL) coconut on top before baking.

* Date Bars: Combine 1 ½ cups (375 mL) chopped, pitted dates, and 1 ½ cups (375 mL) water or orange juice in a pot and cook for about 10 minutes, until the mixture is thick and jam-like. Remove it from the heat and stir in 1 tsp (5 mL) vanilla extract. Use the date mixture in place of the berry filling and bake as directed.

Cakes

Most cakes are made for sharing to mark special occasions. Birthdays, weddings, showers, Christmas…all seem to require special cakes to commemorate them and to help people celebrate. Of course, there isn't anything wrong with eating cake on a perfectly average day when you aren't celebrating anything. That's where humble, homey cakes come into play. It's no wonder cake is such a universal comfort food—there's a hardly a day that can't be made better by a slice.

Fortunately, cakes can be easily mixed together from scratch and need not be elaborated on with icing and other decoration. Of course, a plain cake can always be topped with fruit, whipped cream, or a drizzle of chocolate or caramel syrup from a jar.

How to bake a cake

The thought of stirring up a cake from scratch makes a lot of people nervous, but in reality cakes made from scratch can be as easy as cakes made with a mix. Most cakes utilize the "creaming method," a process by which the butter and sugar are first beaten together until they're light and fluffy. Beating rubs the grains of sugar against the fat, which aerates (incorporates air into) the mixture. These tiny air bubbles later expand in the oven with the help of leavening agents, making whatever it is you're baking rise. Creaming butter and sugar is most easily done with an electric mixer, but you can do it by hand in a pinch. When you're baking a cake, adding the dry and wet ingredients alternately helps to create a tender crumb. Cake and pastry flour is often used because of its lower gluten content, but it's not necessary—all-purpose flour works just fine for most cakes.

Always use the pan size called for in a recipe—if your pan is too big, the batter will be spread too thin and will bake too quickly. If a pan is too small, it may not accommodate the amount of batter and could overflow in the oven or not bake all the way through. If you do substitute baking pans, make sure their volumes are comparable, and adjust baking times if necessary. For example, most cake batters can be baked in muffin tins to make cupcakes, but because cupcakes are smaller they will bake much more quickly than full-sized cakes. To give you an idea, cupcakes usually bake in half to two-thirds of the suggested baking time of a regular 8-inch or 9-inch cake.

If you use a glass baking pan to bake your cake in, you may need to decrease your oven temperature by 25°F (14°C), since glass conducts heat much more efficiently than metal does.

Unless a recipe specifies otherwise, spray your pans with non-stick spray (do this outside—the fat is not good for you to breathe in) or rub them with softened butter, margarine, or shortening. Bundt pans, with all their nooks and crannies, require particular attention when greasing. Angel food cakes are the exception—you shouldn't grease the pan at all, so that the airy batter can cling to the sides and rise high. Some recipes suggest flouring the pans after they're greased—this is just extra insurance against sticking, and will give the cake a slightly thicker crust, but it's not necessary. To flour greased baking pans, sprinkle them with a spoonful of flour and tap the edge of the pan, shaking the flour around until it coats the entire surface. Dump out any extra.

As with any baked goods, cakes (with the exception of cheesecakes) are best stored covered at room temperature for a few days. Some last longer than others, but virtually all cakes freeze well for up to 6 months. Before freezing, cool the cake completely and wrap it tightly in plastic wrap, then in foil. Thaw it on the countertop, still wrapped so that the cake is protected from any condensation, or frost frozen cake layers—by the time it's decorated and has been admired for awhile the cake will have thawed nicely.

Old-Fashioned Banana Cake

Ingredients

¼ cup (60 mL) butter or margarine, softened

1 ½ cups (375 mL) sugar

2 large eggs

2 very ripe bananas (you'll need about a cup (250 mL) of mashed banana)

1 tsp (5 mL) vanilla extract

2 cups (500 mL) all-purpose flour

1 tsp (5 mL) baking powder

1 tsp (5 mL) baking soda

½ tsp (2.5 mL) salt

¾ cup (185 mL) buttermilk or sour milk (see page 45)

Chances are one day you'll find yourself with overripe bananas you don't know what to do with. If you aren't in the mood to bake, throw them in the freezer whole. When you want to make a banana cake, thaw them on the counter or in a bowl of warm water and squeeze the mushy bananas out of their skins and into your cake batter.

Method

1   Preheat the oven to 350°F (175°C). Spray two 8-inch or 9-inch round cake pans or one 9- × 13-inch pan with non-stick spray.

2   In a large bowl, beat the butter and sugar with an electric mixer for a minute, until it's well blended and has the consistency of wet sand. Add the eggs one at a time, beating well after each. Add the bananas and vanilla and beat well, but don't worry about getting all the lumps of banana out.

3   In a small bowl, stir together the flour, baking powder, baking soda, and salt. Add about one-third of it to the banana mixture and beat on low speed just until it's combined. Add half the buttermilk in the same manner, then another third of the flour, the rest of the buttermilk, and the rest of the flour. Beat the batter on low speed just until it's combined.

4   Divide the batter between the prepared pans, smoothing the tops. Bake them for 30–35 minutes, until the cakes are golden, the edges are begin to pull away from the sides of the pan, and the tops are springy to the touch.

5   Cool the cakes in their pans for about 10 minutes, then run a knife around the edges and invert them onto a wire rack. Cool completely before you frost them with any of the icings or frostings on pages 284–85.

Makes two 8-inch or 9-inch layers or one 9- × 13-inch cake

 What to do with the leftovers

*   Keep them covered at room temperature for up to 3 days, or wrap them well and freeze for up to 6 months. Frost frozen cake layers or leave them on the countertop to thaw first.

Other things to do with it

*   Stir ½ cup (125 mL) chocolate chips or chopped walnuts or pecans into the batter along with the final addition of flour.

*   Banana Cupcakes: Fill greased or paper-lined muffin tins with batter and bake them for 25–30 minutes, until the tops are golden and springy to the touch. Makes about 1 ½ dozen cupcakes.

Classic White Cake

Ingredients

2 ½ cups (625 mL) all-purpose flour

2 tsp (10 mL) baking powder

¼ tsp (2.5 mL) salt

½ cup (125 mL) butter or margarine, softened

1 ½ cups (375 mL) sugar

3 large eggs

1 tsp (5 mL) vanilla extract

1 ¼ cups (310 mL) milk

Everyone should have a good basic cake recipe in their repertoire, and this simple recipe with its endless potential flavoring and frosting combinations can be called into service for any occasion that calls for cake. Plain batter can be flavored with lemon or orange zest, poured over fruit to make Upside-Down Cake, or baked in layers or as cupcakes and slathered with any of the icings and frostings on pages 284–85.

Method

1 Preheat the oven to 350°F (175°C). Spray two 8-inch or 9-inch round cake pans or one 9- × 13-inch pan with non-stick spray.

2 In a medium bowl, stir together the flour, baking powder, and salt. In a larger bowl, beat the butter with an electric mixer for about half a minute, until it's pale and creamy. Pour in the sugar and continue to beat for 3–4 minutes, until the mixture is light and fluffy. Add the eggs one at a time, beating well after each. Scrape down the sides of the bowl whenever it needs it.

3 Stir the vanilla into the milk. Add about one-third of the flour mixture to the butter mixture and stir it in by hand or with the electric mixer on low speed, just until it's combined. Add about half the milk in the same manner, then another third of the flour, the rest of the milk, and the rest of the flour, mixing just until the batter is blended.

4 Divide the batter between the greased cake pans, and tap the bottoms a few times on the countertop to remove any air bubbles. To prevent a domed top, spread the top of the batter with a spatula, creating a slight dent in the middle and a raised edge. This compensates for the way a cake tends to rise higher in the middle.

5 Bake for 30–35 minutes for round layers or 40–45 minutes for a 9- × 13-inch cake, until golden, the edges pull away from the sides of the pan, and the tops are springy to the touch. Let them cool for about 10 minutes before running a knife around the edge of the pans and inverting them onto a wire rack. Cool completely before you frost them.

Makes two 8-inch or 9-inch layers or one 9- × 13-inch cake

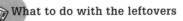

What to do with the leftovers

* Keep them covered at room temperature for up to 3 days, or wrap them well and freeze for up to 6 months. Frost frozen cake layers or leave them on the countertop to thaw first.

Other things to do with it

* Fill greased or paper-lined muffin tins with batter and bake them for 25–30 minutes, until the tops are golden and springy to the touch.

* Coconut Cream Cake: Stir ½ cup (125 mL) shredded coconut into the batter with the final addition of flour. Flavor Fluffy White Frosting (page 285) with coconut extract; use it to frost the cake and then sprinkle with toasted coconut. (Toast coconut in a dry pan set over medium heat; shake the pan until the coconut is golden and fragrant.)

* Spice Cake: Add 1–2 tsp (5–10 mL) cinnamon and ¼–½ tsp (1–2 mL) each allspice, ginger, and cloves to the flour mixture.

* Upside-Down Cake: Line the bottoms of well-greased pans with slices of pineapple or halved apricots, peaches, or plums, putting the fruit close together as it will shrink a little as it cooks. In a small pot or microwave-safe bowl, melt ¼ cup (60 mL) butter with ¾ cup (185 mL) packed brown sugar and stir until the mixture is smooth. Pour the mixture evenly over the fruit and then pour the cake batter over top. Bake as directed, increasing the baking time by about 10 minutes.

Chocolate Cake

Ingredients

1 ¾ (435 mL) cups all-purpose flour

1 ¾ (435 mL) cups sugar

¾ cup (185 mL) cocoa

1 ½ tsp (7 mL) baking powder

1 ½ tsp (7 mL) baking soda

½ tsp (2.5 mL) salt

1 cup (250 mL) milk

½ cup (125 mL) canola oil

2 large eggs

2 tsp (10 mL) vanilla extract

1 cup (250 mL) hot coffee or boiling
    water

There's likely no food as universally loved as chocolate cake. Although this is a very rich and densely chocolatey cake, it's important to note that most of the fat it contains is canola oil, which is made up of primarily heart-healthy mono- and polyunsaturated fats.

Method

1 Preheat oven to 350°F (185°C). Spray two 8-inch or 9-inch round cake pans or one Bundt pan with non-stick spray.

2 In a large bowl, stir together the flour, sugar, cocoa, baking powder, baking soda, and salt, breaking up any lumps of cocoa. Add the milk, oil, eggs, and vanilla and beat with an electric mixer on medium speed for 2 minutes, until smooth. Stir in the coffee (the batter will be thin), and pour the batter into the prepared pans.

3 Bake for 30–35 minutes for cake layers, or 50–55 minutes for a Bundt cake, until the top is springy to the touch. Let them cool for about 10 minutes before running a knife around the edge of the pans and inverting them onto a wire rack. Cool completely before you frost them.

Makes two 8-inch or 9-inch layers or one Bundt cake

What to do with the leftovers

*   Keep them covered at room temperature for up to 3 days, or wrap them well and freeze for up to 6 months. Frost frozen cake layers or leave them on the countertop to thaw first.

Other things to do with it

*   Chocolate Cupcakes: Fill greased or paper-lined muffin tins with batter and bake them for 25–30 minutes, until the tops are golden and springy to the touch.

*   Black Forest Cake: Split cooled cake layers in half horizontally, and spread each layer with cherry pie filling. Frost the cake with sweetened whipped cream (beat 3 cups/750 mL of whipping cream with ⅓ cup/80 mL confectioners' sugar just until stiff peaks form) and sprinkle with chocolate curls made by scraping a vegetable peeler over a bar of chocolate.

Carrot Cake

Ingredients

3 cups (750 mL) all-purpose flour

2 cups (500 mL) sugar (or half white, half brown sugar)

1 Tbsp (15 mL) baking soda

2 tsp (10 mL) cinnamon

1 tsp (5 mL) salt

1 cup (250 mL) canola oil

4 large eggs

1 tsp (5 mL) vanilla extract

2 cups (500 mL) (packed) grated carrots (about 3 carrots)

1 cup (250 mL) applesauce (sweetened or unsweetened)

1 cup (250 mL) chopped walnuts, pecans, raisins, or dried cranberries, or a combination

This is the best carrot cake recipe I know—I've been making it for years. It does contain a lot of oil (still less than most carrot cake recipes do), but keep in mind that canola oil contains healthy mono- and polyunsaturated fats, the kind we want to include in our diets. Carrot cake is, of course, best slathered with Cream Cheese Frosting (see page 284).

Method

1 Preheat the oven to 325°F (170°C). Spray a Bundt pan or two 9-inch round cake pans with non-stick spray.

2 In a large bowl, stir together the flour, sugar, baking soda, cinnamon, and salt. In a smaller bowl, stir together the oil, eggs, and vanilla. Add the oil mixture, grated carrots, and applesauce to the dry ingredients and stir by hand until almost combined. Add the nuts and dried fruit and stir just until the batter is blended.

3 Pour the batter into the prepared pan(s). Bake for 1 hour and 15 minutes for a Bundt cake, or for 40–45 minutes for layer cakes, until the tops are cracked and springy to the touch and the edges pull away from the sides of the pan. Cool the cake(s) in the pan for 10–15 minutes, then loosen the edge with a knife, and invert onto a wire rack to cool completely. If you decide to frost the cake, make sure it's completely cool first, or the frosting will melt and slide down the sides.

Makes one Bundt cake or two 9-inch round layers

What to do with the leftovers

* Keep them covered at room temperature for a few days, or them wrap well and freeze for up to 6 months.

Other things to do with it

* Flavor the batter with the grated zest of an orange by stirring it into the oil mixture.

* Carrot Cupcakes: Fill greased or paper-lined muffin tins with batter and bake them for 25–30 minutes, until the tops are golden and springy to the touch. Makes about 2 dozen cupcakes.

* Sweet Potato Cake: Replace the carrots and applesauce with 2 cups (500 mL) mashed sweet potatoes. (Pierce sweet potatoes with a fork and microwave them or bake them at 350°F/175°C until they're very tender; let them cool and mash them.)

Angel Food Cake

Ingredients

1 cup (250 mL) cake and
 pastry flour

1 ⅓ cups (330 mL) sugar
 (granulated or superfine)

Pinch salt

1 ½ cups (375 mL) egg whites (about
 12 large egg whites)

1 tsp (5 mL) cream of tartar

1 Tbsp (15 mL) lemon juice (optional)

2 tsp (10 mL) vanilla extract

Angel food is essentially a meringue made sturdy with the addition of flour and baked into a light and airy low-fat cake. There are infinite ways you can flavor and serve an angel food cake. Try adding grated lemon or orange zest, or 2 tsp (10 mL) instant coffee dissolved in 2 tsp (10 mL) water in place of the vanilla. If you don't have cake and pastry flour, use a scant cup (250 mL) of all-purpose flour instead. If you have superfine (also known as berry) sugar in the cupboard, use it instead of the regular (granulated) sugar—it will dissolve more easily into the meringue. This cake is delicious frosted with the Chocolate Whipped Cream Frosting on page 285, which is light and won't weigh down the cake.

Method

1 Preheat the oven to 350°F (175°C).

2 Sift together the flour, ⅓ cup (80 mL) of the sugar, and salt onto a plate or piece of waxed paper.

3 Put the egg whites into a clean glass or stainless steel bowl and beat them with an electric mixer on medium speed until they're foamy. Add the cream of tartar, lemon juice, and vanilla and beat until soft peaks form when you lift the beater. Gradually beat in the remaining cup of sugar, pouring in about 2 Tbsp (30 mL) at a time, and continue to beat until the peaks are stiff and glossy but not dry.

4 Shake about one-quarter of the flour mixture over the egg whites and gently fold it in with a spatula, being careful not to deflate the egg whites. (For more about folding, see page 233). Repeat with the remaining flour, folding it in a quarter at a time. Gently pour the batter into an ungreased tube pan and run a rubber spatula or long knife through it to eliminate any large air bubbles.

5 Bake for 45–50 minutes, until the cake is golden and springy to the touch. When you take it out of the oven, invert it onto a bottle (put the neck of the bottle through the hole of the pan—it will balance!) or stand it upside-down on its legs if your pan has them. Cooling the cake upside-down will help maintain its airiness. Once the cake is cool, turn it right side up and run a long, thin knife around the outer edge of the cake and around the center tube to loosen it. Remove the outer rim of the pan if it's removable, and invert the cake onto a plate.

6 Serve slices plain, topped with berries and whipped cream, or frosted with the Chocolate Whipped Cream Frosting on page 285.

Makes one cake; serves 8

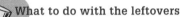

What to do with the leftovers

* Keep them covered or wrapped at room temperature for up to 3 days, or wrap them well in plastic wrap and freeze them for up to 4 months.

Other things to do with it

* Cut the cake horizontally into two layers and fill the middle with homemade or bottled lemon curd. Replace the top and spread the cake with sweetened whipped cream.

* Chocolate Angel Food Cake: Sift ¼ cup (60 mL) cocoa into the flour mixture. Sifting the cocoa gets rid of any lumps.

* Coconut Angel Food Cake: Use coconut extract in place of the vanilla. Top the cake with sweetened whipped cream and sprinkle it with toasted coconut. (Toast coconut in a dry pan over medium heat for a few minutes; shake the pan occasionally until the coconut is golden and fragrant.)

Sour Cream Pound Cake

Ingredients

1 tsp (5 mL) baking soda

1 ½ cups (375 mL) sour cream (light or regular, not fat-free)

½–¾ cup (125–185 mL) butter or stick margarine, softened

Grated zest of 1 or 2 lemons (optional)

2 ½ cups (625 mL) sugar

5 large eggs

2 tsp (10 mL) vanilla extract

4 cups (1 L) all-purpose flour, or 4 ½ cups (1.125 L) cake and pastry flour

½ tsp (2.5 mL) salt

Glaze (optional)

1 ½ cups (375 mL) icing sugar

¼ cup (60 mL) lemon juice

Pound cakes are moist, dense, and sturdier than most cakes. They were named during a time when the recipe called for a pound of butter, a pound of flour, a pound of eggs, and so on. Pound cakes usually aren't frosted, and are served in slices or wedges, often topped with fruit. Because pound cake isn't as fragile as other cakes, cubes of it are perfect for chocolate fondue, the base of a trifle, or threading onto skewers with chunks of fresh fruit to throw on the grill. Use the smaller amount of butter if you're concerned about fat.

Method

1   Preheat the oven to 325°F (170°C). Spray a 10-inch tube pan or two 8- × 4-inch loaf pans with non-stick spray.

2   Stir the baking soda into the sour cream and set it aside. In a large bowl, beat the butter with an electric mixer for a minute or so, until it's fluffy and light. Add the lemon zest (if using) and sugar and beat for another minute. Beat in the eggs one at a time, and then the vanilla.

3   In a medium bowl, stir together the flour and salt and stir one-third of it by hand into the butter mixture. (A spatula works best for this—you can scrape the sides and bottom of the bowl as you stir.) Add half the sour cream, then another third of the flour mixture, the rest of the sour cream, and the rest of the flour, stirring just until the batter is combined.

4   Pour the batter into the prepared pan(s). Bake for 1 ½ hours for a tube pan or 1 hour for loaf pans, until the cake is golden and cracked on top and springy to the touch. If you want to glaze it, stir together the icing sugar and lemon juice and brush the top of the warm cake with the syrupy mixture as soon as it comes out of the oven. Let the cake absorb the lemon syrup and brush it again until it has all been absorbed.

5   Let the cake cool in the pan for about 20 minutes, then run a knife around the edge and invert it onto a plate or wire rack to cool. Serve the cake in slices, as is, or topped with fresh or thawed frozen berries.

Makes one 10-inch tube cake or 2 loaves

What to do with the leftovers

* Keep them covered at room temperature for a few days, or wrap them well in plastic wrap and freeze for up to 6 months.

Other things to do with it

* Grill thick slices of pound cake until they're toasted and grill-marked, and serve them topped with a scoop of ice cream and fresh or thawed frozen berries.

* Lemon-Berry Pound Cake: Gently stir 2 cups (500 mL) fresh or frozen (unthawed) berries into the batter after the final addition of flour.

* Lemon-Poppy Seed Pound Cake: Add ¼ cup (60 mL) poppy seeds to the batter along with the final addition of flour.

* Chocolate Pound Cake: Replace ¾ cup (185 mL) of the flour with cocoa powder. Omit the lemon zest and glaze.

* Chocolate Marble Pound Cake: Omit the lemon zest and glaze. Stir ¼ cup (60 mL) cocoa powder into ¼ cup (60 mL) sugar. Remove about a cup of the finished batter and gently stir the cocoa mixture into it. Spread half the white batter in the bottom of the cake pan. Top with the chocolate batter, then the remaining white batter. Swirl a knife through all the layers to create a marbled effect and bake as directed.

* Orange-Chocolate Chip Pound Cake: Replace the lemon zest with orange zest, and gently stir 1 cup (250 mL) chocolate chips or chunks into the batter with the final addition of flour.

Cheesecake

Ingredients

Crust

1 cup (250 mL) graham cracker
crumbs or chocolate wafer
crumbs

3 Tbsp (45 mL) butter, melted

2 Tbsp (30 mL) sugar (optional)

Filling

1 ½ lb (three 8 oz/250 g packages)
cream cheese, regular or light

1 cup (250 mL) sugar

3 Tbsp (45 mL) all-purpose flour

Grated zest of 1 lemon (optional)

2 Tbsp (30 mL) lemon juice

½ tsp (2.5 mL) vanilla extract

3 large eggs

There are essentially two types of cheesecake: those you bake and those you don't. The unbaked ones usually get their structure from gelatin and firm up in the fridge. Baked cheesecakes have a different texture altogether; they're denser and cheesier, but are just as easy to make. Regular cream cheese produces the creamiest results, but light cream cheese works very well, too. Fat-free cream cheese just doesn't cut it.

Slices of plain cheesecake can be dressed up with anything you can think of: fresh berries tossed with a little sugar, thawed frozen berries in syrup, caramel sauce, or a drizzle of bottled chocolate sauce as is, or spiked with 1–2 Tbsp (15–30 mL) Kahlua.

Method

1   Preheat the oven to 325°F (170°C).

2   To make the crust, combine the graham crumbs, butter, and sugar and press the mixture into the bottom of an ungreased 9-inch springform pan. Bake the crust for 10 minutes, then set it aside. Turn the oven up to 425°F (220°C).

3   To make the filling, beat the cream cheese in a large bowl with an electric mixer until there are no lumps left. Add the sugar, flour, lemon zest, lemon juice, and vanilla and beat it again, just until it's smooth. Add the eggs one at a time, beating well after each one. Pour the batter over the crust.

4   Bake the cheesecake for 10 minutes, then reduce the heat to 250°F (130°C) and continue to bake for another 30–35 minutes. (If you have trouble with the top of your cheesecakes cracking, spray some water inside the oven with a spray bottle before you put your cheesecake in, or place a pan of water on the rack below the cheesecake to keep the oven humid inside as it bakes.) You can tell when the cheesecake is done when it's barely firm around the edges and the center is just slightly jiggly. It will firm up as it cools. Immediately run a thin knife around the edge to loosen it from the pan, but allow it to cool completely and then refrigerate it for at least an hour before you remove the sides of the springform pan.

Makes one 9-inch cheesecake

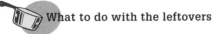

What to do with the leftovers

* Keep them covered in the fridge for up to 4 days, or wrap them well in plastic wrap and freeze for up to 4 months. (I put a dinner plate on top of the springform pan to cover it in the fridge—easy access.)

Other things to do with it

* Pumpkin Cheesecake: Replace half the sugar with brown sugar. Stir 1 ½ cups (375 mL) canned pure pumpkin, 1 ½ tsp (7.5 mL) cinnamon, and ½ tsp (2.5 mL) each ground ginger and nutmeg into the eggs and stir the mixture into the cream cheese batter at the end, instead of adding the eggs one at a time.

* Coconut Cheesecake: Omit the lemon zest, juice, and vanilla. Add ½ cup (125 mL) shredded coconut to the crumb crust mixture. When making the filling, replace the flour with cornstarch and add 1 cup (250 mL) coconut cream (not coconut milk). If you have it, ½ tsp (2.5 mL) of coconut extract also helps boost the flavor. Serve the cheesecake as is, or top it with sliced fresh strawberries.

Cakes

Sunken Chocolate Cake

Ingredients

8 oz (250 g) semisweet or bittersweet chocolate, coarsely chopped

½ cup (125 mL) butter, softened or cut into chunks

6 large eggs

1 cup (250 mL) sugar

Topping

1 ½ cups (375 mL) whipping cream

3 Tbsp (45 mL) confectioners' sugar

1 tsp (5 mL) vanilla extract

Chocolate for curls (optional)

This cake is heavenly—intensely chocolate, visually stunning, and ridiculously easy to make, which makes it the ideal cake to draw into service for birthdays and other special occasions. The cake rises in the oven and then sinks in the middle when you take it out, creating a perfect vessel for a mound of whipped cream. Not only does the cream ease the intensity of the chocolate, it counts as decoration so there's no need for frosting. If you want to fancy it up a bit, top the cake with a dusting of cocoa or chocolate curls. Sparklers are perfect—candles are easily lost in the cloud of cream.

Method

1 Preheat the oven to 350°F (175°C). Line the bottom of a 9-inch springform pan with a circle of waxed paper or parchment—use the bottom of the pan to trace a circle on the paper, then cut it out with scissors. Don't grease the pan—the batter needs to be able to cling to the sides as it rises.

2 Gently melt the chocolate with the butter in a glass or stainless steel bowl set over a bowl or pot of hot or gently simmering water. (If you have a double boiler, use it, but it's not essential.) The thing to remember when melting chocolate is to do it gently, and not let it come in contact with intense heat; chocolate scorches and can seize up easily.

3 Separate 4 of the eggs, putting the yolks and whites in separate medium-sized bowls. Add the remaining 2 eggs and half of the sugar to the egg yolks. Whisk in the warm chocolate mixture and stir until it's smooth.

4 Beat the egg whites with an electric mixer until foamy. Gradually add the remaining sugar, beating until the egg whites form soft mounds but aren't yet stiff. Fold about one-quarter of the egg whites into the chocolate mixture to lighten it, and then gently fold in the rest, without deflating the egg whites. (To read more about folding, see page 233). Pour the batter into the prepared pan and smooth the top.

5 Bake for 35–40 minutes, until the cake is puffy and cracked on top, and the middle isn't wobbly. Cool the cake completely in the pan without loosening the sides; the batter needs to cling to the sides of the pan as it cools so that it can properly sink in the middle and keep its high edges.

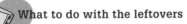

6 When you're ready to serve the cake, beat the cream, sugar, and vanilla until soft peaks form and mound the whipped cream in the middle of the cake. Run a thin knife around the edge of the pan to loosen the cake, remove the sides of the pan and transfer it to a serving plate, leaving the cake on the pan bottom. To make chocolate curls, run a vegetable peeler along the edge of a square of room-temperature chocolate and sprinkle the curls over the cream.

Makes one 9-inch cake

What to do with the leftovers

* Keep them covered at room temperature or in the fridge (if the cake is topped with cream) for up to 3 days, or wrap them well in plastic wrap and freeze for up to 3 months. Eat frozen slices straight out of the freezer in the middle of the night.

Other things to do with it

* Flavor the cake batter by stirring the grated zest of an orange or 2 Tbsp (30 mL) Grand Marnier into the melted chocolate mixture.

Upside-Down Pear Gingerbread

Ingredients

Gingerbread

¼ cup (60 mL) butter or margarine, softened

½ cup (125 mL) packed brown sugar

1 large egg

½ cup (125 mL) buttermilk or sour milk (see page 45)

¼ cup (60 mL) dark molasses

1–2 Tbsp (15–30 mL) grated fresh ginger, or 1 tsp (5 mL) powdered ginger

1 cup (250 mL) all-purpose flour

1 tsp (5 mL) baking soda

½ tsp (2.5 mL) cinnamon

¼ tsp (1 mL) salt

¼ tsp (1 mL) allspice

¼ tsp (1 mL) nutmeg

Topping

1 Tbsp (15 mL) butter or margarine

1–2 Tbsp (15-30 mL) corn syrup

⅓ cup (80 mL) packed brown sugar

2 ripe but firm pears or tart apples, peeled and thinly sliced

One of the biggest selling points of an upside-down cake is the fact that it needs no decorating. When you invert the cake the pear slices end up on top, making it look gratifyingly complete with no need for frosting. It does, however, scream for ice cream or whipped cream—provide a bowl of it alongside for people to serve themselves, or put a dollop on each slice. Pear gingerbread is also great with thick vanilla yogurt. It even works for breakfast.

Method

1 Preheat the oven to 350°F (175°C). Spray an 8-inch or 9-inch round cake pan with non-stick spray.

2 To make the topping, melt the butter, corn syrup, and brown sugar in a small pot over medium heat or microwave it until it's smooth. Pour the mixture over the bottom of the prepared pan and arrange the pear slices on top, placing them tightly together. Keep in mind that they shrink a bit as they cook, so you can even get away with overlapping them.

3 To make the gingerbread batter, beat the butter and brown sugar in a medium bowl until well blended. Add the egg, buttermilk, molasses, and ginger and beat until thoroughly combined.

4 In a small bowl, stir together the flour, baking soda, cinnamon, salt, allspice, and nutmeg. Add the dry ingredients to the egg mixture and stir by hand or on the lowest speed of an electric mixer just until the batter is combined. Pour the batter over the sliced pears.

5 Bake the cake for about 40 minutes, until the top is springy to the touch. Let it stand for 5 minutes, then run a knife around the edge of the cake and invert it onto a plate while it's still hot. If it cools too much and sticks to the pan, warm it in the oven again before you try to invert it. Don't fret if any pear slices stick to the bottom of the pan—simply peel them out and place them back on top of the cake where they belong.

Makes one 8-inch or 9-inch cake

 What to do with the leftovers

* Keep them covered in the fridge for up to 3 days, or wrap them well in plastic wrap and freeze for up to 3 months.

Other things to do with it

* Blueberry Gingerbread: Omit the topping and stir 1 cup (250 mL) of fresh or frozen (unthawed) blueberries into the batter. Bake as directed in an 8-inch square pan and cut it into squares.

Apple, Plum, or Berry
Crumble Cake

Ingredients

Crumble

½ cup (125 mL) all-purpose flour

⅓ cup (80 mL) packed brown sugar

¼ tsp (1 mL) cinnamon (optional)

2–3 Tbsp (30–45 mL) butter or
  margarine, chilled

Cake

1 ½ cups (375 mL) all–purpose flour

1 tsp (5 mL) baking powder

¼ tsp (1 mL) salt

¼ cup (60 mL) butter or margarine,
  softened

¾ cup (375 mL) sugar

1 large egg

1 tsp (5 mL) vanilla

½ cup (125 mL) sour cream or yogurt

1 large apple, peeled, cored
  and sliced or cut into chunks,
  3 plums, pitted and thickly
  sliced, 2 peaches or nectarines,
  pitted and sliced, or 1 cup
  (250 mL) fresh or frozen
  (unthawed) berries

Eat-straight-from-the-pan cakes are the epitome of comfort food—with this recipe you get the best of both worlds with cake and fruit crumble all in one. It's not too sweet, easy to eat with a fork or your fingers, and can be made with any kind of fruit you have around, even if it's getting wrinkly or has soft spots.

Method

1 Preheat the oven to 350°F (175°C). Spray an 8-inch square or round pan with non-stick spray.

2 To make the crumble, stir together the flour, brown sugar, cinnamon, and butter and blend it with a fork or your fingers until the mixture is well combined and crumbly. Set aside.

3 To make the cake, combine the flour, baking powder, and salt in a small bowl. In a medium bowl, beat the butter and sugar with an electric mixer until it's light and fluffy. Beat in the egg and vanilla. Add half the flour mixture and stir by hand just until it's combined. Stir in the sour cream, then the remaining flour mixture, stirring until it's just blended.

4 Spread the batter into the prepared pan. Spread the apples, plums, peaches, or berries on top and sprinkle with the crumble mixture. Bake for about 40 minutes, until the cake is golden and springy to the touch. (Springiness may be difficult to test with the fruit in the way—you could also test it by sticking a toothpick or bamboo skewer into the cake. If it comes out with moist, not gooey, crumbs sticking to it, it's done.)

Makes one 8-inch cake

What to do with the leftovers

* Keep them covered at room temperature for a few days or wrap them well in plastic wrap and freeze for up to 4 months. Leftovers are delicious warmed up in the microwave and topped with a scoop of vanilla ice cream.

Other things to do with it

* Add the grated zest of an orange to the batter, and scatter a few fresh, frozen or dried cranberries among the chopped apples.

Fixes for mixes

Even though mixing up a cake from scratch is really, really easy, sometimes it's quicker or somehow more appealing in a nostalgic sort of way to doctor up a mix. Or perhaps you picked up a few when they were on sale and need to transform them into something more interesting that you might even be able to pass off as your own. Cakes made from mixes were all the rage when they were new to store shelves, so these might remind you of something Mom or Grandma used to make.

Ambrosia Cake: Mix one yellow cake mix with 2 large eggs, ½ cup (125 mL) water, ½ cup (125 mL) canola oil, and a drained can of mandarin oranges. Bake in a greased 9- × 13-inch pan according to the package directions. Stir together a container of Cool Whip, a 113 g package of dry butter pecan instant pudding mix and a small drained can of crushed pineapple to frost the cake with.

Carrot Cake: Mix a yellow cake mix with ⅔ cup (160 mL) orange juice, ½ cup (125 mL) canola oil, 4 large eggs, and 2 tsp (10 mL) cinnamon. Beat until well blended and then stir in 3 cups (750 mL) grated carrots and ½ cup (125 mL) each raisins and/or chopped walnuts or pecans. Pour the batter into a greased Bundt pan and bake at 325°F (170°C) for 1 hour and 10 minutes, until the top is springy to the touch.

Chocolate or Yellow Banana Cake: Beat a chocolate or yellow cake mix with a 113 g package instant chocolate or vanilla pudding mix, 1 cup (250 mL) water, 2 large eggs, 2 mashed very ripe bananas and ½ cup (125 mL) canola oil. Stir in ½ cup (125 mL) chocolate chips or chopped walnuts or pecans. Pour into a greased Bundt pan and bake at 350°F (175°C) for 50–55 minutes, until the top is springy.

Cinnamon Bun Cake: Mix a yellow cake mix with ½ cup (125 mL) canola oil, ¼ cup (60 mL) milk or water, 4 large eggs, and 1 cup (250 mL) light sour cream. In a small bowl, stir together ½ cup (125 mL) packed brown sugar and 1 Tbsp (15 mL) cinnamon. Pour half the cake batter into a greased 9- × 13-inch pan. Sprinkle the batter with the cinnamon sugar and top with remaining batter. Swirl a knife through both batters to create a marbled effect and bake according to the package directions.

Dump Cake (presumably named because you dump everything into the bowl): Beat together a chocolate or devil's food cake mix, a 113 g package instant chocolate pudding mix, 4 large eggs, 1 cup (250 mL) sour cream and ¼ cup (60 mL) orange juice or milk. (If you're using juice, you can add the grated zest of an orange as well for a more intense flavor.) Stir in 1 cup (250 mL) chocolate chips and pour the batter into a greased Bundt pan. Bake at 350°F (175°C) for an hour, until the top is springy to the touch.

Frosting a cake

The great thing about icings and frostings, besides licking off the beaters, is that they don't have to be paired with specific types of cake. Chocolate frosting is delicious on a banana cake, and chocolate cake is fantastic with cream cheese frosting. Don't be afraid to mix and match your flavors.

Only frost cakes that have completely cooled; a warm cake will melt any icing you attempt to spread over it. Brush away any crumbs from the surface of the cake before you begin—cake crumbs in frosting are like flies in paint. If you want some extra insurance against crumbs, spread the top and sides of the cake layers with a thin layer of frosting and chill or freeze to firm up the frosting. This is called a crumb coat—the chilled frosting will trap any loose crumbs and provide a smooth surface for the rest of your frosting. Make sure you use room-temperature frosting; when it's chilled it's usually too stiff to spread easily.

If you're having trouble stacking domed cake layers, slice the domed part off with a serrated knife so that it's level, and flip the cake upside down to minimize crumbs from the cut part. To keep your serving plate clean, tuck strips of waxed paper under the edges of the cake before you frost it, and then pull them out when you're done.

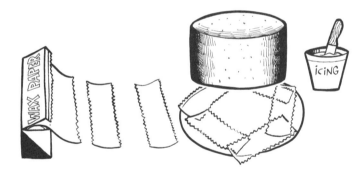

Basic Butter Icing

This will make enough frosting to cover two cake layers. All the measurements are approximate—if you start with a lump of soft butter and add confectioners' sugar and a drizzle of milk or other liquid (and cocoa if you want it to be chocolate) until you have a spreadable mixture, you have frosting. Tint it with a few drops of food coloring or spike it with flavored extract if you like.

Ingredients

¼–½ cup (60–125 mL) butter or margarine, softened

4 cups (1 L) confectioners' sugar, plus a little extra if needed

¼ cup (60 mL) milk or other liquid, plus a little extra if needed

1–2 tsp (5–10 mL) vanilla, coconut, maple, or other flavored extract

Method

1 In a large bowl, beat the butter with an electric mixer until creamy. Gradually add the confectioners' sugar, milk, and vanilla, beating until the mixture is creamy and well blended. Add a little more sugar or milk if necessary to achieve a spreadable frosting.

Makes about 4 ½ cups; enough to cover two cake layers or 2 dozen cupcakes

Chocolate Icing: Replace about ½ cup (125 mL) of the confectioners' sugar with cocoa.

Coffee Icing: Use cold strong coffee as your liquid, or dissolve 1 Tbsp (15 mL) instant coffee granules into the milk. Replace ½ cup (125 mL) of the confectioners' sugar with cocoa as well to make Mocha Icing.

Peanut Butter Icing: Use smooth or crunchy peanut butter in place of the butter.

Orange Icing: Use orange juice in place of the milk, and add the finely grated zest of an orange.

Cream Cheese Frosting: Use only ¼ cup (60 mL) butter and add an 8 oz (250 g) package regular or light cream cheese. Try not to overbeat cream cheese frosting. Mixing too hard for too long tends to break down the cream cheese.

For Lemon Cream Cheese Frosting add 2 Tbsp (30 mL) or more lemon juice and reduce the amount of milk accordingly.

Maple Icing: Replace about half the milk with real maple syrup. Use maple extract, if you have some, instead of the vanilla. Because of the maple syrup, you can usually get away with cutting back on the butter even more.

Penuche (Brown Sugar) Icing: Melt the butter with ½ cup (125 mL) packed brown sugar and the milk in a small pot. When it's melted and smooth, let it cool slightly and beat in enough confectioners' sugar to create a spreadable frosting.

Fluffy White Frosting

Known in my grandma's battered cookbooks as 7 Minute Frosting or Boiled Icing, this is a light, creamy, meringue-like frosting that is beaten in a double boiler over simmering water in order to cook the egg whites. The light and creamy texture makes it easy to spread, and as a bonus, it's fat-free. It also takes on flavorings and food coloring very well. Add a few drops of color to the water to tint the frosting, or drop it in at the end to create a swirled effect.

Ingredients

1 ½ cups (375 mL) sugar

1 Tbsp (15 mL) light corn syrup

⅓ cup (80 mL) water

2 large egg whites

1 tsp (5 mL) vanilla, coconut, maple, mint, or other flavored extract

Method

1   In the top of a double boiler or in a clean stainless steel bowl set over a pot of simmering water, combine the sugar, corn syrup, water, and egg whites. Make sure the simmering water doesn't touch the bottom of the bowl or double boiler—you only need 1–2 inches of water in the pot. Beat the sugar mixture with an electric mixer on high speed for about 7 minutes, until it stands in billowy peaks. Remove it from the heat and beat in the vanilla.

Makes 2 ½ cups, enough to frost 2 cake layers or 24 cupcakes.

Fluffy Brown Sugar Frosting: Substitute packed dark or golden brown sugar for the white (granulated) sugar.

Chocolate Whipped Cream Frosting

This light topping is perfect for angel food cakes, which tend to get weighed down by regular frosting.

Ingredients

1 cup (250 mL) confectioners' sugar

½ cup (125 mL) cocoa

¼ cup (60 mL) milk

Pinch cream of tartar

2 cups (500 mL) whipping cream

Method

1   In a large bowl, whisk together the confectioner's sugar, cocoa, milk, and cream of tartar until smooth. Cover and refrigerate it for about an hour, until it's well chilled. (This can be done a few hours ahead of time.)

2   Using an electric mixer, gradually beat the cream into the chocolate mixture, and continue beating until stiff peaks form.

Makes 4 cups, enough to frost an angel food cake.

Pies

Baking a pie from scratch is one of the most intimidating culinary tasks, primarily because of the crust factor. Baking pies used to be the norm—any home cook could turn one out, and did so on a regular basis. Most pie bakers were taught by their mothers or grandmothers, who baked pies from scratch for reasons of necessity and economy. These days, with the availability of frozen pie crusts and ready-made pies, pie baking has some-how turned into a daunting and unnecessary hassle. But it's easier than you think, and well worth the effort. Treat not-so-perfect attempts as learning experiences rather than wasted time and ingredients, and remember that tying your shoes seemed like an impossible task once.

How to bake a pie

Mixing

The only way to learn how to make a pie is by just doing it. Pastry is simply a combination of flour, fat, and water, but the method by which you combine them is vital to the end result. The two rules my grandma reinforced as she deftly rolled perfect "never-fail" pastry for her butter tarts were: keep the dough cold, and don't handle it too much. Once you get the hang of it, you'll wonder what all the fuss was about.

The secret to making tender, flaky pastry is in the mixing and handling of the dough. When mixing pastry from scratch, it's important to keep the ingredients—primarily the fat—cold. When butter and shortening begin to melt, they can become greasy and produce a heavy crust. Cold fat particles produce flaky layers. Cooks employ many techniques to accomplish this: freezing the butter and grating it into the flour, chilling or freezing the dry ingredients after the fat has been added, making sure the water is ice-cold, or using a pastry blender or food processor to cut in the butter or shortening so that their warm fingers don't melt the fat as it's blended in.

When you add the butter and shortening to the flour mixture, the mixture should be blended so that the bits of fat range from the size of bread crumbs to the size of small peas. Smaller pieces make your pastry tender, and the larger pieces make it flaky. This part can be done quickly and easily in a food processor—just make sure you pulse it only until the mixture is crumbly. Don't blend it to the point where it becomes completely homogeneous.

Once the fat has been added, or "cut in," you'll need to add your liquid. Using ice-cold water will keep the small particles of fat from melting. Many pie bakers swear by a teaspoon (5 mL) of white vinegar in their pastry to keep it tender by preventing the formation of gluten—strands of protein that make pastry tough. It's not necessary, but if you decide to add vinegar, stir it into the water.

The amount of water you'll need to hold your pastry together will vary depending on factors like humidity and the flour you use, so sprinkle a little at a time over the dry ingredients, just until the dough comes together. If you want to do this part in the food processor, pulse just until the mixture starts to clump together, then gather it into a ball by hand. Your next goal should be to handle the dough as little as possible—mixing, kneading, and rolling also develops the gluten in flour, making it tough.

Rolling out pastry dough

The first thing to do once you've mixed your pastry dough is to gather it into a ball, flatten it into a disk shape, wrap it in plastic wrap, and refrigerate it for at least 30 minutes. This isn't absolutely necessary, but the resting period will give the gluten a chance to relax, making the pastry more tender and preventing it from shrinking as it bakes. At this point pastry can be refrigerated for up to 2 days, or frozen for up to 4 months. Since it's exactly as much work to make enough pastry for 2 pies, you can double the amount of ingredients and freeze half for another pie.

If your pastry is coming straight out of the fridge, let it sit on the countertop for about 10 minutes to make it more malleable. To keep it from sticking, lightly dust the countertop with flour. Try to use as little flour as you can get away with; you don't want the pastry to absorb too much excess flour. You could also roll the pastry out between two sheets of waxed or parchment paper.

Dust your dough and rolling pin lightly with a little flour, and keep the flour canister close by so you can reach more if you need it. Begin at the center of your dough and roll outward toward the edges, using long, gentle strokes. Roll up and down from the center, not back and forth, and rotate the dough a quarter turn every couple of rolls to make sure it isn't sticking. If it starts to stick to the counter, sprinkle a little more flour underneath. If it sticks to the rolling pin, sprinkle the pin with a little more flour.

Continue to roll the dough, keeping it as evenly thick and round as possible, until it's a few inches larger than the pie plate or tart pan, and between 1⁄16–1⁄8 inch (1.5–3 mm) thick. If it cracks or tears, patch it up with your fingers, using a little extra dough from around the edge if you need to. Never gather up and reroll pastry, or it will end up shrunken and tough.

Lining the pan

The easiest way to transfer the dough to the pie plate is to fold it gently into quarters, then transfer the wedge of dough to the plate, placing the corner in the middle, and unfold it. Or you could drape the dough over the rolling pin to help lift it over. Unfold the dough onto the plate, center it, and gently fit the dough into the plate without stretching it. Trim the edge of the dough to within 1⁄2 inch (1 cm) of the plate rim with scissors or a knife. Fold the edge of the dough under itself so that it's

Pies

flush with the rim of the plate, and crimp the border with your fingers or press it down with the tines of a fork. For best results, refrigerate the shell for another 30 minutes before filling or baking it. To make tart shells, cut circles of rolled-out dough with a biscuit cutter, glass rim, or the open end of a can, and fit them into regular or mini muffin pans.

If you don't have a pie plate, most fruit fillings that aren't too juicy can be baked into a free-form tart—roll the dough into a 12- to 14-inch (30–35 cm) circle and transfer it to a rimmed baking sheet. Pile the fruit filling onto the middle of the pastry, leaving a 2-inch border. Fold the dough border in toward the center—it won't cover the fruit completely. Bake at 350°F (175°C) until the crust is golden, about 40 minutes.

Blind baking a pie crust

Some pie crusts need to be "blind baked," meaning they are baked without any filling. Crusts can be partially baked for recipes in which the pie requires additional baking once the filling is added, or completely baked for recipes in which the filling is cooked separately. Since custard-type fillings don't require a long baking time, partially baking the crust first ensures it won't turn out soggy. And since some fillings, such as chocolate mousse or lemon curd, don't require any baking at all, the crusts must be baked completely before they're filled.

To blind bake a pie crust you need to prick it all over with a fork, then line it with aluminum foil and fill it with pie weights, dried beans, or rice before baking it. Lining the unbaked shell and weighing it down helps it hold its shape and keeps it from puffing up as it bakes. You could also line it with a second pie plate, if you have one of the same size. Tart shells don't need to be lined before they're blind baked; just prick them all over with a fork.

Blind bake the pie shell at 400°F (200°C) for about 10 minutes, until the edges are set. Gently remove the weights and the foil and continue to bake for another 5–7 minutes, until the crust is dry and just barely golden. If it starts to puff up, use a dish towel to gently tap the bubble down. Partially blind-baked shells should be just slightly colored when they come out of the oven. For a fully baked crust, continue to bake it for another 10–12 minutes, until it's golden. Let either crust cool completely before adding the filling, so that the warm pastry doesn't steam and become soggy.

Basic Pie Crust

Ingredients

For a single crust pie:

1 ⅓ cups (330 mL) all-purpose flour

1 Tbsp (15 mL) sugar

¼ tsp (1 mL) salt

¼ cup (60 mL) butter, chilled and cut into small pieces

¼ cup (60 mL) vegetable shortening, chilled and cut into small pieces

3–4 Tbsp (45–60 mL) ice water

For a double crust pie, or two single pie crusts:

2 ½ cups (625 mL) all-purpose flour

2 Tbsp (30 mL) sugar

½ tsp (2.5 mL) salt

¾ cup (185 mL) butter, chilled and cut into small pieces

¼ cup (60 mL) vegetable shortening, chilled and cut into small pieces

6–8 Tbsp (90–125 mL) ice water

When making pastry, you need to use a solid fat. Lard used to be the fat of choice, and will produce very flaky pastry, but shortening has become the norm for health reasons. (If you want to convert your recipes to use lard, or vice versa, you'll need only three-quarters as much lard as vegetable shortening.) You can use all butter or all shortening in your pastry, or a combination of the two. Butter will give you the best flavor, but the crust won't be as flaky as it would be if it was made with shortening, which is used for flakiness but doesn't add any flavor. A combination of both gives you the best of both worlds. All-purpose flour will produce great results—there's no need to buy cake and pastry flour, which is popular because of its lower gluten content.

Method

1 In a large bowl or the bowl of a food processor, stir together the flour, sugar, and salt. Add the butter and shortening and use a fork, pastry blender, wire whisk, or the "pulse" motion of the food processor to blend the mixture until it resembles coarse meal, with lumps of fat no bigger than a pea. Drizzle the minimum amount of water over the mixture and stir until the dough comes together, adding a little more a bit at a time if you need it.

2 Gather the dough into a ball, flatten it into a disk, wrap it in plastic, and chill for at least half an hour. If you're making a double crust pie, divide the dough in half, making one half slightly larger than the other, since it will take slightly more pastry to line a pie plate than to top a pie. (The pastry can be prepared up to this point and frozen for up to 4 months; let it thaw on the countertop when you need it.)

3 Follow the instructions on pages 288–89 to roll the dough and line your pie plate.

Makes 1 crust for a single or double crust pie

Other things to do with it

* Nut Pastry: Add ¼ cup (60 mL) (for a single crust) to ½ cup (125 mL) (for a double crust) finely chopped or ground pecans, hazelnuts, walnuts, or almonds to the dry ingredients before you cut in the butter and shortening.

* Lemon Pastry: Add the finely grated zest of a lemon to the dry ingredients before you cut in the butter and shortening.

Crumb Crust

Ingredients

1 ⅓–1 ½ cups (330–375 mL) finely crushed graham cracker or other cookie crumbs

2 Tbsp (30 mL) sugar

¼ cup (60 mL) butter or margarine, melted, or 2 Tbsp (30 mL) butter and 2 Tbsp (30 mL) honey or corn syrup

Crumb pie crusts need not be made only out of graham crumbs; gingersnaps, digestive cookies, oatmeal biscuits, and vanilla or chocolate wafers all make fantastic crusts. All you need is enough melted butter, or a combination of melted butter and honey or corn syrup, to hold the crumbs together.

Method

1 Preheat the oven to 350°F (175°C).

2 In a medium bowl, combine the cookie crumbs and sugar, then stir in the butter and blend until the mixture is well combined. Add a little extra butter or honey if you need to hold the crumbs together, or a few extra crumbs if the mixture seems too wet. Press firmly into the bottom and up the sides of a 9-inch pie plate.

3 Bake for 10–12 minutes, until the crust is pale golden and set. Cool on a wire rack.

Makes 1 single pie crust

Other things to do with it

* Chocolate Crumb Crust: Finely chop 1 square (1 oz/25 g) semisweet chocolate and melt it with the butter, then stir the chocolate mixture into the crumbs. Press into the pie plate and freeze for 30 minutes, until firm. This crust is best used for ice cream pies and other no-bake fillings.

* Nut Crumb Crust: Use ½ cup (125 mL) finely ground toasted almonds, pecans, or other nuts in place of ½ cup (125 mL) of the crumbs.

Apple Pie

Ingredients

Pastry for a single or double crust pie, chilled (see page 290)

Filling

2–3 lb (1–1.5 kg) Granny Smith, Braeburn, McIntosh, or other tart apples (5 or 6 large apples)

1 Tbsp (15 mL) lemon juice

⅓ cup (80 mL) sugar

2 Tbsp (30 mL) all-purpose flour

¼ tsp (1 mL) cinnamon

Streusel Topping (optional, if making a single crust pie)

¼ cup (60 mL) packed brown sugar

¼ cup (60 mL) all-purpose flour

3 Tbsp (45 mL) butter, chilled and cut into pieces

¼ cup (60 mL) chopped walnuts or pecans (optional)

Apple pie is the quintessential comfort food, and probably the simplest pie to prepare because apples are so easy to handle. Tart apples have the most flavor and hold their shape well. Use a combination of your favorite varieties for a more complex flavor. Remember that fruit shrinks quite a bit as it cooks, so expect to produce a large mound of peeled and sliced apples for each pie.

Serve wedges warm with vanilla ice cream or cold with a chunk of cheddar cheese. If you like the apple-cheddar combination, try grating some old cheddar into the dry ingredients when you make your pie pastry.

Method

1 Preheat the oven to 450°F (230°C).

2 If your dough is coming straight from the fridge, let it sit on the countertop for about 10 minutes, until it's malleable. If you're making a double crust pie, divide the pastry in half, making one piece just slightly larger than the other.

3 On a lightly floured surface, roll the pastry (the bigger half, if you're making a double crust pie) out into a 12-inch (30 cm) circle. Gently fold the dough into quarters to transfer it into a 9-inch (23 cm) pie plate. Unfold the dough onto the plate, center it, and gently fit the dough into the plate without stretching it, leaving the edges hanging over.

4 Peel, core, and slice the apples into a large bowl and toss them with the lemon juice. In a small dish combine the sugar, flour, and cinnamon and sprinkle it over the apples; toss them well to coat. Pour the apples into the pie shell, mounding them in the middle. Don't panic if it seems like a lot!

5 If you're using a top crust, roll out the second piece of dough on a lightly floured surface into a 12-inch (30 cm) circle. Lay it over the apples and press around the edges to seal. Trim both layers of excess pastry with scissors or a knife so that the overhang is about ½ inch (1 cm) around the pie plate. Tuck the edges of the pastry under itself so that it's even with the edge of the pie plate, and flute it all around the edge with your fingers. Cut a few slits in the top crust to allow steam to escape as the pie bakes.

6 To top the pie with streusel instead of a top crust, blend the sugar, flour, butter, and walnuts together with a fork until well combined and crumbly. Sprinkle evenly over the apples. Trim and flute the edge of the bottom crust.

7 Place the pie on a baking sheet (to catch any drips) and bake for 20 minutes. Reduce the oven temperature to 350°F (175°C) and bake it for another 20–25 minutes, until the crust is golden and the apples are tender. If the crust is browning too quickly, cover it loosely with a piece of foil. Cool the pie on a wire rack and serve warm, at room temperature, or cold.

Makes 1 pie

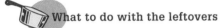

What to do with the leftovers

* Keep them covered in the fridge for up to 3 days, or wrap them well and freeze for up to 3 months.

Other things to do with it

* Add ½ cup (125 mL) dried sour cherries, cranberries, or raisins to the apple mixture.

* Make a lattice top crust by cutting the second circle of dough into even strips and weaving them over the apples. Seal, trim, and flute the edge and bake as directed.

* Free-form Apple Pie: On a lightly floured surface, roll out enough pastry for a single crust pie into a 14-inch (35 cm) circle and transfer it to a parchment-lined baking sheet. Spread 2 Tbsp (30 mL) apricot or peach preserves over the dough, leaving a 2-inch (5 cm) border around the edge. Spoon the apple mixture over the dough and sprinkle with the crumble mixture. Fold the edges of dough over the filling, letting it crease wherever it folds naturally. It won't completely cover the apples. Press the folds of the dough to help it hold its shape. Bake the pie for about 25 minutes, and then reduce the heat to 325°F (170°C) and bake for another 30–40 minutes, until the apples are tender. If the pastry is browning too quickly, cover it loosely with foil.

Peach Pie

Ingredients

Pastry for a double crust pie, chilled
 (see page 290)

Filling:

5 lb (2.25 kg) ripe peaches
 or nectarines (about 8)

¾ cup (185 mL) sugar

¼ cup (60 mL) all-purpose flour

¼ tsp (1 mL) cinnamon

Pinch nutmeg (optional)

There's no better use for ripe peaches than a homemade peach pie, topped with pastry or sweet and crunchy streusel. Being able to make a peach pie will win you a lot of friends and admirers. Nectarines work just as well as peaches, and either will get along well with a handful of berries added to the filling.

Method

1 Preheat the oven to 400°F (200°C).

2 If your dough is coming straight from the fridge, let it sit on the countertop for about 10 minutes, until it's malleable. Divide the pastry in half, making one piece just slightly larger than the other.

3 On a lightly floured surface, roll the bigger piece of pastry out into a 12-inch (30 cm) circle. Gently fold the dough into quarters to transfer it into a 9-inch (23 cm) pie plate. Unfold the dough onto the plate, center it, and gently fit the dough into the plate without stretching it, leaving the edges hanging over.

4 To peel the peaches, drop them into a large pot of boiling water for about 30 seconds; remove them with a slotted spoon and plunge them into cold water. The skins should slip right off. Slice them thickly into a large bowl, removing the pits.

5 In a small bowl, stir together the sugar, flour, cinnamon, and nutmeg. Sprinkle over the peaches and toss gently to coat them with the flour mixture. Pour the peaches into the crust, mounding them in the middle.

6 On a lightly floured surface, roll out the second piece of pastry into a 12-inch (30 cm) circle. Lay it over the peaches and press around the edges to seal. Trim both layers of excess pastry with scissors or a knife so that the overhang is about ½ inch (1 cm) around the pie plate. Tuck the edges of the pastry under itself so that it's even with the edge of the pie plate, and flute it all around the edge with your fingers. Cut a few slits in the top crust to allow steam to escape as the pie bakes.

7 Bake for 1 hour and 10 minutes, until the pie is golden and the juices are bubbling through the slits. If the pastry is browning too quickly, cover it loosely with a piece of foil. Cool the pie on a wire rack for 2–3 hours before you cut it. Serve warm, at room temperature, or cold.

Makes 1 pie

What to do with the leftovers

* Keep them covered in the fridge for up to 2 days, or wrap them well and freeze for up to 3 months.

Other things to do with it

* Make a lattice top crust by cutting the second circle of dough into even strips and weaving them across the top of the pie. Seal, trim, and flute the edge and bake as directed.

* Fill a single pie crust with the peach mixture and top with the streusel recipe on pages 296–97.

* Cherry Pie: Replace the flour with cornstarch, and increase the sugar to 1 cup (250 mL). Use 6 cups (1.5 L) fresh pitted cherries instead of the peaches and top them with a lattice crust. Bake at 425°F (220°C) for 15 minutes, then reduce the oven temperature to 375°F (190°C) and bake for another 50 minutes, until golden and bubbly.

Fresh Berry Pie

Ingredients

Pastry for a single or double crust pie
(see page 290)

Filling

5–6 cups (1.25–1.5 L) fresh
blackberries, blueberries, and
raspberries

1 Tbsp (15 mL) lemon juice

3–4 Tbsp (45–60 mL) quick-
cooking tapioca, cornstarch,
potato starch, or flour

1 cup (250 mL) sugar

Pinch salt

Streusel (optional, if making a single crust pie)

⅓ cup (80 mL) packed brown sugar

¼ cup (60 mL) all-purpose flour

¼ cup (60 mL) oats

¼ cup (60 mL) butter, chilled and cut
into pieces

Having tasted only ruby red, cornstarch-thickened, diner-style berry pie until my early twenties, my first introduction to fresh berry pie was a revelation. But I feared making my own, worrying that the berries would be too juicy and I'd end up with berry soup. On the other hand, you don't want to add too much flour or cornstarch and end up with a gummy, cloudy pie. But now I know people welcome the fresh juices, especially when they get to mingle with melting vanilla ice cream. The amount of thickener you use will depend on the juiciness of your berries; blueberries tend not to be as juicy as strawberries, raspberries, and blackberries. The trick is to thicken them just enough to bind the juices so that they're neither watery nor stodgy. Using a combination of berries is best for flavor and texture, and starches are much more effective thickeners than flour, which means you won't need as much.

Method

1 Preheat the oven to 450°F (230°C).

2 If your dough is coming straight from the fridge, let it sit on the countertop for about 10 minutes, until it's malleable. If you're making a double crust pie, divide the pastry in half, making one piece just slightly larger than the other.

3 On a lightly floured surface, roll the bigger piece of pastry out into a 12-inch (30 cm) circle. Gently fold the dough into quarters to transfer it into a 9-inch (23 cm) pie plate. Unfold the dough onto the plate, center it, and gently fit the dough into the plate without stretching it, leaving the edges hanging over.

4 In a large bowl, gently toss the berries with the lemon juice. Pulverize the tapioca, if you're using it, in a food processor or spice grinder, or with a mortar and pestle. In a small bowl, combine it with the sugar and salt. Sprinkle the mixture over the berries and gently toss to coat. Pour the berries into the crust, sprinkling any of the sugar left over in the bottom of the bowl on top.

5 On a lightly floured surface, roll out the second piece of pastry into a 12-inch (30 cm) circle. Lay it over the berries and press around the edges to seal. Trim both layers of excess pastry with scissors or a knife so that the overhang is about ½ inch (1 cm) around the pie plate. Tuck the edges of the pastry under itself so that it's even with the edge of the pie plate, and flute it all around the edge with your fingers. Cut a few slits in the top crust to allow steam to escape as the pie bakes.

6 To top the pie with streusel instead of a top crust, blend the sugar, flour, oats, and butter together with a fork until well combined and crumbly. Sprinkle evenly over the berries. Trim and flute the edge of the bottom crust.

7 Place the pie on a baking sheet and bake for 15 minutes. Reduce the oven temperature to 375°F (190°C) and bake for another 40–45 minutes, until the crust is golden and the filling is bubbly. If the pastry is browning too quickly, cover it loosely with a piece of foil. Cool the pie on a wire rack for at least 3 hours to allow it to set before cutting it. Serve warm, at room temperature, or cold.

Makes 1 pie

 What to do with the leftovers

* Keep them covered in the fridge for up to 3 days. Berry pie doesn't freeze as well as others.

 Other things to do with it

* Coarsely grate a tart apple into the berry mixture.

* Make a lattice top crust by cutting the second circle of dough into even strips and weaving them across the top of the pie. Seal, trim, and flute the edge and bake as directed.

* Peach-Berry Pie: Use 6 large, ripe but firm peaches and 1 cup (250 mL) berries. To peel the peaches, drop them into boiling water for about 30 seconds; remove them with tongs or a slotted spoon and plunge them into cold water. The skins should slip right off. Thickly slice the peaches and toss them with the berries, sugar, and cornstarch, using only ⅔ cup (160 mL) sugar. Top with streusel or a second crust and bake as directed.

Lemon Meringue Pie

Ingredients

1 single pastry or crumb pie crust,
    fully baked (see pages 290–91)

Filling

1 cup (250 mL) sugar

⅓ cup (80 mL) cornstarch

¼ tsp (1 mL) salt

1 ½ cups (375 mL) water

5 large egg yolks, lightly beaten

½ cup (125 mL) fresh lemon juice

Grated zest of 1 large lemon

2 Tbsp (30 mL) butter

Meringue

5 large egg whites

¼ tsp (1 mL) cream of tartar

Pinch salt

½ cup (125 mL) sugar

For advice on how to maximize the volume of your egg whites, see page 232. To keep the meringue from weeping, make sure the filling is hot when you top it with the meringue, and allow the pie to cool completely after baking and before putting it in the fridge.

Method

1 Preheat the oven to 400°F (200°C).

2 To make the filling, whisk together the sugar, cornstarch, and salt in a heavy pot set over medium heat. Stir in the water. Cook, whisking constantly, until the mixture comes to a boil. Boil it for a minute, until it thickens, then remove it from the heat.

3 Slowly whisk about ¼ cup (60 mL) of the hot mixture into the egg yolks in a small bowl to warm them up, and then slowly pour the egg mixture back into the pot, whisking constantly until the mixture is smooth. Whisk in the lemon juice, zest, and butter and return the pot to the heat. Bring to a boil and cook, stirring constantly, for a minute or until it has thickened. Pour it into the pie crust.

4 To make the meringue, put the egg whites in a clean glass or stainless steel bowl with the cream of tartar and salt and beat them with an electric mixer on high speed until soft peaks form. Add the sugar in a slow stream or sprinkle in a little at a time, beating until it's glossy and holds stiff peaks.

5 Spread the meringue over the filling, covering it completely, and making sure the meringue is touching the pastry on all sides of the pie. Spread it into a dome shape, with a peaked top. Put the pie back in the oven, making sure there's room for the meringue, and bake it for 8–10 minutes, until the meringue is golden. Cool it completely on a wire rack and then chill for an hour (or up to 4 hours) before serving.

Makes 1 pie

Other things to do with it

* Add ½ cup (125 mL) finely chopped or ground pecans to the crust, whether you make a pastry or a crumb crust.

What to do with the leftovers

* Keep them in the fridge for up to 3 days. These pies are difficult to cover, but you could stick toothpicks in the meringue to support a tent of plastic wrap, cover it with a cake dome or leave it uncovered.

Pies

Pumpkin Pie

Ingredients

1 single pie crust (see pages 290)

1 14 oz (398 mL) can pure pumpkin

¾ cup (185 mL) half and half,
    evaporated 2% milk, or
    whipping cream

½ cup (125 mL) sugar

½ cup (125 mL) packed brown sugar

3 large eggs

1 Tbsp (15 mL) molasses

1 tsp (5 mL) vanilla extract

½–1 tsp (2.5–5 mL) cinnamon

¼ tsp (1 mL) salt

¼ tsp (1 mL) ground allspice

¼ tsp (1 mL) ground ginger (optional)

Pinch nutmeg (optional)

There are few foods in the world more closely associated with holiday celebrations than pumpkin pie. During the winter you can find them in every grocery store and supermarket, but if you're having people over, wouldn't you prefer to have your house smelling heavenly? And if you're going somewhere, wouldn't you rather bring a pie you baked yourself? Luckily, pumpkin pie is one of the fastest and easiest kinds to make from scratch. If you're really ambitious, you could cut your trimmed scraps of pastry into tiny leaves, with "veins" made gently with the tip of a sharp knife, bake them separately on a cookie sheet and then lay them on top of the baked pie.

Some people are under the misconception that fresh pumpkin is better than canned for making pie—it isn't. Using canned pumpkin purée is infinitely easier, and it contains 20 times the beta carotene of fresh pumpkin.

Method

1   Preheat the oven to 350°F (175°C).

2   In a large bowl, whisk together the pumpkin, cream, sugars, eggs, molasses, vanilla, cinnamon, salt, allspice, ginger, and nutmeg and mix until well blended and smooth. Pour into the pie crust.

3   Bake for 50–60 minutes, until the filling is set but still just a little wobbly in the middle and the crust is golden. If the crust is browning too quickly, cover the pie lightly with a sheet of foil as it bakes. Cool completely in the pan on a wire rack and then refrigerate it for at least an hour, or up to a day. Serve the pie at room temperature with whipped cream, sweetened with a little sugar or maple syrup.

Makes 1 pie

 What to do with the leftovers

* Keep them covered in the fridge for up to 5 days. Eat them cold, or warm them in the microwave.

 Other things to do with it

* As soon as it comes out of the oven, sprinkle the hot pie with a mixture of ½ cup (125 mL) chopped and toasted pecans and 1 bashed up Skor bar. The chocolate, toffee, and nuts will melt slightly and sink into the surface of the warm filling.

* Maple Pumpkin Pie: Replace the brown and white sugars with ¾ cup (185 mL) maple syrup. (Grade B is cheaper and more intensely flavored than grade A, which makes it ideal for baking.) Bake the pie as directed.

Pies

Chocolate Cream Pie

Ingredients

1 single crumb or pastry crust,
    any flavor, baked (see pages
    290–91)

¾ cup (185 mL) sugar

⅓ cup (80 mL) cocoa

3 Tbsp (45 mL) cornstarch

Pinch salt

1 large egg

2 cups (500 mL) milk (whole,
    2% or 1%, not skim)

2 oz (56 g) semisweet chocolate,
    grated or finely chopped

1 tsp (5 mL) vanilla extract

¾ cup (185 mL) whipping cream,
    chilled

1 Tbsp (15 mL) sugar

Cream pies like chocolate, banana, and coconut are rarely made from scratch anymore, even though it's just as easy as cooking a powdered pudding mix on the stovetop to fill a crust. Only the crust, which can be a crumb crust or pastry, needs to be baked—the filling is cooked on the stovetop and then poured into the crust and chilled.

To make chocolate curls to sprinkle on top, scrape a vegetable peeler across the side of a chunk of room-temperature chocolate, or grate it on the coarse side of a box grater.

Method

1 Preheat the oven to 350°F (175°C).

2 To make the filling, combine the sugar, cocoa, cornstarch, and salt in a medium pot. Stir in the egg and about ¼ cup (60 mL) of the milk and whisk until it's smooth. Set the pot over medium heat and whisk in the rest of the milk. Cook, stirring constantly, until it comes to a boil. Turn the heat down a bit but keep it bubbling gently for 1–2 minutes, until the mixture is thick. Remove it from the heat and stir in the grated chocolate and vanilla, stirring until the chocolate melts.

3 Immediately pour the filling into the crust. Cover with a piece of plastic wrap to prevent a skin from forming, and refrigerate for 2 hours, or up to a day.

4 Whip the cream with the sugar with an electric mixer on medium-high speed, beating just until stiff peaks form. Spread the whipped cream over the pie and serve right away, or chill it for up to 3 hours. If you like, top your pie with chocolate curls.

Makes 1 pie

What to do with the leftovers

* Keep them in the fridge for up to a day, or cover them with plastic wrap and freeze for up to 3 months.

Other things to do with it

* Mocha Cream Pie: Dissolve 1 Tbsp (15 mL) instant coffee or espresso granules into the milk before you add it to the pot.

* Chocolate Banana Cream Pie: Slice 2 bananas. Add half the filling to the crust, top with the banana slices, and pour the remaining filling over them. Chill the pie as directed and top with the whipped cream. If you like, you can replace 2 Tbsp (30 mL) of the butter in the crust with 2 Tbsp (30 mL) mashed ripe banana to give the crust a banana flavor, too.

* Coconut Cream Pie: Omit the cocoa and chocolate and make your crust with graham crackers, vanilla wafers, or digestive biscuits. Use ½ cup (125 mL) sugar and 2 eggs. Add 1 cup (250 mL) sweetened shredded or flaked coconut along with the milk (try using coconut milk instead of regular milk) and cook the filling as directed. When you remove the filling from the heat, add ½ tsp (2.5 mL) coconut extract along with the vanilla. Toast another ½ cup (125 mL) sweetened coconut in a dry pan set over medium heat until it's golden and fragrant; cool and sprinkle the toasted coconut over the pie after topping it with whipped cream.

Pecan Pie

Ingredients

1 single pie crust, partially
  blind baked (see pages 289–90)

Filling

2 cups (500 mL) pecan halves

1 cup (250 mL) packed brown sugar

2–4 Tbsp (30–60 mL) butter, melted

3 large eggs

¾ cup (185 mL) corn syrup

2 tsp (10 mL) vanilla extract

½ tsp (2.5 mL) salt

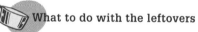

What to do with the leftovers

* Keep them covered in the fridge
  for up to 5 days. Eat them cold or
  warm them in the microwave.

Other things to do with it

* Sprinkle ½ cup (125 mL) chopped chocolate or
  chocolate chips over the bottom of the pie shell before
  pouring in the filling.

* Maple Pecan Pie: Replace the brown sugar with ½ cup
  (125 mL) maple sugar, and use maple syrup in place
  of the corn syrup. (You can get away with using grade
  B maple syrup, which is much cheaper and perfect for
  baking.)

OK, pecan pie is deliriously rich and high in fat and in calories, so if you're going to have some you might as well make a really good one. Just make sure you don't eat it all at once. You can get away with cutting back on the butter to about 2 tablespoons (30 mL), and take comfort in the fact that almost all of the fat in pecans is the healthy kind.

Method

1 Preheat the oven to 350°F (175°C).

2 Place the pecans on a baking sheet and toast them for 5–7 minutes, shaking the pan occasionally, until they're fragrant. Keep a close eye on them so that they don't burn.

3 In a medium bowl, stir together the sugar, melted butter, eggs, corn syrup, vanilla, and salt; stir until well blended and smooth, making sure you get rid of any lumps of brown sugar. Stir in the pecans and pour the mixture into the crust.

4 Bake the pie for 50–60 minutes, until the filling is slightly puffed and set. If the pastry is browning too quickly, cover the pie loosely with a piece of foil. Cool it completely on a wire rack before serving at room temperature.

Makes 1 pie

* Fig Pecan Pie: Stir ¾ cup (185 mL) chopped dried
  Calimyrna figs into the filling along with the pecans.

* Orange-Bourbon Pecan Pie: Stir ¼ cup (60 mL)
  bourbon and the grated zest of an orange into the filling
  mixture.

Puddings and fruit desserts

Dessert is that little reward you get for making it through the day. In England, dessert in general is referred to as "pudding," but in North America, "pudding" refers to soft desserts often associated with nursery food, likely because they're sweet and require little or no chewing. Pudding beyond those that come in a package are rarely made from scratch, which is a shame. A warm bowl of rice pudding or sticky chocolate pudding cake will cure many afflictions, real or imagined. And if you have some fruit in the house, it's easy to turn it into a warm, comforting cobbler or crisp, which has the same qualities of a pudding, with its soft, melting fruit and crunchy-sweet topping.

Real Chocolate Pudding

Ingredients

½ cup (125 mL) sugar

⅓ cup (80 mL) cocoa

3 Tbsp (45 mL) cornstarch

Pinch salt

2 cups (500 mL) milk or light cream

3 oz (85 g) chopped semisweet chocolate or ½ cup (125 mL) chocolate chips (optional)

1 tsp (5 mL) vanilla extract

Real chocolate pudding takes no longer to make than pudding from a package. My mom used to make this when there was nothing else in the house for dessert—chances are you have the ingredients in your cupboard already. It can be made with any kind of milk, even soy milk, or if you're feeling really indulgent, light cream. The chopped chocolate isn't necessary, but it adds intensity to the flavour and creates an even creamier texture.

Method

1 In a medium pot, whisk together the sugar, cocoa, cornstarch, and salt. Stir in about a cup of the milk and whisk until the mixture is smooth and well blended, then whisk in the remaining milk. Set the pan over medium heat and cook, whisking constantly, for about 5 minutes or until the mixture bubbles and thickens. Continue to cook the pudding for another minute.

2 Remove the pot from the heat and stir in the chocolate and vanilla. Let it sit for a few minutes to let the chocolate melt, and stir until it's smooth.

3 Divide the pudding between 4 small bowls. Let it cool for about 20 minutes and serve warm, or put it in the fridge for at least half an hour (or several hours) and serve it cold. If you don't like pudding "skin," cover the surface with plastic wrap before you chill it.

Serves 4

 What to do with the leftovers

* Keep them covered in the fridge for up to 4 days. Pudding can also be frozen—try pouring it into popsicle moulds to make pudding pops.

 Other things to do with it

* Give the pudding a mocha or orange flavor by adding 1 tsp (5 mL) instant coffee to the milk or the grated zest of an orange to the sugar mixture.

Rice Pudding

Ingredients

½ cup (125 mL) long- or
    short-grain white rice

4 cups (1 L) milk

½ cup (125 mL) sugar

1 tsp (5 mL) vanilla extract

Pinch salt

1 large egg (optional)

½ cup (125 mL) half and half or whip-
    ping cream (optional)

Raisins (optional)

Cinnamon (optional)

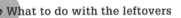

What to do with the leftovers

* Keep them covered in the fridge
  for up to 4 days. Rice pudding
  doesn't freeze very well.

Other things to do with it

* Use brown rice for added fiber.

* Use the ½ cup (125 mL) whipping cream, and whip it
  until soft peaks form. Let the pudding cool completely,
  and then fold the whipped cream into it.

There are two ways to make rice pudding: in a pot on the stovetop or in a baking dish in the oven. The stovetop varieties are stirred as they cook and tend to be creamier; baked rice puddings are firmer. People either love raisins in their rice pudding or hate them—the same goes for cinnamon—so use either or both only if you want to. The egg and cream are also optional—they will make the pudding creamier but aren't essential.

Method

1 Combine the rice, milk, sugar, vanilla, and salt in a large pot and set it over medium-high heat. Bring the mixture to a boil, then turn down the heat, and simmer, stirring often, for about an hour or until the rice is very tender.

2 If you're using it, whisk the egg lightly in a small bowl with a fork or wire whisk. Remove the pot of rice pudding from the heat and quickly whisk about ½ cup (125 mL) of the hot pudding into the egg. Return the egg mixture to the pot and stir it well. The heat of the pudding will cook the egg, even though it's been taken off the stove. Stir in the half and half or whipping cream.

3 If you want to add raisins, stir in as many as you like. Refrigerate the pudding for about 2 hours, or until it's well chilled. Sprinkle cinnamon on top before you serve it.

Serves 4

* Coconut Rice Pudding: Use a 14 oz (398 mL) can light or regular coconut milk in place of 1 ½ cups (375 mL) of the milk, and coconut extract instead of the vanilla. Top each bowl of pudding with shredded coconut that has been toasted in a dry pan until golden and fragrant.

Tiramisù

Ingredients

1 cup (250 mL) strong black coffee or
   espresso, cooled

¼ cup (60 mL) Kahlua or Marsala
   (optional)

1 cup (250 mL) mascarpone or an
   8-oz (250-g) tub light cream
   cheese

⅓ cup (80 mL) packed brown sugar

¼ cup (60 mL) sugar

1 cup (250 mL) whipping cream or
   ½ tub Cool Whip

2 Tbsp (30 mL) sugar (optional,
   if using whipping cream)

20 ladyfingers

Cocoa and/or 1 oz (25 g)
   semisweet chocolate to make
   curls (optional)

Tiramisù is often described as an Italian trifle. It's composed of sponge cake or ladyfingers dipped in a boozy coffee mixture, then layered with mascarpone (an ultra-rich Italian cream cheese) or cream cheese, and topped with grated chocolate. Packages of ladyfingers can usually be found in the cookie aisle, or at Italian grocery stores.

Method

1 In a shallow bowl, mix the coffee and Kahlua. In a medium bowl, beat the cream cheese with both sugars until the mixture is completely smooth. In another medium bowl, beat the whipping cream with the sugar on high speed with an electric mixer until softly stiff peaks form. Using a rubber spatula, gently fold the whipped cream into the cream cheese mixture. (For more about folding, see page 233).

2 Dip 10 of the ladyfingers in the coffee-Kahlua mixture and use them to line the bottom of an 8-inch square pan. Don't soak them for too long, or they may fall apart.

3 Once the bottom of the pan is covered with ladyfingers (you may have to break some of them to get them to fit), spread half the cream cheese mixture over top of them. Repeat with a second layer of dipped ladyfingers and the rest of the cream cheese mixture.

4 To make chocolate curls, scrape a vegetable peeler across a block or bar of room-temperature chocolate (chocolate tends to crumble when it's cold), or grate it on the coarse side of a box grater, which will make smaller curls. Sprinkle the top of the tiramisù with cocoa and/or chocolate curls.

5 Put the tiramisù in the fridge for an hour, or for up to 6 hours, to allow the flavors to mingle.

Serves 6

Puddings
and fruit
desserts

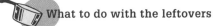 **What to do with the leftovers**

* Keep them in the fridge, covered with plastic wrap, for up to 2 days, or wrap them well and freeze for up to 3 months. The frozen tiramisù can be thawed at room temperature or eaten frozen.

Other things to do with it

* Layer the ladyfingers and cream cheese mixture in individual parfait glasses or bowls instead of in a pan.

* Tiramisù Trifle: In a large glass bowl, layer cubes of pound cake, drizzled with the coffee-Kahlua mixture, with layers of the cheese mixture. Top with whipped cream and sprinkle with chocolate curls.

* Chocolate Tiramisù: Use cream cheese instead of mascarpone, and beat ¼–½ cup (60–125 mL) chocolate syrup into it along with the sugar. Bash up 2 Skor bars and sprinkle one over the first layer and the second over top of the finished tiramisù.

Trifle

Ingredients

Base

1 pound cake (see page 274), cut into cubes

Fruit

2 10 oz (283 g) packages frozen raspberries in syrup, thawed and drained with ½ cup (125 mL) syrup reserved

¾ cup (185 mL) raspberry jam

Custard

3 Tbsp (45 mL) custard powder (such as Bird's)

3 Tbsp (45 mL) sugar

2 ½ cups (625 mL) milk

Topping

1 ½ cups (375 mL) whipping cream

1 Tbsp (15 mL) sugar

1 tsp (5 mL) vanilla

What to do with the leftovers

* Keep them covered in the fridge for up to 3 days and eat them directly from the bowl with a spoon.

You don't make a trifle so much as assemble it. It comes across as very involved and stunning to look at but in reality it's nothing more than layers of cake, fruit, custard, and cream. A trifle is best made with plain cake, fruit, and cream, but really can be made with ingredients limited only by your imagination. Best of all, it can be assembled a day before you need it and you don't have to worry about it falling or burning or any kitchen disasters beyond maybe scorching the custard on the stove, which won't happen if you don't leave it alone.

Method

1 Place half of the chunks of pound cake in a large glass bowl. (If it's a large cake, you may not need the whole thing—just make one layer on the bottom of the bowl.)

2 Combine the thawed raspberries, syrup, and raspberry jam. Layer half over the pound cake.

3 Prepare the custard according to the package directions; let it cool slightly and pour half over the berries.

4 Add another layer of pound cake, the remaining fruit, and the remaining custard. Whip the cream, sugar, and vanilla in bowl until the mixture holds peaks. Top the trifle with whipped cream, and a few fresh berries, if you have some around.

Serves 6

Other things to do with it

* Roasted Apple and Pear Trifle: Toss 3 large Granny Smith apples, peeled, cored and sliced, 3 Bartlett or Bosc pears, peeled, cored and sliced, 2 Tbsp (30 mL) lemon juice, and 2 Tbsp (30 mL) melted butter and spread on a large rimmed baking sheet. Roast at 400°F (200°C) for about an hour, turning every 15 minutes, until the fruit is soft and golden. Let it cool on the sheet. Use it in place of the raspberries and jam, drizzling with bottled caramel sauce after each layer. To make it festive, use eggnog in place of the milk when making the custard.

Chocolate Pudding Cake

Ingredients

Cake

1 cup (250 mL) all-purpose flour

½ cup (125 mL) sugar

¼ cup (60 mL) cocoa

2 tsp (10 mL) baking powder

¼ tsp (1 mL) salt

½ cup (125 mL) milk, any kind

¼ cup (60 mL) canola oil or melted butter or margarine

1 tsp (5 mL) vanilla extract

Topping

½ cup (125 mL) packed brown sugar

¼ cup (60 mL) cocoa

Pudding cake is cake unlike any other. As it bakes, it creates a rich, creamy, puddingy sauce underneath the batter, which bakes up all crunchy and chewy on top. You eat it in a bowl, with a spoon. Chocolate pudding cake is one of the fastest (in terms of actual work time) and simplest recipes I know, and everyone goes mad for it. Serve it up warm, with a scoop of vanilla ice cream to melt into it.

Method

1 Preheat the oven to 350°F (175°C). Spray an 8-inch square pan with non-stick spray.

2 In a medium bowl, stir together the flour, sugar, cocoa, baking powder, and salt. Add the milk, oil, and vanilla and stir until smooth. Spread the batter into the prepared pan.

3 To make the topping, stir together the sugar and cocoa and sprinkle it over the batter. Pour 1 cup (250 mL) of very hot water over the whole thing, but don't stir it! Bake the pudding cake for 30–35 minutes, until the cake appears done and the sauce is bubbly. Serve it warm.

Serves 6

 What to do with the leftovers

* Keep them covered in the fridge for up to 3 days or wrap well and freeze for up to 3 months. Reheat them in the microwave.

 Other things to do with it

* Stir a handful of chopped walnuts, pecans, or chocolate chips into the batter before you spread it into the pan.

Apple Strudel

Ingredients

½ cup (125 mL) raisins

2 Tbsp (30 mL) apple juice, brandy, Calvados, or water

3–4 medium Granny Smith, McIntosh, or Golden Delicious apples, peeled, cored and thinly sliced

1 Tbsp (15 mL) lemon juice

½ cup (125 mL) dry white bread crumbs or gingersnap cookie crumbs

¼–½ cup (60–125 mL) sugar

¼ tsp (1 mL) cinnamon

6 sheets phyllo pastry, thawed

¼ cup (60 mL) butter, melted

Apple strudel may seem like a lot of work, but it's one of those things that's just demanding enough to make you feel proficient in the kitchen without actually requiring much skill. If you've never worked with phyllo pastry—paper-thin sheets of dough that you can find in the frozen pastry section of the grocery store—don't let it intimidate you. Phyllo is actually very forgiving. Because there are so many layers, you won't be able to tell if a few sheets are torn or cracked. Just make sure the sheets you aren't working with are well wrapped or covered with a tea towel so that they don't dry out. Once you get the hang of phyllo pastry, you can fill it with any kind of filling (sweet or savoury) you like.

Method

1   Preheat the oven to 375°F (190°C). Spray a baking sheet with non-stick spray.

2   Combine the raisins and apple juice in a small bowl and let them stand for about half an hour to plump up. Drain them well. Toss the raisins with the apples and lemon juice in a large bowl. Add the bread crumbs, ¼ cup (60 mL) sugar, and cinnamon and toss everything to blend well.

3   Unroll the phyllo and place one sheet on a clean, dry work surface, with a long side facing you. Keep the remaining phyllo covered with a dish towel or plastic wrap so that it doesn't dry out. Brush the sheet of phyllo very lightly with melted butter (you don't need to completely cover the surface), and sprinkle it with about a teaspoon (5 mL) of sugar. Lay a second sheet on top of the first, brush it with butter and sprinkle with sugar, and repeat with the remaining phyllo.

4   Spread the apple filling in a strip down the length of the phyllo, leaving a 2 ½-inch (6-cm) border along the bottom long edge, and 2 inches (5 cm) on each short side. Fold the short ends of the phyllo over the filling, and fold the long edge closest to you over the apples, as if you were making a burrito. Roll the strudel away from you, jelly roll style. Gently place it seam side down on the prepared baking sheet.

5 Brush the top of the strudel with a little butter if there's any left over, and sprinkle with a little sugar. Cut a few vents across the top with a sharp knife, to allow steam to escape as the strudel bakes. Bake for 30–40 minutes, until it's golden brown. Let it stand for at least 15 minutes before cutting into it. Serve it warm, at room temperature, or refrigerate it for up to 4 hours and serve it cold.

Serves 6

 What to do with the leftovers

* Keep them wrapped in the fridge for up to 2 days, or wrap them well and freeze for up to 4 months.

 Other things to do with it

* Use pears instead of apples, and/or other chopped dried fruit in place of the raisins.

* Phyllo Turnovers: After brushing with butter, cut each sheet of phyllo lengthwise into 4 strips. Place a spoonful of filling (the apple filling, any prepared pie filling, or mincemeat) onto the end of the strip and fold a corner of phyllo over to cover it. Continue folding the strip like a flag, maintaining the triangle shape so that you end up with a triangle-shaped package. Brush the turnovers with a little butter and bake them on an ungreased baking sheet for about 20 minutes, until golden.

Fruit Crisp

Ingredients

Filling

3 Granny Smith apples, peeled, cored, and thickly sliced or cut into chunks

3 McIntosh apples, peeled, cored, and thickly sliced or cut into chunks

2 Tbsp (30 mL) lemon juice

2–4 Tbsp (30–60 mL) sugar

Crumble topping

½ cup (125 mL) all-purpose flour

½ cup (125 mL) oats

½ cup (125 mL) packed brown sugar

Pinch cinnamon (optional)

Pinch salt

¼ cup (60 mL) butter or margarine, chilled

½ cup (125 mL) sliced almonds or chopped pecans (optional)

Puddings and fruit desserts

Fruit crisps have all the charm of pie with none of the hassles of pastry. Plums, peaches, pears, berries, or a combination of fruits in season all peeled and chopped and tossed with sugar make wonderful fruit crisps.

When making apple crisp, tart, flavorful apples such as Granny Smith and McIntosh are the best choice, and are more likely to hold their shape after being cooked. The amount of sugar you need will depend on the sweetness of the apples you use; taste them first and add sugar according to your taste. The best ways to eat fruit crisp are warm with vanilla ice cream and cold with vanilla yogurt the next morning for breakfast.

Method

1 Preheat the oven to 350°F (175°C).

2 To make the filling, toss the apples with the lemon juice in a shallow baking dish. (The shallower the baking dish, the more surface area for crumble!) Sprinkle them with sugar and toss to coat well.

3 To make the crumble, combine the flour, oats, brown sugar, cinnamon, and salt in a medium bowl. Blend in the butter with a fork or your fingers until the mixture is well combined and crumbly. If it isn't crumbly enough, add 1–2 Tbsp (15–30 mL) of honey, or a little extra butter. Stir in the nuts.

4 Sprinkle the crumble mixture over the apples, squeezing it to make bigger clumps as you go. Bake for 45–50 minutes, until golden on top and bubbly around the edges. Serve warm or at room temperature.

Serves 4–6

What to do with the leftovers

* Keep them covered in the fridge for up to 4 days or wrap them well and freeze for up to 3 months. Reheat them in the microwave or eat them cold.

Other things to do with it

* Peach Berry Crisp: Use 2 large peaches or nectarines, peeled, pitted, and sliced, and 4 cups (1 L) fresh or frozen mixed berries (blueberries, blackberries, strawberries, and raspberries) in place of the apples. Add 2 Tbsp (30 mL) flour to the sugar before tossing the fruit with it.

* Plum Crisp: Replace the apples with 8 plums, pitted and cut into thick wedges. Add 2 Tbsp (30 mL) flour to the sugar before tossing the fruit with it. Taste the plums as you cut them up—you may have to increase the sugar a bit if they're very tart.

Blackberry-Blueberry Cobbler

Ingredients

Filling

½ cup (125 mL) sugar

1 Tbsp (15 mL) cornstarch

2 cups (500 mL) blackberries (about 1 pint)

2 cups (500 mL) blueberries (about 1 pint)

1 Tbsp (15 mL) lemon juice

Cobbler

1 cup (250 mL) all-purpose flour

2 Tbsp (30 mL) sugar

1 tsp (5 mL) baking powder

½ tsp (2.5 mL) baking soda

Pinch salt

2 Tbsp (30 mL) butter, softened

½ cup (125 mL) buttermilk or thin yogurt

If you're lucky to live in an area that has wild blackberries in August, this is a great way to use them. If not, any other juicy berry will do, and frozen berries are a fine substitute. Since cobbler is essentially drop biscuits baked on top of juicy fruit, this makes a wonderful breakfast. Why not?

Method

1 Preheat the oven to 350°F (175°C).

2 To make the filling, combine the sugar and cornstarch in a medium bowl. Add the berries and lemon juice and toss them to coat. Transfer to a baking dish (about 2 L) or pie plate and bake for 20 minutes, until bubbly around the edges.

3 In a medium bowl, combine the flour, sugar, baking powder, baking soda, and salt. Add the butter and blend until the mixture is well combined and crumbly. Add the buttermilk and stir just until you have a soft, sticky dough.

4 Remove the berries from the oven and drop spoonfuls of the cobbler dough over top. If you like, sprinkle the dough with a little extra sugar. Return to the oven for about 30 minutes, or until the biscuits are golden and the fruit is bubbly. Serve warm.

Serves 4

What to do with the leftovers

* Keep them covered in the fridge for up to a day, or transfer to a tightly sealed container and freeze for up to 4 months. Eat them cold or warm them up in the oven or microwave.

Other things to do with it

* Peach or Plum Berry Cobbler: Replace half the berries with 4 sliced plums, or 2 peeled and sliced peaches or nectarines.

Dried Fruit Compote

Ingredients

1 cup (250 mL) apple cider or juice

1 cup (250 mL) water

½ cup (125 mL) sugar

2 cinnamon sticks, broken in half

2 cups (500 mL) dried Calimyrna figs, stemmed and halved lengthwise

1 cup (250 mL) sliced dried apricots

1 cup (250 mL) dried tart cherries

4 dried pear halves, chopped

Serve this sweet, sticky compote warm over pancakes or vanilla ice cream, or chill it and make breakfast parfaits, layered with granola and vanilla yogurt. It's also great with roast pork, chicken, or turkey.

Method

1 In a large pot set over medium heat, combine the apple cider, water, sugar, and cinnamon sticks. Cook, stirring, until the sugar dissolves and it comes to a boil. Reduce the temperature to low, add the figs, and simmer for 3 minutes.

2 Add the apricots, cherries, and pears and simmer, uncovered, for about 10 minutes, until the fruits are tender but still retain their shape. Remove the pan from the heat and set it aside to cool. Serve the compote at room temperature, or refrigerate until it's chilled and serve cold.

Makes about 4 cups (1 L)

 What to do with the leftovers

* Store them in a container in the fridge for up to a week. This compote doesn't freeze well.

* Serve the compote cold or warmed in the microwave over ice cream, pound cake, pancakes, or waffles, swirled into thick vanilla yogurt, or layered with yogurt and granola.

 Other things to do with it

* Experiment with different combinations of dried fruit, or add one or two whole pods of star anise along with the cinnamon sticks.

Damage control

All cooks screw up from time to time, even the professional ones. Here are a few solutions to emergencies you might otherwise call your mom for help with.

Cookies are burning on the bottom: This is one of the most common cookie-baking problems, and can usually be blamed on your oven being too hot or on dark cookie sheets that conduct heat better than light-colored sheets. Cookies are best baked on light-colored cookie sheets that have been sprayed with non-stick spray or lined with parchment or a silicone baking mat, unless a recipe instructs otherwise. If you still have a problem with cookie bottoms burning, try doubling up the cookie sheet and placing a few pennies in between the two layers to insulate the cookies from the heat of the oven.

Cookies aren't chewy: This is almost always caused by overbaking. People often wait until cookies are golden and set all the way through before taking them out of the oven. If you wait this long they'll be overdone. Remember that cookies firm up as they cool, so if they're set all the way through when you take them out, they'll be even firmer before they're cool enough to eat. Make sure you check them at the earliest suggested baking time. If they're too soft to remove from the cookie sheet they're probably not quite done, but cookies should be barely golden and set around the edges, and still nice and soft in the middle if you want them to be chewy once they cool down. Remove them from the cookie sheet and transfer them to a wire rack to cool immediately if you have one—cookies can continue to cook for a few minutes longer as they sit on a hot cookie sheet. If you are certain overbaking isn't the problem, you may have overmixed your dough. Stirring develops gluten, which can make cookies tough. Once flour has come into contact with liquid ingredients, it should be stirred gently, just until the dough is combined.

Cookies aren't spreading enough: Chances are your oven is too hot, and the cookie dough is setting too quickly on the outside before the cookies have a chance to spread. It could also be caused by dough that has had too much flour added and is too thick as a result—read up on measuring your ingredients, and try to stir the flour to aerate it before measuring it (see page 230). This will ensure you aren't adding too much.

Cookies are spreading too much and resemble pancakes more than cookies: Chances are your oven is too cool, and the cookie dough is melting onto the sheet before it has a chance to set properly.

Fat or grease in a pan starts on fire: Turn off the heat and cover the pan with a lid to cover it completely and cut off the oxygen supply.

Fires outside of a pan: Douse the flames by pouring on a handful of baking soda or salt. Never pour water on flaming fat or oil—you'll spread the fire.

Gravy or sauce is too thin: Slowly simmering a sauce allows it to reduce, which means excess moisture will evaporate and the remainder will be more concentrated in flavor. Just make sure you don't overseason your sauce before you reduce it, or it could end up too salty or spicy. You could also thicken a sauce with a cornstarch "slurry"—whisk 1 Tbsp (15 mL) cornstarch into 2 Tbsp (30 mL) cold water, and then whisk it into the sauce. Bring to a simmer and cook for 1 minute to maximize the thickening potential.

Gravy or sauce is lumpy: Try to break up the lumps by whisking vigorously. If this doesn't work, pour the gravy through a mesh sieve or purée it in a blender or food processor. To prevent lumps in the first place, dissolve any flour or cornstarch you need to add in a little cold water or other liquid before you add it to your gravy or sauce.

Muffins are too dry and have tunnels: The batter may have been overmixed, the muffins overbaked (as a result of too much time or an oven that was too hot), or too much flour was added. It's important to stir or sift flour before it is lightly spooned into a measuring cup when you measure it—just like brown sugar, flour can get packed down as it settles in its bag or canister, so 1 scooped cup (250 mL) could actually be 1 ¼ cups (310 mL). Remember to level it off with a knife or other flat edge so that you don't have a heaping cup, either.

Muffins don't rise enough: Your oven may be too cool or your leavener inactive. To test your baking powder or soda, see page 235. To test your oven temperature, buy an inexpensive oven thermometer at any department store. If you find that your oven temperature is off, compensate by adjusting the temperature accordingly—there's usually no need to have it professionally calibrated.

Muffins stick to the pan: The pan wasn't greased properly, or the muffins cooled completely in the pan. Tip them on an angle in the pan while they're still warm to allow steam to escape, and so they don't stick as they cool.

Oversalted gravy or sauce: Add one or two peeled potatoes to absorb some of the salt. Remove them once they have cooked through.

Overwhipped cream: If you've overwhipped your cream, gently fold in 2–3 Tbsp (30–45 mL) of cream or milk to restore the proper consistency.

Overwhipped egg whites: If you have overwhipped your egg whites, beat a fresh one until it's frothy, fold it into the overwhipped whites and beat again until they're just the right consistency.

How to
do your laundry

Doing your own laundry isn't really that hard, is it?
Not really, but you may be baffled before you even get your clothes
into the machine. These steps walk you through
your first few loads, until you get the hang of it.

Washing clothes

1   If you care about your clothes, read their labels. If you're not sure what they mean, there's a guide on page 323.

2   Separate your darks and whites! Washing whites with anything but other whites can make them dingy, and you could turn them pink if you wash them with red clothes. If you have room, buy two laundry hampers to toss clothes into—this saves you sorting them when it's time to do laundry.

3   Check your clothes for stains. If you miss one and it ends up in the dryer, the stain will set. Spot treat any stains using the guide on page 321.

4   You don't ever need to wash your clothes in hot water. Always use the warm or cold setting. If you have your own washer and dryer, this also saves you a lot of money! When washing dark clothes for the first time, use cold water and a handful of salt in the water. This helps to set the color.

5   Once you have chosen the temperature setting, set the machine for the type and size of load you are doing. The options are usually pretty self-explanatory: large or small, heavy duty or delicates. There are often instructions printed inside washing machine lids.

6   Measure the detergent according to the package directions (although you usually don't need quite as much as they say), and add it first, allowing it to dissolve in the water before putting the clothes in the washer. Sometimes powder detergents don't break up properly, and can make your clothes cloudy white. Liquid detergents dissolve much better.

7   When you're washing whites, bleach will help brighten your load. Add the bleach to the water before adding your clothes to avoid getting pure bleach on anything.

8   When you add your clothes, make sure they're evenly distributed around the basin of the washing machine, and leave about 3 inches between the top of the clothes and the top of the basin.

9   The easiest way to add fabric softener is in the form of a dryer sheet, rather than in the washing machine, in which case you have to go back and add it during the rinse cycle. If you do use liquid fabric softener, follow the instructions on the bottle.

How to dry your clothes

1   Tear dryer sheets in half—they work just as well. (Used dryer sheets are also great for dusting.)

2   Try to remember to empty the lint trap every time you use the dryer.

3   Some articles of clothing, particularly cotton ones, are better off being hung or laid flat to dry, so that they don't shrink. Don't worry about cotton socks and underwear though—they can go in the dryer. Clothes such as T-shirts and sweats that have been washed and dried a lot already are probably fine, too.

4   For clothes that do go in the dryer, follow the care instructions on their labels (see page 323). Some clothes may shrink if they go into the dryer at excessive heat.

5   Take clothes out of the dryer as soon as they're done—they'll get wrinkled sitting in a pile in the dryer if you leave them for too long.

Other laundry tips

* Once in awhile, wash your washing machine by hand using hot water and white vinegar, or run the normal cycle using hot water, and add a small bottle of vinegar to clean any soap film that has built up inside.

* Some people like to wash and dry their clothes inside out to prevent fading.

* Pilling is caused by clothes rubbing against each other when you wear them and in the washer and dryer. Prevent it by turning clothes inside out before you wash them.

* Use a safety pin to pin your socks together so they don't lose each other.

* Many garments labeled "dry clean only" can be safely washed by hand using mild soap (like Woolite) and cold water. Lay them flat to dry.

* To wash delicates by hand, put them in the sink or a large Tupperware container with warm water and about a teaspoon (5 mL) of liquid laundry detergent or dishwashing liquid. Swish them around in the sink, or seal and shake the container for a few minutes, then rinse well and lay flat or hang to dry.

* If you have fragile items such as lingerie or beaded clothes that you don't want to wash by hand, put them in a pillow case and tie the top closed before you throw it in the wash.

* If your black clothes fade after several washings, add a box of black fabric dye every 8–10 washes to restore their color, or add some coffee or strong black tea to the rinse cycle. (Always wash the machine thoroughly after using fabric dye in it.)

* To prevent jeans from fading, soak them for an hour in a mixture of 2 Tbsp (30 mL) salt and 1 gallon (4 L) of cold water. Turn them inside out and wash as usual using cold water.

* When whites get dingy, cut half a lemon into slices and put them in a basin of boiling hot water. Soak your dingy clothes for at least half an hour, then wash them as usual.

* To prolong the life of pantyhose, soak them in water before you wear them for the first time, then wring them out and freeze them solid in a plastic bag. Let them thaw and dry completely before wearing them. When rinsing pantyhose, add 2 Tbsp (30 mL) of white vinegar to the rinse water to increase elasticity.

* If you don't have any bleach, try adding ¼–½ cup (60–125 mL) lemon juice, ¼ cup (60 mL) white vinegar, or 3 Tbsp (45 mL) hydrogen peroxide to your wash instead.

* If you're out of fabric softener, try adding ¼ cup (60 mL) white vinegar to the last rinse cycle. It softens and also brightens colors, but won't come out smelling like vinegar! You could also substitute ¼–½ cup (60–125 mL) hair conditioner.

* To clean suede garments, sponge them with a soft cloth dipped in white vinegar.

How to remove stains

No matter what caused the stain, it's important that you act quickly! If you need to take your clothes to the dry cleaner, do it soon and make sure you point out the stain. If you know what caused it, tell them.

If you use stain removal products, follow the instructions carefully. Test them on an inconspicuous spot first, to make sure it doesn't change the color of the fabric. Some suggest removing the stain from the back. Place the garment with the stain inside out on top of a clean white cloth. Apply stain treatment to the back of the stain, and move it to a fresh spot as the stain begins to remove itself from the clothing and onto the cloth. When removing stains, always remember to dab, not rub.

Blood

Rinse or presoak the item in cold water and wash in cold water using your regular laundry detergent.

Chocolate

Spot clean or prewash the item in warm water with a cleaning product that contains enzymes. Wash as usual.

Coffee

Soak in cold water and apply a stain-removing product. Wash as usual and lay flat or hang to dry—don't put it in the dryer. Repeat the procedure if the stain remains.

Grass

Presoak the item in warm water with a detergent containing enzymes. Wash as usual, using bleach if it's safe and appropriate for the fabric.

Gum

Hold an ice cube on the gum to harden it, then pick off as much as you can with a dull knife and your fingers. Use a stain-removing stick or a little laundry soap or liquid laundry detergent on the spot before you wash it if a stain remains.

Ink

Pull the piece of fabric with the stain on it over the mouth of a jar or glass. Hold it tight (use your hand or an elastic band) and drop rubbing alcohol through the stain so that the ink will drop with it into the container. Rinse well and use a stain-removing prewash spray or a little laundry soap or liquid laundry detergent on the spot before you wash it. Wash as usual but check the stain before you dry it. If it's still there, repeat the procedure.

Juice

Soak the item in cold water, then apply a stain-treating product. Wash as usual but check the stain before you dry it. If it's still there, repeat the procedure. Some suggest pouring rubbing alcohol over red juice stains to treat them before washing.

Make-up

Spot clean the area with laundry soap, liquid laundry detergent, or a stain treatment. Use Vaseline (petroleum jelly) to remove lipstick stains. Some people swear by rubbing the area with the heel of a loaf of bread. Wash as usual.

Mud

Brush off as much of the surface dirt as possible. Presoak in warm water with laundry detergent and wash as usual.

Perspiration

Apply a stain treatment or white vinegar to the stains and let it sit for half an hour. Rinse and then wash as usual using bleach (if it's appropriate for the fabric) and hot water.

Red Wine

Cover the area with salt to absorb excess liquid. Some suggest rubbing with a paste made with salt and water. Dab with club soda or soak in a solution of cold water and borax for half an hour. Wash as usual.

Ring around the collar

Use an old toothbrush to wash collars with hair shampoo or dish detergent, both which break up natural oils. Wash as usual.

Tomato sauce

Gently spot clean the area using warm water and liquid laundry soap or dish detergent and an old toothbrush. Rinse and wash as usual.

Urine

Cover the area with salt to absorb excess liquid. Rinse in cold water. If a stain remains, spot clean with white vinegar. Wash as usual.

Fabric Care Symbols

Symbol	Name	Description
	Machine wash	If there are dots in the water, the number of dots indicates water temperature: 1 dot = cool, 2 dots = warm, 3 dots = hot
	Indicates delicate/ gentle cycle	If there are dots in the water, the number of dots indicates water temperature: 1 dot = cool, 2 dots = warm, 3 dots = hot
	Hand wash	
	Chlorine bleach may be used	
	Do not bleach	
	Tumble dry	If there are dots in the circle, the number of dots indicates heat setting: 1 dot = low, 2 dots = medium, 3 dots = high
	Line dry/ Hang to dry	
	Lay flat to dry	
	Iron	If there are dots in the iron, the number of dots indicates iron temperature: 1 dot = low (110°C–200°C) 2 dots = warm (150°C–230°C), 3 dots = high (200°C–390°C)
	Do not iron	

Glossary of cooking terms

Al dente: An Italian term meaning "to the tooth," *al dente* refers to pasta cooked so that it's firm but tender, not mushy.

Baste: To drizzle or spoon juices, sauces, or other liquid over something as it cooks.

Barbecue: Barbecuing differs greatly from grilling; true barbecue is a long, slow method of cooking meat, usually involving indirect heat and smoke.

Beat: To mix ingredients briskly until they're well blended.

Blanch: To plunge food, usually fruits and vegetables, briefly into boiling water, then run them under cold water to stop the cooking process. Used to brighten the color of vegetables or to loosen skins (particularly with peaches and tomatoes) for easier peeling.

Blind bake: To precook a pie crust that will be filled with cooked filling, or to ensure proper cooking when the filled pie requires a short cooking time.

Boil: Heating liquid or cooking food in liquid that has been heated to the point where bubbles break the surface.

Braise: To cook food by first browning in a little fat, then adding a small amount of liquid and cooking, tightly covered, over low heat for a long time. Braising can be done in the oven or on the stovetop and works well to tenderize tough cuts of meat.

Broil: To cook food directly under a high heat source; the opposite of grilling.

Caramelize: Heating sugar to the point where it melts and turns golden to deep brown. Foods can also be caramelized when they're cooked to the point where their natural sugars turn golden brown.

Chop: To cut food into pieces ranging in size from large to small. Very fine chopping is called mincing.

Deglaze: A technique used after sautéing meat or other food. After finishing the sauté, remove the food and excess fat from the pan. Add a small amount of liquid (wine, stock, juice, or even water) to the pan and cook, scraping up the browned bits that have stuck to the bottom. Heat and stir until the liquid has reduced to the consistency you want.

Dice: To cut food into small cubes of roughly equal size.

Dutch oven: A large, deep pot with a tight-fitting lid.

Emulsion: When blending two ingredients that don't easily combine, most commonly oil and vinegar, you'll need a blender to blend it to the point where it's stable for hours. Alternatively, shake it in a jar to blend the ingredients for a short period of time. Using an emulsion such as egg or mustard will bind together substances that normally don't combine well.

Fillet: A boneless piece of fish, chicken, or other meat.

Fold: A blending technique used to combine light, airy mixtures. Usually done with a spatula, the purpose is to gently mix ingredients while retaining their volume.

Glaze: To coat food with a liquid that will make it glossy or shiny, such as a thin icing or egg wash.

Grate: To shred food using a box grater or food processor. The sides of a box grater have different sized holes to provide varying textures.

Grill: To cook food on a rack over direct heat, usually on a barbecue.

Grind: To break down food into small pieces, usually using a food processor, grinder, or mortar and pestle.

Julienne: To cut food (usually vegetables) into thin matchstick-like sticks.

Knead: To blend and mix pliable dough, developing the gluten and creating a smooth, elastic consistency. To knead by hand, press down into the dough with the heels of both hands, then push away, fold in half, and turn a quarter turn. Repeat the process for 5–15 minutes, until the dough is smooth and elastic.

Leavening agent: An ingredient that causes batter or dough to rise, such as yeast, baking powder, baking soda, and eggs.

Marinate: To soak meat or vegetables in a seasoned liquid to season and tenderize it.

Mince: To finely chop food into tiny pieces.

Parboil: To partially cook food, usually vegetables, briefly in boiling water. This helps ingredients that require longer to cook than other ingredients in the same dish—for example, carrots in a stir-fry.

Poach: To cook food in very gently boiling liquid.

Purée: To finely blend to a smooth, lump-free consistency. Usually done in a blender, food processor, food mill, or using a hand-held immersion blender.

Reduce: To boil or simmer a liquid until it reduces in volume.

Roast: To cook food, usually meat or vegetables, in an open pan in the oven.

Sauté: To quickly cook food in a small amount of butter or oil over medium-high heat.

Score: To cut shallow incisions into the surface of foods, often meat and baked goods. This is done to tenderize less tender cuts of meat, to assist with flavor absorption when marinating, to allow excess fat to drain during cooking, or as a decoration.

Sear: To brown meat in a very hot pan to caramelize the exterior, creating a crunchy crust and flavor. It doesn't "seal in the juices," as is commonly believed.

Sift: To pass dry food (usually flour) through a fine mesh to remove lumps.

Slice: To cut food into long, flat pieces.

Steam: To cook food over boiling or simmering water in a covered pan.

Stew: To slowly cook food covered in liquid in a covered pot or pan. Very similar to braising.

Stir-fry: To quickly cook chopped food (usually meat and vegetables) in a small amount of fat over high heat. Very similar to sautéing.

Toast: To brown food by cooking over or under direct heat.

Whip: To vigorously beat ingredients such as cream or egg whites, incorporating air into them in order to increase their volume.

Whisk: To blend ingredients using a wire whisk.

Zest: The colorful outermost layer of the peel of citrus fruits.

Planning your menus

Food you can make ahead

Foods that make great leftovers

(keep in the fridge, freeze well, or can be turned into other things)

Baked Beans 194

Baked Ham 134

Bean Salad 198

Chili 192

Easy Ravioli (freeze them before boiling) 173

Macaroni & Cheese 176

Maple Roast Pork Tenderloin with Apples 136

Meatloaf 120

Mushroom Lentil Burgers 196

Roast Beef 122

Roast Chicken 153

Roast Pork Loin 137

Spinach and Feta Rice or Orzo Salad 93

Party food

Any of the cookies, bars, cakes and pies

Bean Salad 198

Chicken Satay 152

Chili 192 (with Corn Bread 247)

Frittata (cut into squares and served cold) 56

Oven Fries 226

Oven-Roasted Barbecue Ribs 132

Potato Salad 90

Spicy Garlic Pan-Seared Shrimp 166

Spinach and Feta Rice or Orzo Salad 93

Sticky Honey-Garlic or Buffalo Chicken Wings 143

Food to feed a crowd

Baked Beans 194

Baked Ham 134

Baked Wild Rice Pilaf with Pecans 184

Basic Lemon-Parmesan Risotto 186

Bean Salad 198

Chicken Satay 152

Chicken, Shrimp, and Sausage Jambalaya 109

Chili 192

Corn Bread 247

Greek Lamb Kebabs with Tzatziki 139

Lasagna 174

Oven-Roasted Barbecue Ribs 132

Pork Cassoulet 102

Pot Roast 118

Potato Salad 90

Roast Beef 122

Roast Chicken(s) 153

Roast Pork Loin 137

Scalloped Potatoes 227

Spinach and Feta Rice or Orzo Salad 93

Sticky Oven-Roasted Chicken Pieces 148

When you need to feed only one or two

Big Noodle Bowl 81

Burgers 126 (freeze extra patties to cook later)

Easy Ravioli 173

Grilled Portobello Burgers 214

Muesli 65

Omelet 54

Pad Thai 108

Pan-Seared Steak 116

Portobello Pizzas 213

Red Beans and Rice 195

Sautéed (or Pan-Fried) Whitefish Fillets 159

Sautéed, Grilled, or Broiled Chicken Breasts 144

Smoothies 66

Stuffed or Twice-Baked Potatoes 221

Steamed or Grilled Corn 208

Food you can bring with you for lunch

Any muffins, quick breads, biscuits, or
  scones 234
Baked Beans 194
Beef Stew 99
Black Bean Soup 79
Chicken, Shrimp, and Sausage
  Jambalaya 109
Chili 192
Corn, Chicken, and Cheddar
  Chowder 77
Ginger-Sesame Noodle Salad 91
Granola 64
Meatloaf 120
Peanut Noodles with Chicken
  and Veggies 179
Poached Salmon 162
Pork Cassoulet 102
Red Beans and Rice 195
Rice Salad 94
Rigatoni with Mushroom Sauce 172
Spinach and Feta Rice or Orzo Salad 93
Tabbouleh 96
White Beans with Tomatoes, Spinach,
  and Pancetta 197

Fast food

Big Noodle Bowl 81
Biscuits 250
Black Bean Soup 79
Couscous 187
Couscous Salad 95
Crunchy Chicken Fingers
  with Honey Mustard 150
Dried Fruit Compote 314
Easy Ravioli 173
Fish Cakes 161
Fried Rice 185
Grilled Portobello Burgers 214
Pad Thai 108
Peanut Noodles with Chicken and
  Veggies 179
Potato Pancakes 228
Real Chocolate Pudding 304
Roasted Asparagus 200
Sloppy Joes 125
Spicy Garlic Pan-Seared Shrimp 166
Spinach, Bean, and Pasta Soup 72
Steamed or Grilled Corn 208
Tabbouleh 96
Thai Coconut Soup with Chicken
  or Seafood 80
Tiramisù 306
White Beans with Tomatoes,
  Spinach, and Pancetta 197
Wilted Kale with Bacon 212
Wilted Spinach with Bacon
  Vinaigrette 215

Menu ideas

Having company for dinner?

When you want to impress someone

(Your date or your mom)
Potato and Leek Soup 75
Braised Lamb Shanks 140
Parmesan Polenta 188
Vegetables in season
Tiramisù 306

Chicken Stuffed with Brie, Caramelized
    Onions, and Garlic 146
Baked Wild Rice Pilaf with Pecans 184
Green Salad 83 with vinaigrette 85
Chocolate Pudding Cake with vanilla
    ice cream 309

Roasted Chicken 153
Lemon-Parmesan Risotto 186
Braised Cabbage with Apples 204
Roasted Asparagus 200
Lemon Meringue Pie 298

Summer barbecue

Grilled Portobello Burgers 214
Greek Lamb Kebabs with Tzatziki 139
Spinach and Feta Rice or Orzo Salad 93
Marinated Corn and Beans 210
Peach or Berry Pie 295/296
Grilled Sour Cream Pound Cake with fresh
    fruit 274

Sunday brunch

Frittata 56
Home Fries 57
Carrot Apple Morning Glory Muffins 239
    or Cinnamon Sticky Buns 252
Smoothies 66

Index

Index

Index

Index

Index

Index

Index

Index

Index